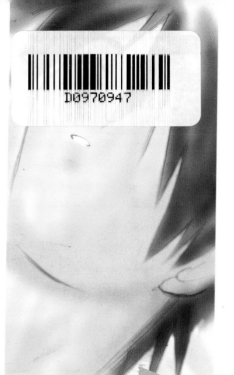

CONTENTS

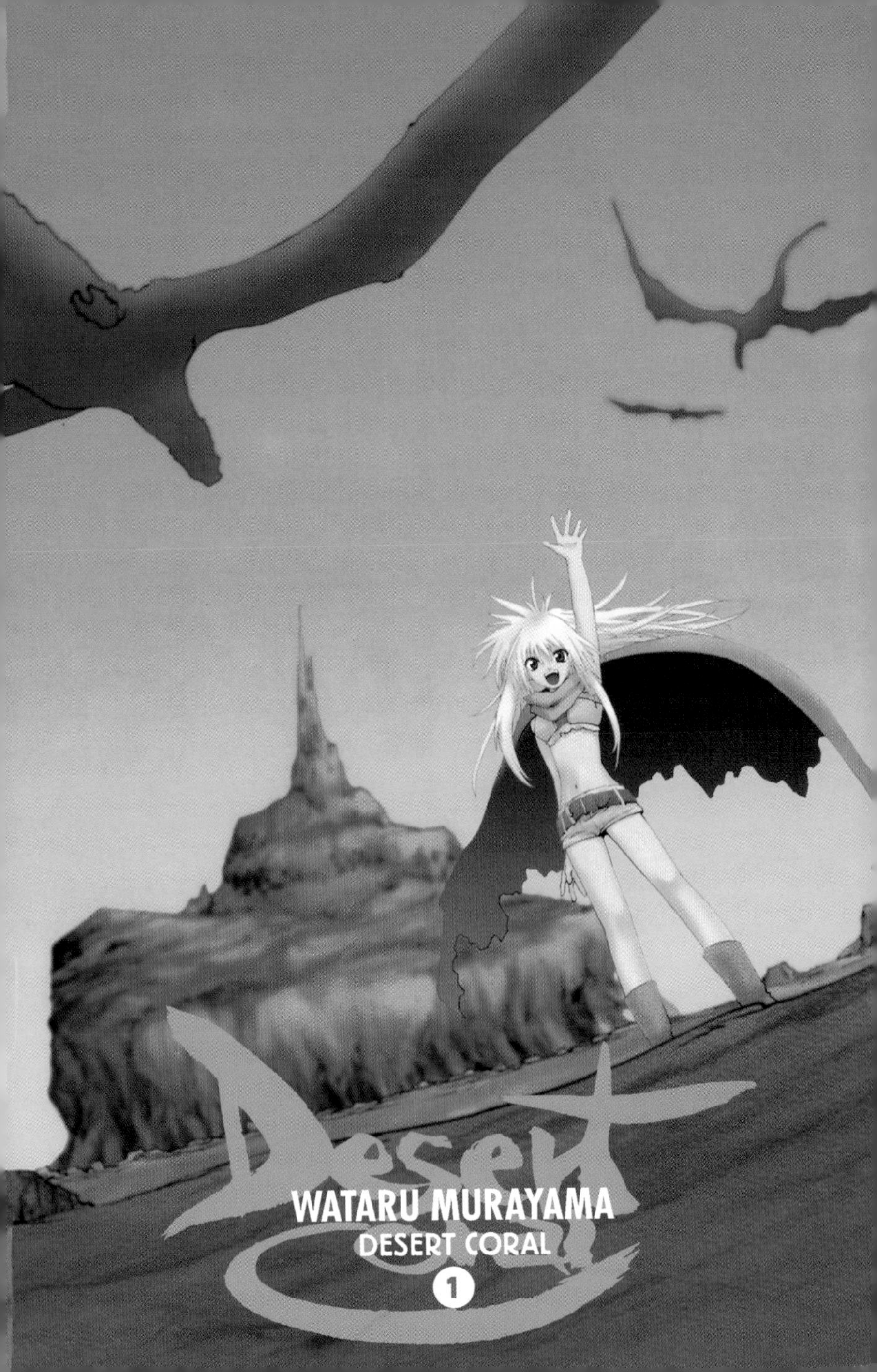
Desert
WATARU MURAYAMA
DESERT CORAL
1

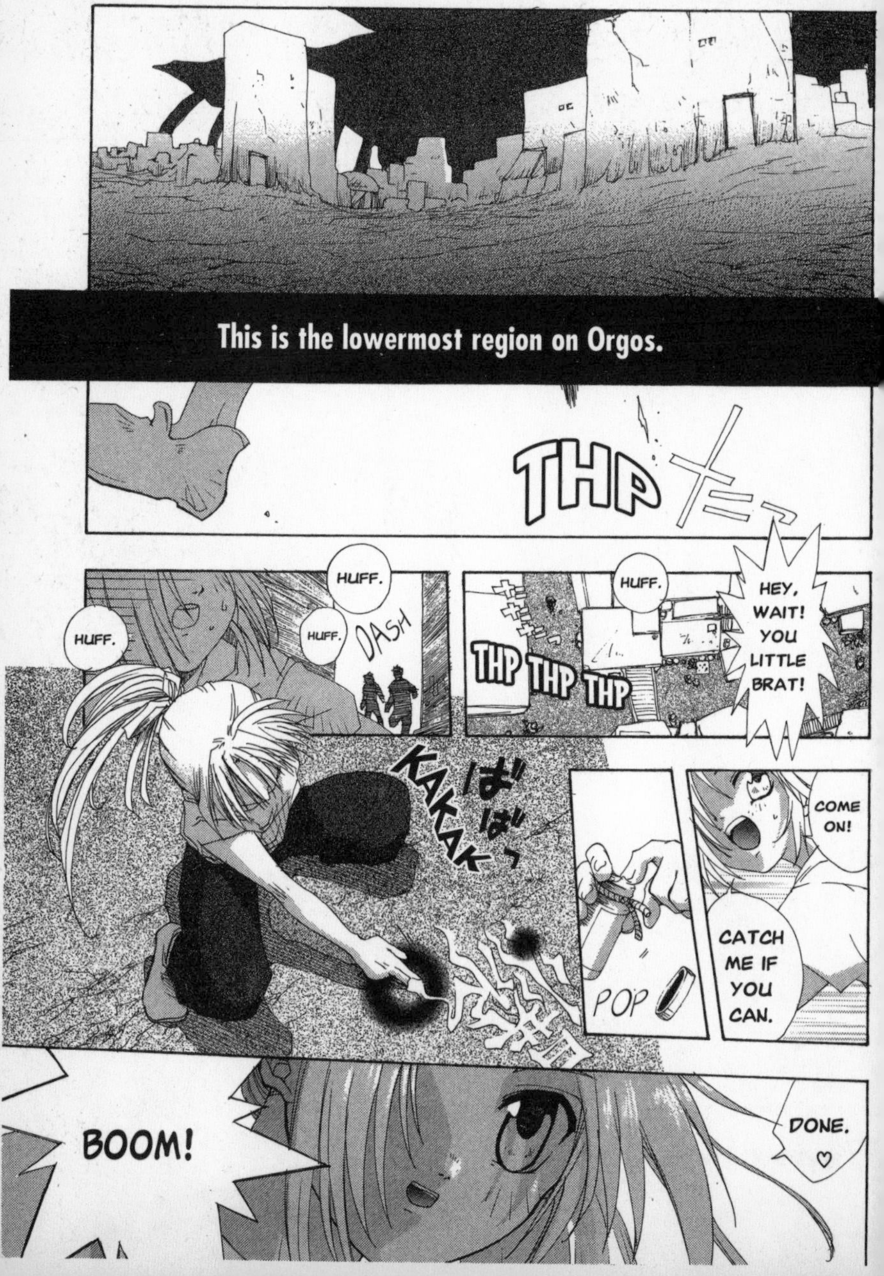
This is the lowermost region on Orgos.
THP
HEY, WAIT! YOU LITTLE BRAT!
HUFF.
THP THP THP
HUFF.
HUFF.
DASH
HUFF.
COME ON!
CATCH ME IF YOU CAN.
POP
KAKAK
ばばっ
DONE. ♡
BOOM!

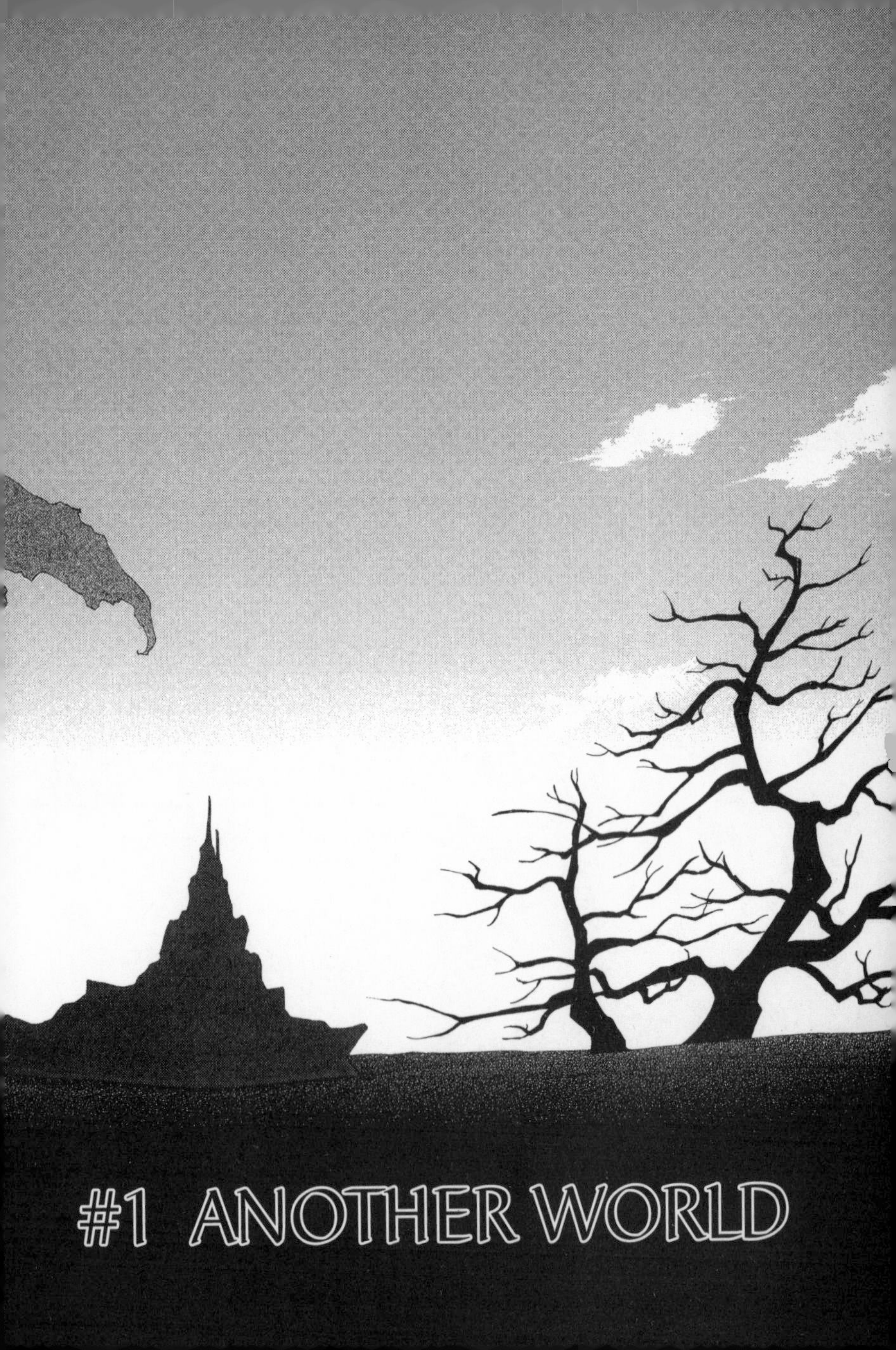

#1 ANOTHER WORLD

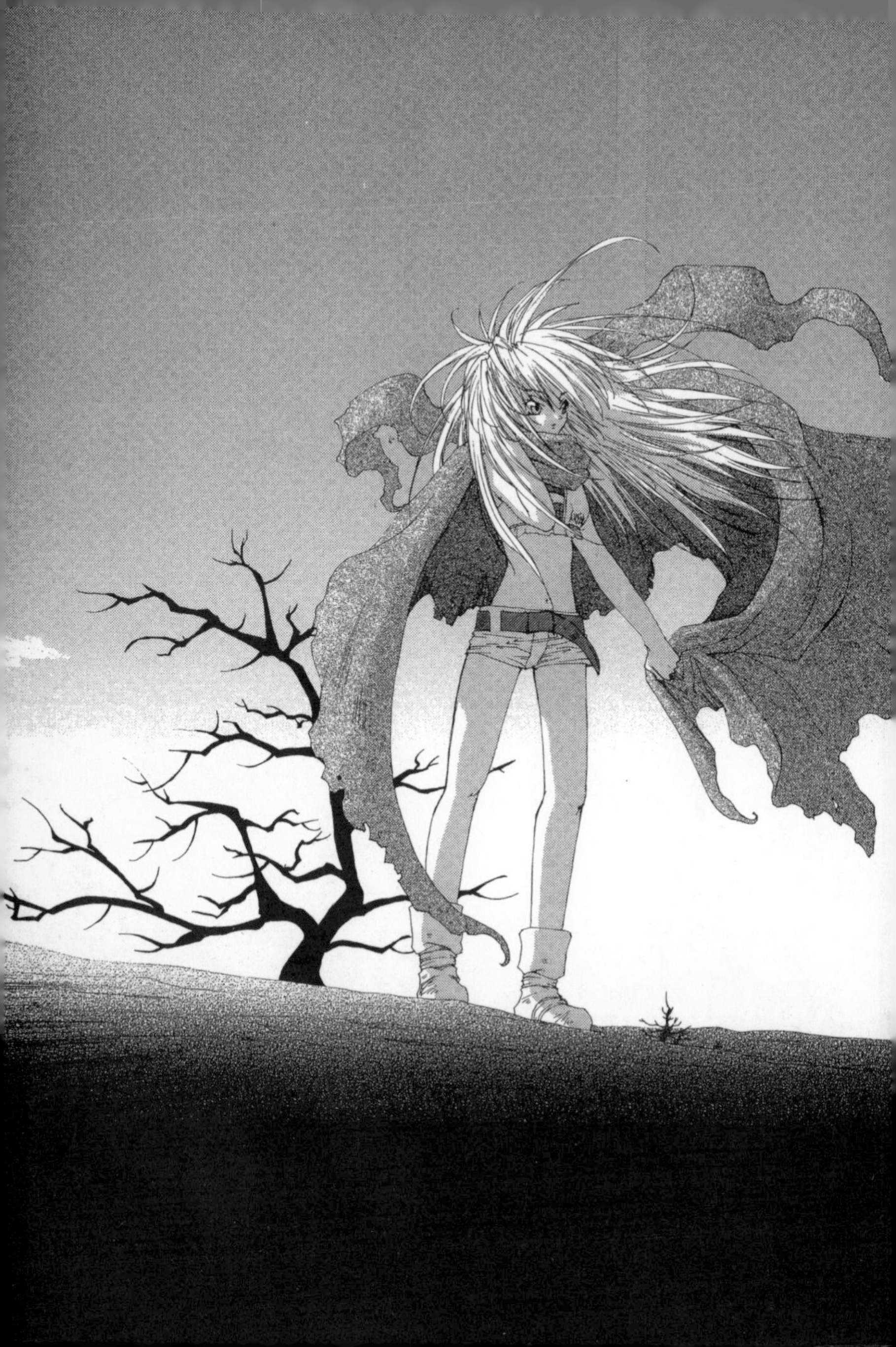

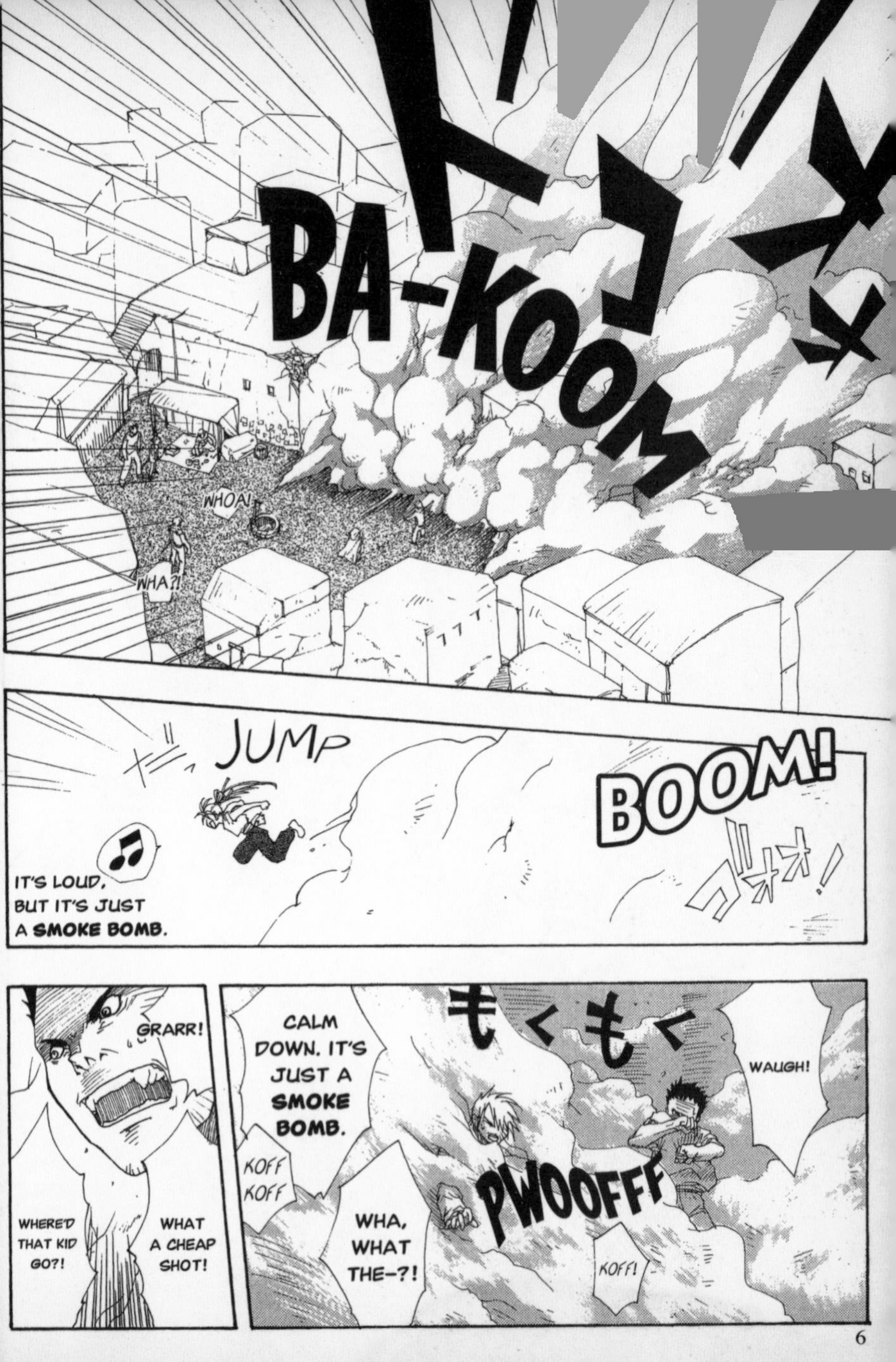
BA-KOOM
WHOA!
WHA?!
BOOM!
JUMP
IT'S LOUD, BUT IT'S JUST A SMOKE BOMB.
もくもく
WAUGH!
CALM DOWN. IT'S JUST A SMOKE BOMB.
PWOOFFF
KOFF KOFF
WHA, WHAT THE-?!
KOFF!
GRARR!
WHAT A CHEAP SHOT!
WHERE'D THAT KID GO?!

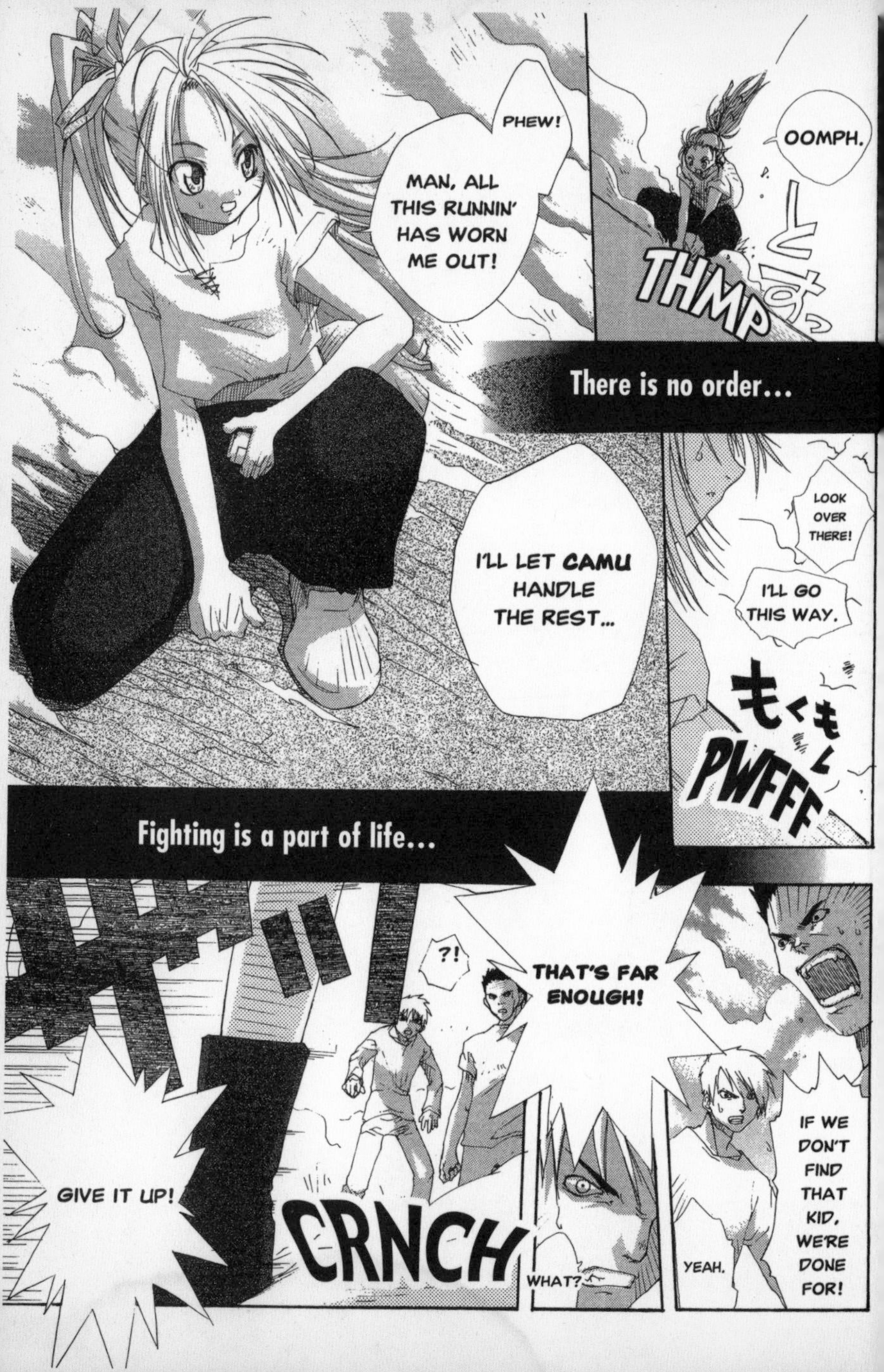
OOMPH.
とすっ
THMP
There is no order...
LOOK OVER THERE!
I'LL GO THIS WAY.
もくもく
PWFFF
PHEW!
MAN, ALL THIS RUNNIN' HAS WORN ME OUT!
I'LL LET CAMU HANDLE THE REST...
Fighting is a part of life...
IF WE DON'T FIND THAT KID, WE'RE DONE FOR!
YEAH.
THAT'S FAR ENOUGH!
?!
WHAT?
CRNCH
GIVE IT UP!

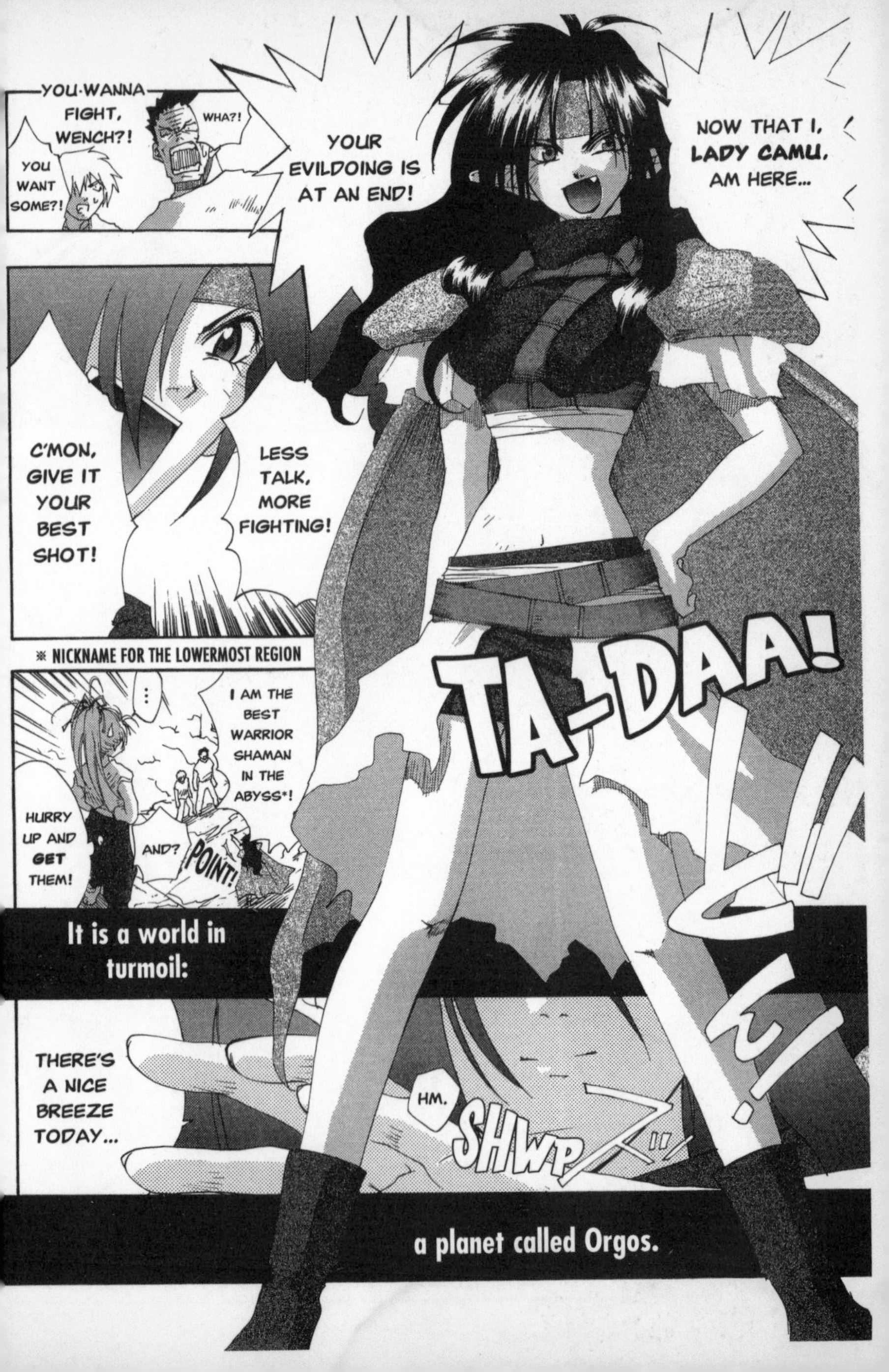
NOW THAT I, LADY CAMU, AM HERE...
YOUR EVILDOING IS AT AN END!
TA-DAA!
YOU·WANNA FIGHT, WENCH?!
WHA?!
YOU WANT SOME?!
LESS TALK, MORE FIGHTING!
C'MON, GIVE IT YOUR BEST SHOT!
※ NICKNAME FOR THE LOWERMOST REGION
I AM THE BEST WARRIOR SHAMAN IN THE ABYSS*!
...
AND?
POINT!
HURRY UP AND GET THEM!
It is a world in turmoil:
HM.
SHWP
THERE'S A NICE BREEZE TODAY...
a planet called Orgos.

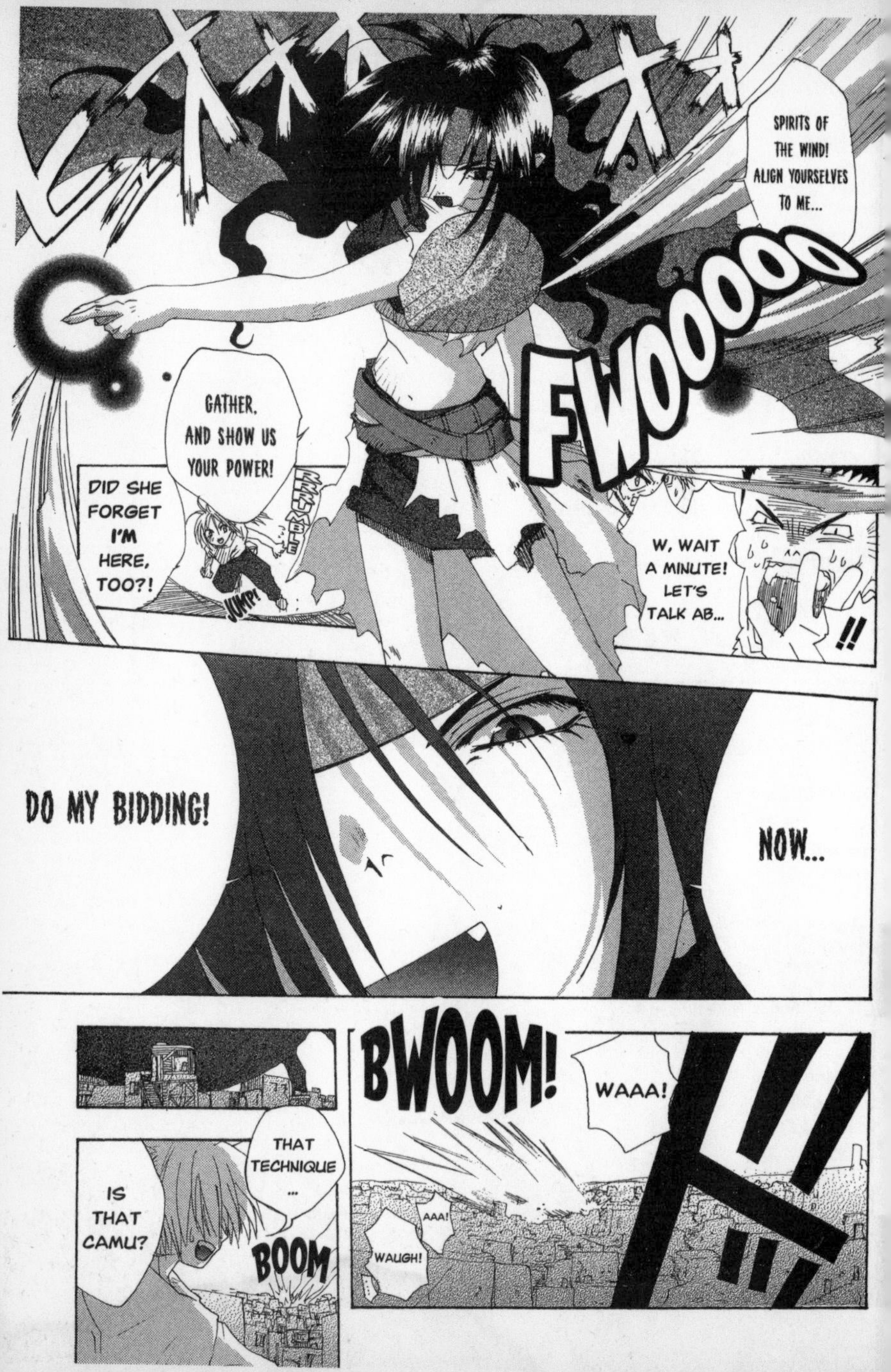
SPIRITS OF THE WIND! ALIGN YOURSELVES TO ME...
FWOOOOO
GATHER, AND SHOW US YOUR POWER!
W, WAIT A MINUTE! LET'S TALK AB...
!!
DID SHE FORGET I'M HERE, TOO?!
RRRUMBLE
JUMP!
NOW...
DO MY BIDDING!
BWOOM!
WAAA!
AAA!
WAUGH!
THAT TECHNIQUE ...
IS THAT CAMU?
BOOM

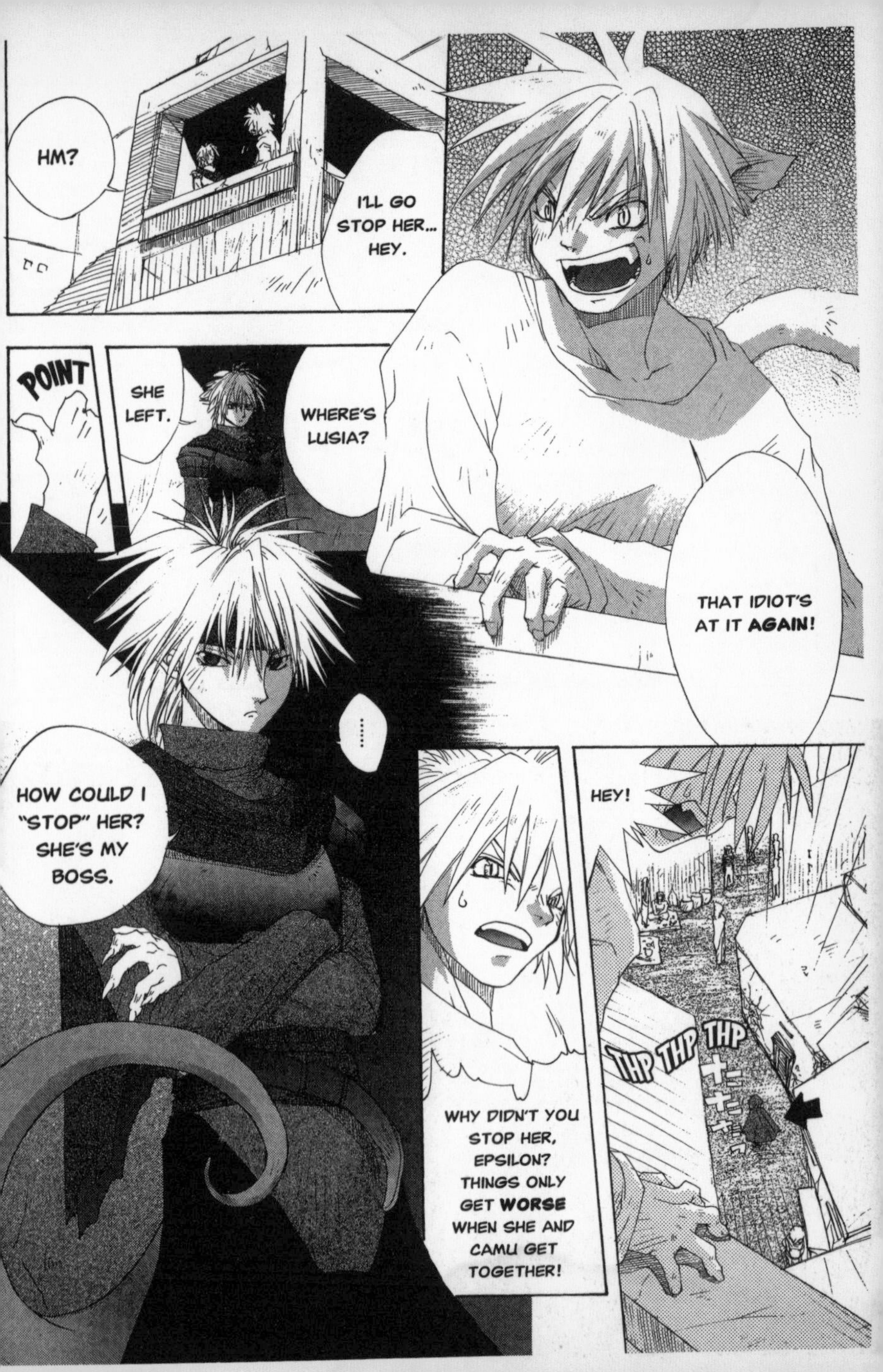
THAT IDIOT'S AT IT AGAIN!
I'LL GO STOP HER... HEY.
HM?
WHERE'S LUSIA?
SHE LEFT.
POINT
HEY!
WHY DIDN'T YOU STOP HER, EPSILON? THINGS ONLY GET **WORSE** WHEN SHE AND CAMU GET TOGETHER!
THP THP THP
......
HOW COULD I "STOP" HER? SHE'S MY BOSS.

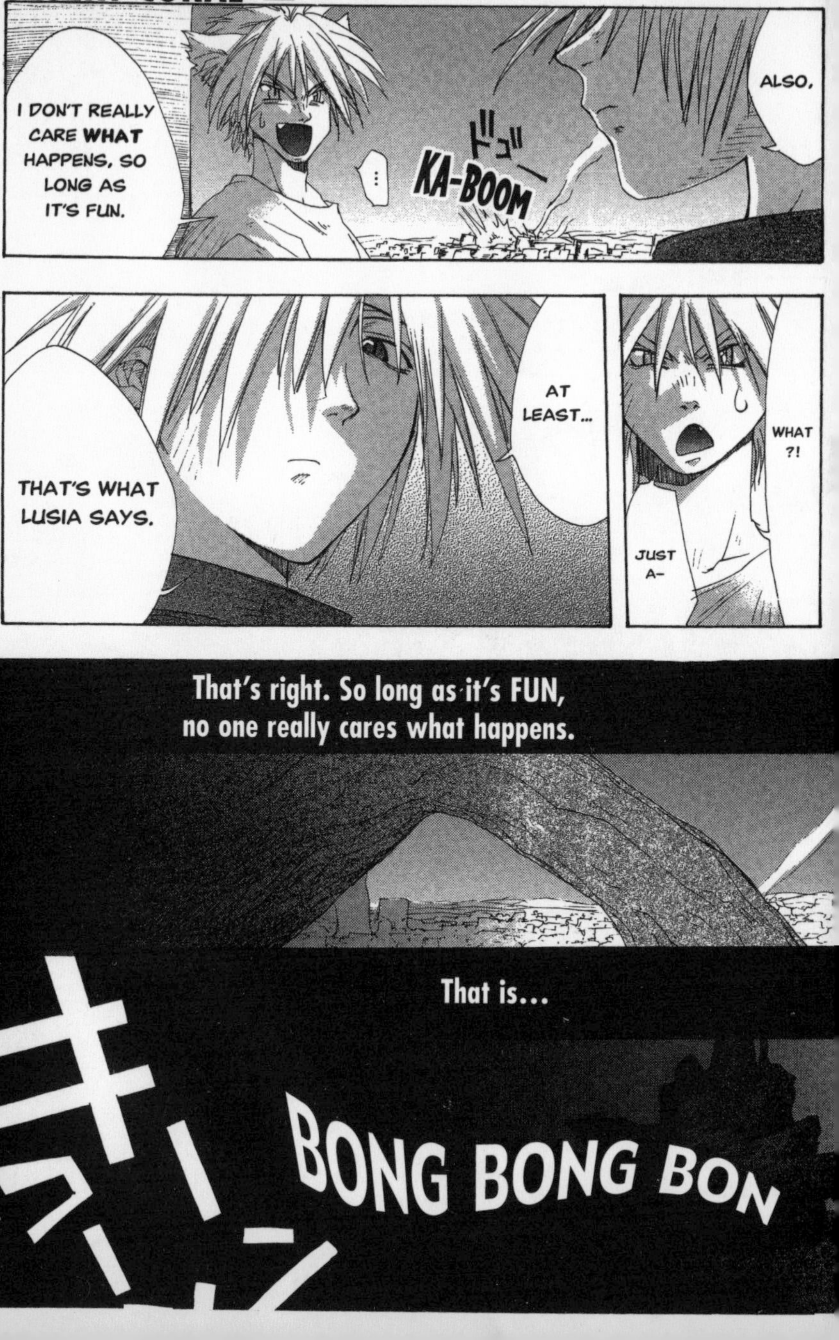
ALSO,
KA-BOOM
...
I DON'T REALLY CARE **WHAT** HAPPENS, SO LONG AS IT'S FUN.
WHAT ?!
JUST A-
AT LEAST...
THAT'S WHAT LUSIA SAYS.
That's right. So long as it's FUN, no one really cares what happens.
That is...
BONG BONG BON

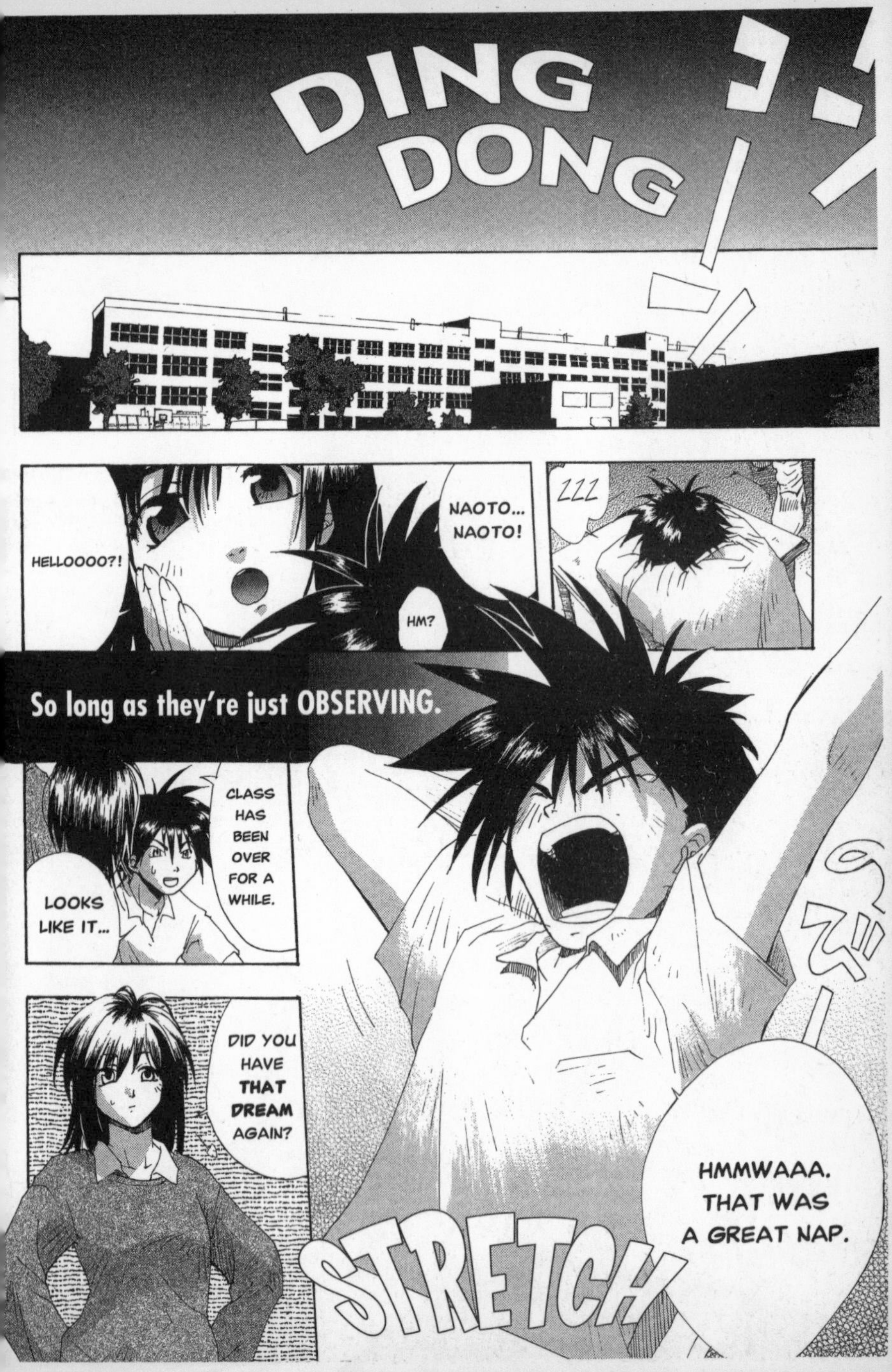
DING DONG
ZZZ
NAOTO... NAOTO!
HELLOOOO?!
HM?
So long as they're just OBSERVING.
STRETCH
HMMWAAA. THAT WAS A GREAT NAP.
CLASS HAS BEEN OVER FOR A WHILE.
LOOKS LIKE IT...
DID YOU HAVE THAT DREAM AGAIN?

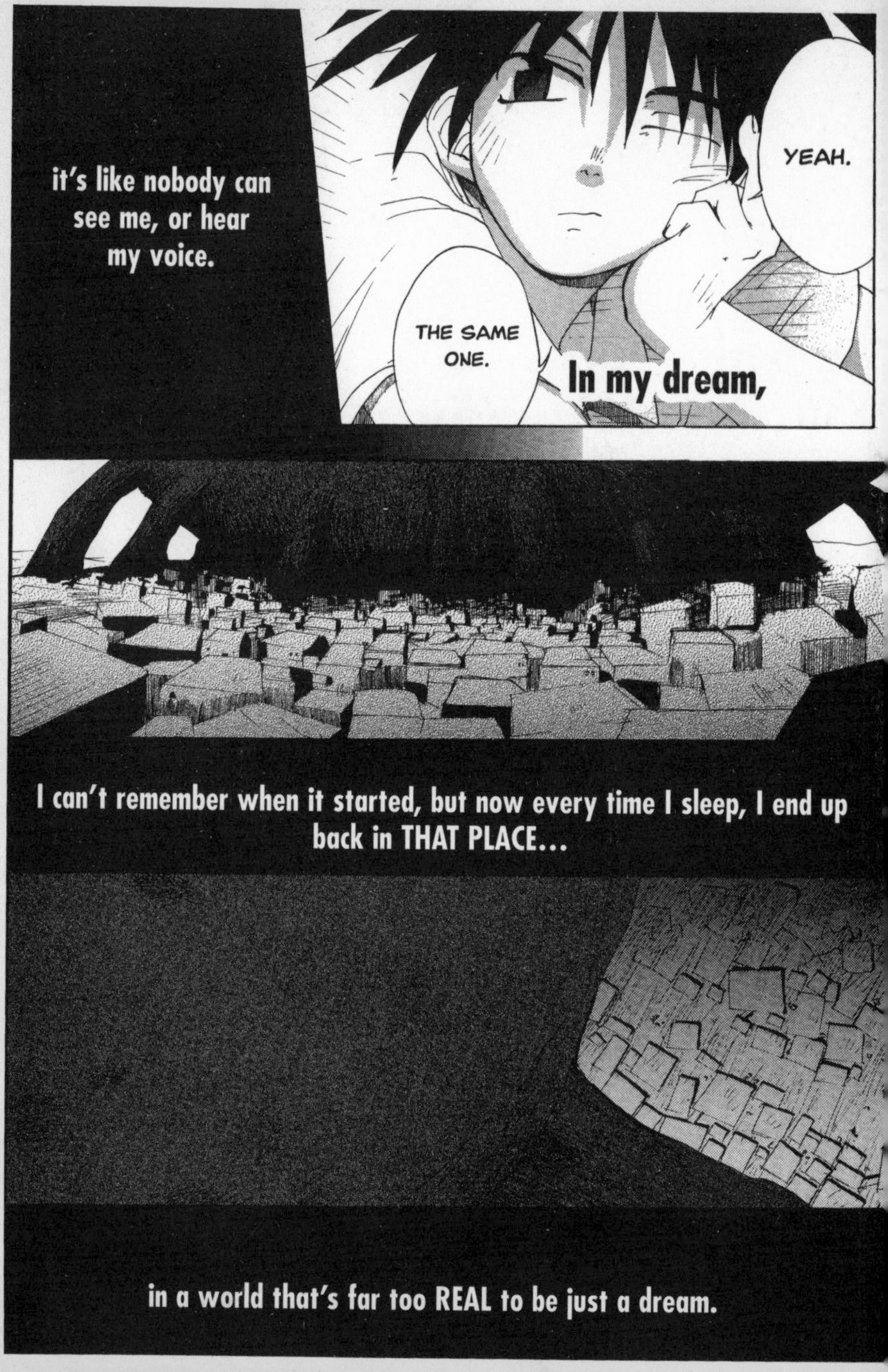
YEAH.
THE SAME ONE.
In my dream,
it's like nobody can see me, or hear my voice.
I can't remember when it started, but now every time I sleep, I end up back in THAT PLACE...
in a world that's far too REAL to be just a dream.

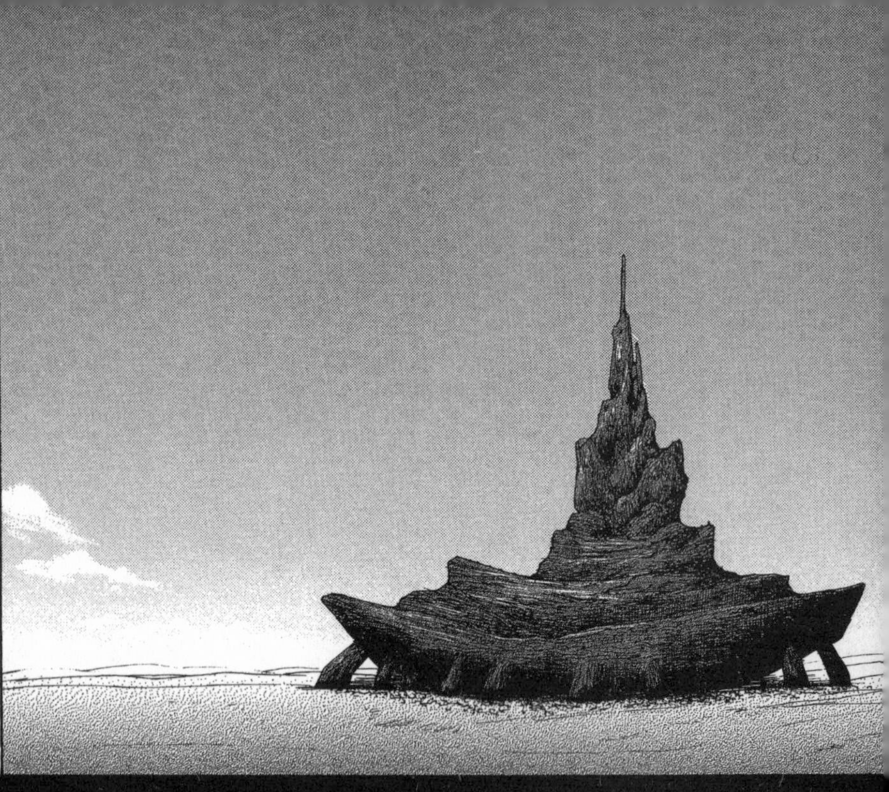

This is my OTHER world.

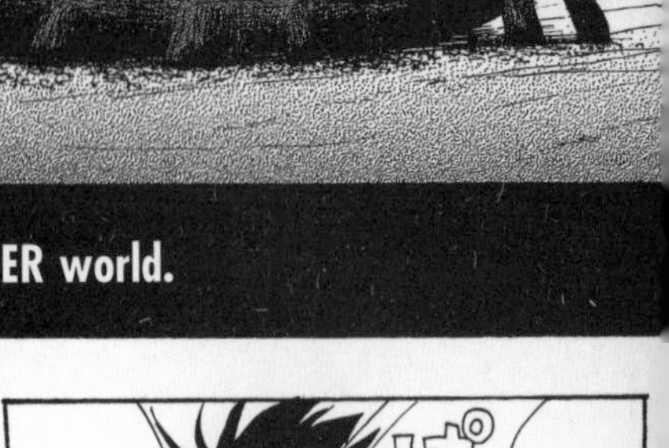
YAAAWN. WELL THEN,
ぱた
G'NIGHT.
PLOP

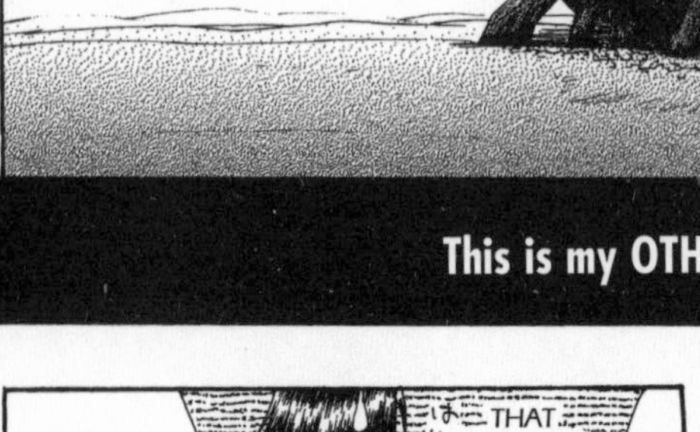
THAT WAS FAST.
ZZZZ
UH, THE NEXT CLASS'S GONNA START SOON.

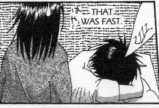

Orgos—the kingdom of the ELPHIS, the desert people.

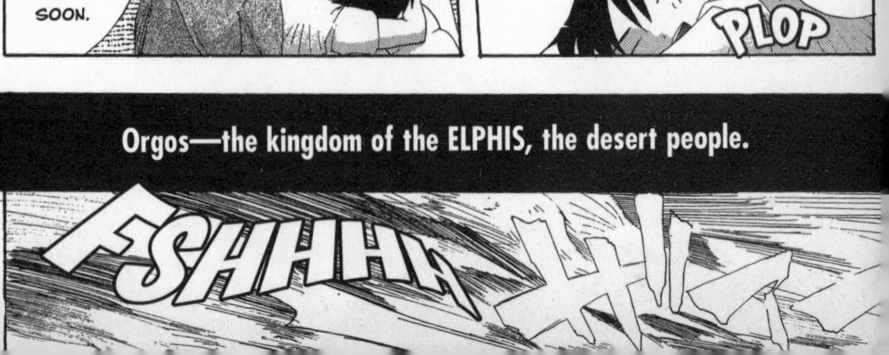
FSHHHA

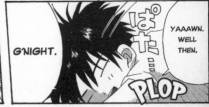

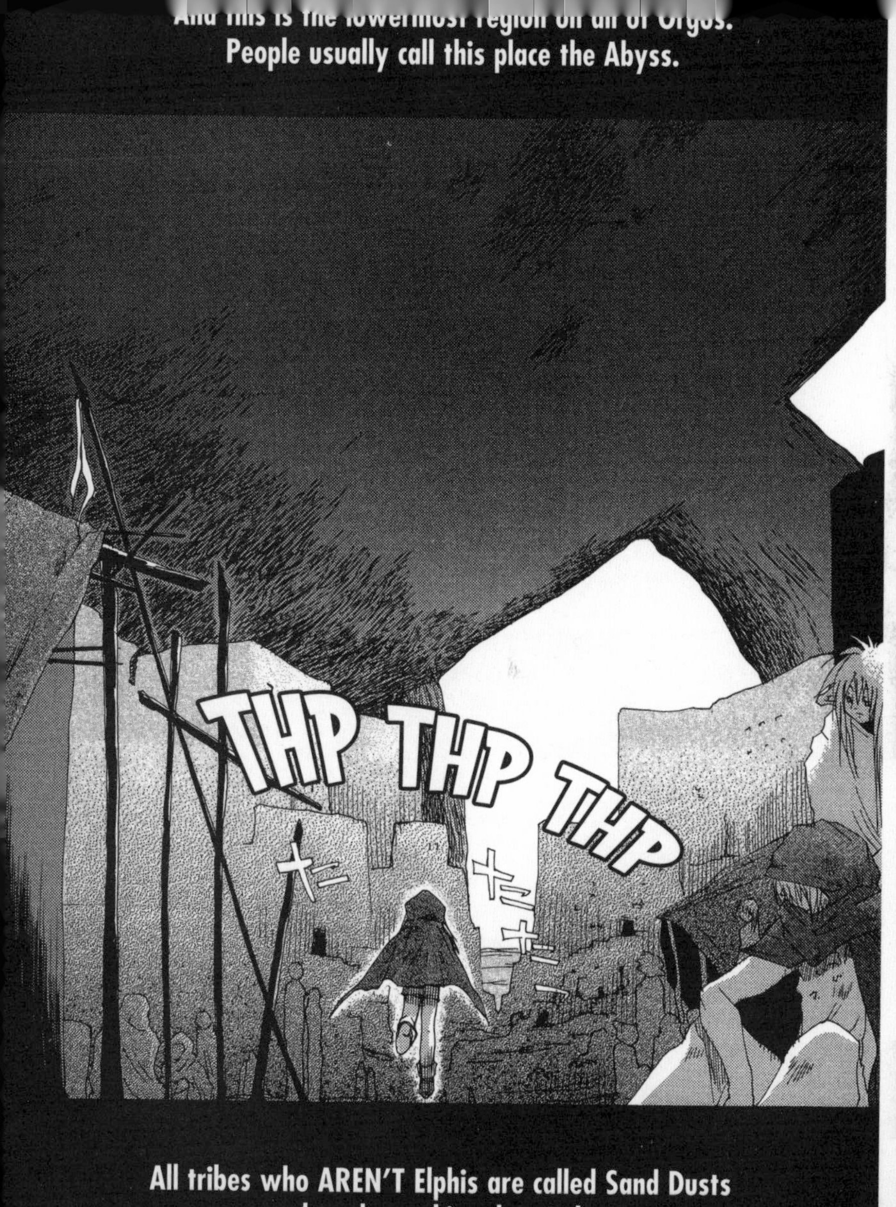
And this is the lowermost region on all of Orgos.
People usually call this place the Abyss.
THP THP THP
All tribes who AREN'T Elphis are called Sand Dusts
—and to them, this place is home.

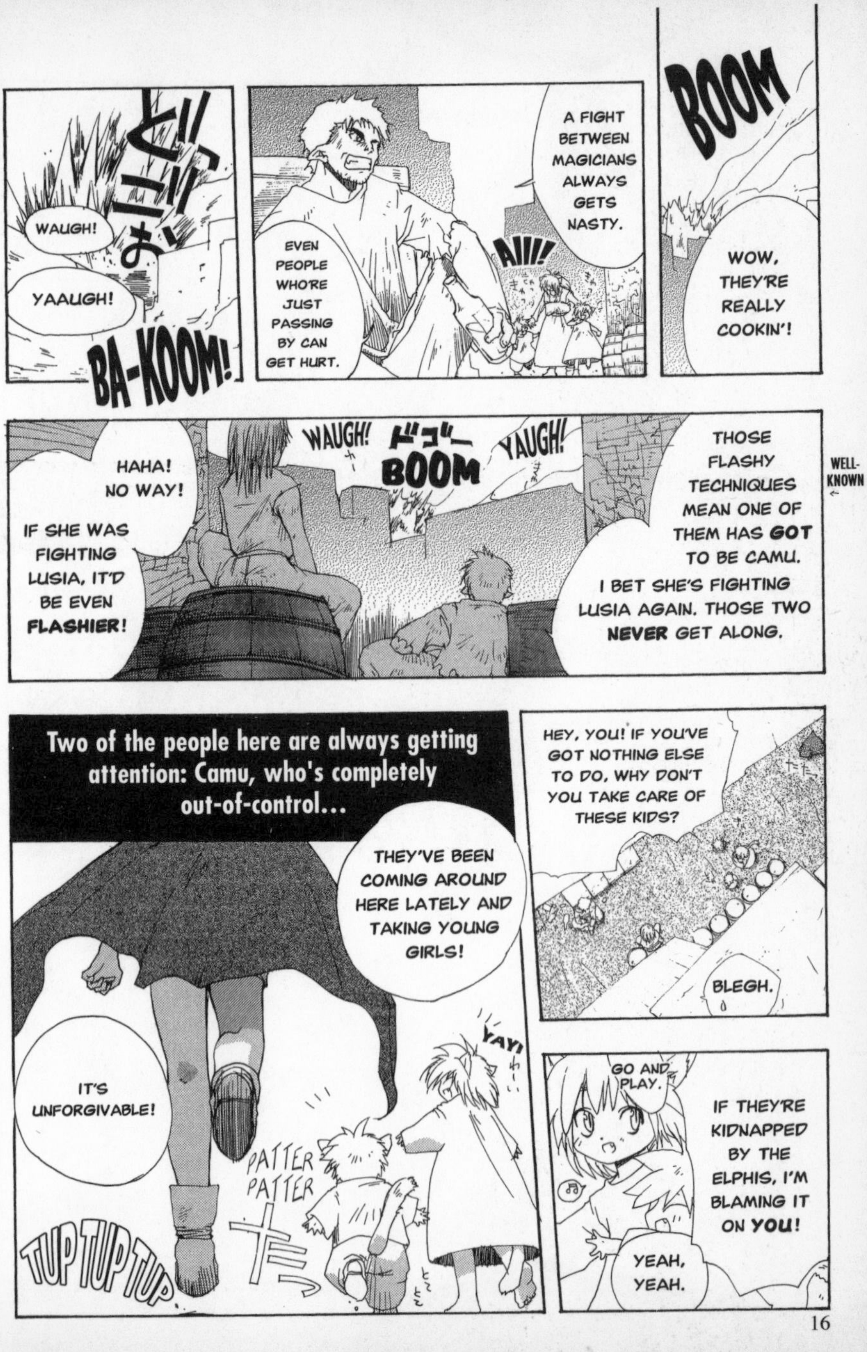
BOOM
WOW, THEY'RE REALLY COOKIN'!
A FIGHT BETWEEN MAGICIANS ALWAYS GETS NASTY.
AIII!!
EVEN PEOPLE WHO'RE JUST PASSING BY CAN GET HURT.
WAUGH!
YAAUGH!
BA-KOOM!
THOSE FLASHY TECHNIQUES MEAN ONE OF THEM HAS GOT TO BE CAMU.
WELL-KNOWN ←
I BET SHE'S FIGHTING LUSIA AGAIN. THOSE TWO NEVER GET ALONG.
YAUGH!
BOOM
WAUGH!
HAHA! NO WAY!
IF SHE WAS FIGHTING LUSIA, IT'D BE EVEN FLASHIER!
HEY, YOU! IF YOU'VE GOT NOTHING ELSE TO DO, WHY DON'T YOU TAKE CARE OF THESE KIDS?
BLEGH.
GO AND PLAY.
IF THEY'RE KIDNAPPED BY THE ELPHIS, I'M BLAMING IT ON YOU!
YEAH, YEAH.
Two of the people here are always getting attention: Camu, who's completely out-of-control...
THEY'VE BEEN COMING AROUND HERE LATELY AND TAKING YOUNG GIRLS!
IT'S UNFORGIVABLE!
YAY!
PATTER PATTER
TUP TUP TUP

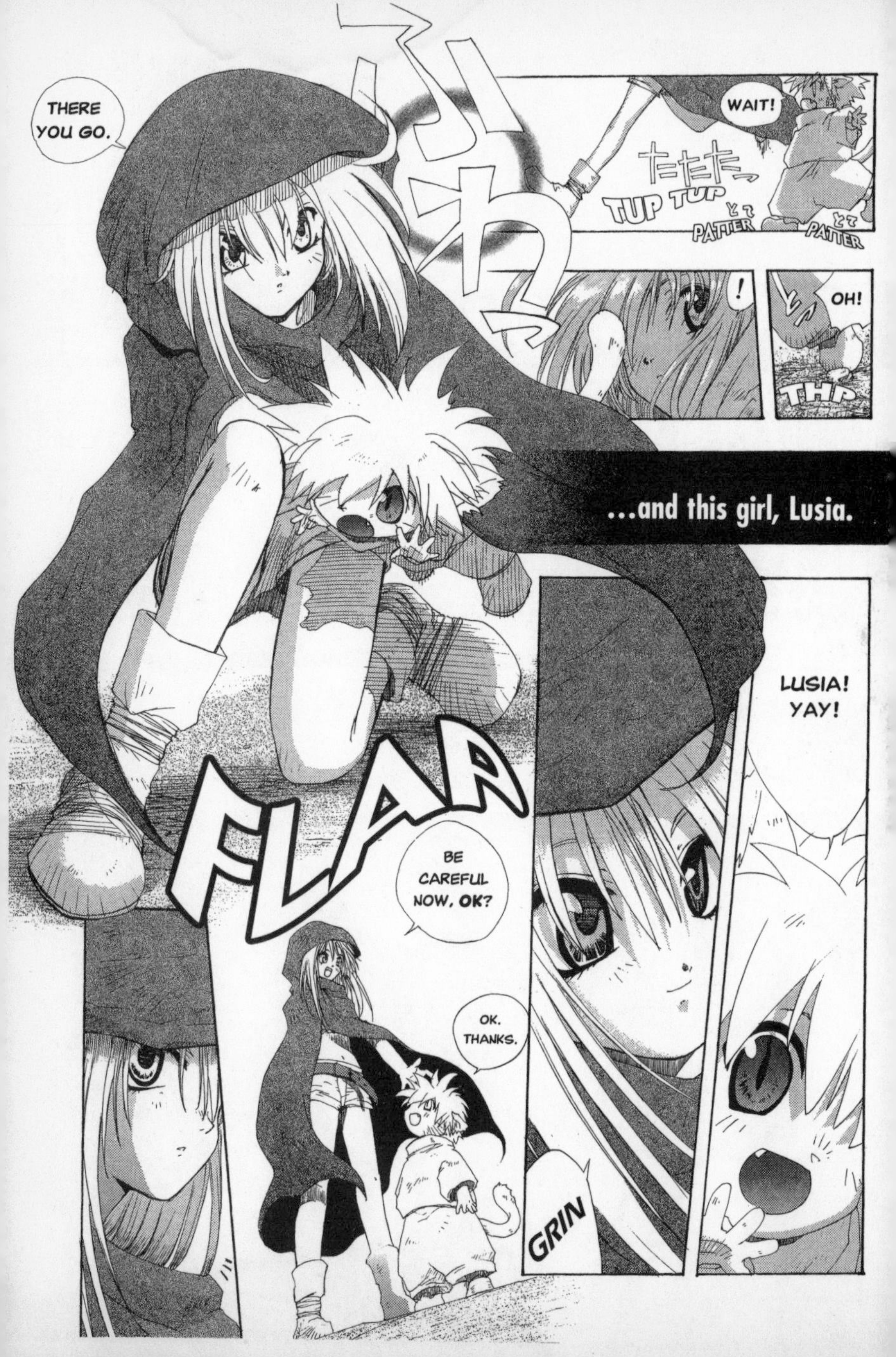

WAIT!
たたたたっ
TUP TUP
とて
PATTER
とて
PATTER
OH!
THP
!
ふわっ
THERE YOU GO.
...and this girl, Lusia.
LUSIA! YAY!
GRIN
FLAP
BE CAREFUL NOW, OK?
OK. THANKS.

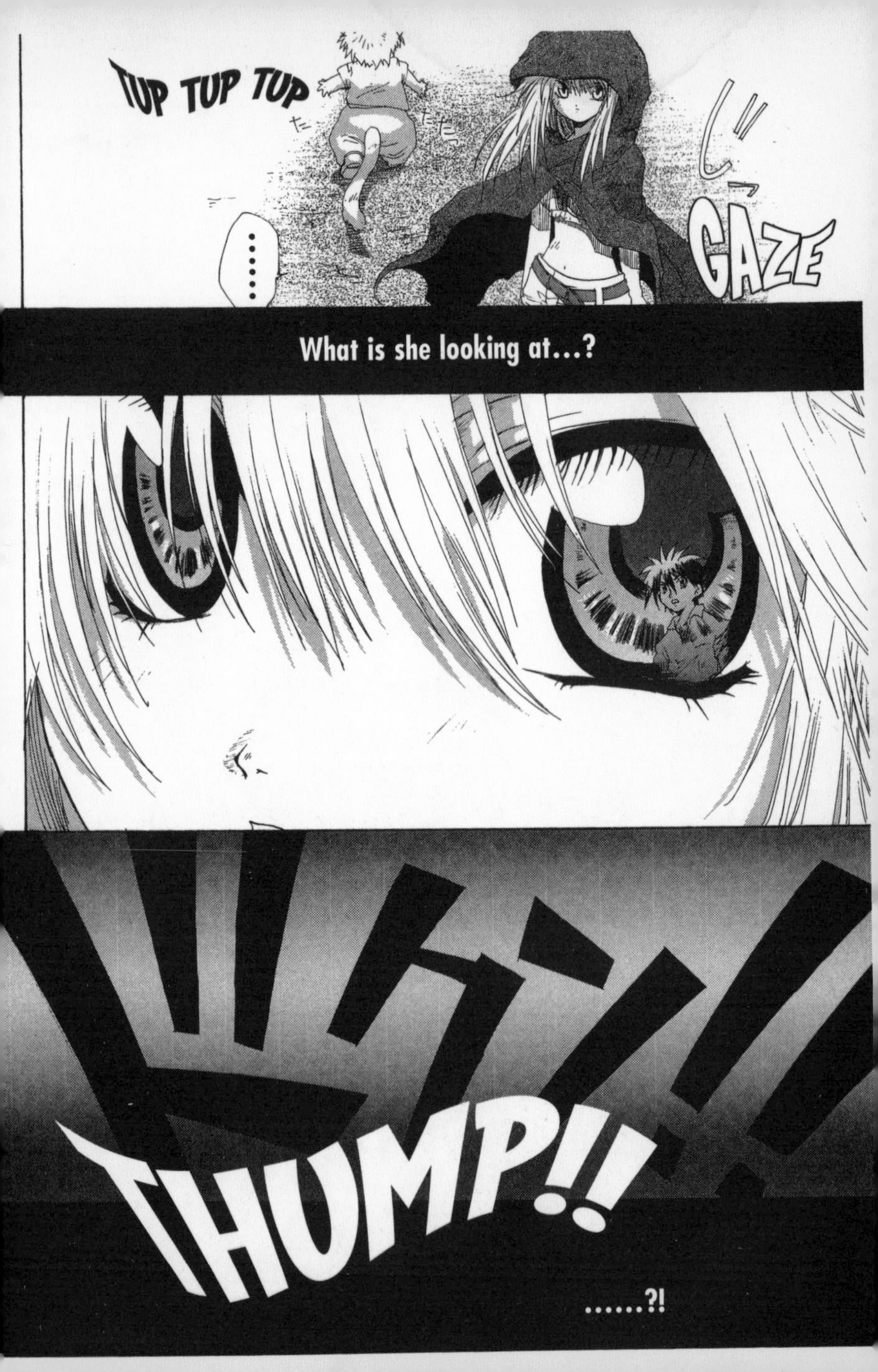
GAZE
......
TUP TUP TUP
What is she looking at...?
THUMP!!
......?!

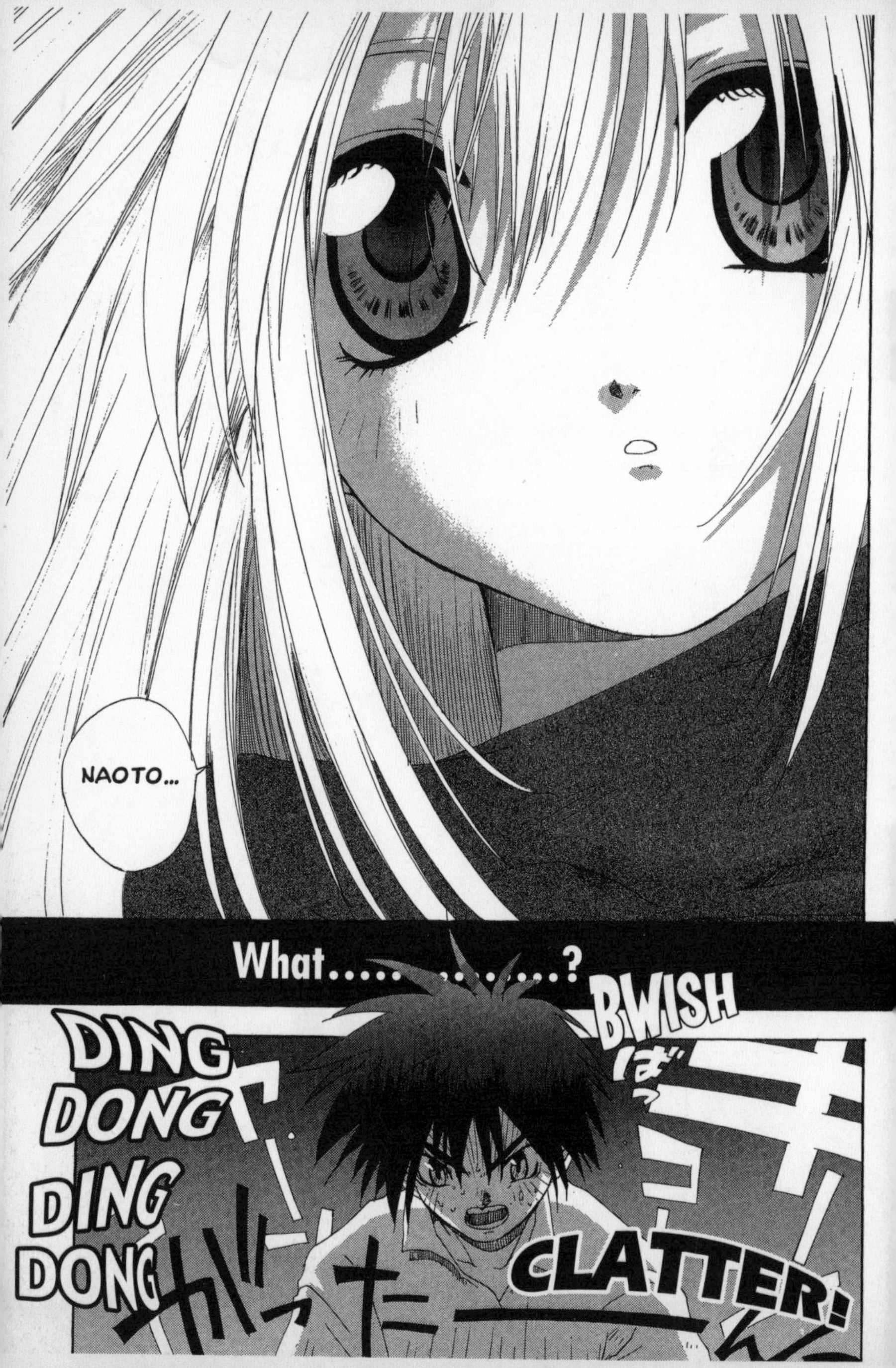
NAOTO...
What..... ....?
BWISH
ばっ
CLATTER!
DING DONG DING DONG

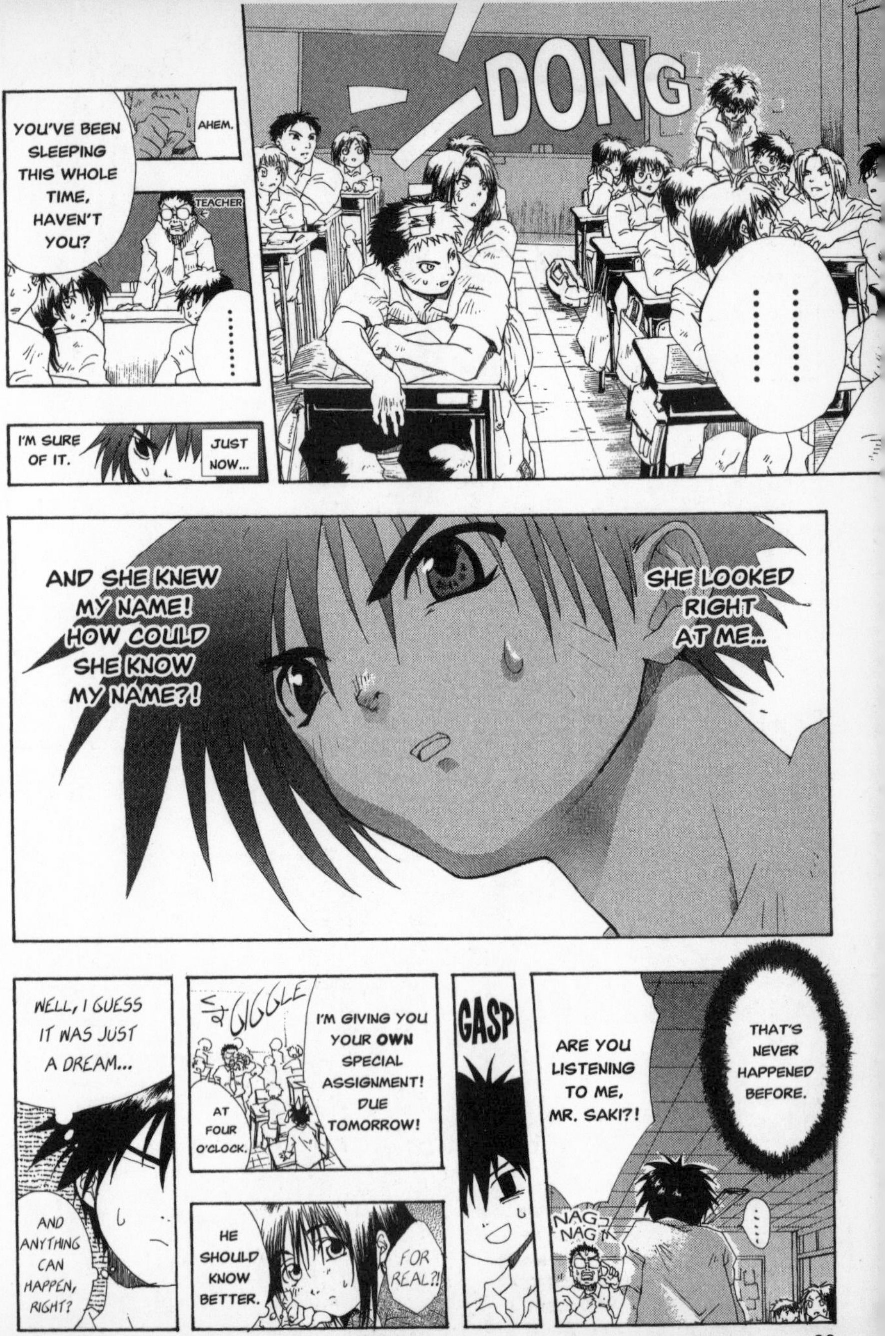
DONG
......
AHEM.
TEACHER
YOU'VE BEEN SLEEPING THIS WHOLE TIME, HAVEN'T YOU?
......
JUST NOW...
I'M SURE OF IT.
SHE LOOKED RIGHT AT ME...
AND SHE KNEW MY NAME! HOW COULD SHE KNOW MY NAME?!
THAT'S NEVER HAPPENED BEFORE.
ARE YOU LISTENING TO ME, MR. SAKI?!
NAG NAG
.....
GASP
I'M GIVING YOU YOUR OWN SPECIAL ASSIGNMENT! DUE TOMORROW!
GIGGLE
AT FOUR O'CLOCK.
FOR REAL?!
HE SHOULD KNOW BETTER.
WELL, I GUESS IT WAS JUST A DREAM...
AND ANYTHING CAN HAPPEN, RIGHT?

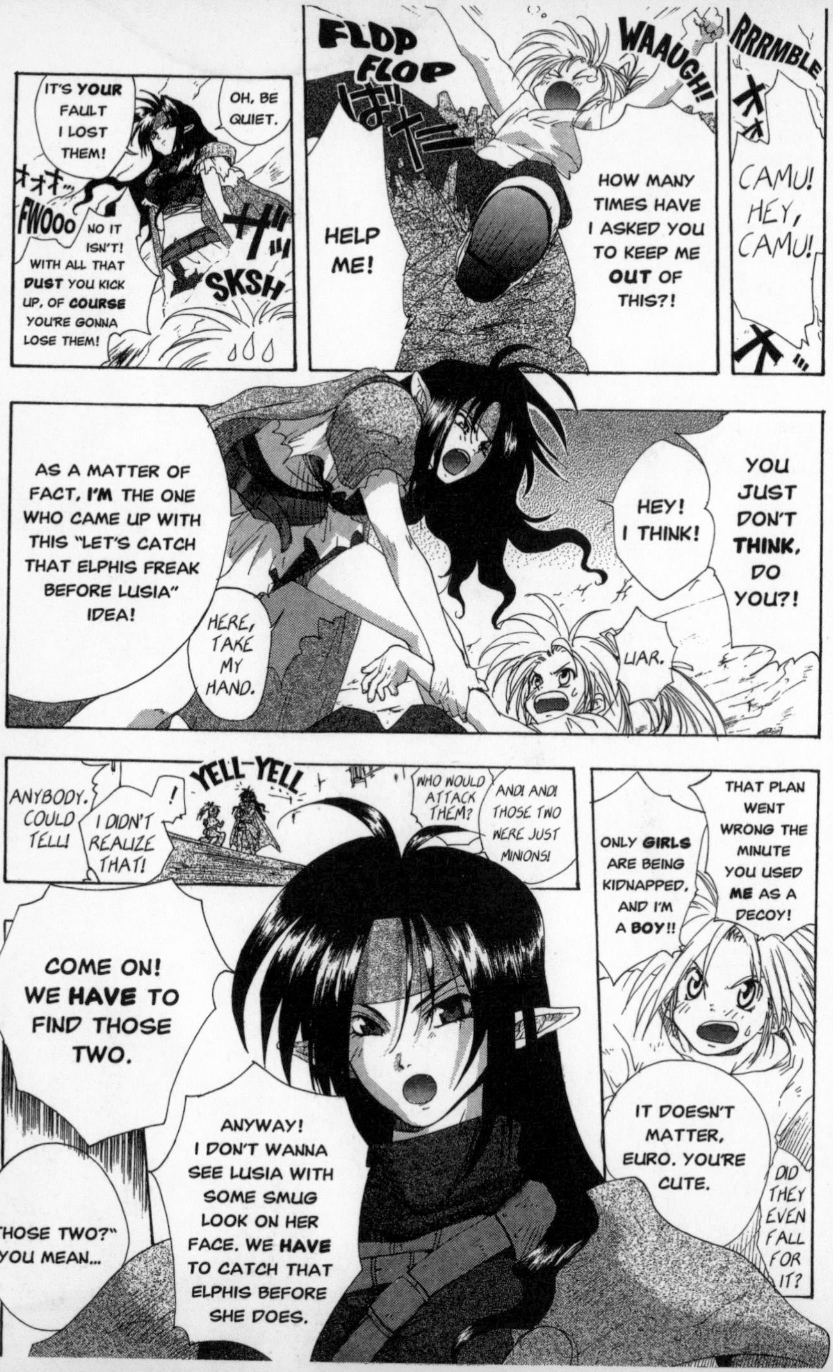
RRRMBLE
CAMU! HEY, CAMU!
FLOP FLOP
WAAUGH!
HOW MANY TIMES HAVE I ASKED YOU TO KEEP ME OUT OF THIS?!
HELP ME!
IT'S YOUR FAULT I LOST THEM!
OH, BE QUIET.
FWOOO
NO IT ISN'T! WITH ALL THAT DUST YOU KICK UP, OF COURSE YOU'RE GONNA LOSE THEM!
SKSH
YOU JUST DON'T THINK, DO YOU?!
HEY! I THINK!
AS A MATTER OF FACT, I'M THE ONE WHO CAME UP WITH THIS "LET'S CATCH THAT ELPHIS FREAK BEFORE LUSIA" IDEA!
LIAR.
HERE, TAKE MY HAND.
THAT PLAN WENT WRONG THE MINUTE YOU USED ME AS A DECOY!
ONLY GIRLS ARE BEING KIDNAPPED, AND I'M A BOY!!
AND! AND! THOSE TWO WERE JUST MINIONS!
WHO WOULD ATTACK THEM?
YELL-YELL
!
I DIDN'T REALIZE THAT!
ANYBODY COULD TELL!
IT DOESN'T MATTER, EURO. YOU'RE CUTE.
DID THEY EVEN FALL FOR IT?
COME ON! WE HAVE TO FIND THOSE TWO.
ANYWAY! I DON'T WANNA SEE LUSIA WITH SOME SMUG LOOK ON HER FACE. WE HAVE TO CATCH THAT ELPHIS BEFORE SHE DOES.
"THOSE TWO?" YOU MEAN...

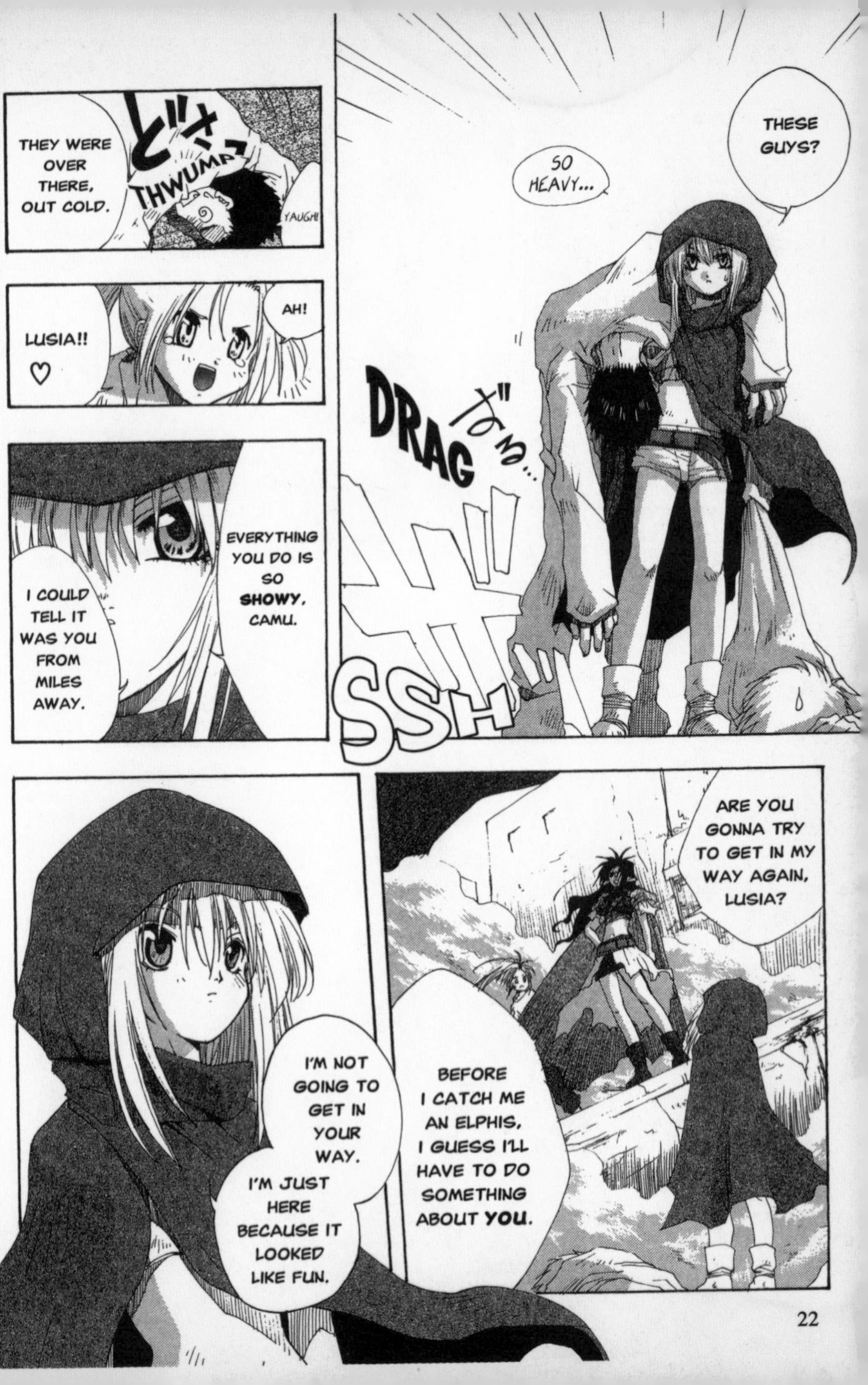
THESE GUYS?
SO HEAVY...
DRAG
SSH
THEY WERE OVER THERE, OUT COLD.
THWUMP
YAUGH!
AH!
LUSIA!! ♡
EVERYTHING YOU DO IS SO SHOWY, CAMU.
I COULD TELL IT WAS YOU FROM MILES AWAY.
ARE YOU GONNA TRY TO GET IN MY WAY AGAIN, LUSIA?
BEFORE I CATCH ME AN ELPHIS, I GUESS I'LL HAVE TO DO SOMETHING ABOUT YOU.
I'M NOT GOING TO GET IN YOUR WAY.
I'M JUST HERE BECAUSE IT LOOKED LIKE FUN.

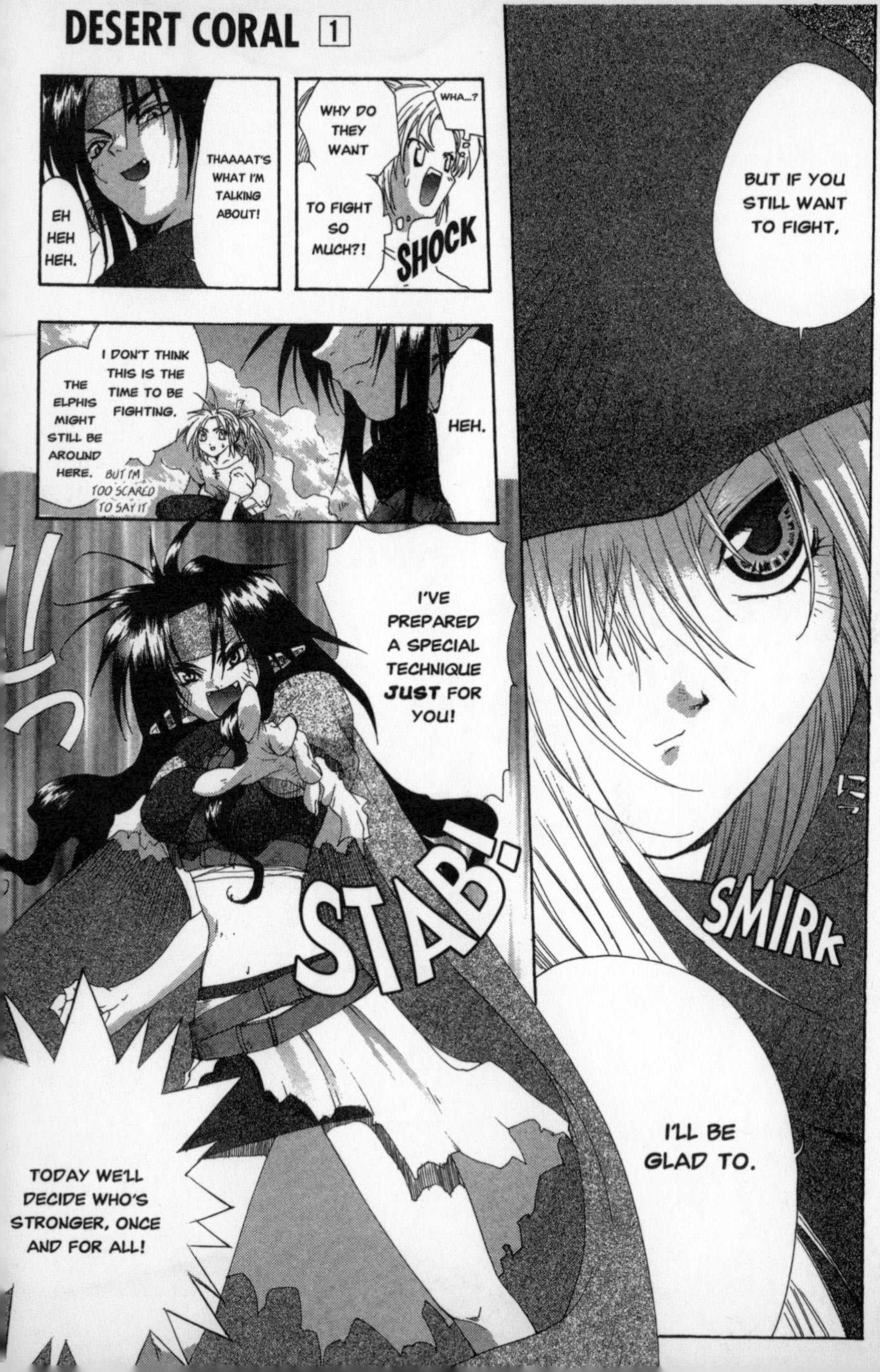
BUT IF YOU STILL WANT TO FIGHT,
SMIRK
I'LL BE GLAD TO.
WHA...?
WHY DO THEY WANT
TO FIGHT SO MUCH?!
SHOCK
THAAAAT'S WHAT I'M TALKING ABOUT!
EH HEH HEH.
HEH.
I DON'T THINK THIS IS THE TIME TO BE FIGHTING.
THE ELPHIS MIGHT STILL BE AROUND HERE.
BUT I'M TOO SCARED TO SAY IT
I'VE PREPARED A SPECIAL TECHNIQUE JUST FOR YOU!
STAB!
TODAY WE'LL DECIDE WHO'S STRONGER, ONCE AND FOR ALL!

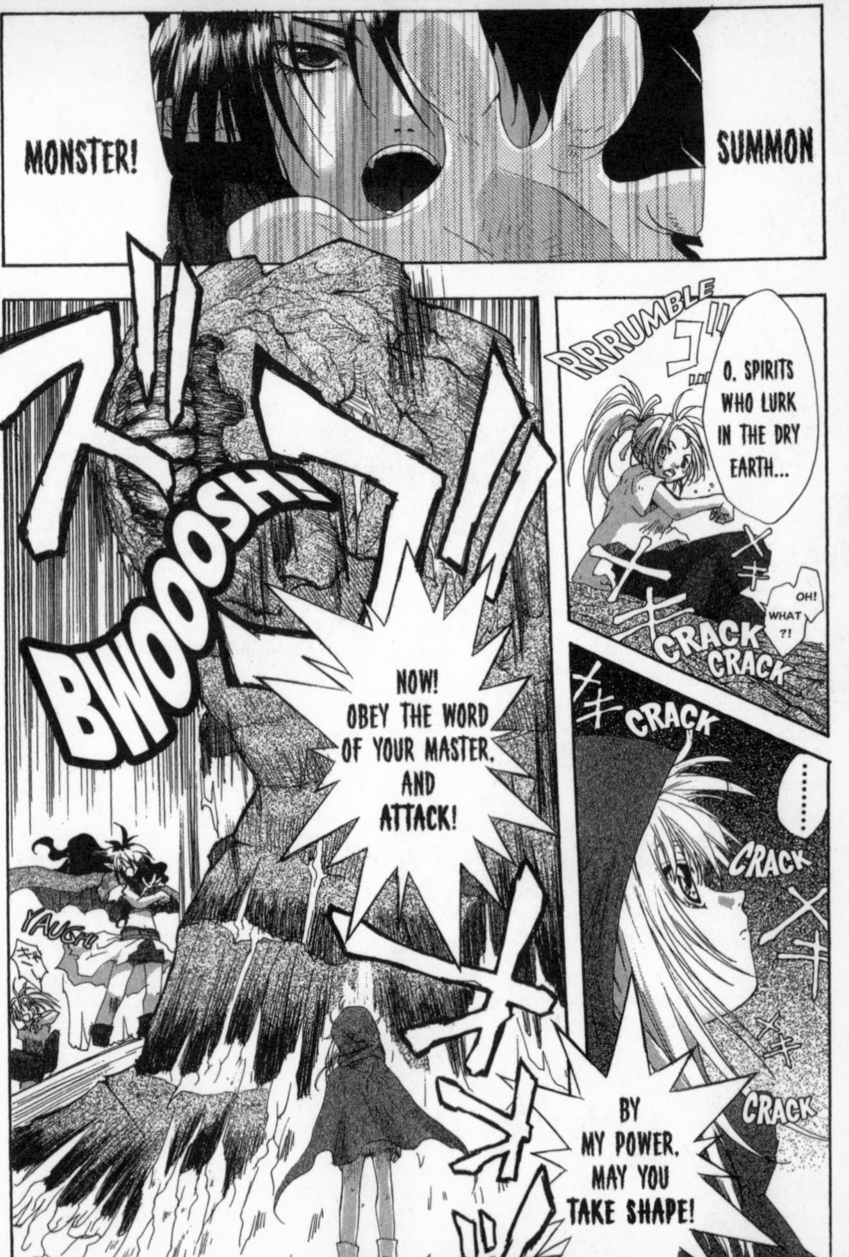
SUMMON
MONSTER!
RRRUMBLE
O. SPIRITS WHO LURK IN THE DRY EARTH...
OH! WHAT?!
CRACK CRACK
CRACK
......
CRACK
CRACK
BY MY POWER, MAY YOU TAKE SHAPE!
BWOOOSH!
NOW! OBEY THE WORD OF YOUR MASTER, AND ATTACK!
YAUGH!

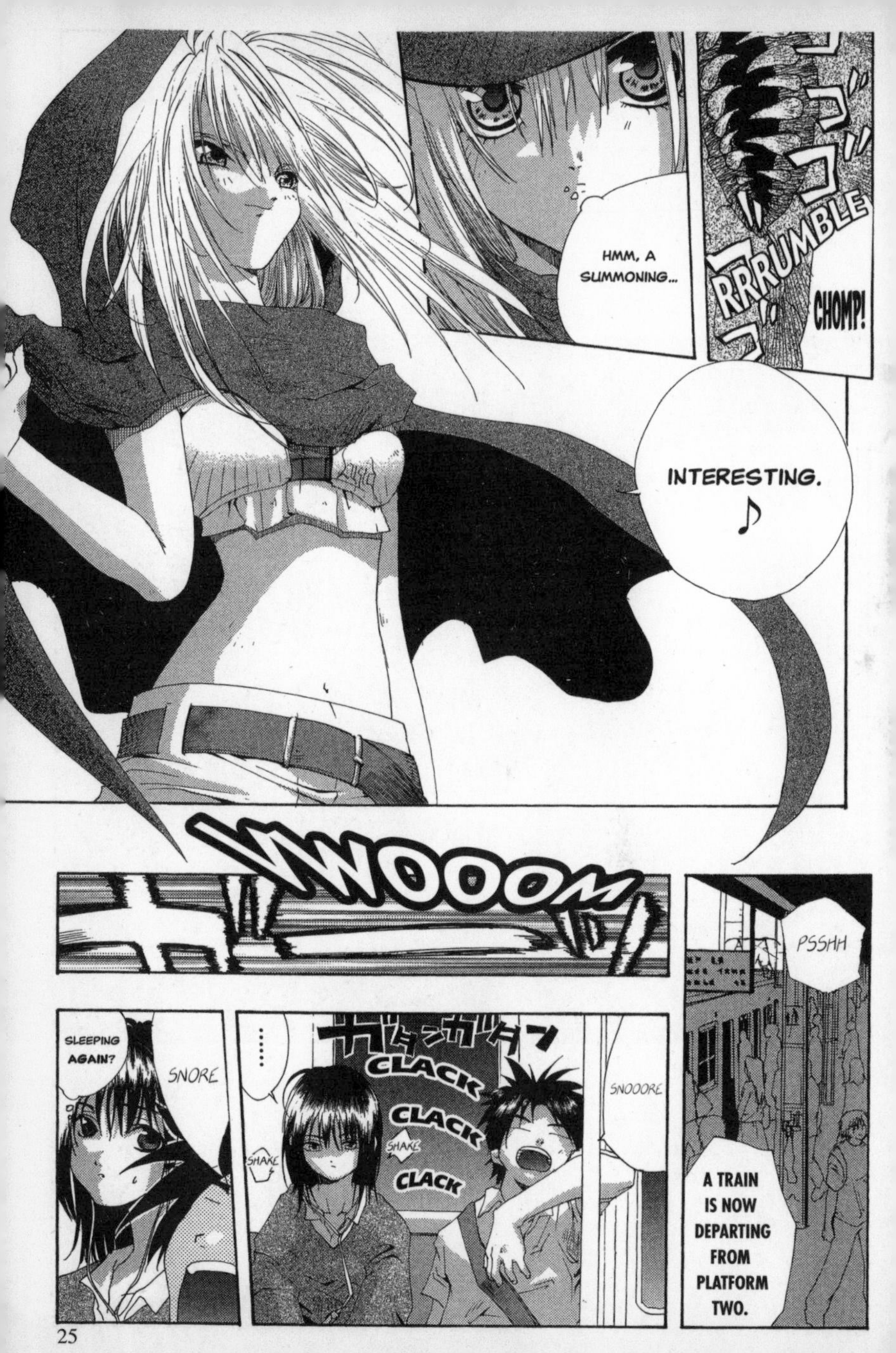
RRRUMBLE
CHOMP!
HMM, A SUMMONING...
INTERESTING. ♪
PSSHH
A TRAIN IS NOW DEPARTING FROM PLATFORM TWO.
WOOOM
......
ガタンガタン
CLACK
CLACK
CLACK
SHAKE
SHAKE
SNOOORE
SLEEPING AGAIN?
SNORE

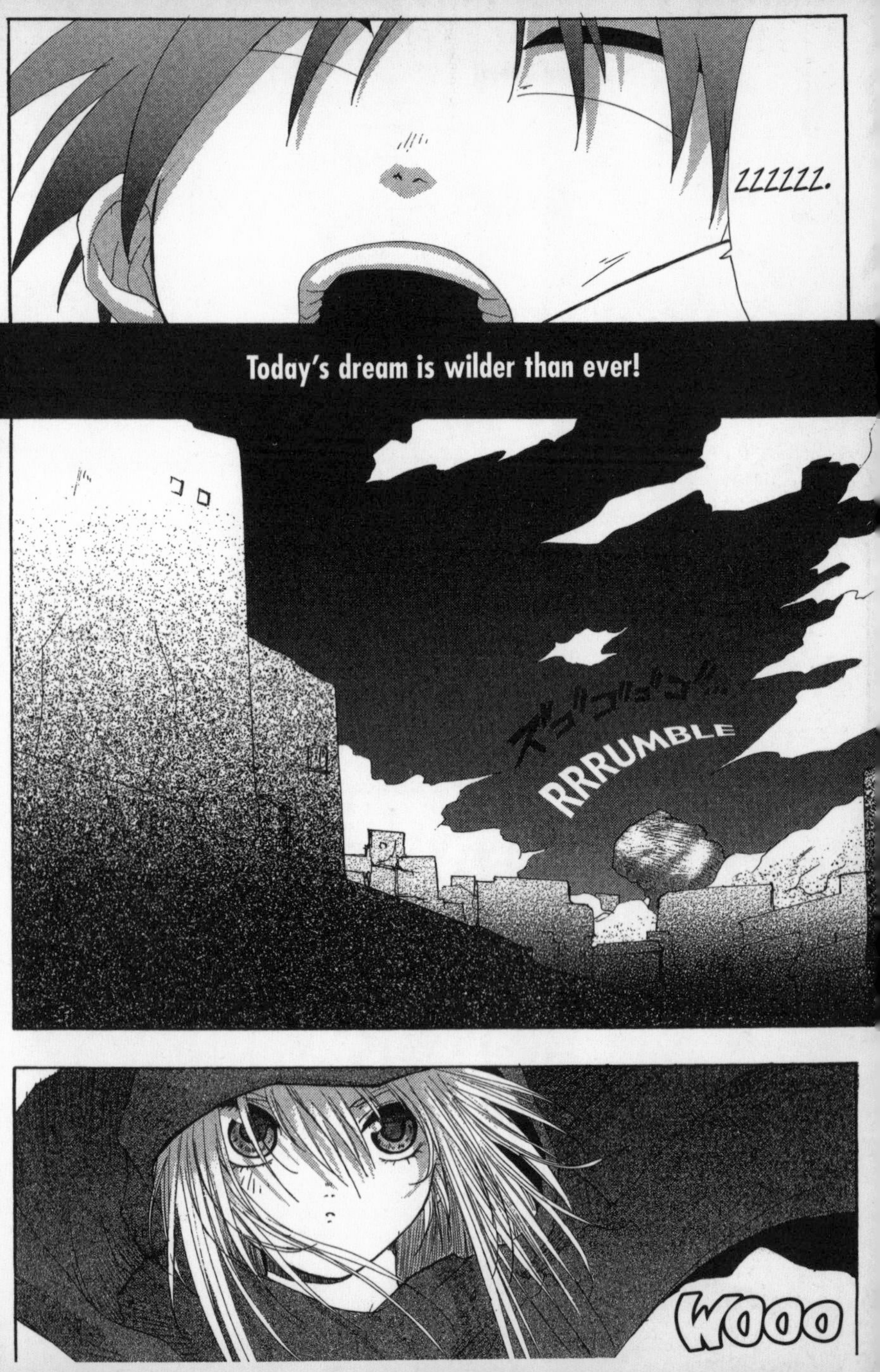
ZZZZZZ.
Today's dream is wilder than ever!
RRRUMBLE
WOOO

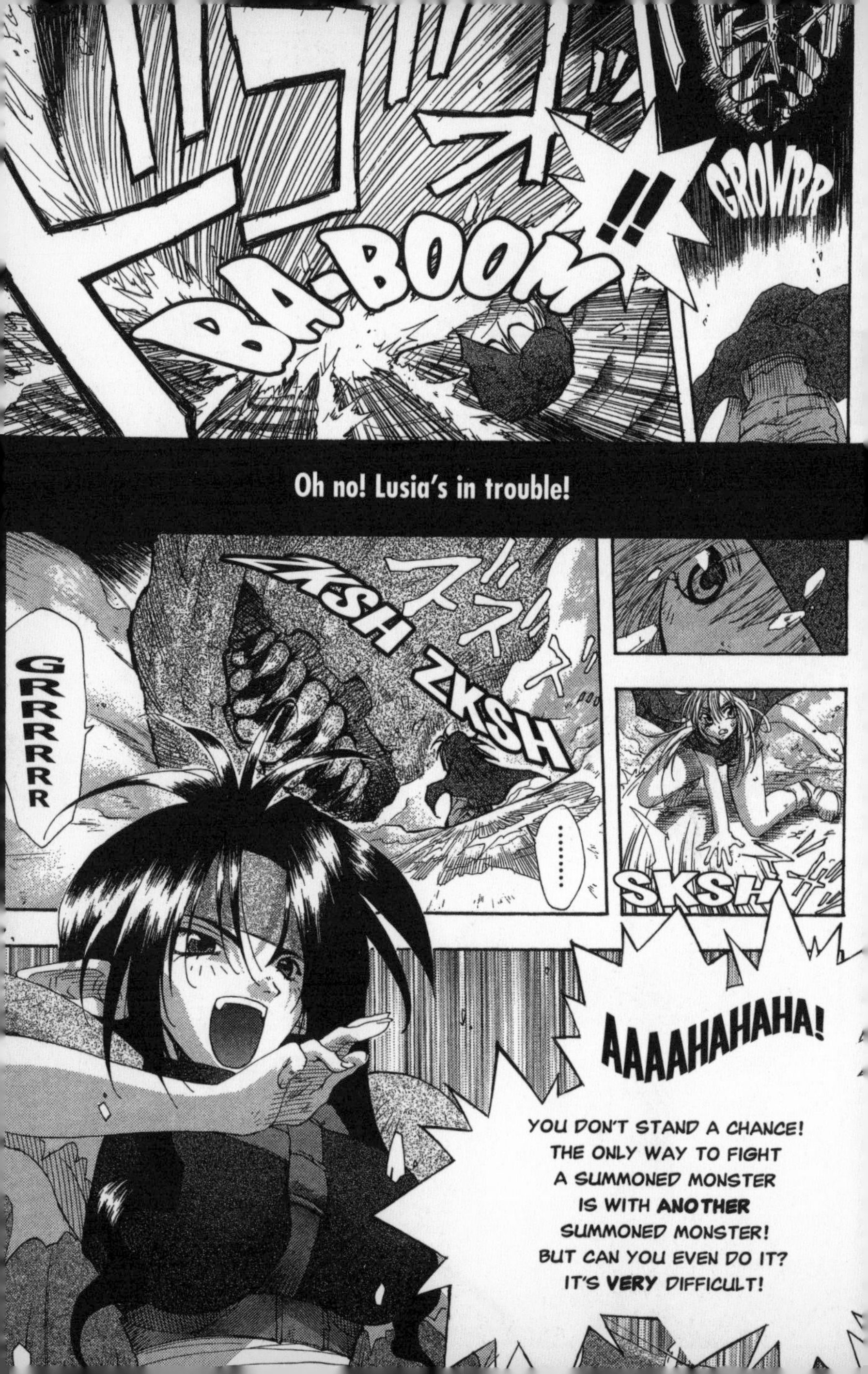

GROWRR
BA-BOOM!!
Oh no! Lusia's in trouble!
SKSH
ZKSH
ZKSH
GRRRRRR
....
AAAAHAHAHA!
YOU DON'T STAND A CHANCE! THE ONLY WAY TO FIGHT A SUMMONED MONSTER IS WITH **ANOTHER** SUMMONED MONSTER! BUT CAN YOU EVEN DO IT? IT'S **VERY** DIFFICULT!

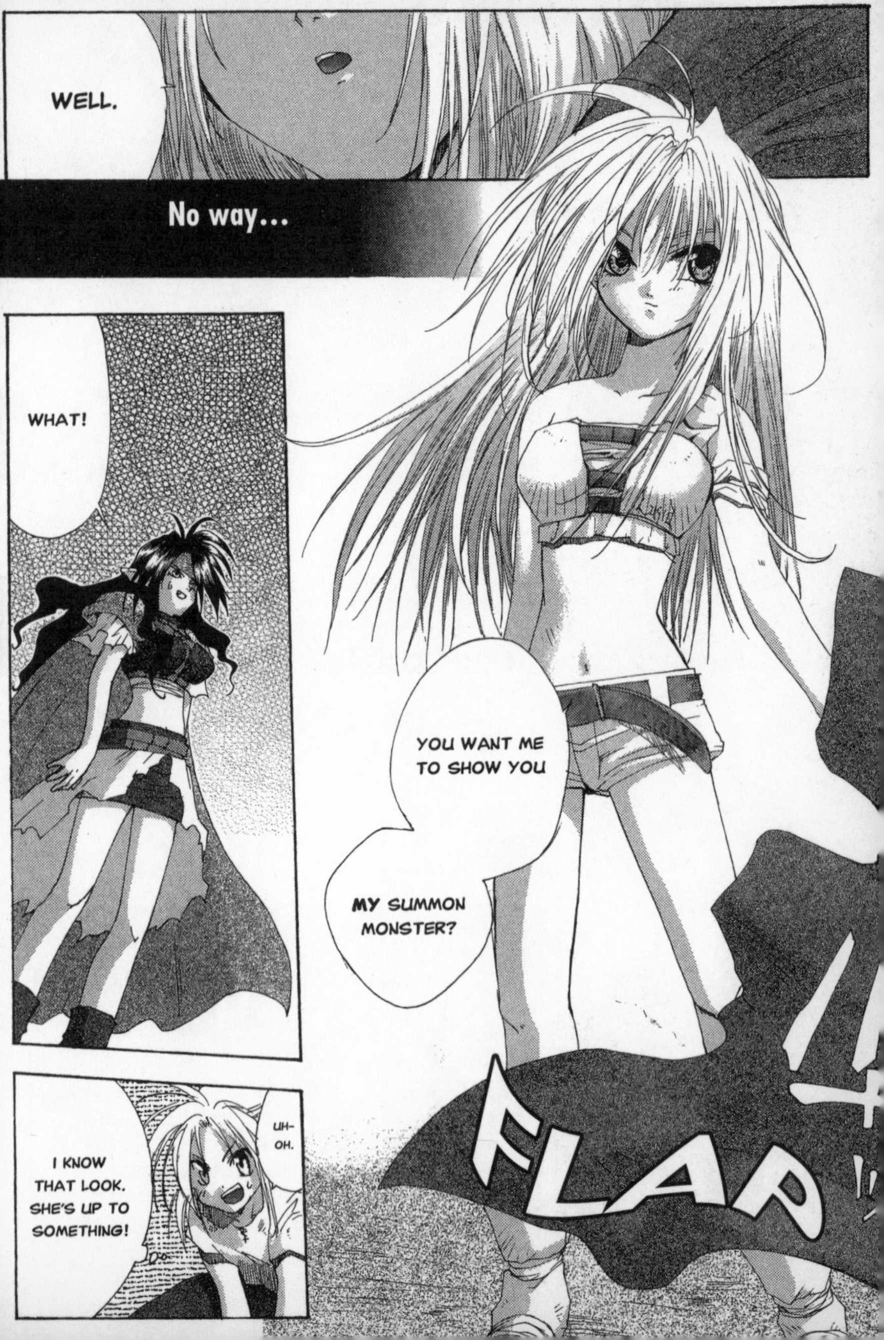
WELL.
No way...
YOU WANT ME TO SHOW YOU
MY SUMMON MONSTER?
FLAP
WHAT!
UH-OH.
I KNOW THAT LOOK. SHE'S UP TO SOMETHING!

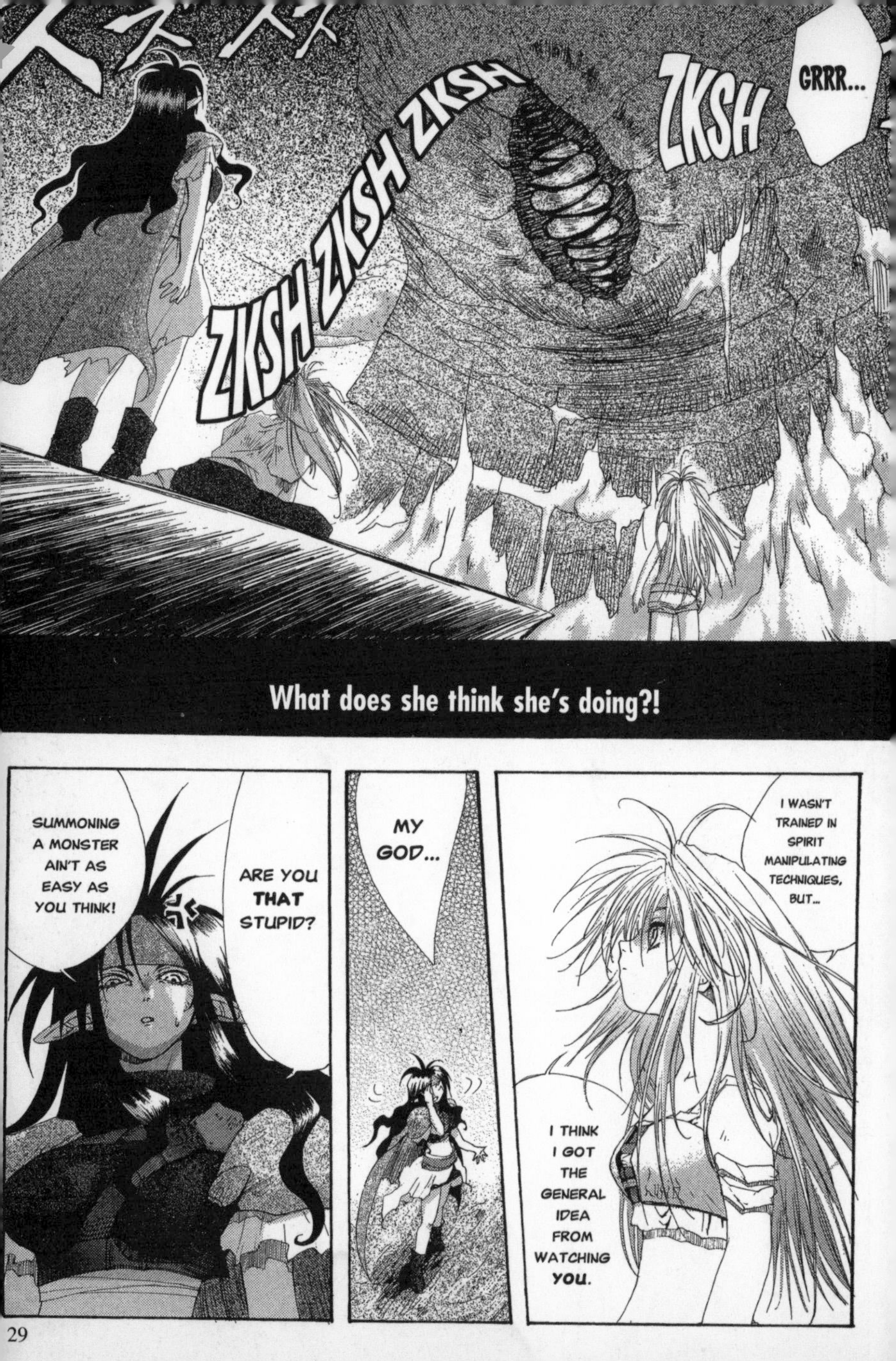
GRRR...
ZKSH
ZKSH ZKSH ZKSH ZKSH
What does she think she's doing?!
I WASN'T TRAINED IN SPIRIT MANIPULATING TECHNIQUES, BUT...
I THINK I GOT THE GENERAL IDEA FROM WATCHING **YOU**.
MY GOD...
ARE YOU **THAT** STUPID?
SUMMONING A MONSTER AIN'T AS EASY AS YOU THINK!

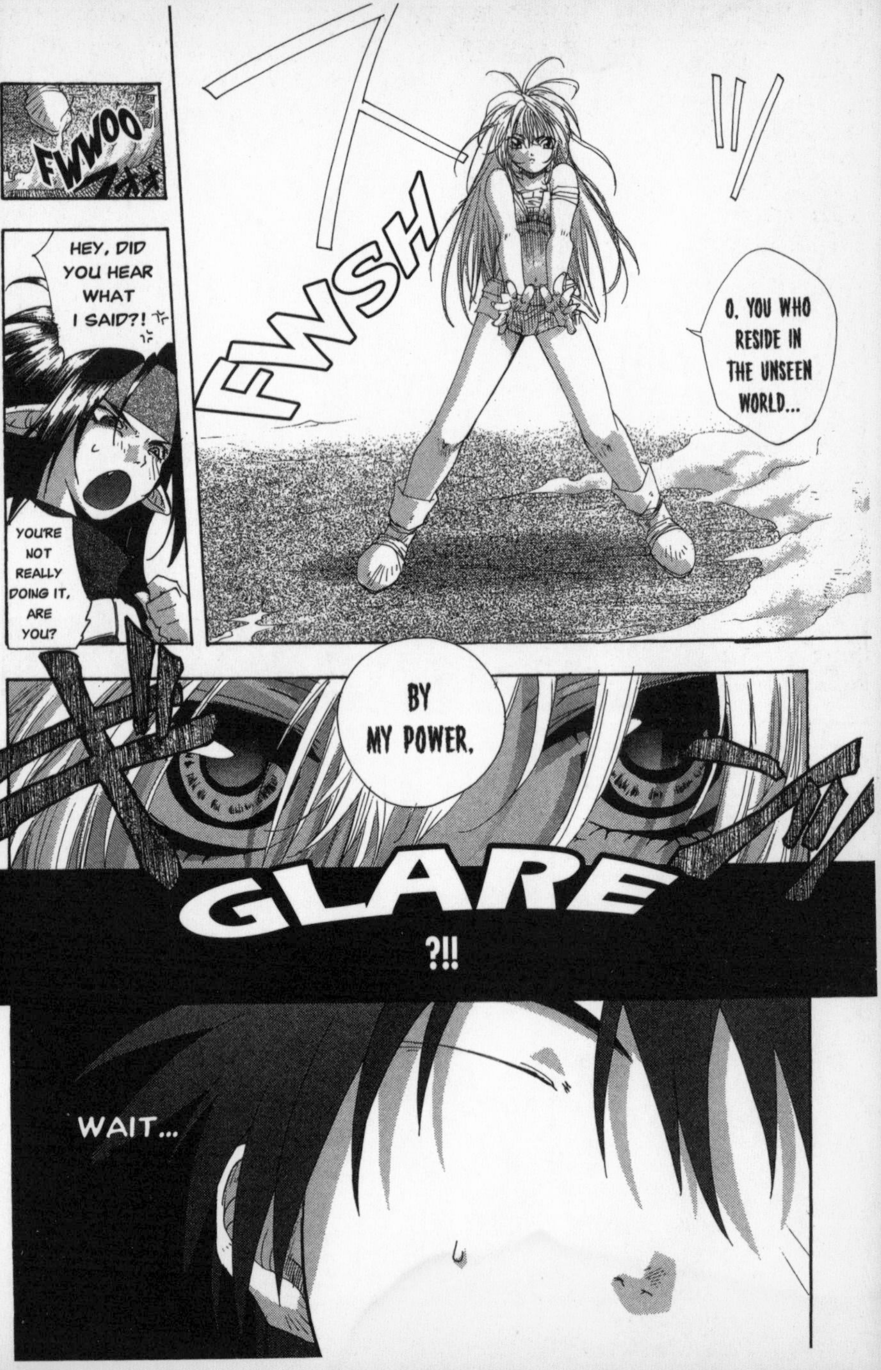
FWSH
O, YOU WHO RESIDE IN THE UNSEEN WORLD...
FWWOO
HEY, DID YOU HEAR WHAT I SAID?!
YOU'RE NOT REALLY DOING IT, ARE YOU?
BY MY POWER,
GLARE
?!!
WAIT...

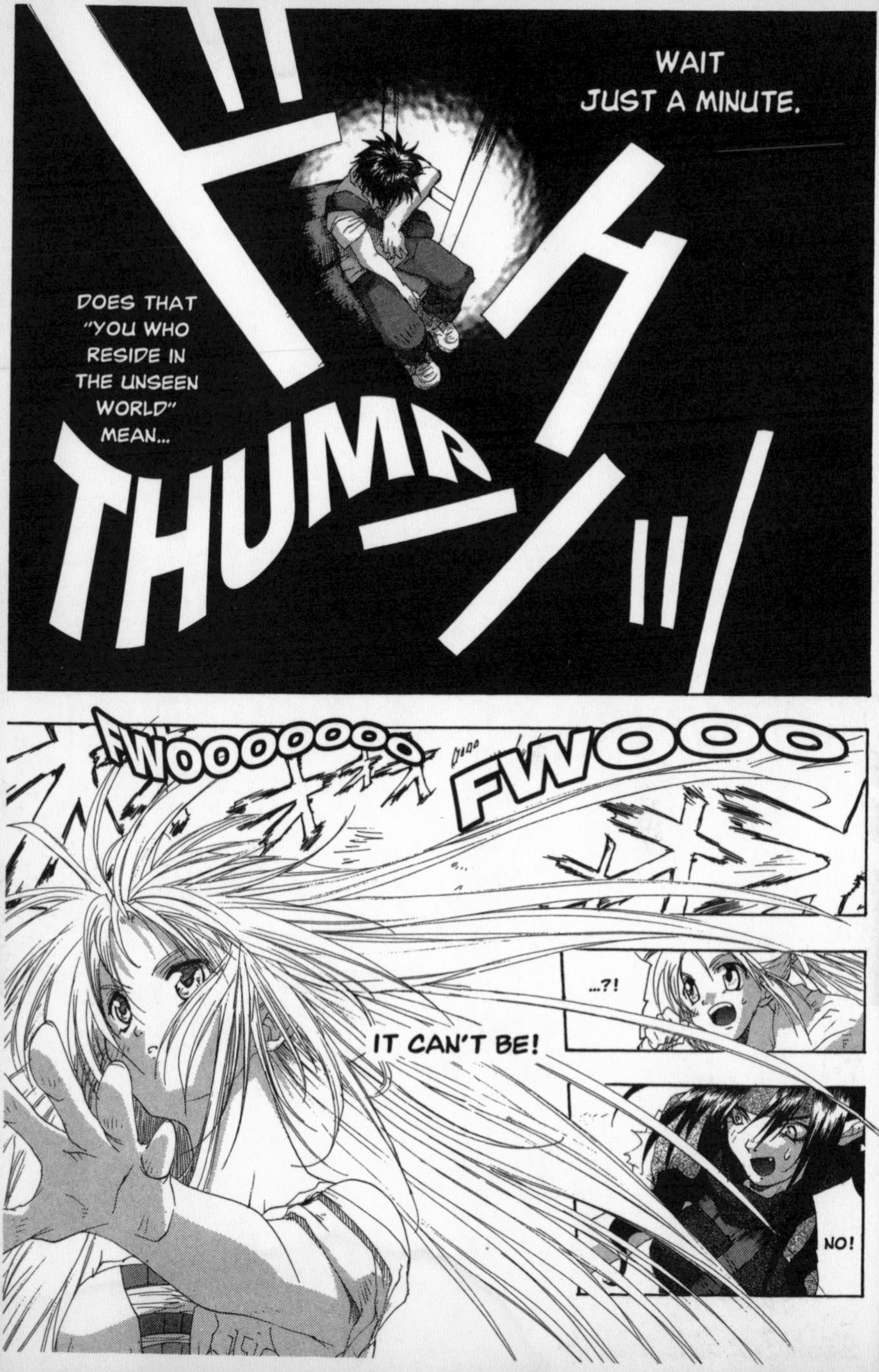
WAIT JUST A MINUTE.
DOES THAT "YOU WHO RESIDE IN THE UNSEEN WORLD" MEAN...
THUMP
FWOOO
FWOOOOOOOO
...?!
IT CAN'T BE!
NO!

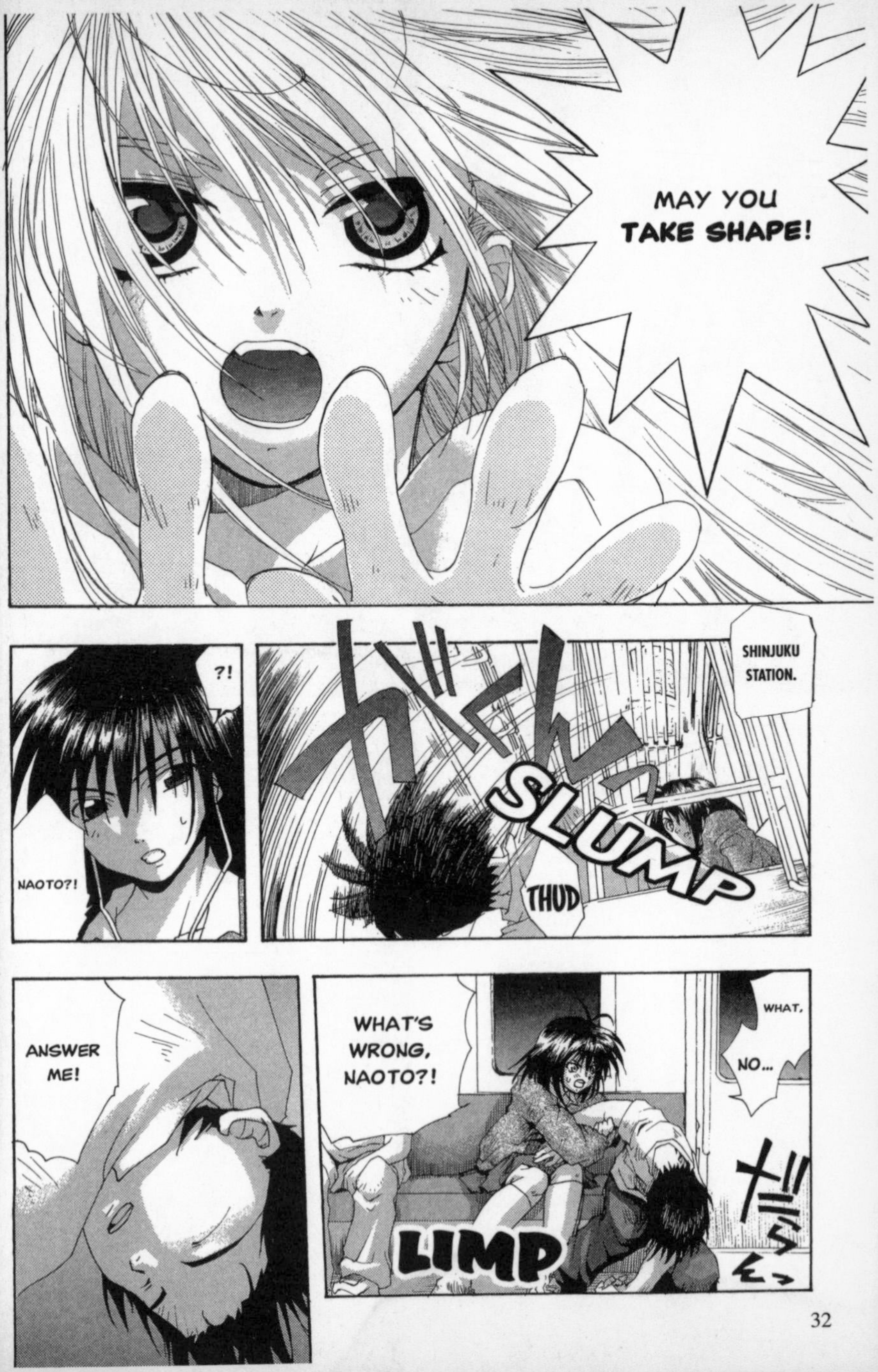
MAY YOU TAKE SHAPE!
SHINJUKU STATION.
SLUMP
THUD
?!
NAOTO?!
WHAT, NO...
WHAT'S WRONG, NAOTO?!
LIMP
ANSWER ME!

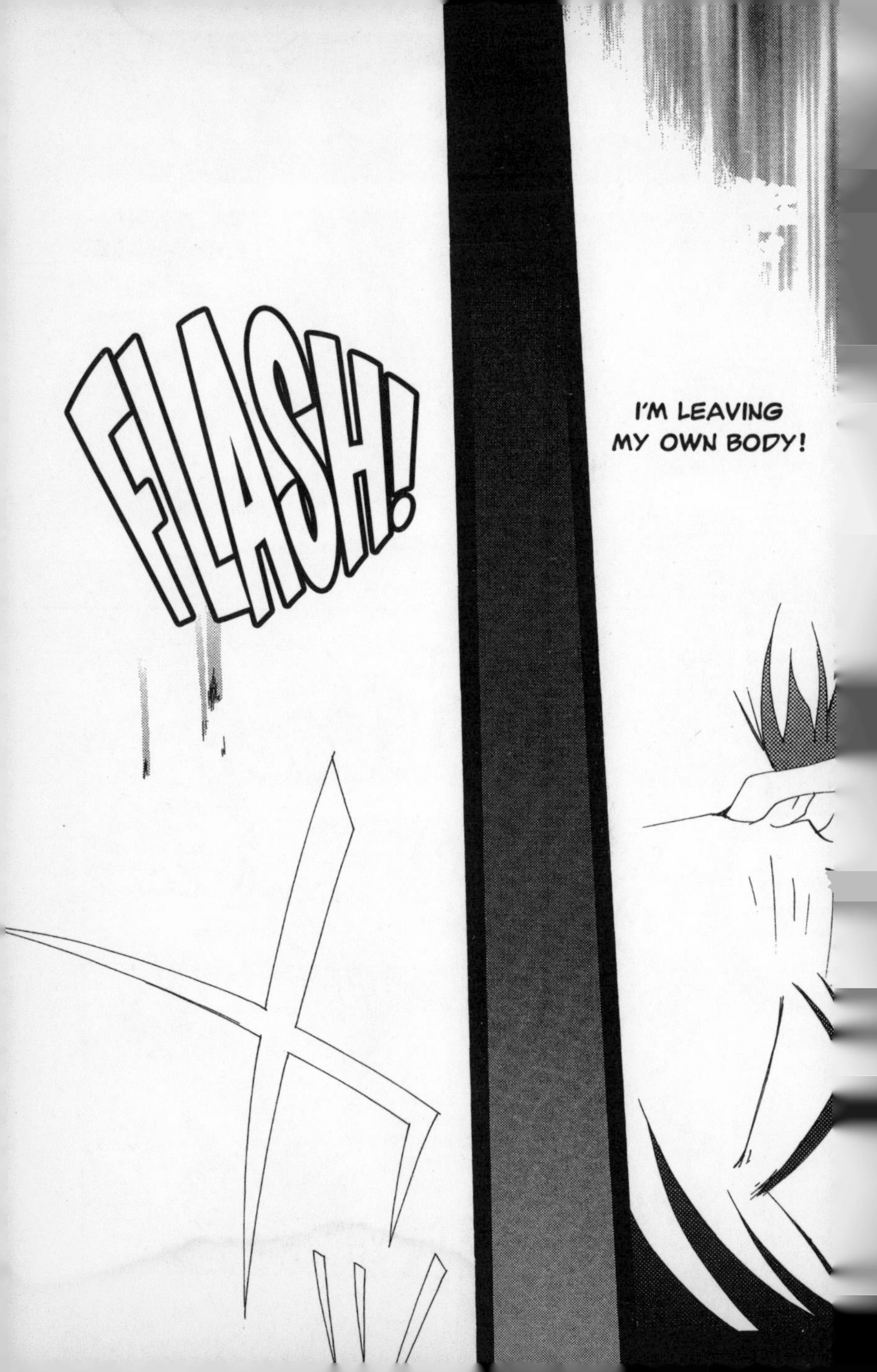
I'M LEAVING MY OWN BODY!
FLASH!

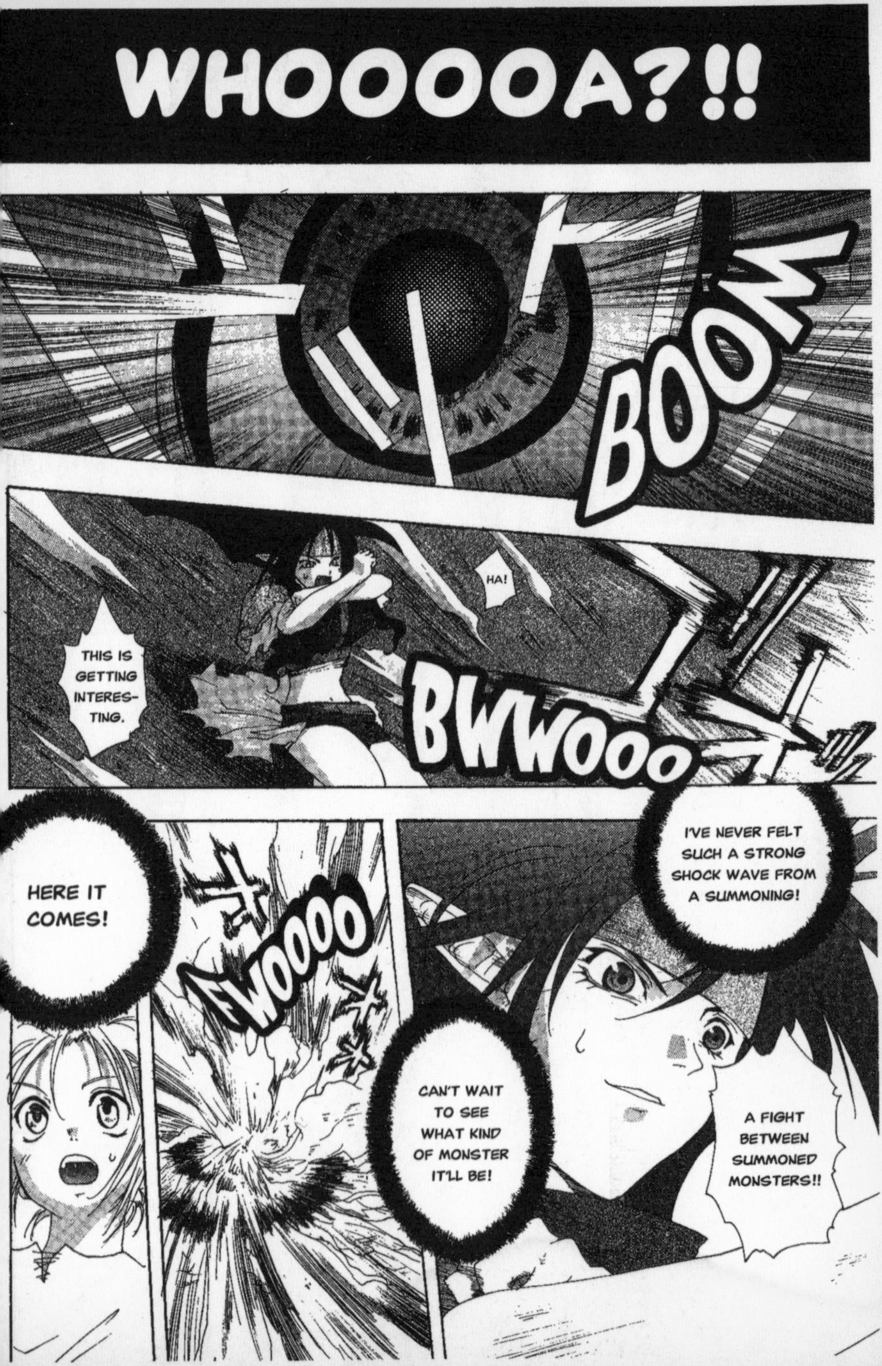
WHOOOOA?!!
BOOM
HA!
BWWOOO
THIS IS GETTING INTERES-TING.
I'VE NEVER FELT SUCH A STRONG SHOCK WAVE FROM A SUMMONING!
A FIGHT BETWEEN SUMMONED MONSTERS!!
CAN'T WAIT TO SEE WHAT KIND OF MONSTER IT'LL BE!
HERE IT COMES!
FWOOOO

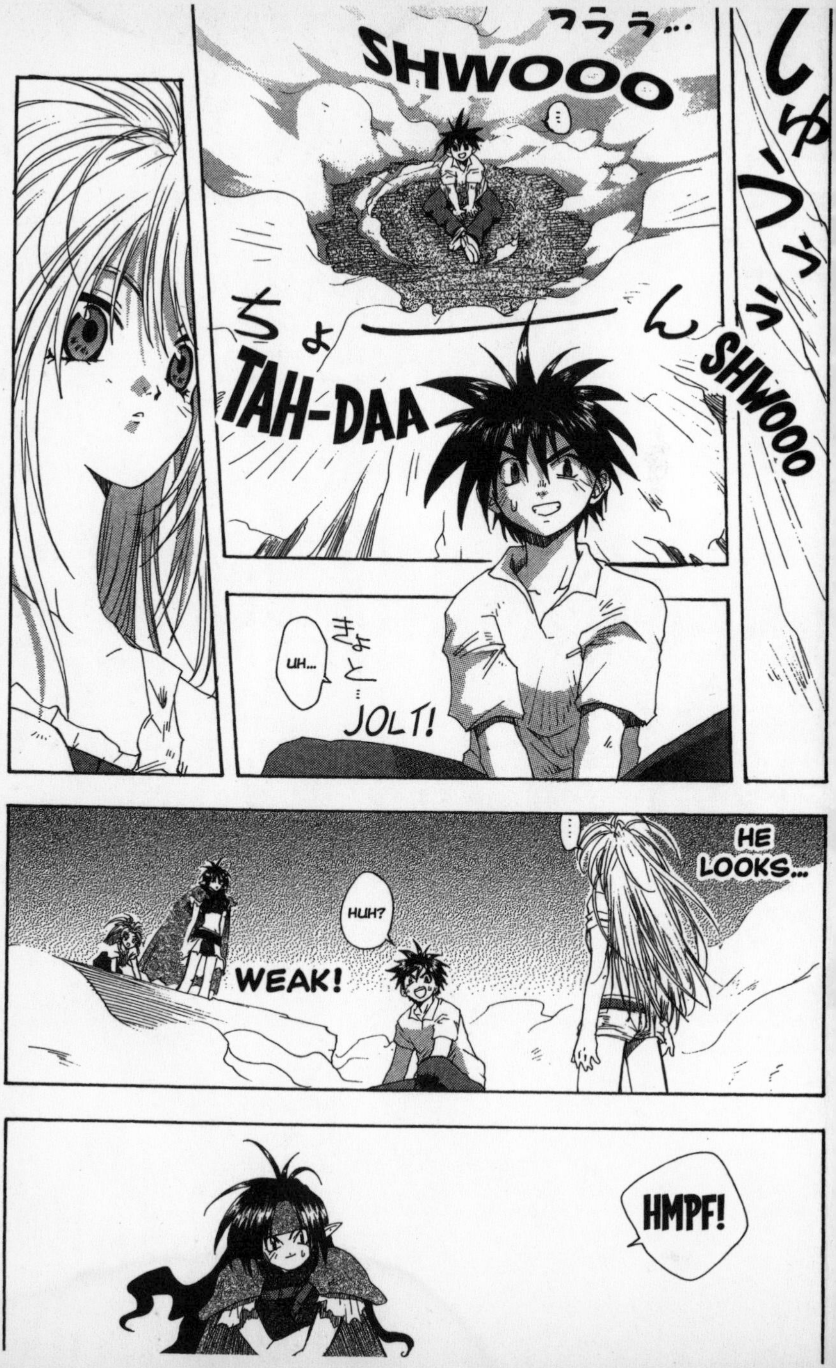
しゅううう
SHWOOO
フうう…
SHWOOO
…
ちょーーーん
TAH-DAA
UH…
きょと
JOLT!
HE LOOKS…
…
HUH?
WEAK!
HMPF!

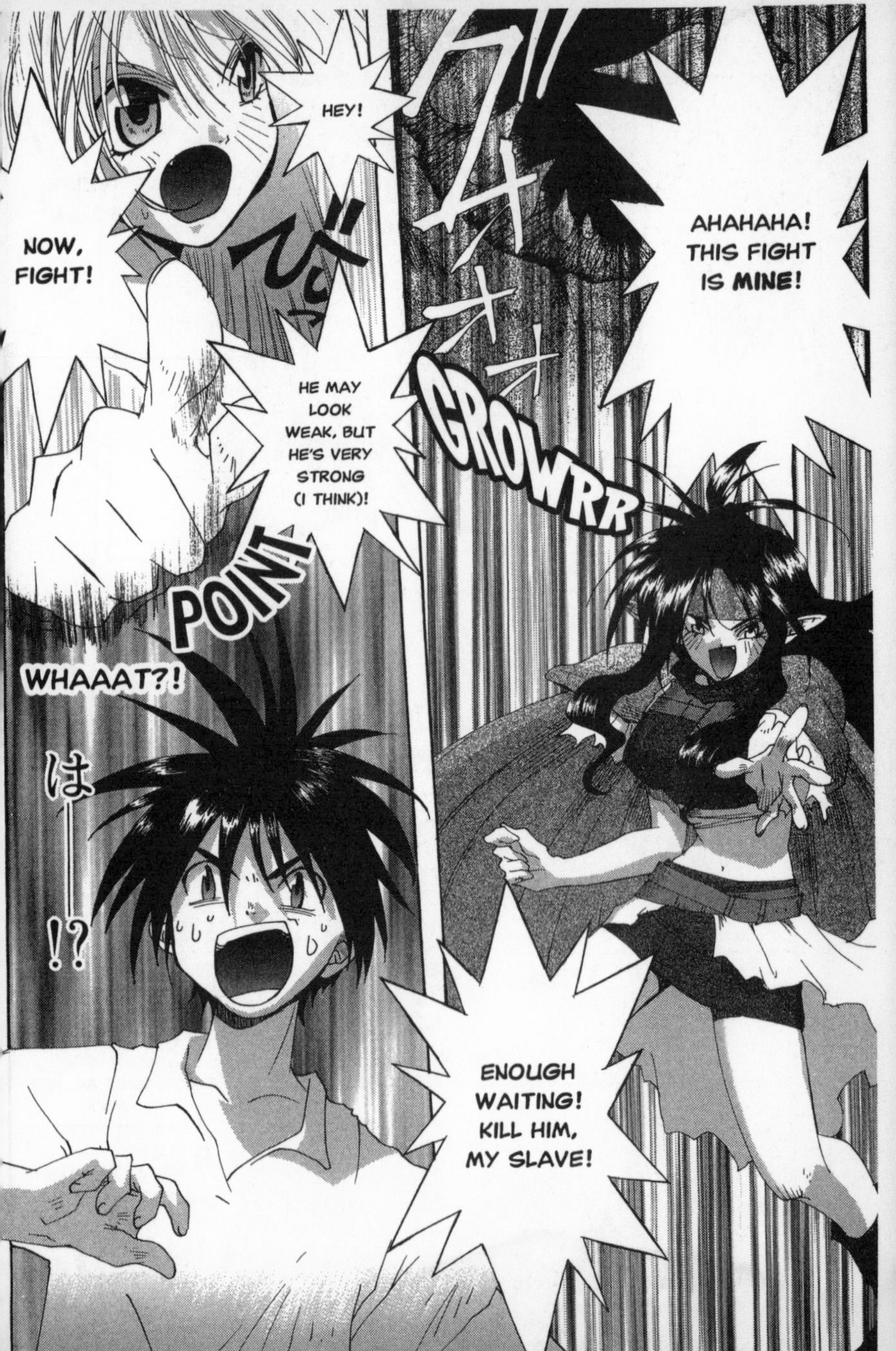
GROWRR
AHAHAHA! THIS FIGHT IS MINE!
HEY!
NOW, FIGHT!
HE MAY LOOK WEAK, BUT HE'S VERY STRONG (I THINK)!
POINT
WHAAAT?!
は——!?
ENOUGH WAITING! KILL HIM, MY SLAVE!

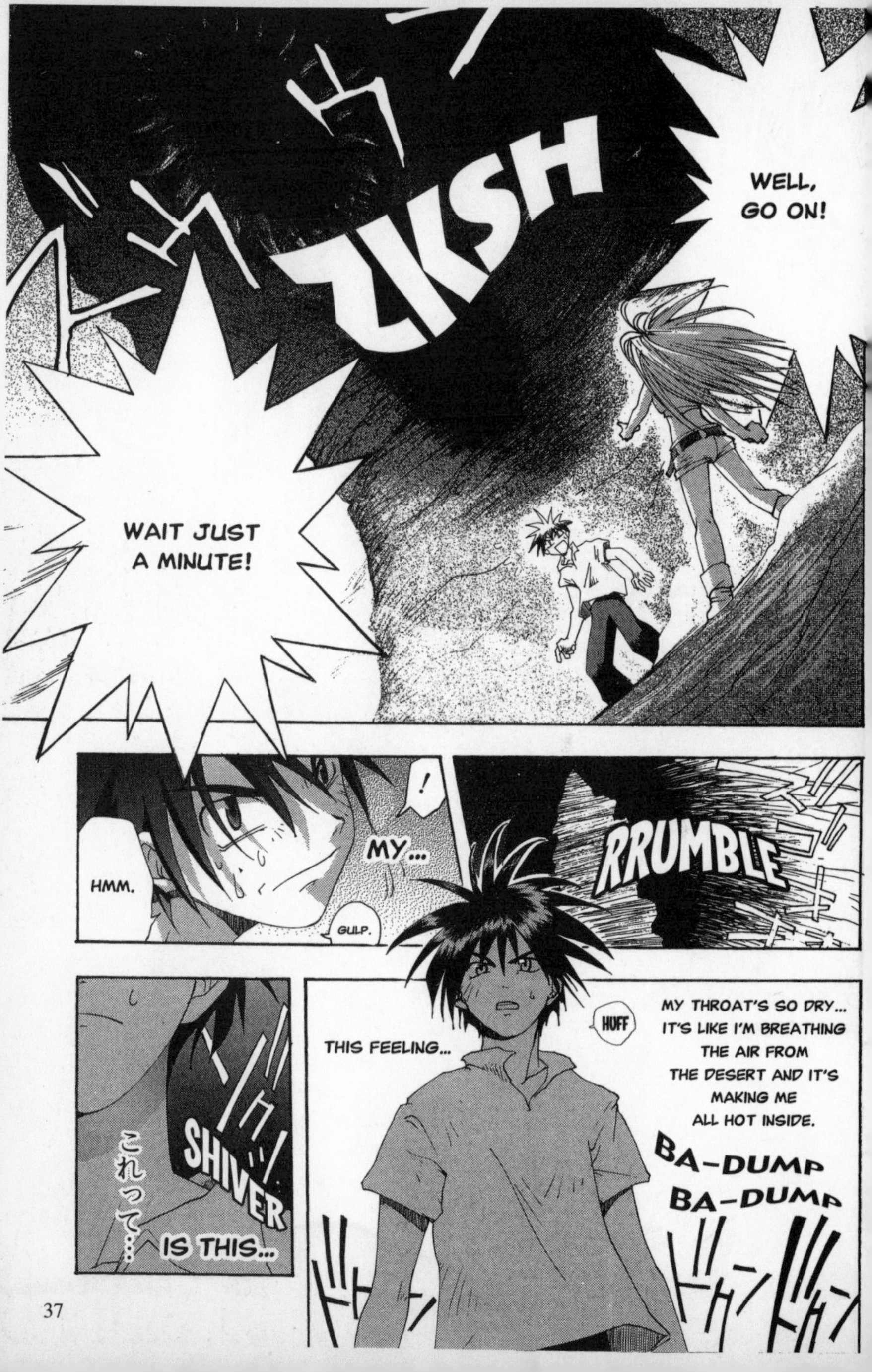
WELL, GO ON!
ZKSH
WAIT JUST A MINUTE!
RRUMBLE
!
MY...
HMM.
GULP.
MY THROAT'S SO DRY... IT'S LIKE I'M BREATHING THE AIR FROM THE DESERT AND IT'S MAKING ME ALL HOT INSIDE.
HUFF
THIS FEELING...
BA-DUMP BA-DUMP
SHIVER
これって…
IS THIS...

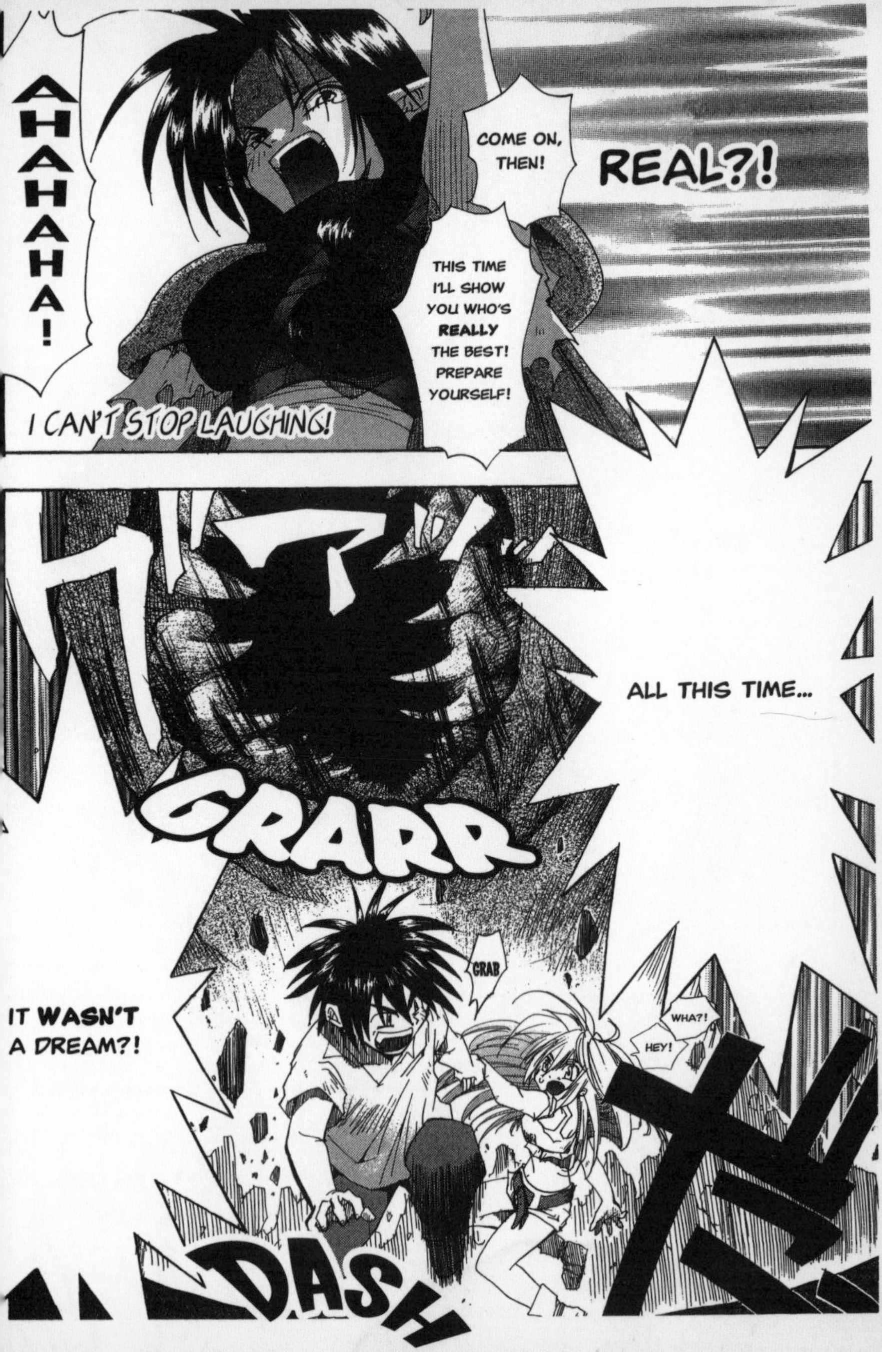
REAL?!
COME ON, THEN!
THIS TIME I'LL SHOW YOU WHO'S **REALLY** THE BEST! PREPARE YOURSELF!
AHAHAHA!
I CAN'T STOP LAUGHING!
ALL THIS TIME...
GRARR
GRAB
WHA?!
HEY!
IT **WASN'T** A DREAM?!
DASH

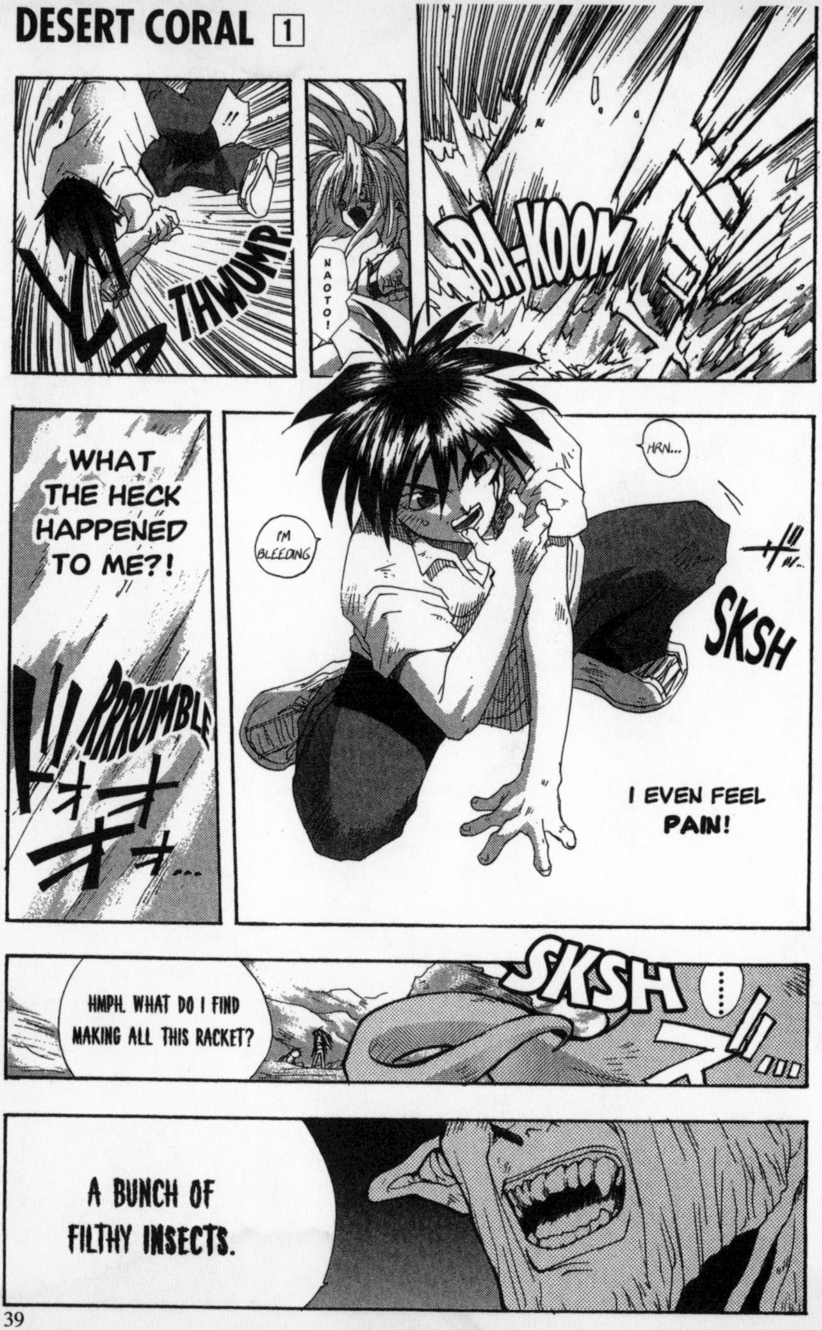
BA-KOOM
NAOTO!
THWUMP!
HRN...
SKSH
I'M BLEEDING
I EVEN FEEL PAIN!
WHAT THE HECK HAPPENED TO ME?!
RRRUMBLE
SKSH
HMPH. WHAT DO I FIND MAKING ALL THIS RACKET?
A BUNCH OF FILTHY INSECTS.

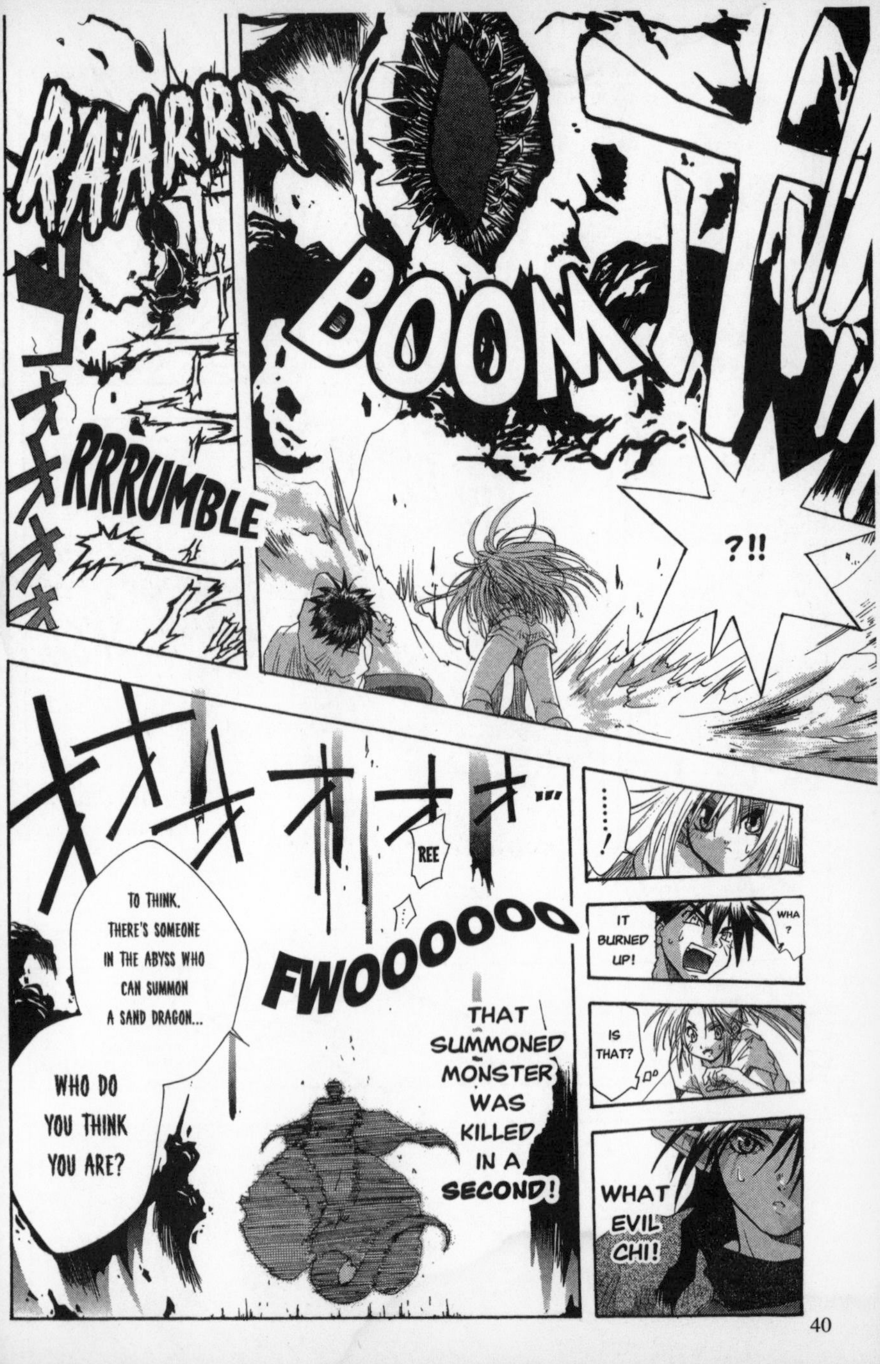
BOOM!
?!!
RAARRR!
RRRUMBLE
......!
WHA ?
IT BURNED UP!
IS THAT?
WHAT EVIL CHI!
REE
FWOOOOOO
THAT SUMMONED MONSTER WAS KILLED IN A SECOND!
TO THINK. THERE'S SOMEONE IN THE ABYSS WHO CAN SUMMON A SAND DRAGON...
WHO DO YOU THINK YOU ARE?

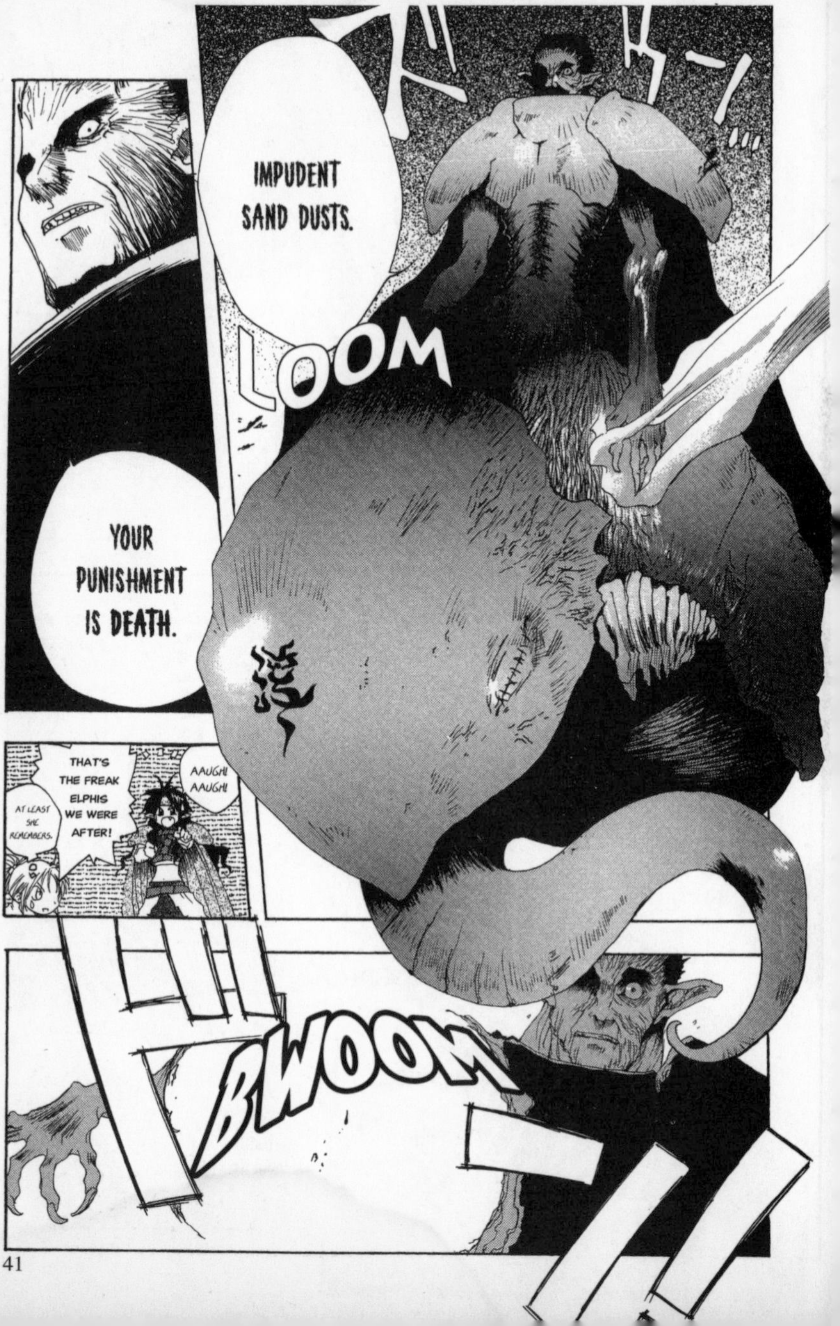
IMPUDENT SAND DUSTS.
LOOM
YOUR PUNISHMENT IS DEATH.
AAUGH! AAUGH!
THAT'S THE FREAK ELPHIS WE WERE AFTER!
AT LEAST SHE REMEMBERS.
BWOOM

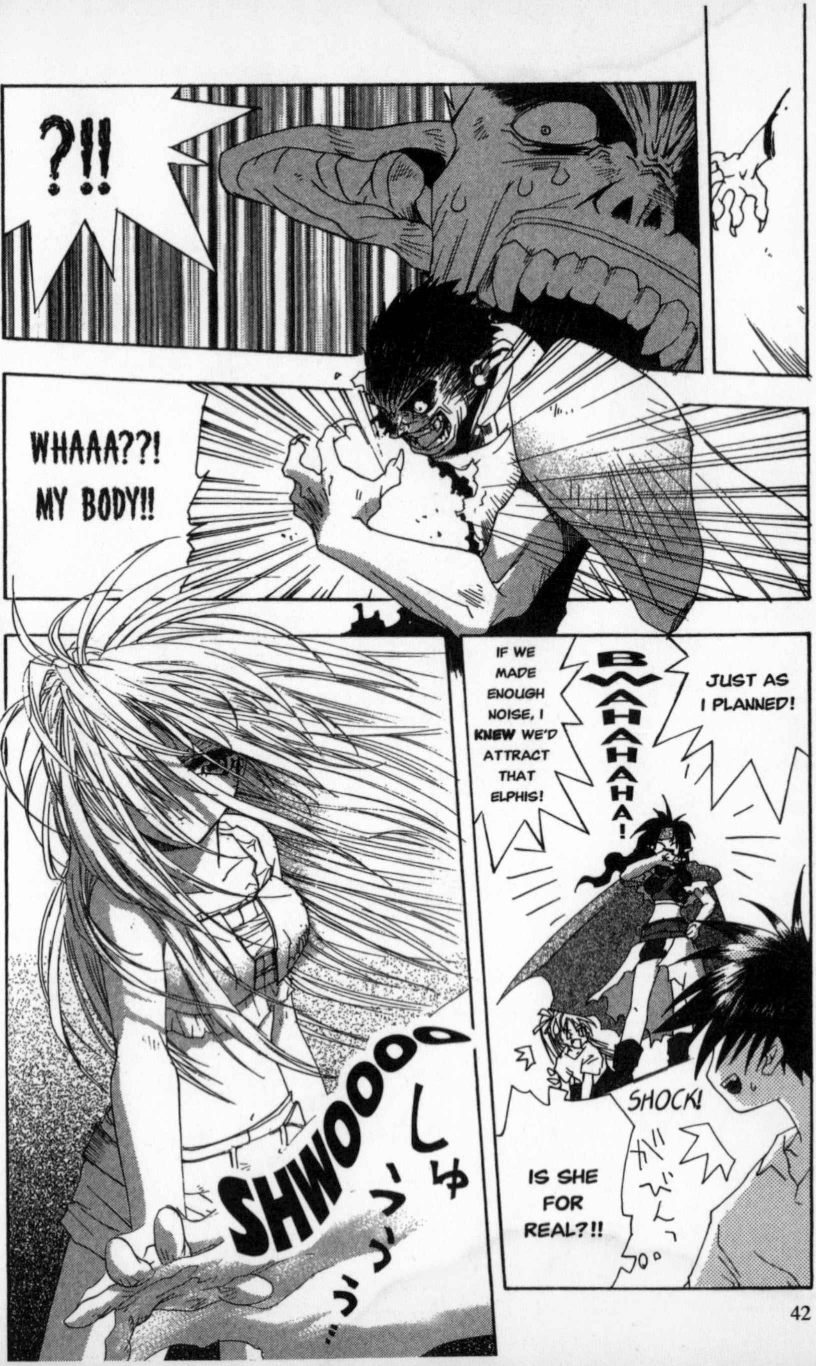
?!!
WHAAA??! MY BODY!!
JUST AS I PLANNED!
BWAHAHAHAHA!
IF WE MADE ENOUGH NOISE, I KNEW WE'D ATTRACT THAT ELPHIS!
SHOCK!
IS SHE FOR REAL?!!
SHWOOOO

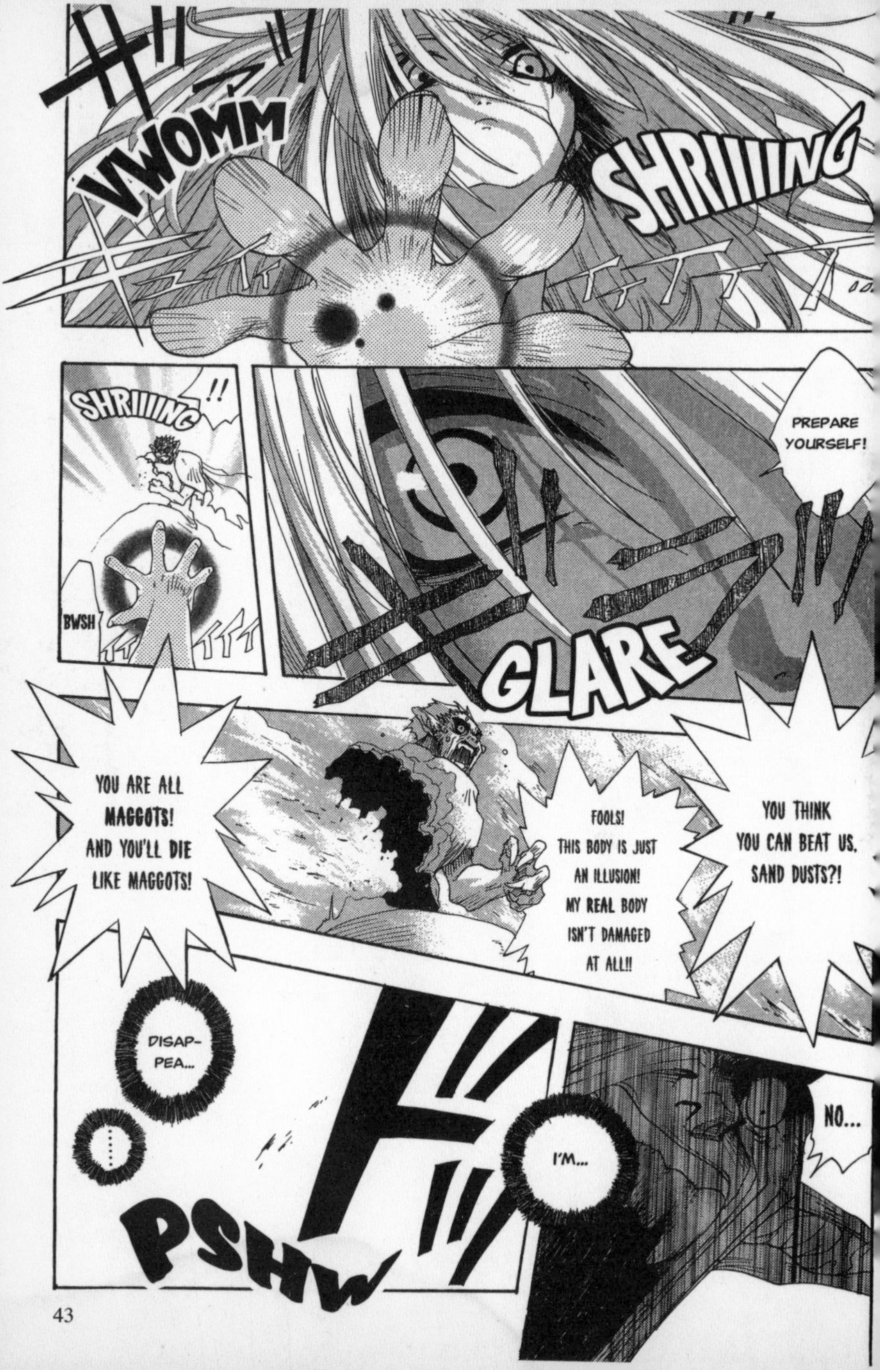
SHRIIIIING
VWOMM
PREPARE YOURSELF!
GLARE
SHRIIIING
!!
BWSH
YOU THINK YOU CAN BEAT US, SAND DUSTS?!
FOOLS! THIS BODY IS JUST AN ILLUSION! MY REAL BODY ISN'T DAMAGED AT ALL!!
YOU ARE ALL MAGGOTS! AND YOU'LL DIE LIKE MAGGOTS!
NO...
I'M...
DISAP- PEA...
......
PSHW

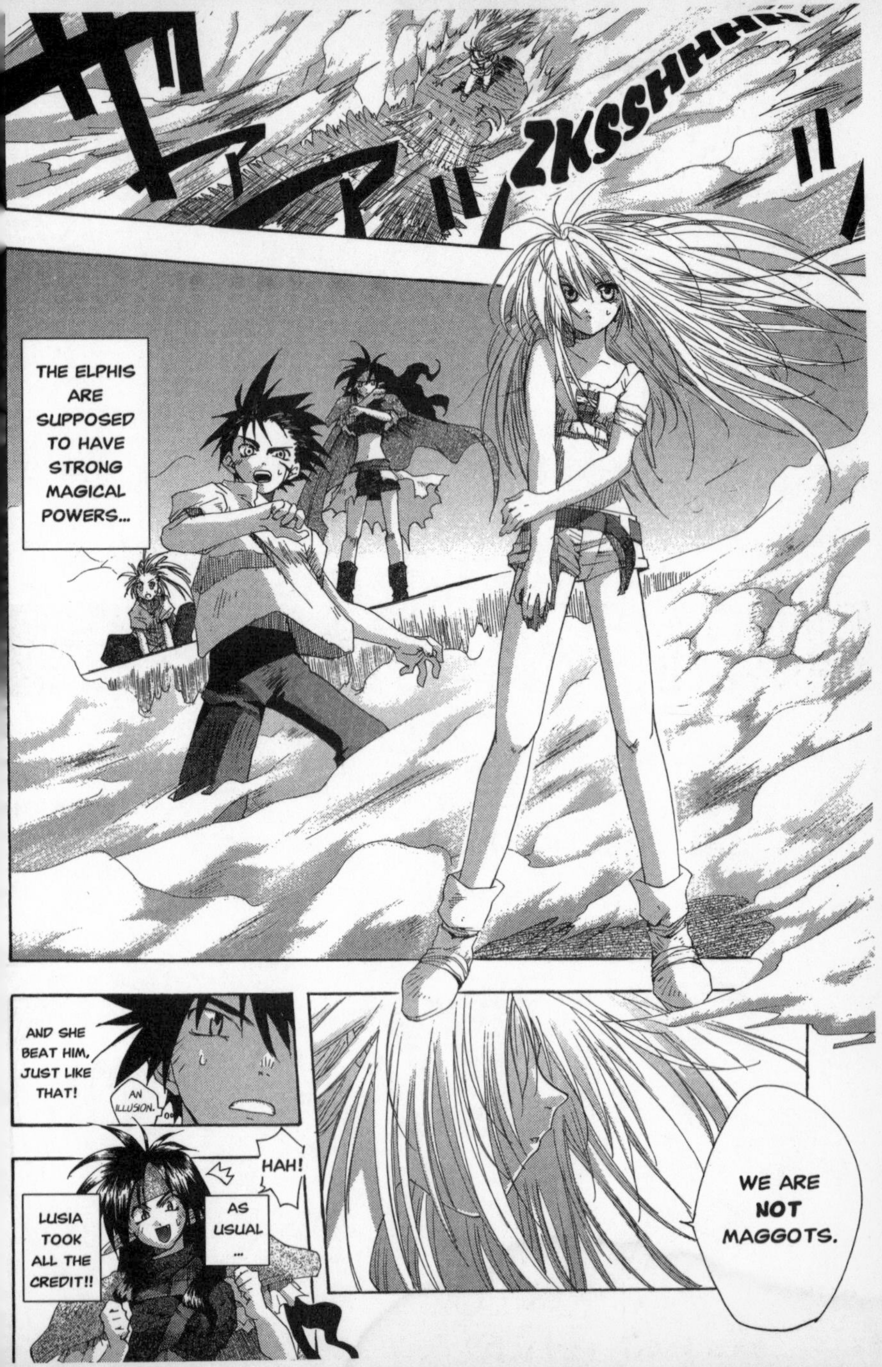
ZKSSHHHH
THE ELPHIS ARE SUPPOSED TO HAVE STRONG MAGICAL POWERS...
WE ARE **NOT** MAGGOTS.
AND SHE BEAT HIM, JUST LIKE THAT!
AN ILLUSION.
HAH!
AS USUAL ...
LUSIA TOOK ALL THE CREDIT!!

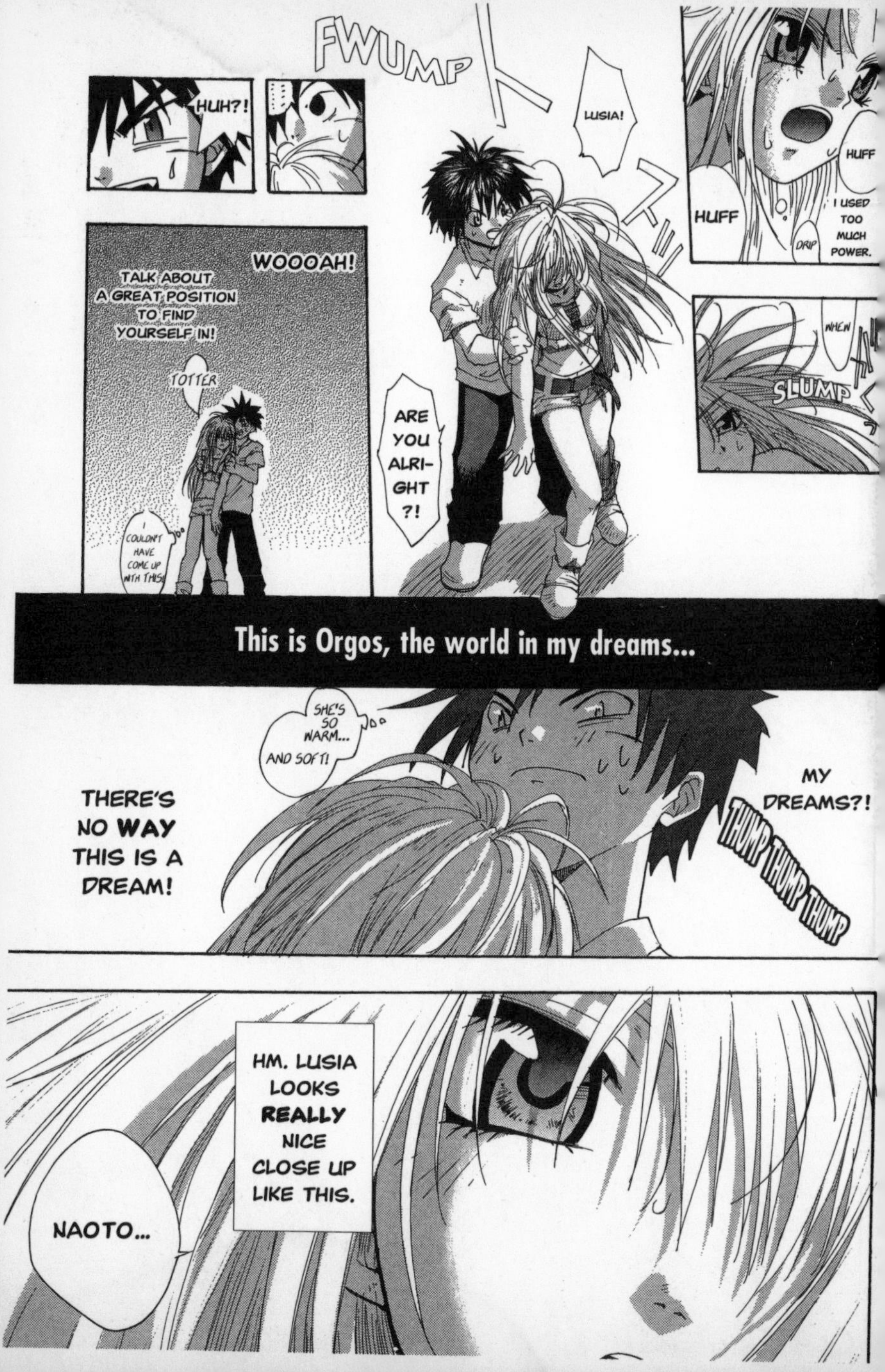
HUFF
HUFF
DRIP
I USED TOO MUCH POWER.
WHEW
SLUMP
FWUMP
LUSIA!
ARE YOU ALRIGHT?!
HUH?!
WOOOAH!
TALK ABOUT A GREAT POSITION TO FIND YOURSELF IN!
TOTTER
I COULDN'T HAVE COME UP WITH THIS!
This is Orgos, the world in my dreams...
MY DREAMS?!
THUMP THUMP THUMP THUMP
SHE'S SO WARM... AND SOFT!
THERE'S NO WAY THIS IS A DREAM!
HM. LUSIA LOOKS REALLY NICE CLOSE UP LIKE THIS.
NAOTO...

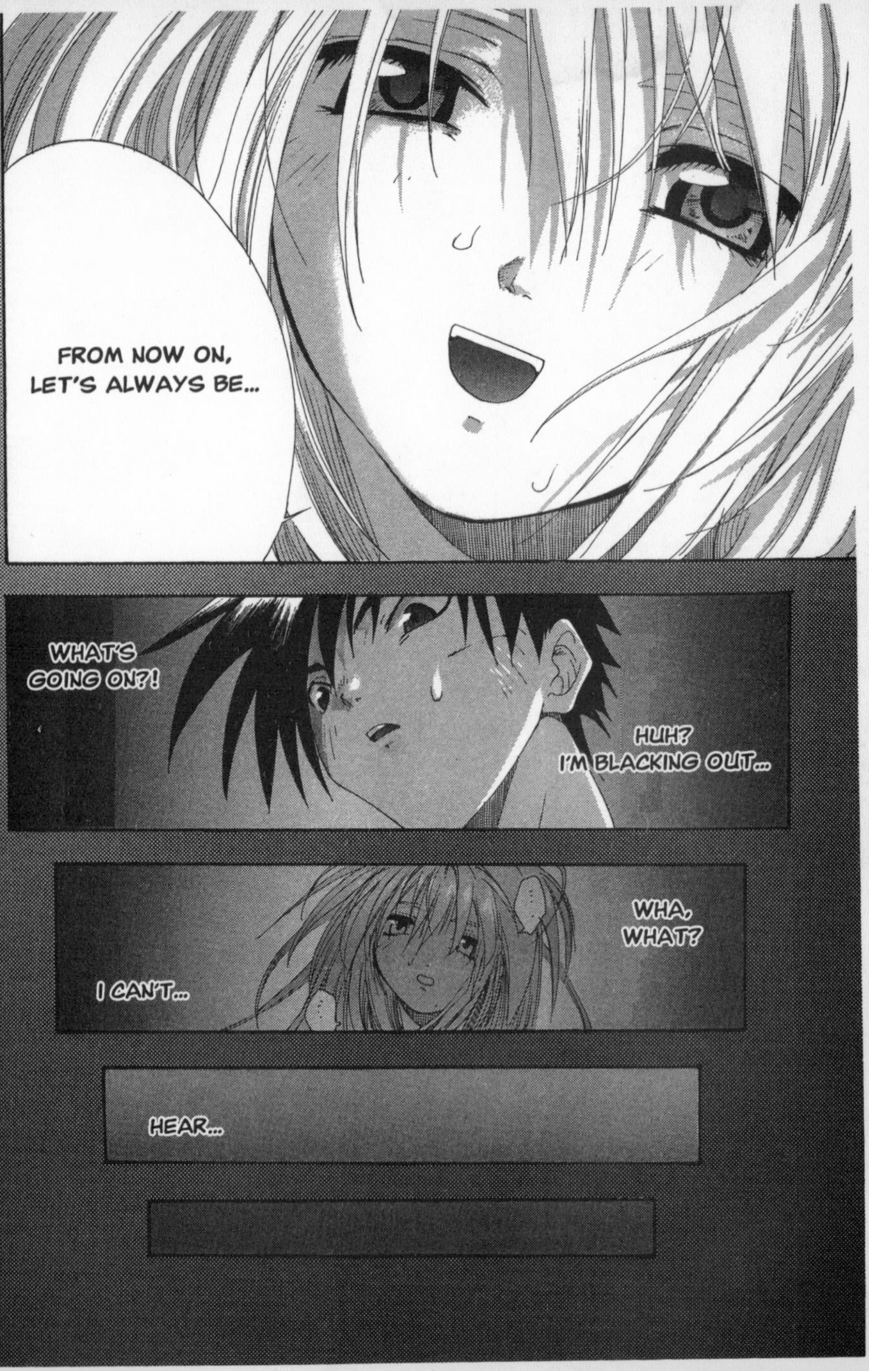
FROM NOW ON, LET'S ALWAYS BE...
HUH? I'M BLACKING OUT...
WHAT'S GOING ON?!
WHA, WHAT?
I CAN'T...
HEAR...

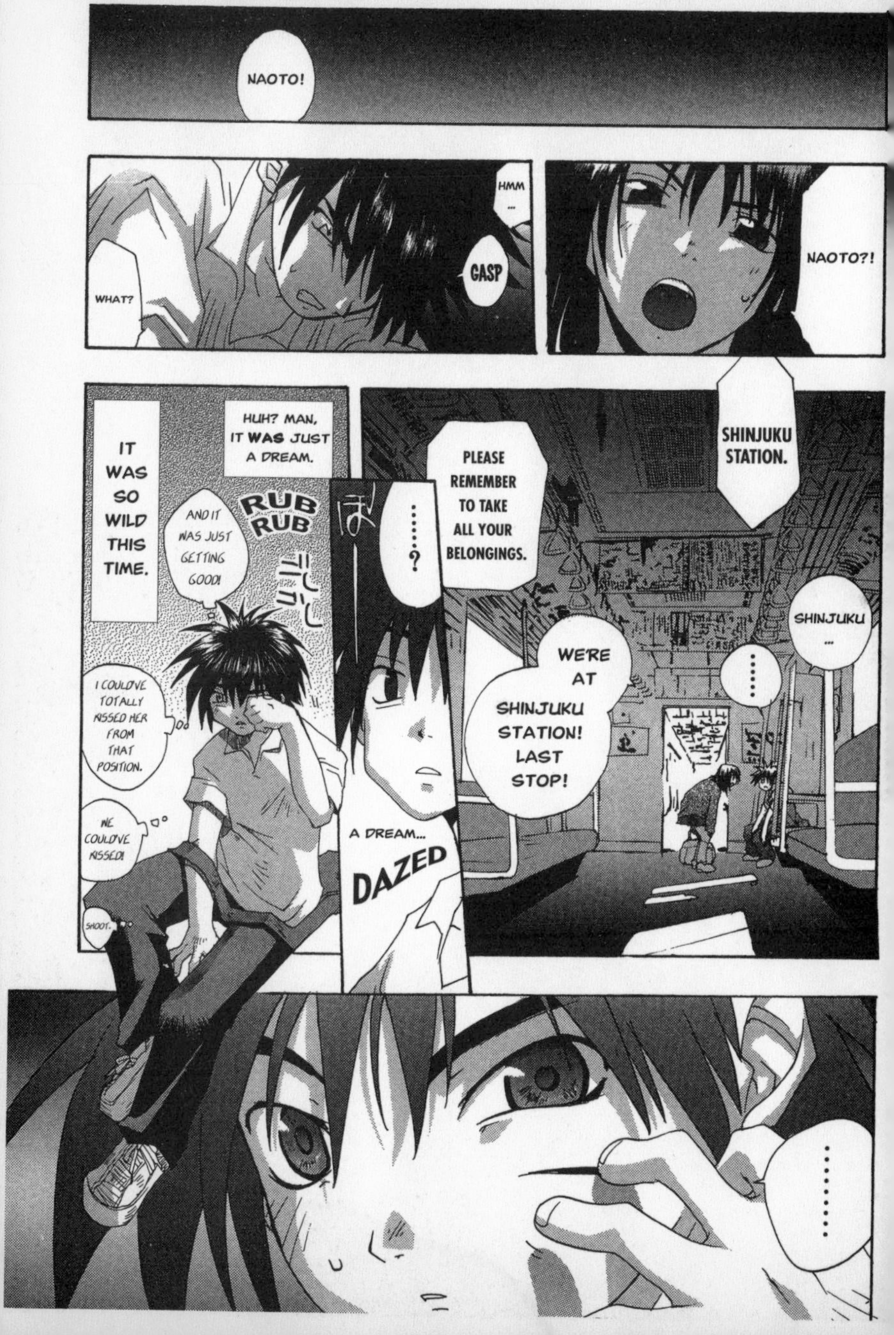
NAOTO!
NAOTO?!
HMM...
GASP
WHAT?
SHINJUKU STATION.
PLEASE REMEMBER TO TAKE ALL YOUR BELONGINGS.
SHINJUKU...
......
WE'RE AT SHINJUKU STATION! LAST STOP!
......?
A DREAM...
DAZED
HUH? MAN, IT WAS JUST A DREAM.
IT WAS SO WILD THIS TIME.
RUB RUB
AND IT WAS JUST GETTING GOOD!
I COULD'VE TOTALLY KISSED HER FROM THAT POSITION.
WE COULD'VE KISSED!
SHOOT.
......

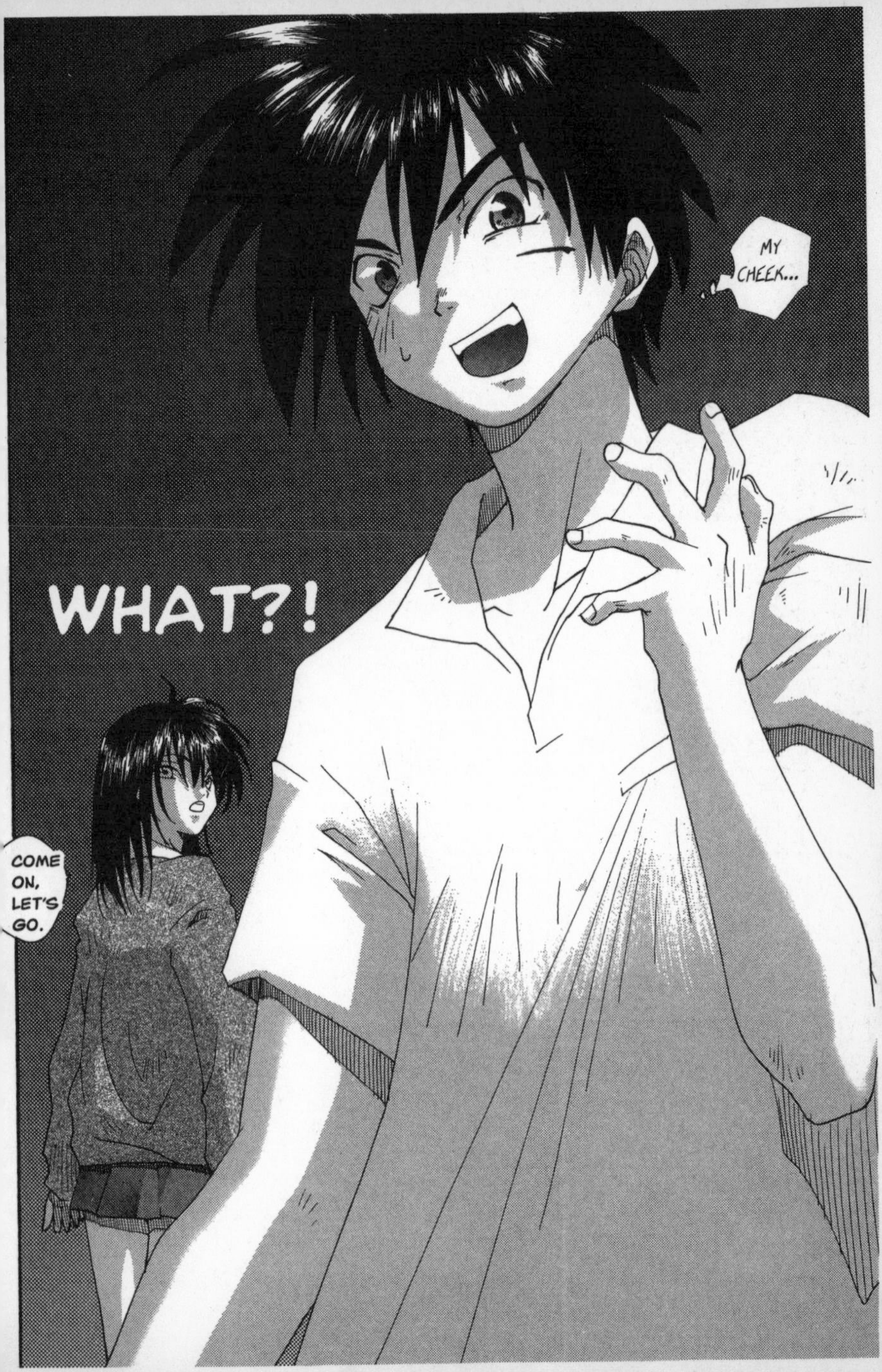
MY CHEEK...
WHAT?!
COME ON, LET'S GO.

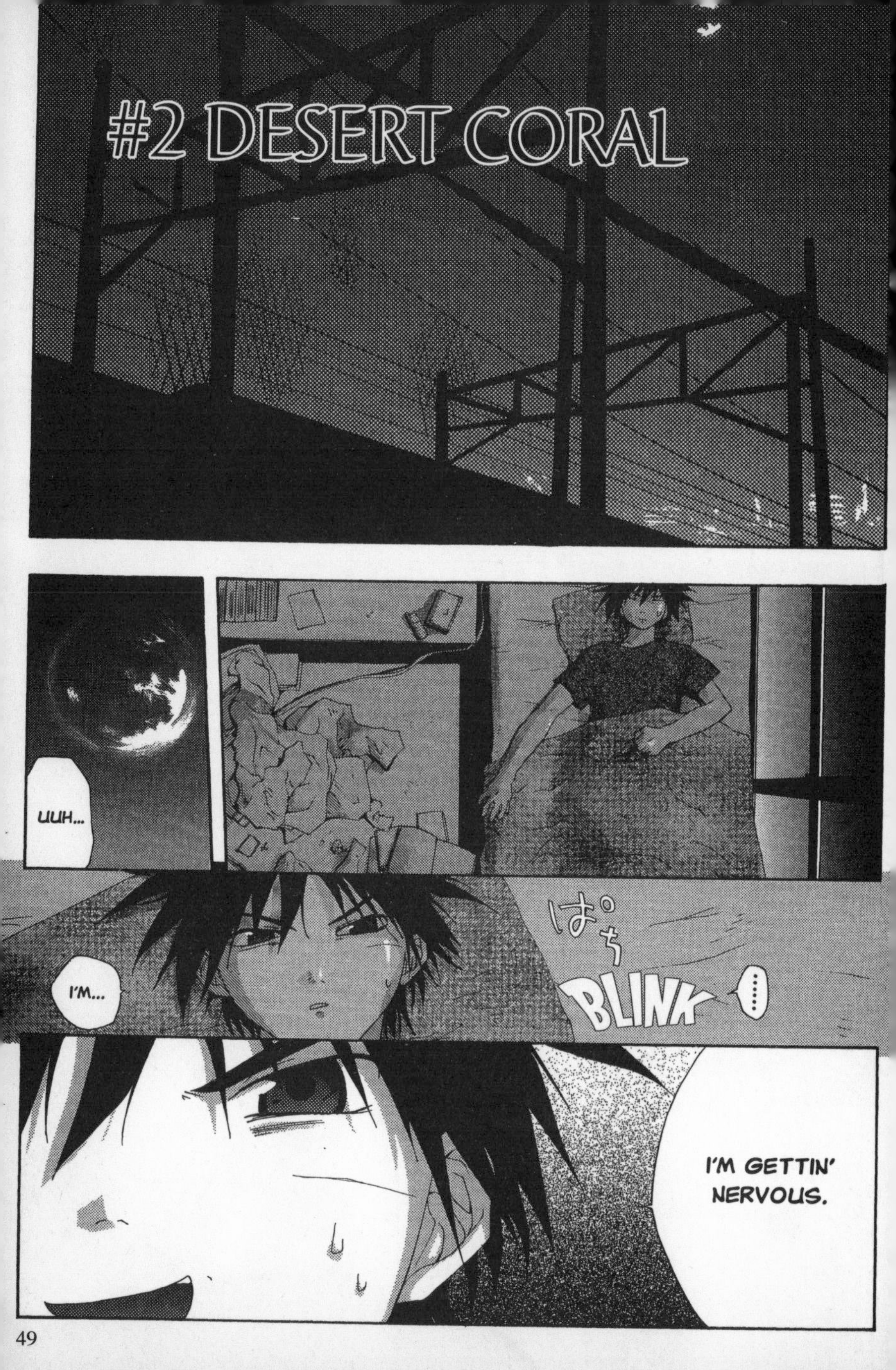
#2 DESERT CORAL
UUH...
......
ぱち
BLINK
I'M...
I'M GETTIN' NERVOUS.

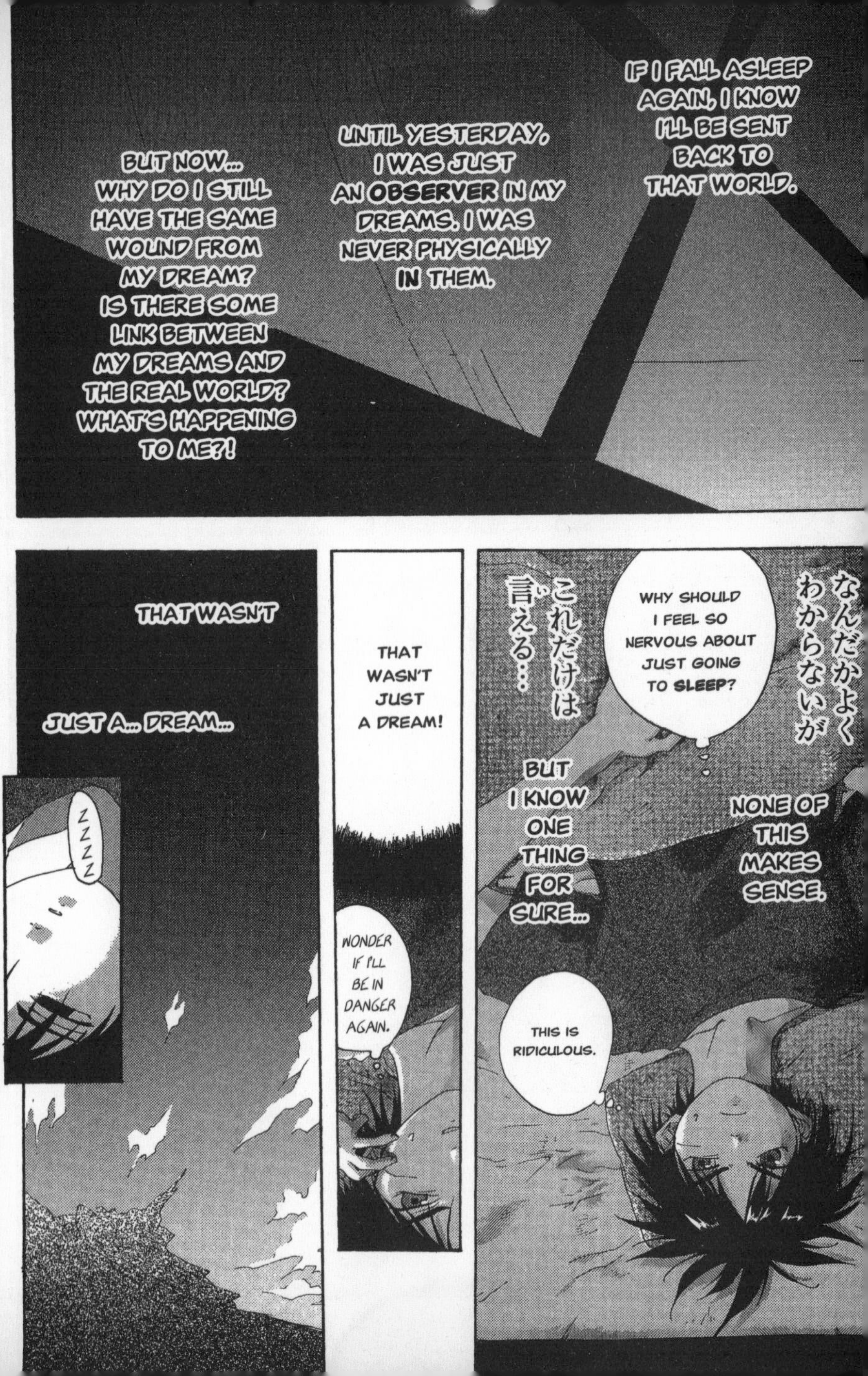
IF I FALL ASLEEP AGAIN, I KNOW I'LL BE SENT BACK TO THAT WORLD.
UNTIL YESTERDAY, I WAS JUST AN **OBSERVER** IN MY DREAMS. I WAS NEVER PHYSICALLY **IN** THEM.
BUT NOW... WHY DO I STILL HAVE THE SAME WOUND FROM MY DREAM? IS THERE SOME LINK BETWEEN MY DREAMS AND THE REAL WORLD? WHAT'S HAPPENING TO ME?!
なんだかよくわからないが
WHY SHOULD I FEEL SO NERVOUS ABOUT JUST GOING TO **SLEEP**?
これだけは言える・・・
NONE OF THIS MAKES SENSE.
BUT I KNOW ONE THING FOR SURE...
THIS IS RIDICULOUS.
THAT WASN'T JUST A DREAM!
WONDER IF I'LL BE IN DANGER AGAIN.
THAT WASN'T
JUST A... DREAM...
ZZZZ

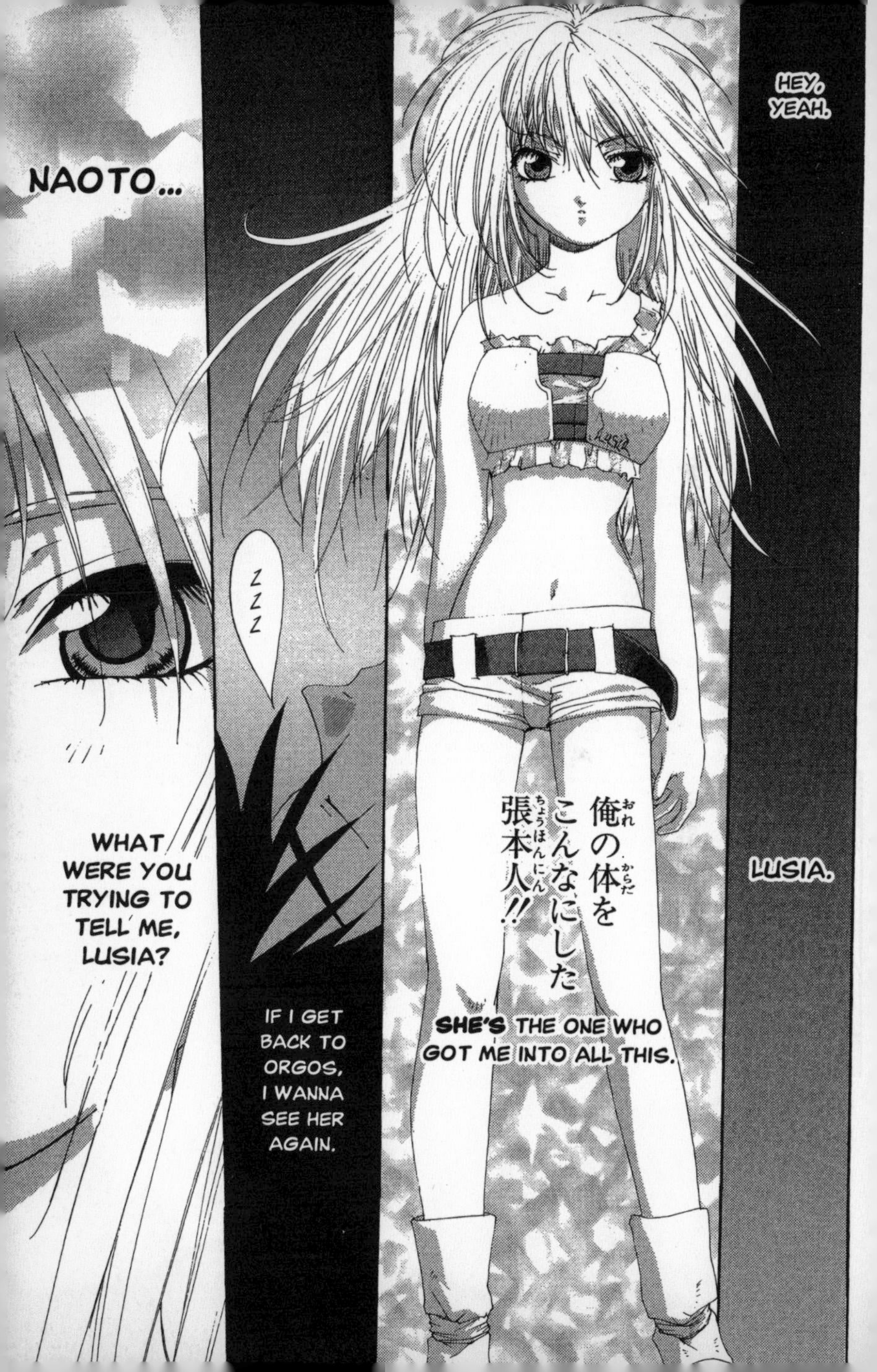
HEY. YEAH.
LUSIA.
俺の体をこんなにした張本人!!
SHE'S THE ONE WHO GOT ME INTO ALL THIS.
Lusia
ZZZ
IF I GET BACK TO ORGOS, I WANNA SEE HER AGAIN.
NAOTO...
WHAT WERE YOU TRYING TO TELL ME, LUSIA?

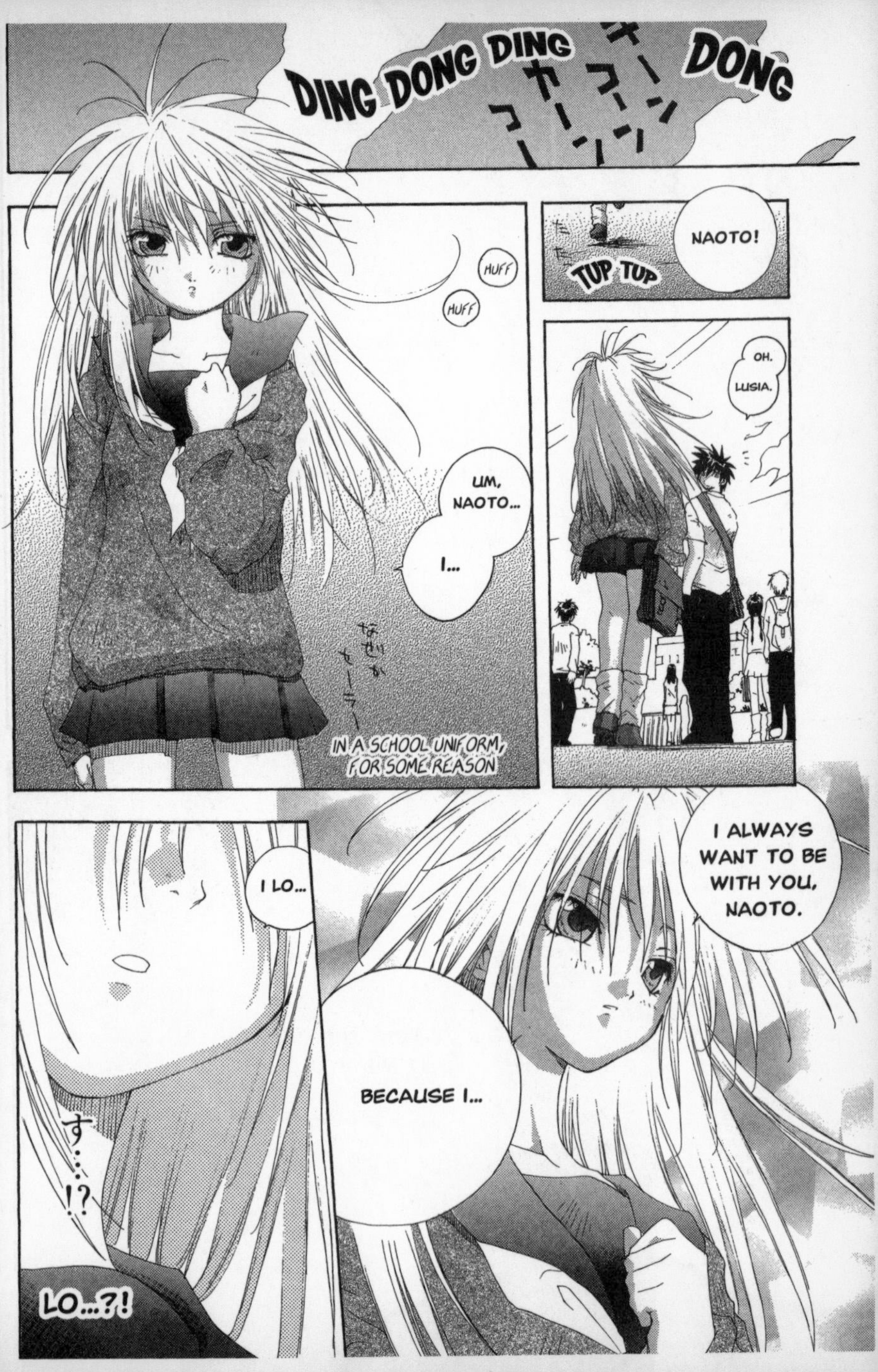
DING DONG DING DONG
TUP TUP
NAOTO!
OH. LUSIA.
HUFF
HUFF
UM, NAOTO...
I...
なぜかセーラー
IN A SCHOOL UNIFORM, FOR SOME REASON
I ALWAYS WANT TO BE WITH YOU, NAOTO.
BECAUSE I...
I LO...
す…!?
LO...?!

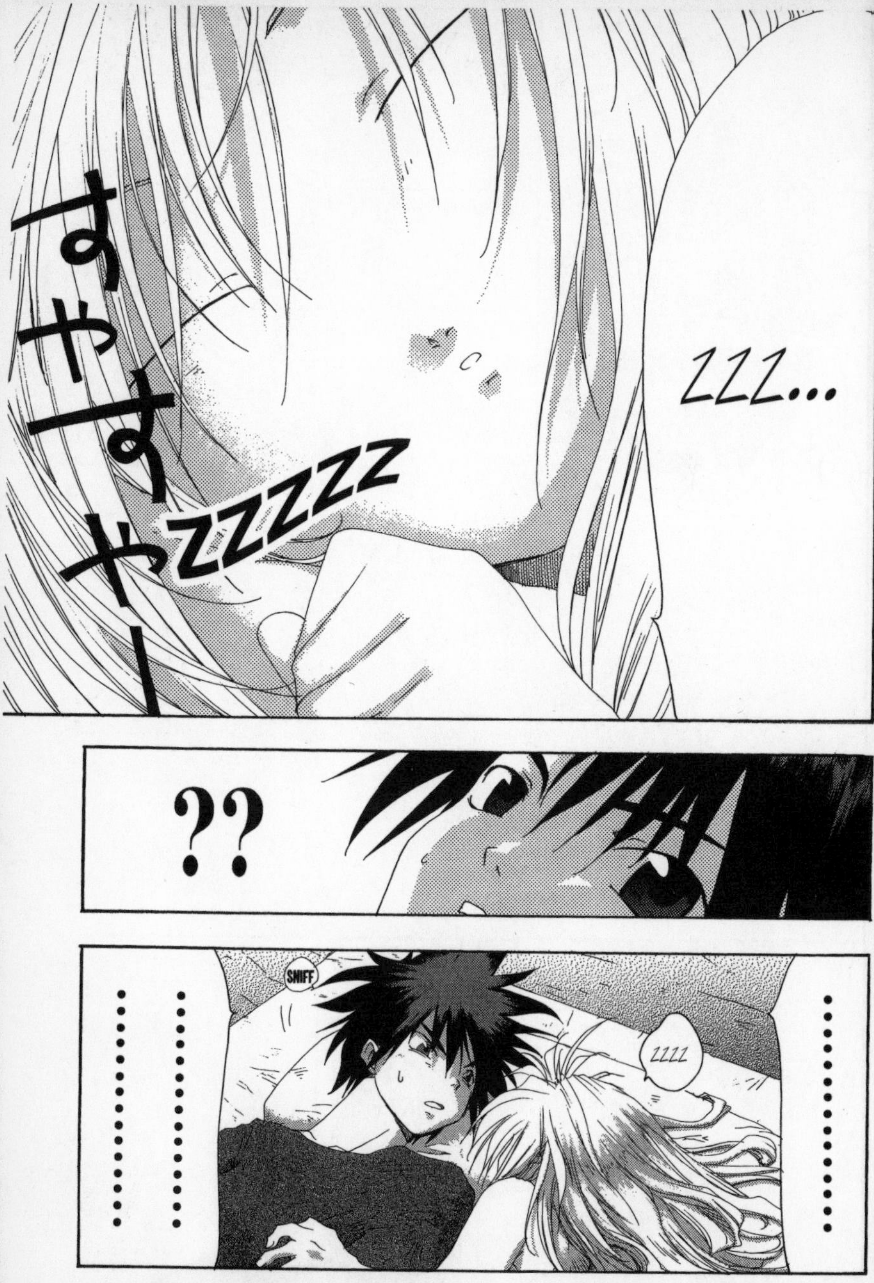

ZZZ...
ZZZZZZ
すやすやー
??
....
ZZZZ
SNIFF
....
....

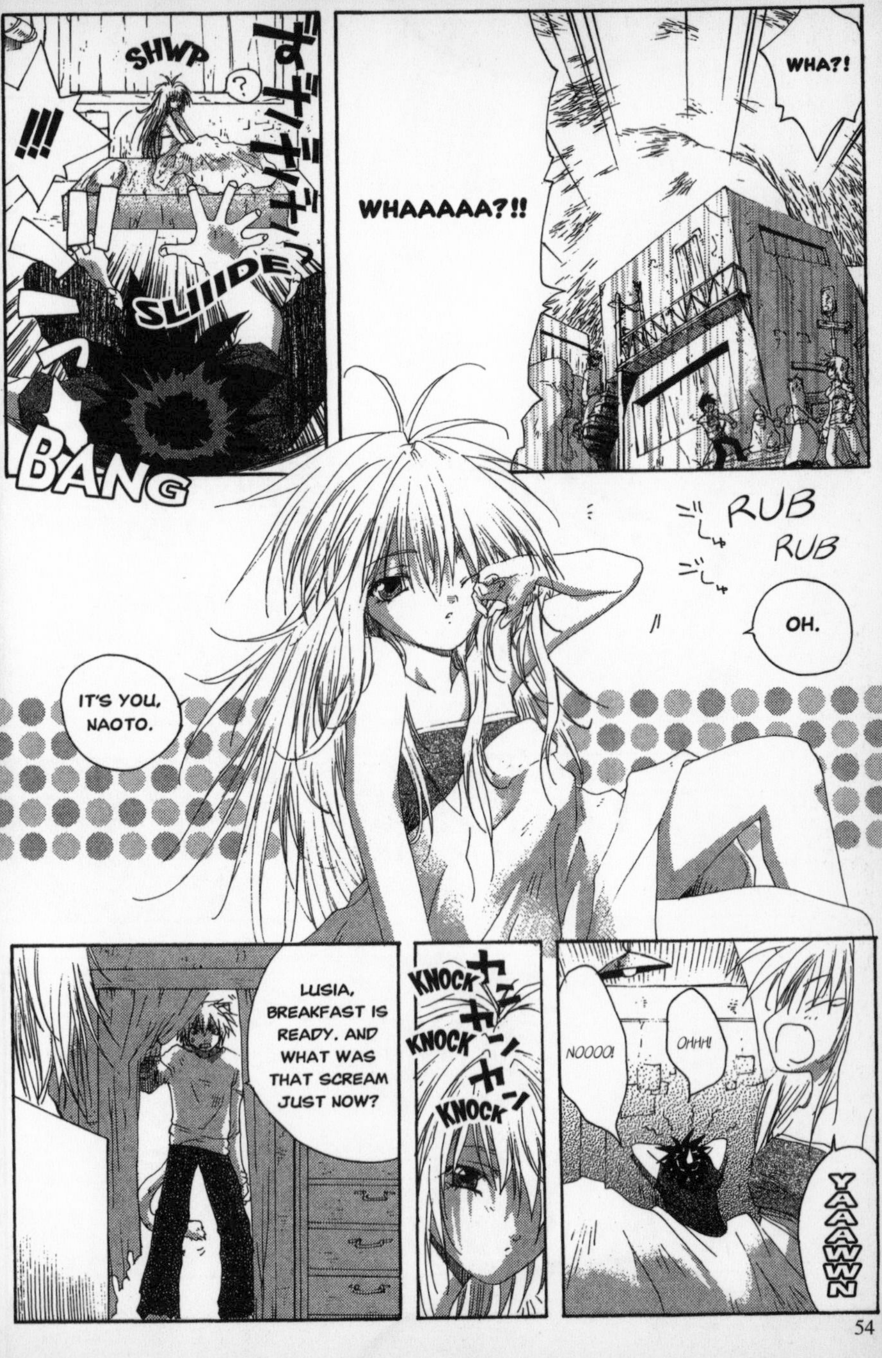

WHA?!
WHAAAAA?!!
SHWP
?
!!!
SLIIIDE
BANG
RUB
RUB
OH.
IT'S YOU, NAOTO.
NOOOO!
OHHH!
YAAAAWWN
KNOCK
KNOCK
KNOCK
LUSIA, BREAKFAST IS READY. AND WHAT WAS THAT SCREAM JUST NOW?

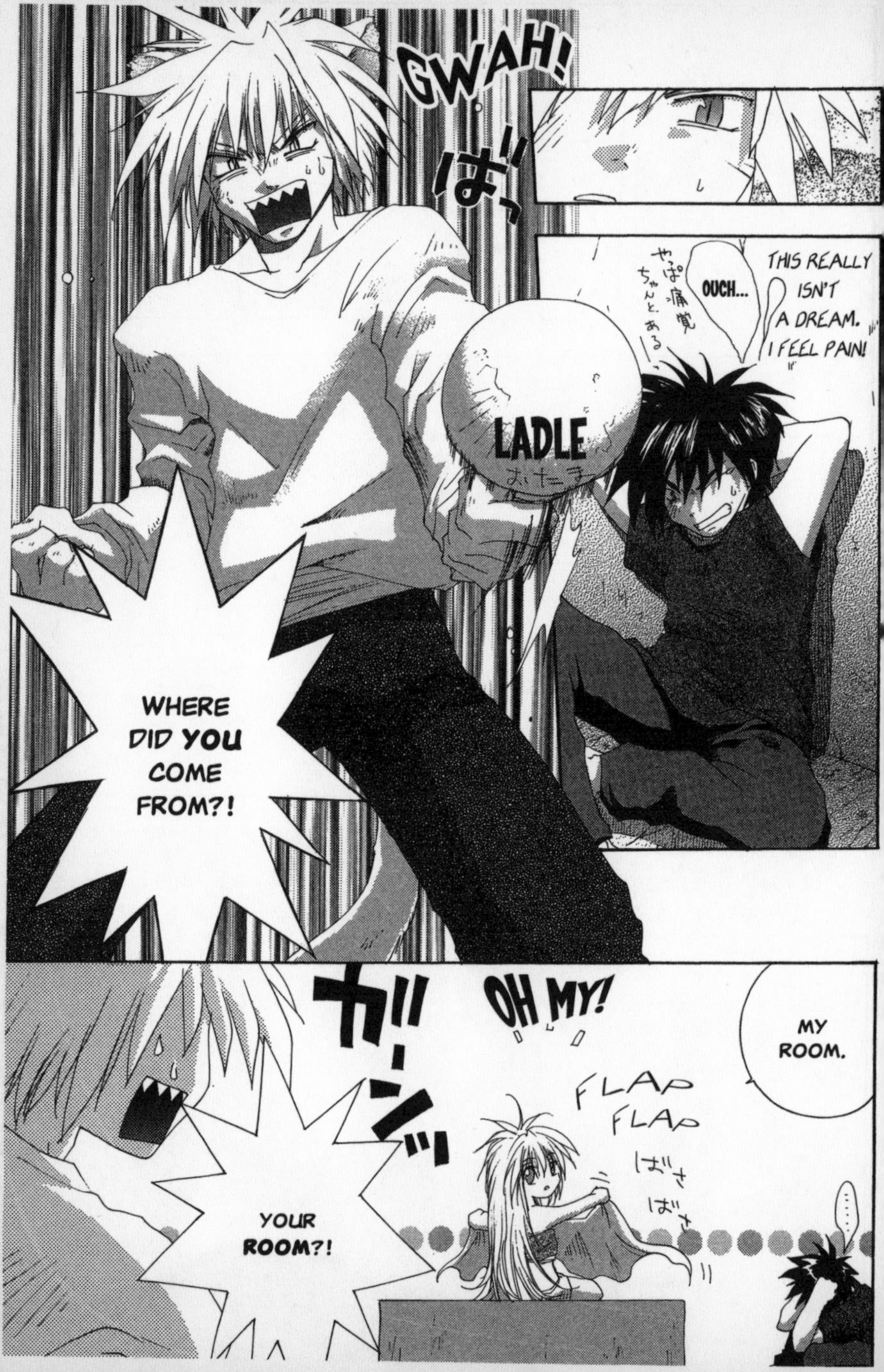

OUCH...
THIS REALLY ISN'T A DREAM. I FEEL PAIN!
やっぱ痛覚ちゃんとある…
GWAH!
ばっ
LADLE
WHERE DID YOU COME FROM?!
MY ROOM.
...
FLAP FLAP
ばさばさ
OH MY!
ガーン
YOUR ROOM?!

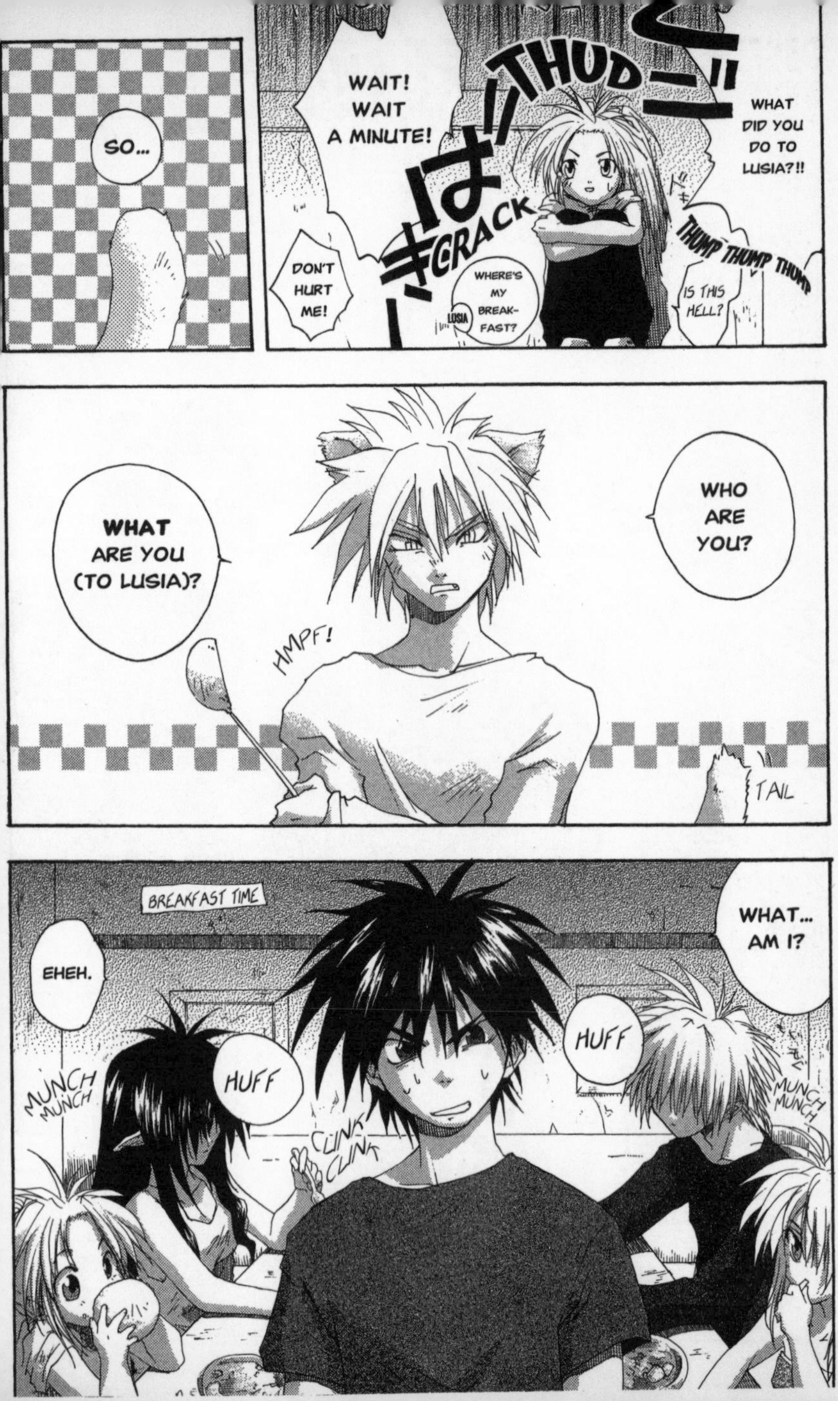
WHAT DID YOU DO TO LUSIA?!!
THUD
WAIT! WAIT A MINUTE!
は
CRACK
THUMP THUMP THUMP
IS THIS HELL?
WHERE'S MY BREAKFAST?
LUSIA
DON'T HURT ME!
SO...
WHO ARE YOU?
WHAT ARE YOU (TO LUSIA)?
HMPF!
TAIL
WHAT... AM I?
BREAKFAST TIME
MUNCH MUNCH
HUFF
EHEH.
HUFF
CLINK CLINK
MUNCH MUNCH

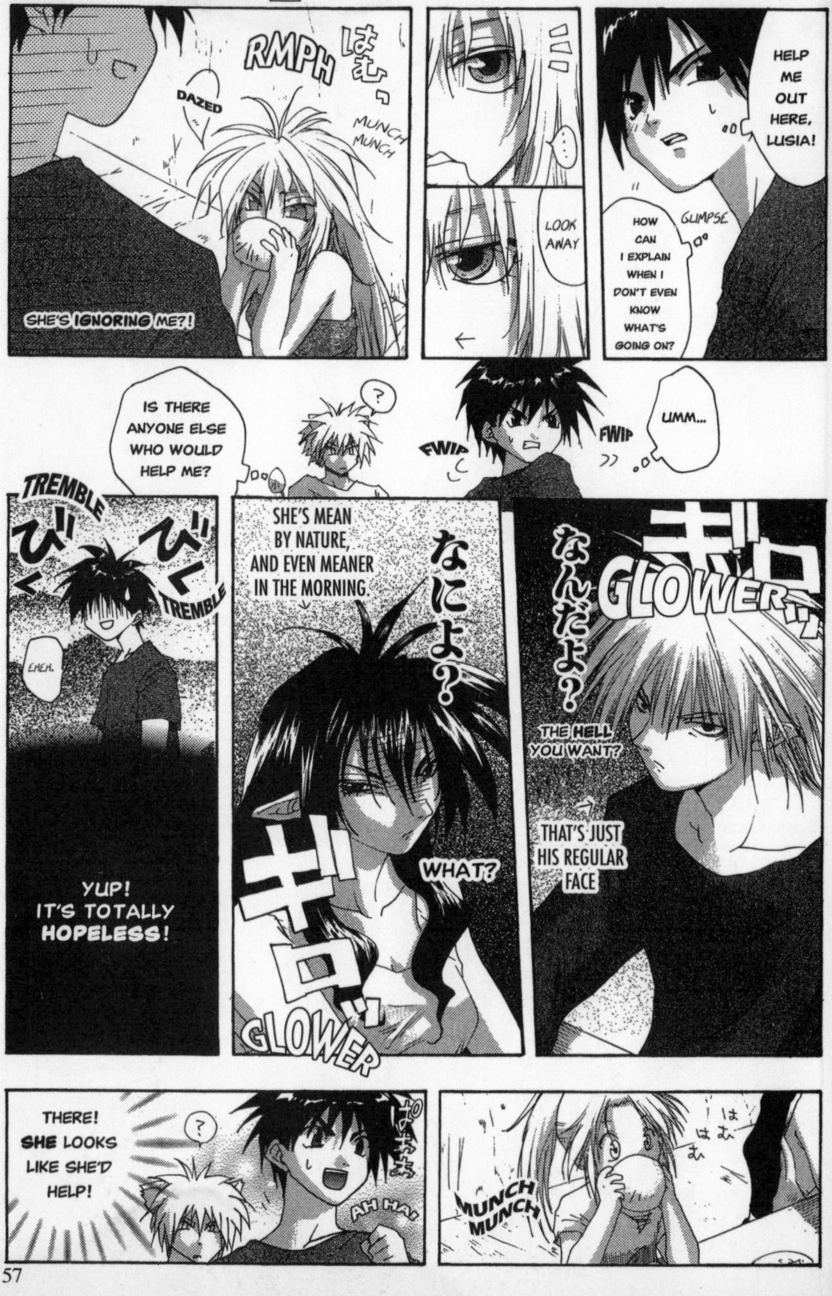
HELP ME OUT HERE, LUSIA!
GLIMPSE
HOW CAN I EXPLAIN WHEN I DON'T EVEN KNOW WHAT'S GOING ON?
...
LOOK AWAY
RMPH
はむっ
MUNCH MUNCH
DAZED
SHE'S IGNORING ME?!
UMM...
FWIP
FWIP
?
IS THERE ANYONE ELSE WHO WOULD HELP ME?
ギロッ
GLOWER
なんだよ?
THE HELL YOU WANT?
THAT'S JUST HIS REGULAR FACE
SHE'S MEAN BY NATURE, AND EVEN MEANER IN THE MORNING.
なによ?
WHAT?
ギロッ
GLOWER
TREMBLE
びく
びく
TREMBLE
EHEH.
YUP! IT'S TOTALLY HOPELESS!
はむはむ
MUNCH MUNCH
THERE! SHE LOOKS LIKE SHE'D HELP!
?
AH HA!

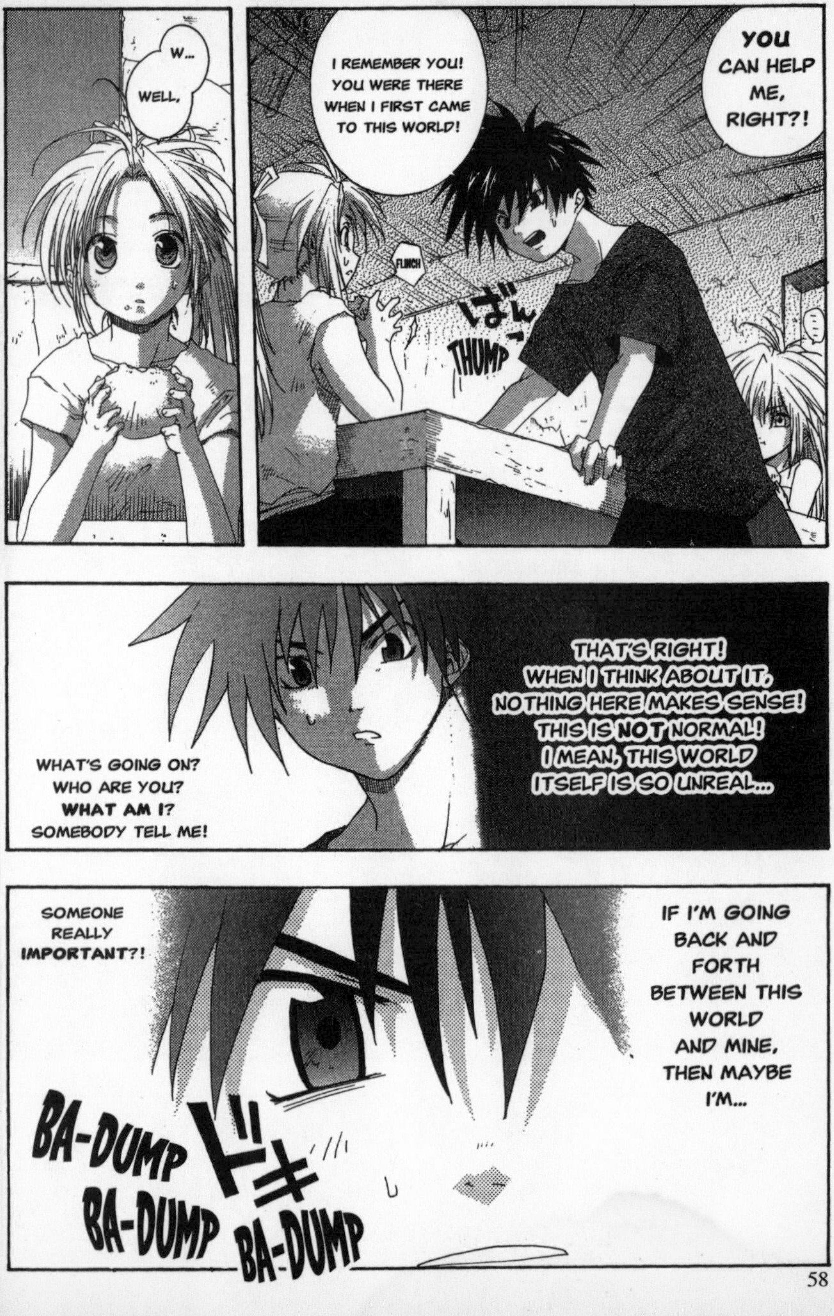
I REMEMBER YOU! YOU WERE THERE WHEN I FIRST CAME TO THIS WORLD!
YOU CAN HELP ME, RIGHT?!
FLINCH
ばん
THUMP
W...
WELL,
THAT'S RIGHT! WHEN I THINK ABOUT IT, NOTHING HERE MAKES SENSE! THIS IS NOT NORMAL! I MEAN, THIS WORLD ITSELF IS SO UNREAL...
WHAT'S GOING ON? WHO ARE YOU? WHAT AM I? SOMEBODY TELL ME!
IF I'M GOING BACK AND FORTH BETWEEN THIS WORLD AND MINE, THEN MAYBE I'M...
SOMEONE REALLY IMPORTANT?!
ドキ
BA-DUMP
BA-DUMP
BA-DUMP

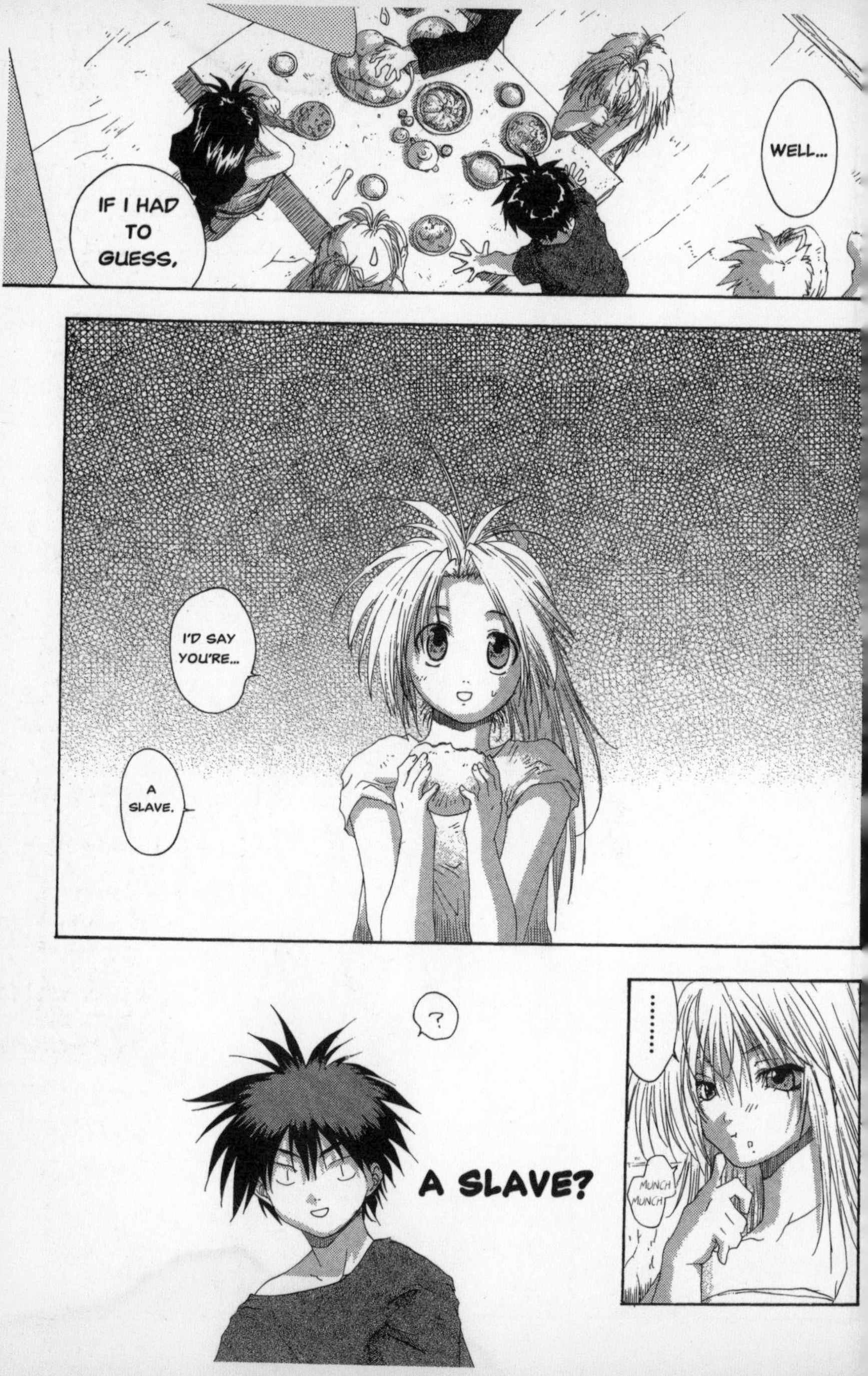
WELL...
IF I HAD TO GUESS,
I'D SAY YOU'RE...
A SLAVE.
......
MUNCH MUNCH
?
A SLAVE?

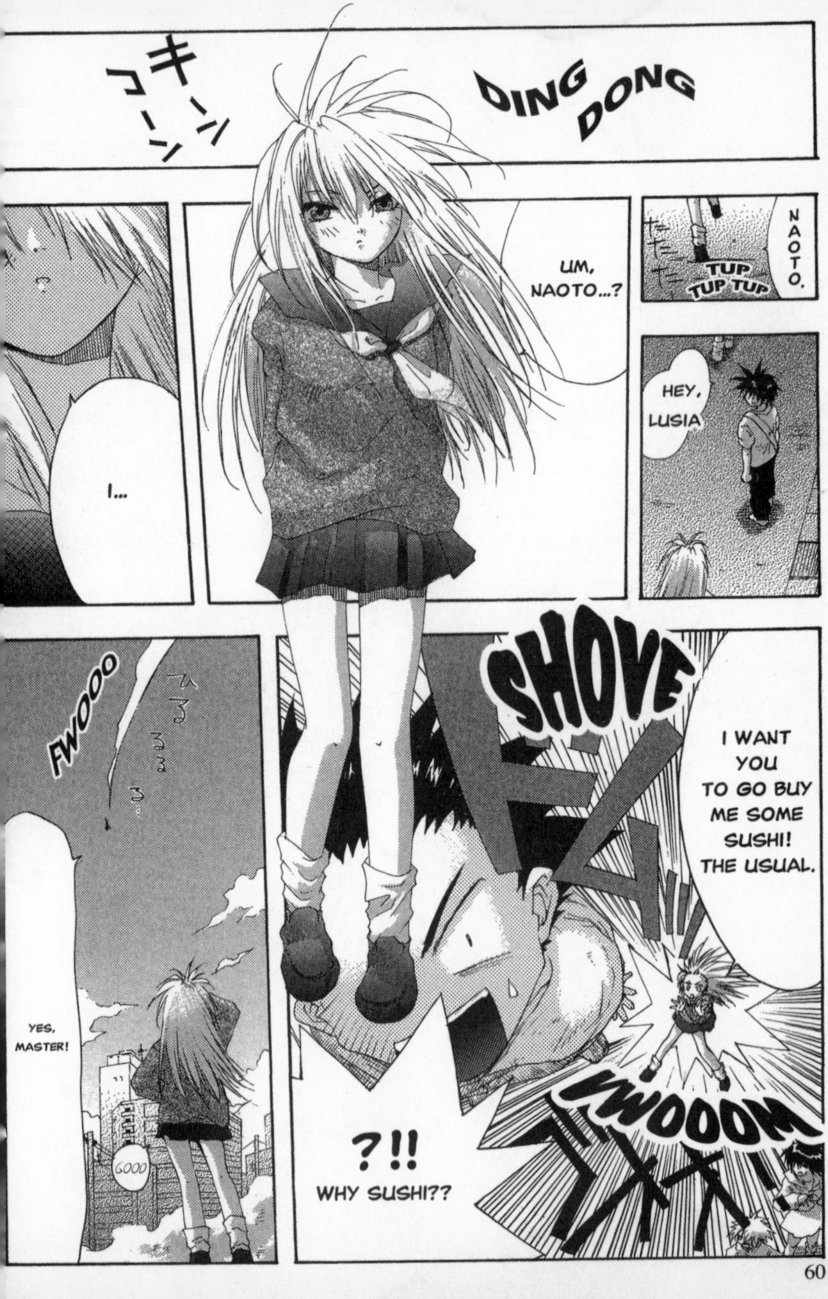
DING DONG
NAOTO.
TUP TUP TUP
HEY, LUSIA
UM, NAOTO...?
I...
SHOVE
I WANT YOU TO GO BUY ME SOME SUSHI! THE USUAL.
VWOOOM
?!!
WHY SUSHI??
FWOOO
YES, MASTER!
GOOD

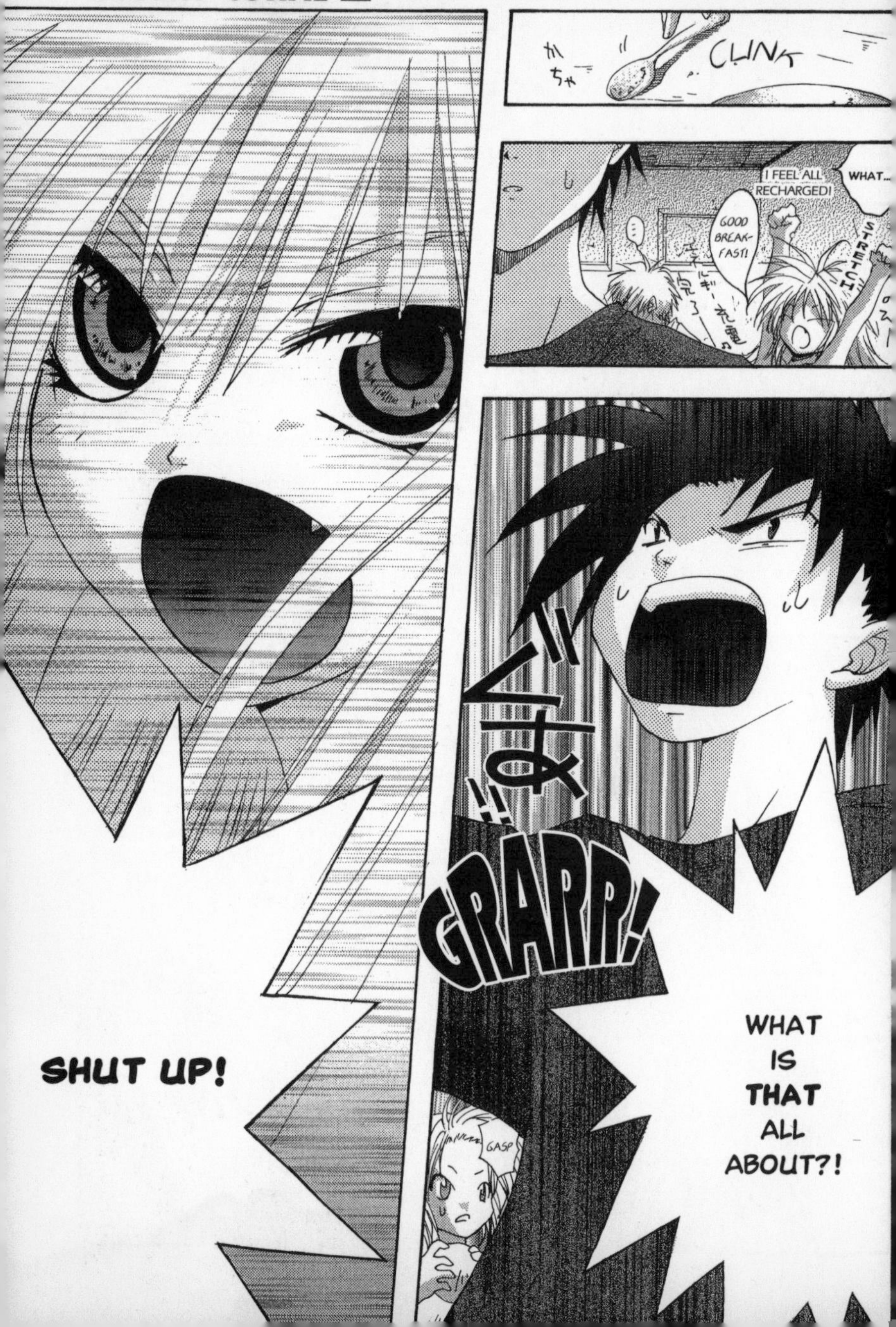
かちゃ
CLINK
WHAT...
STRETCH
I FEEL ALL RECHARGED!
GOOD BREAKFAST!
GRARR!
WHAT IS THAT ALL ABOUT?!
GASP
SHUT UP!

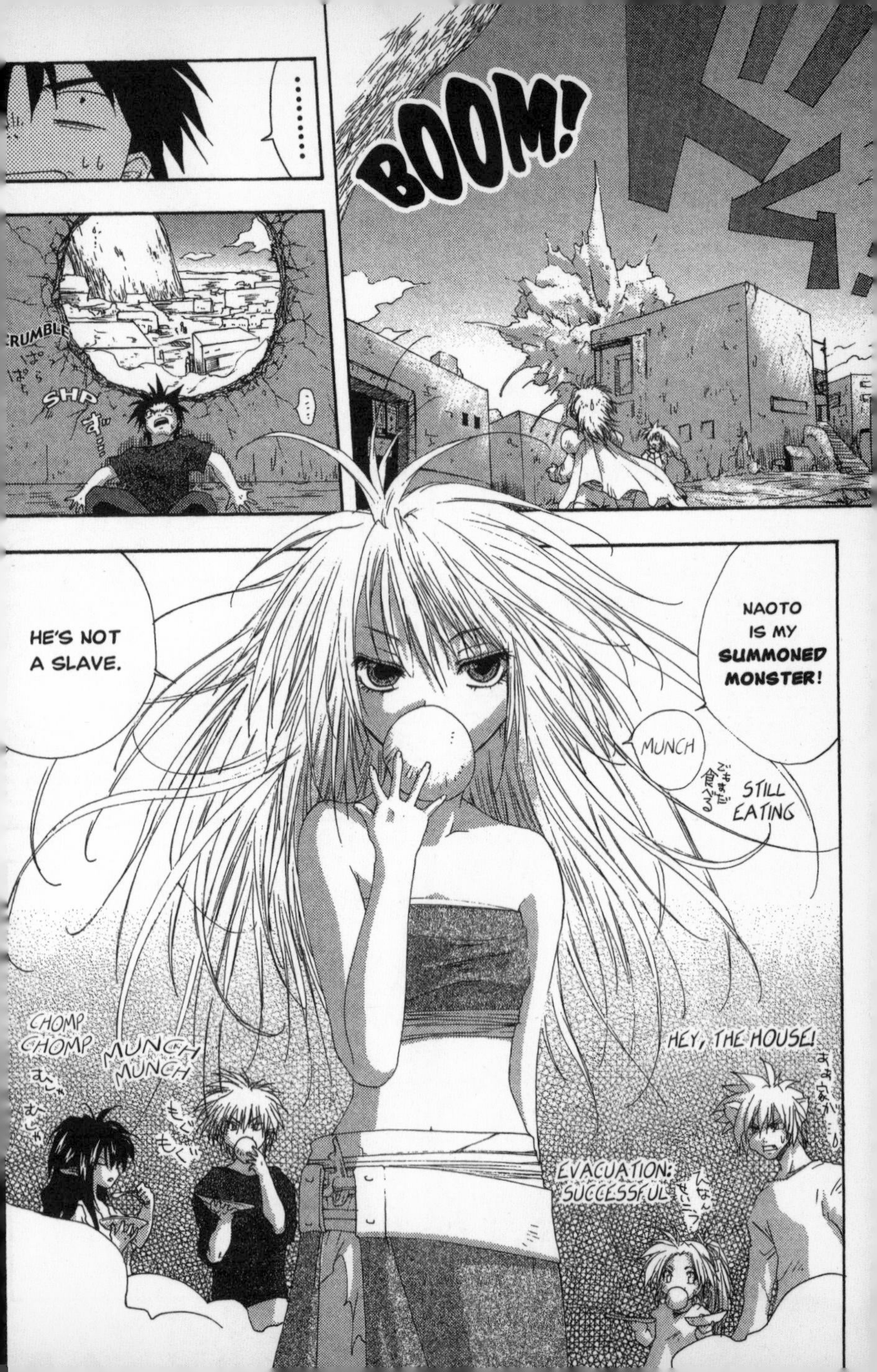
BOOM!
......
CRUMBLE
ぱらぱら
SHP
....
NAOTO IS MY SUMMONED MONSTER!
HE'S NOT A SLAVE.
MUNCH
まだ食べる
STILL EATING
HEY, THE HOUSE!
EVACUATION: SUCCESSFUL
MUNCH MUNCH
もぐもぐ
CHOMP CHOMP
むしゃむしゃ

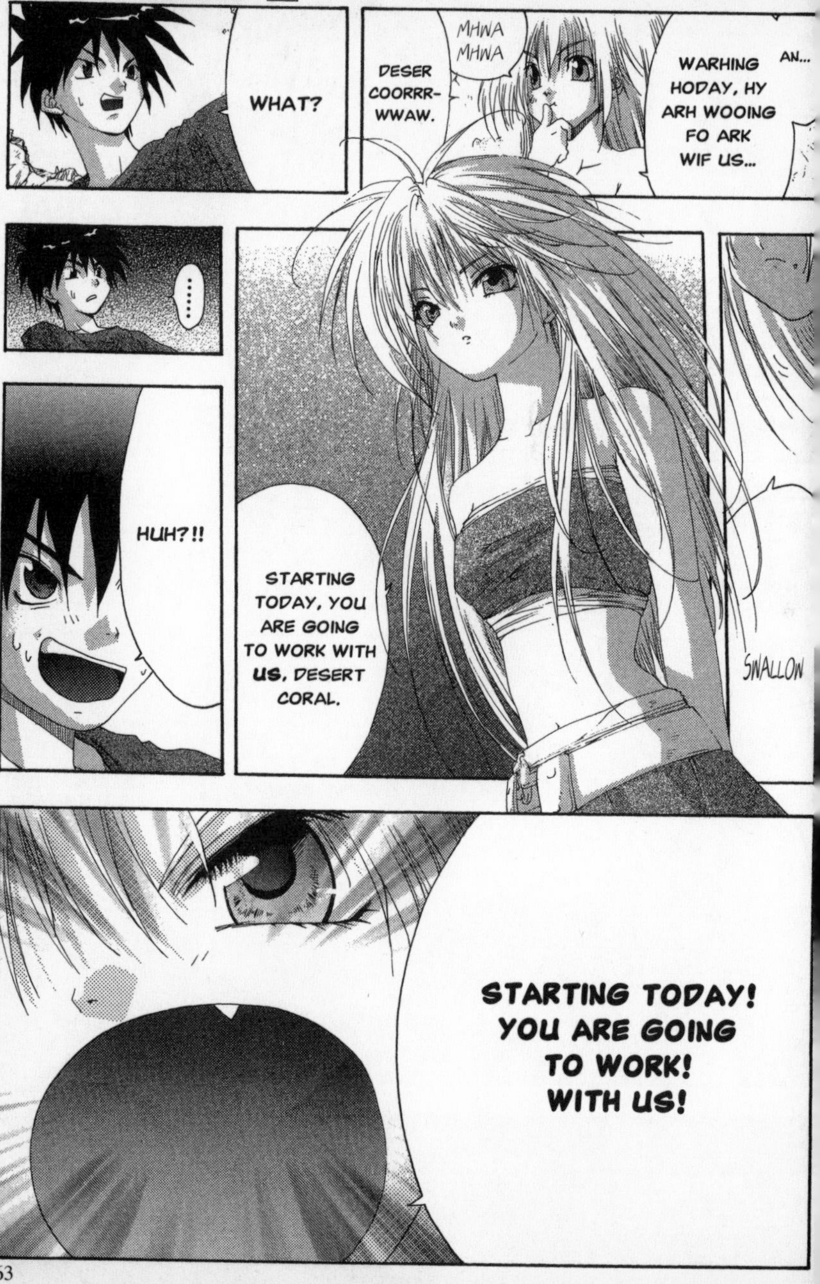
AN...
WARHING HODAY, HY ARH WOOING FO ARK WIF US...
MHWA MHWA
DESER COORRR-WWAW.
WHAT?
SWALLOW
STARTING TODAY, YOU ARE GOING TO WORK WITH US, DESERT CORAL.
......
HUH?!!
STARTING TODAY! YOU ARE GOING TO WORK! WITH US!

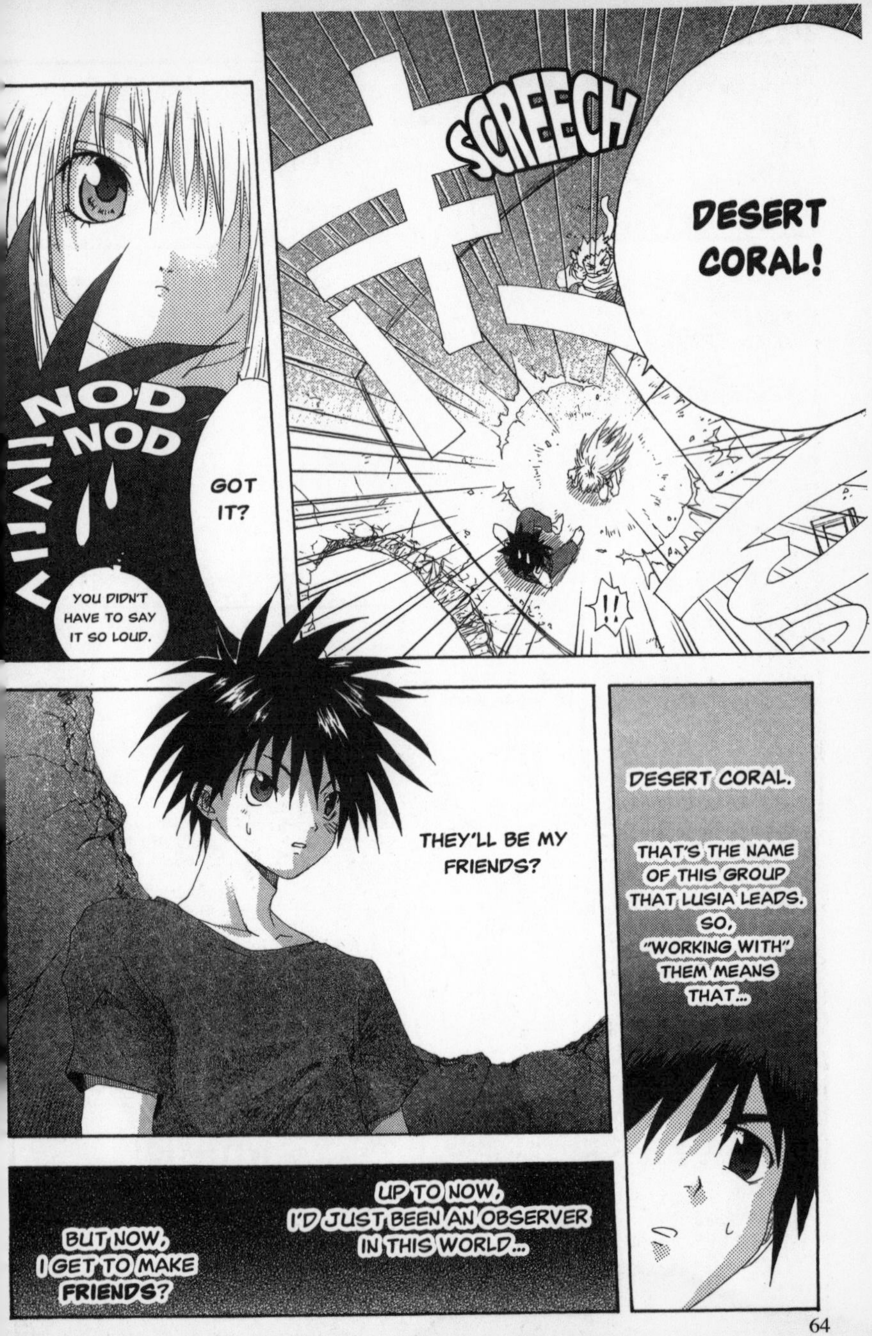
SCREECH
DESERT CORAL!
!!
GOT IT?
NOD NOD
YOU DIDN'T HAVE TO SAY IT SO LOUD.
DESERT CORAL.
THAT'S THE NAME OF THIS GROUP THAT LUSIA LEADS.
SO, "WORKING WITH" THEM MEANS THAT...
THEY'LL BE MY FRIENDS?
UP TO NOW, I'D JUST BEEN AN OBSERVER IN THIS WORLD...
BUT NOW, I GET TO MAKE FRIENDS?

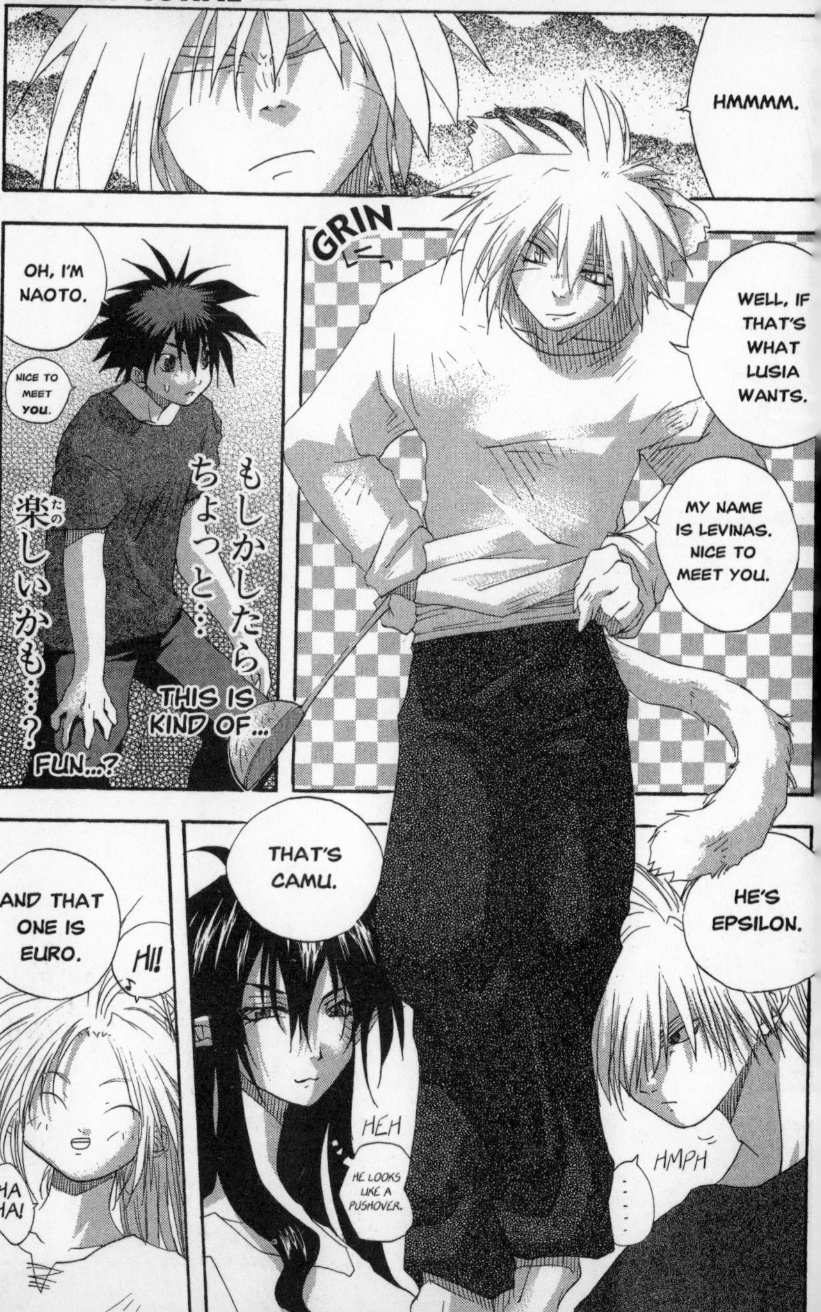
HMMMM.
GRIN
WELL, IF THAT'S WHAT LUSIA WANTS.
MY NAME IS LEVINAS. NICE TO MEET YOU.
OH, I'M NAOTO.
NICE TO MEET YOU.
もしかしたらちょっと…
楽しいかも…?
THIS IS KIND OF...
FUN...?
HE'S EPSILON.
HMPH
......
THAT'S CAMU.
HEH
HE LOOKS LIKE A PUSHOVER.
AND THAT ONE IS EURO.
HI!
HA HA!

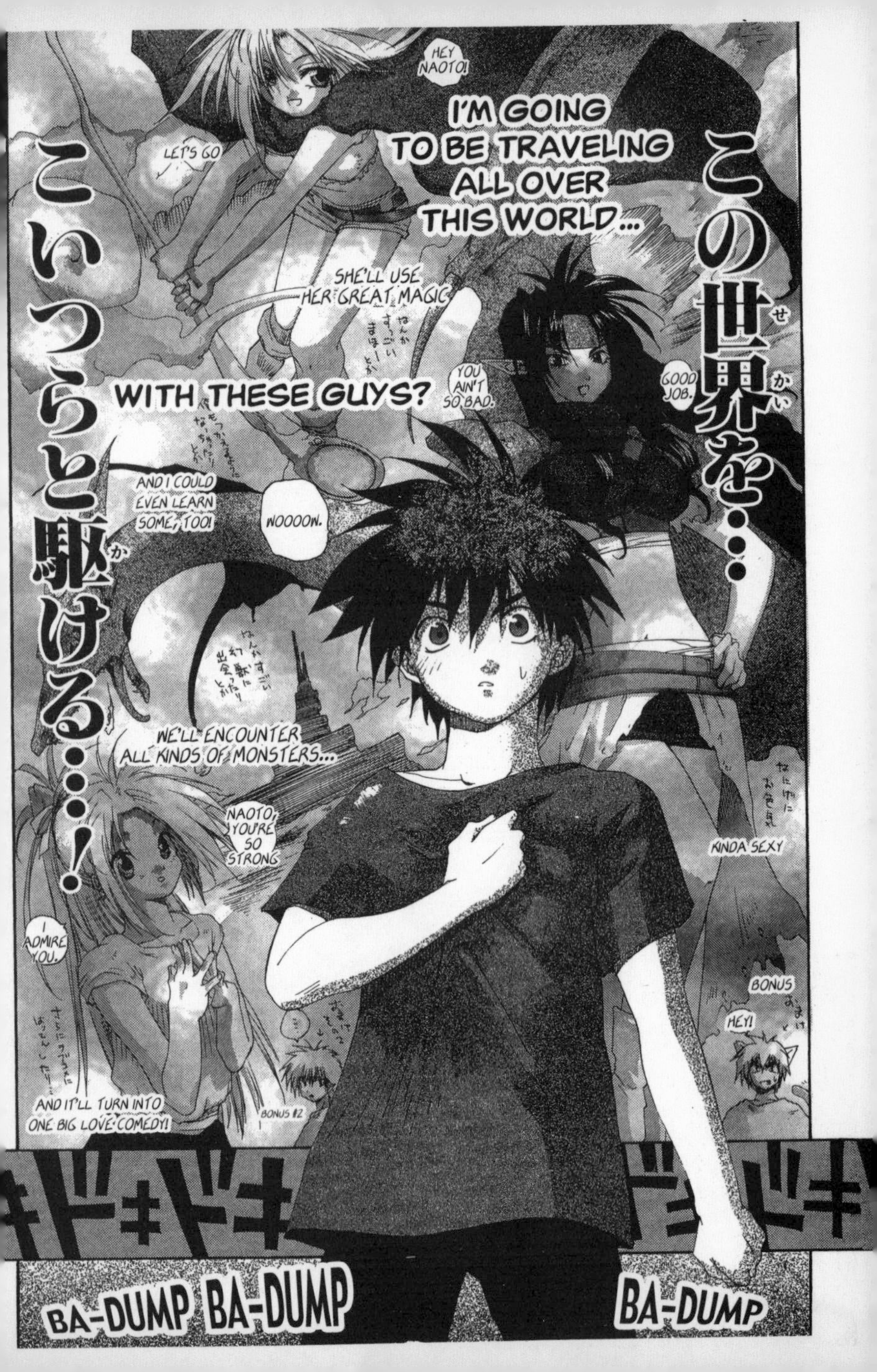
この世界を…
I'M GOING TO BE TRAVELING ALL OVER THIS WORLD...
HEY NAOTO!
LET'S GO
こいつらと駆ける…!
WITH THESE GUYS?
GOOD JOB.
YOU AIN'T SO BAD.
SHE'LL USE HER GREAT MAGIC
AND I COULD EVEN LEARN SOME, TOO!
WOOOOW.
WE'LL ENCOUNTER ALL KINDS OF MONSTERS...
KINDA SEXY
NAOTO, YOU'RE SO STRONG
I ADMIRE YOU.
BONUS
HEY!
BONUS #2
AND IT'LL TURN INTO ONE BIG LOVE COMEDY!
ドキドキ
ドキドキ
BA-DUMP BA-DUMP
BA-DUMP

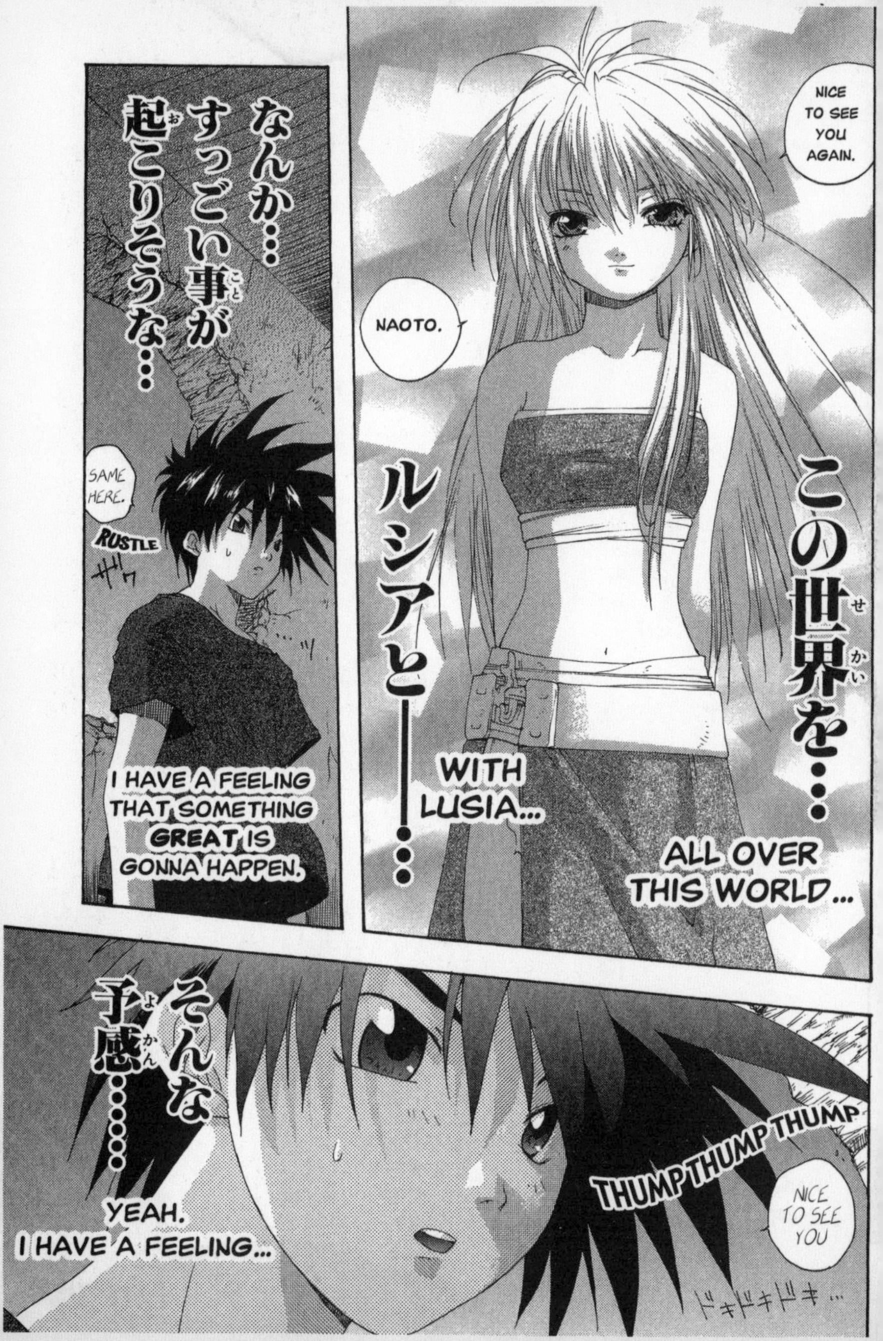
NICE TO SEE YOU AGAIN.
この世界を…
ALL OVER THIS WORLD...
NAOTO.
ルシアと――…
WITH LUSIA...
なんか…すっごい事が起こりそうな…
SAME HERE.
RUSTLE
ザワ
I HAVE A FEELING THAT SOMETHING GREAT IS GONNA HAPPEN.
そんな予感……
YEAH. I HAVE A FEELING...
THUMP THUMP THUMP
NICE TO SEE YOU
ドキドキドキ…

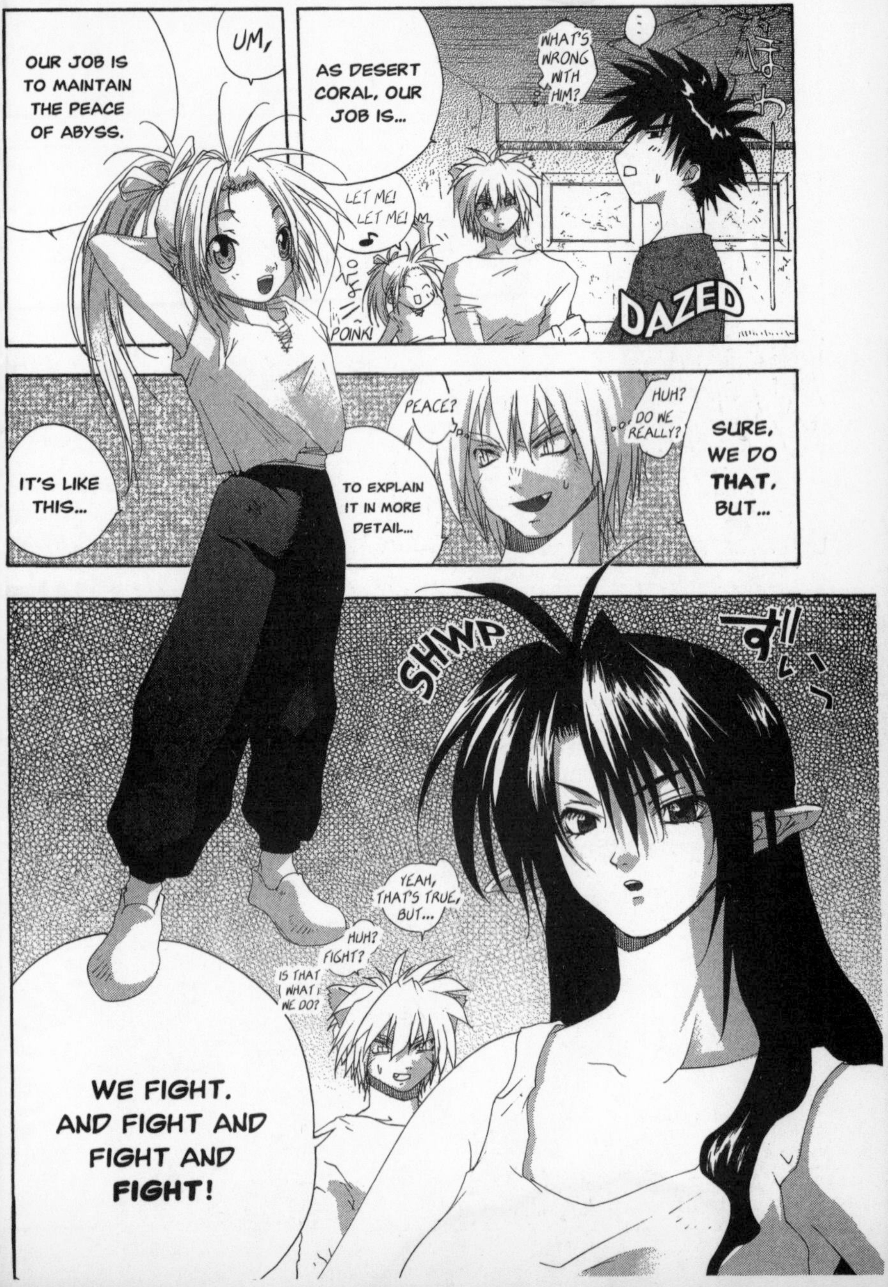
...
WHAT'S WRONG WITH HIM?
DAZED
AS DESERT CORAL, OUR JOB IS...
LET ME! LET ME!
POINK!
UM,
OUR JOB IS TO MAINTAIN THE PEACE OF ABYSS.
SURE, WE DO THAT, BUT...
HUH? DO WE REALLY?
PEACE?
TO EXPLAIN IT IN MORE DETAIL...
IT'S LIKE THIS...
SHWP
YEAH, THAT'S TRUE, BUT...
HUH? FIGHT?
IS THAT WHAT WE DO?
WE FIGHT. AND FIGHT AND FIGHT AND FIGHT!

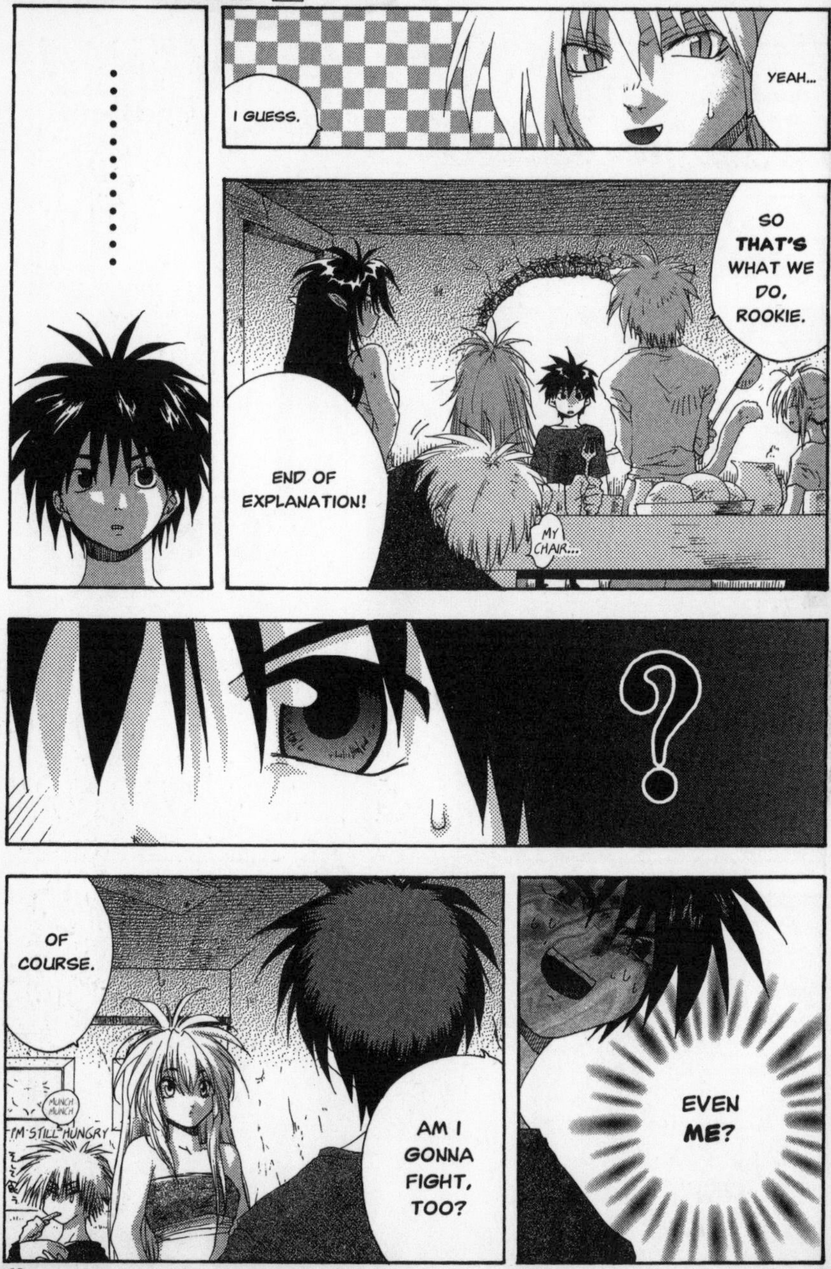
YEAH...
I GUESS.
SO THAT'S WHAT WE DO, ROOKIE.
END OF EXPLANATION!
MY CHAIR...
......
?
EVEN ME?
AM I GONNA FIGHT, TOO?
OF COURSE.
MUNCH MUNCH
I'M STILL HUNGRY

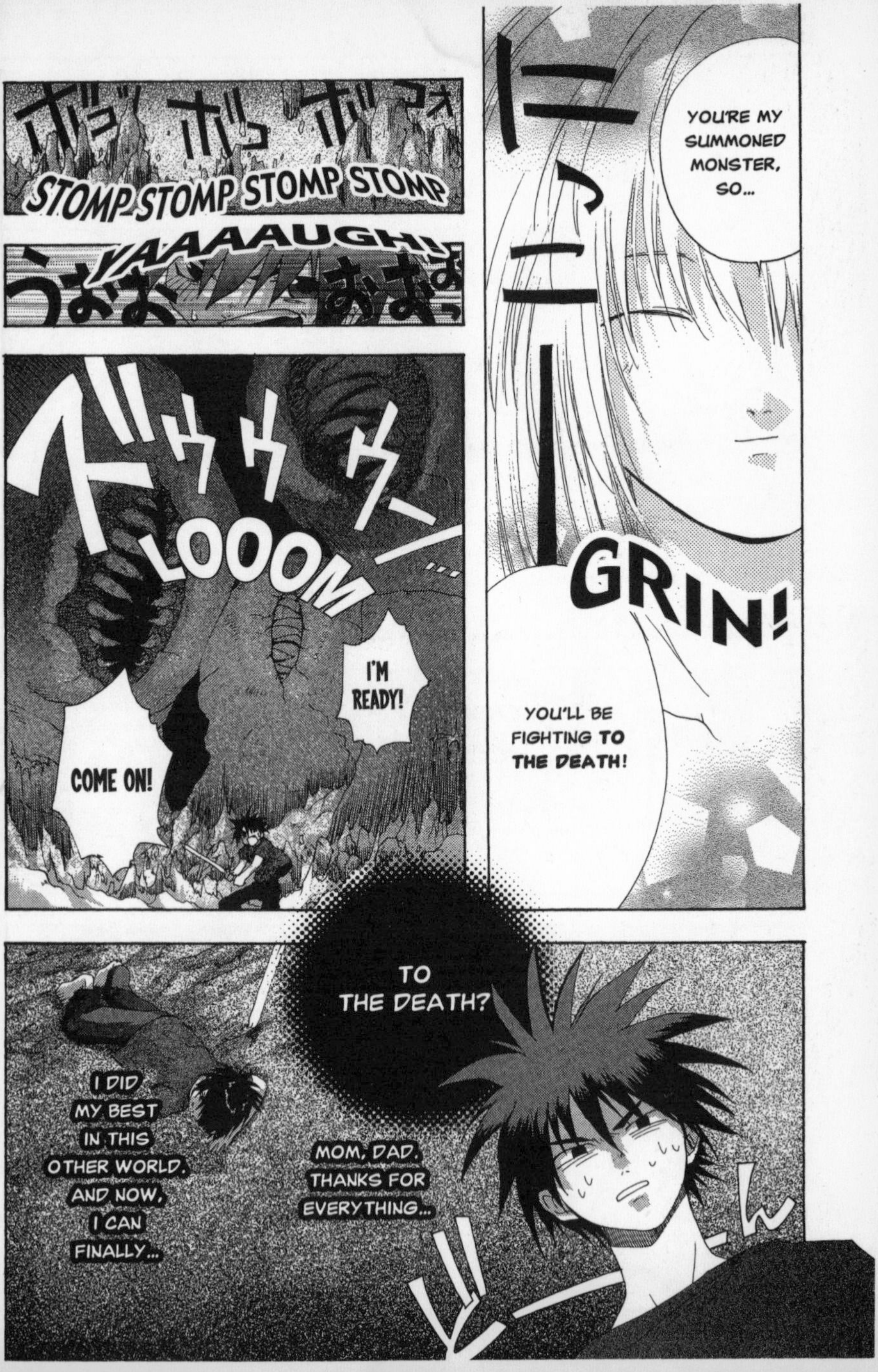
YOU'RE MY SUMMONED MONSTER, SO...
GRIN!
YOU'LL BE FIGHTING TO THE DEATH!
STOMP STOMP STOMP STOMP
YAAAAUGH!
LOOOM
I'M READY!
COME ON!
TO THE DEATH?
MOM, DAD. THANKS FOR EVERYTHING...
I DID MY BEST IN THIS OTHER WORLD. AND NOW, I CAN FINALLY...

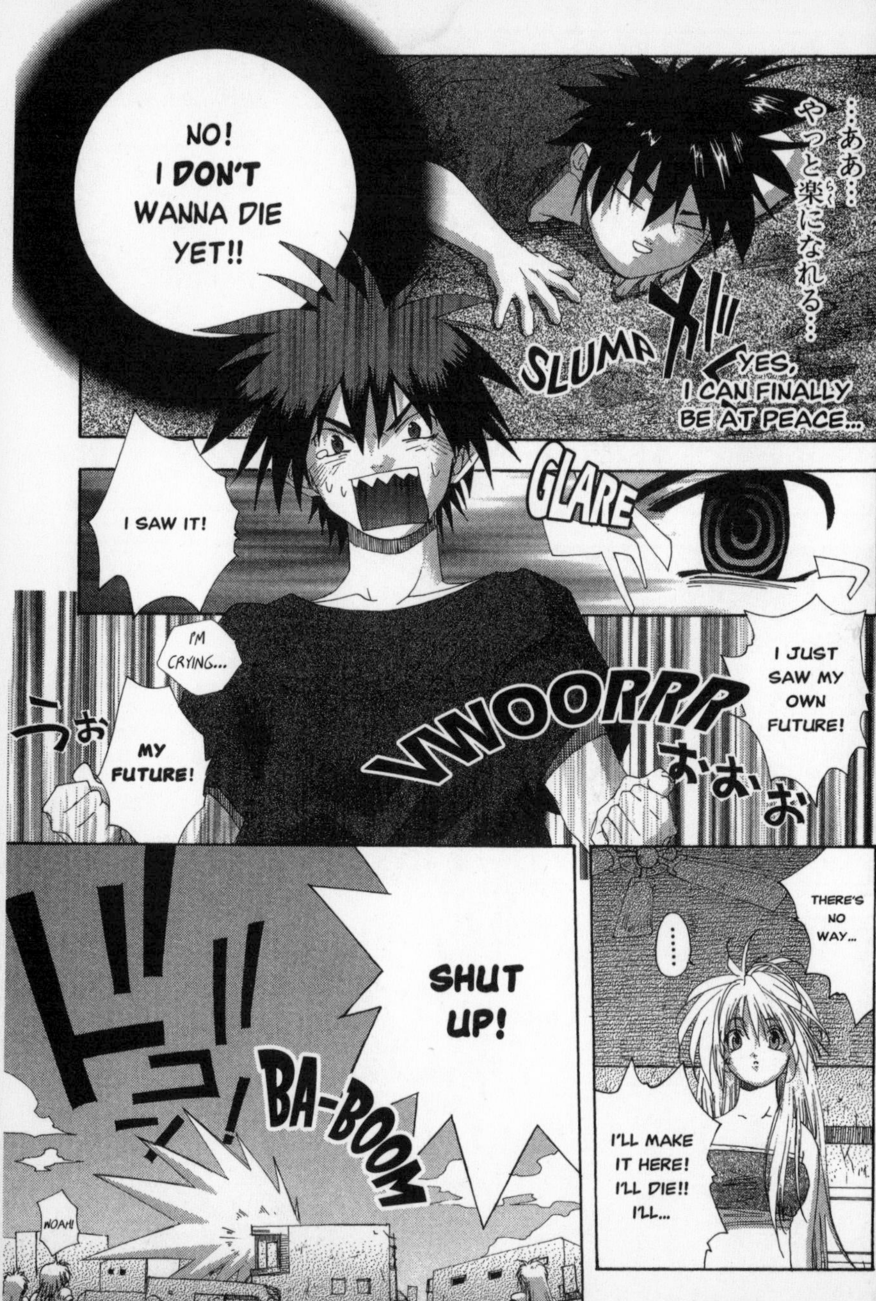
……ああ……やっと楽になれる……
SLUMP
YES, I CAN FINALLY BE AT PEACE...
NO! I DON'T WANNA DIE YET!!
GLARE
I SAW IT!
I JUST SAW MY OWN FUTURE!
VWOORRR
I'M CRYING...
MY FUTURE!
THERE'S NO WAY...
......
I'LL MAKE IT HERE! I'LL DIE!! I'LL...
SHUT UP!
BA-BOOM
WOAH!

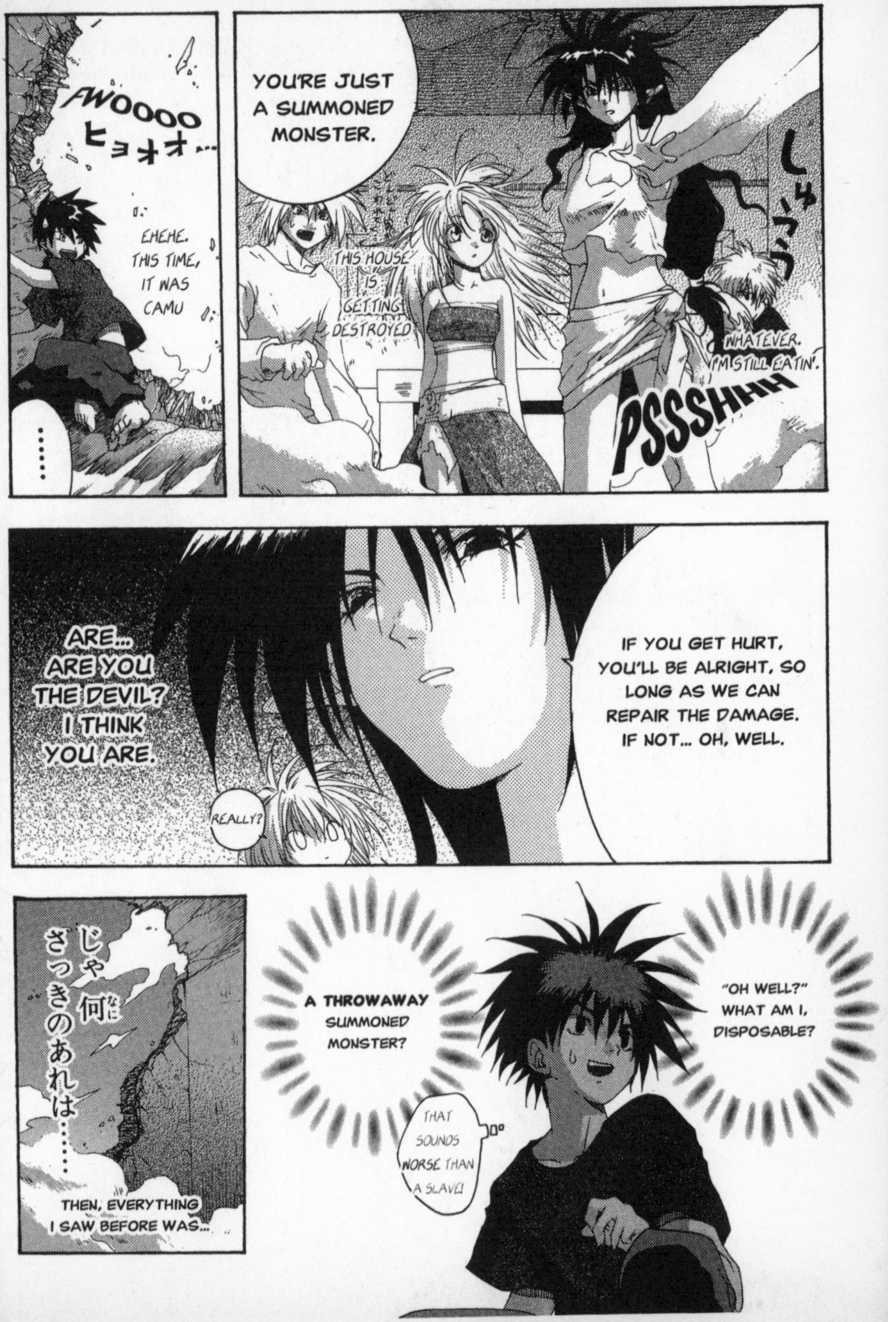
YOU'RE JUST A SUMMONED MONSTER.
WHATEVER. I'M STILL EATIN'.
PSSSHHH
THIS HOUSE IS GETTING DESTROYED
FWOOOO
ヒョオオ…
EHEHE. THIS TIME, IT WAS CAMU
……
IF YOU GET HURT, YOU'LL BE ALRIGHT, SO LONG AS WE CAN REPAIR THE DAMAGE. IF NOT... OH, WELL.
ARE... ARE YOU THE DEVIL? I THINK YOU ARE.
REALLY?
"OH WELL?" WHAT AM I, DISPOSABLE?
A THROWAWAY SUMMONED MONSTER?
THAT SOUNDS WORSE THAN A SLAVE!
じゃ何
さっきのあれは……
THEN, EVERYTHING I SAW BEFORE WAS...

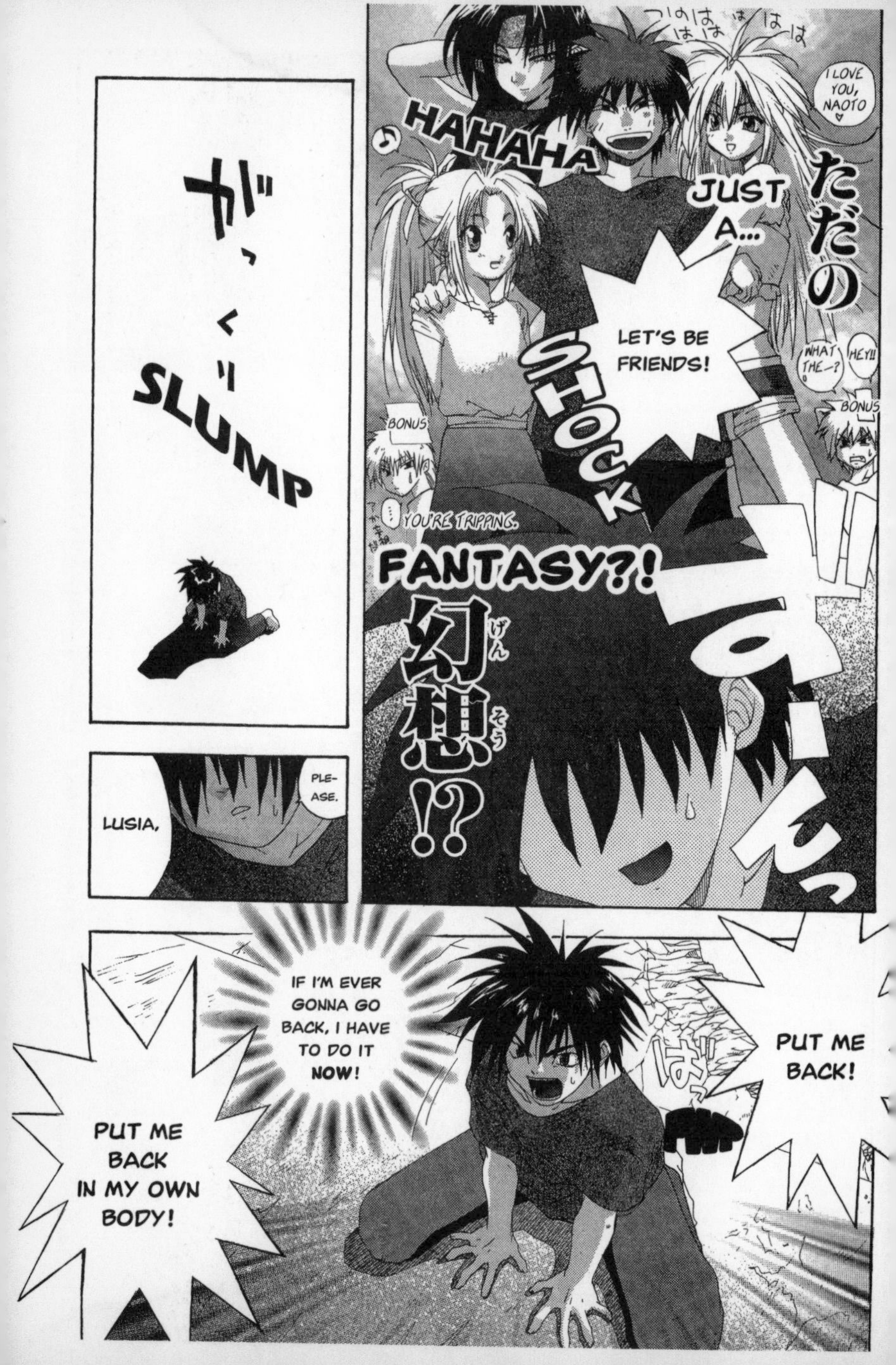
I LOVE YOU, NAOTO ♡
HAHAHA
JUST A...
ただの
LET'S BE FRIENDS!
SHOCK
WHAT THE—?
HEY!!
BONUS
BONUS
...
YOU'RE TRIPPING.
FANTASY?!
幻想!?
がっくり
SLUMP
PLE-ASE.
LUSIA,
PUT ME BACK!
ばっ
IF I'M EVER GONNA GO BACK, I HAVE TO DO IT NOW!
PUT ME BACK IN MY OWN BODY!

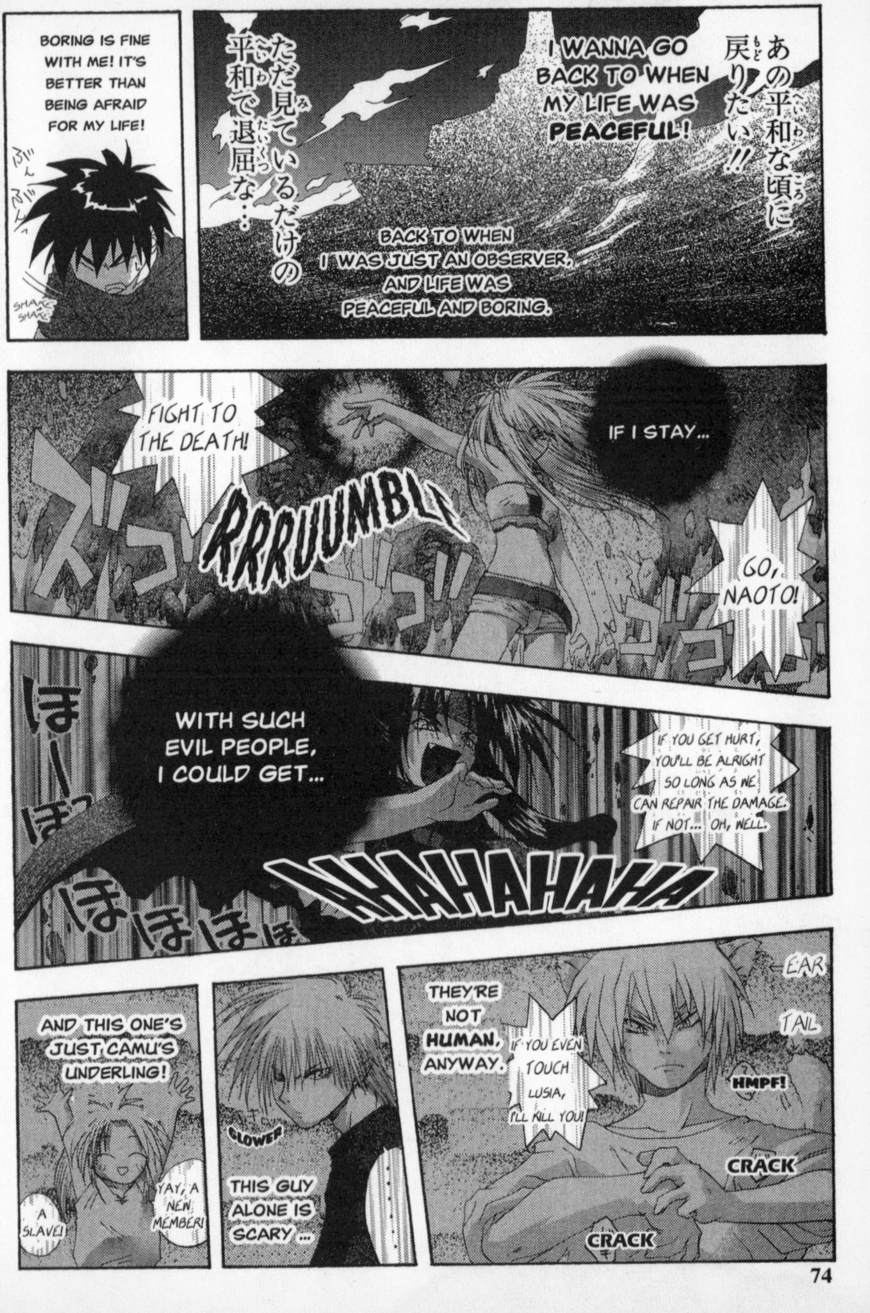
あの平和な頃に戻りたい!!
I WANNA GO BACK TO WHEN MY LIFE WAS **PEACEFUL**!
ただ見ているだけの平和で退屈な…
BACK TO WHEN I WAS JUST AN OBSERVER, AND LIFE WAS PEACEFUL AND BORING.
BORING IS FINE WITH ME! IT'S BETTER THAN BEING AFRAID FOR MY LIFE!
ぶんぶん
SHAKE SHAKE
IF I STAY...
GO, NAOTO!
FIGHT TO THE DEATH!
RRRUUMBLE
IF YOU GET HURT, YOU'LL BE ALRIGHT SO LONG AS WE CAN REPAIR THE DAMAGE. IF NOT... OH, WELL.
WITH SUCH EVIL PEOPLE, I COULD GET...
AHAHAHAHA
EAR
TAIL
HMPF!
THEY'RE NOT **HUMAN**, ANYWAY.
IF YOU EVEN TOUCH LUSIA, I'LL KILL YOU!
CRACK
CRACK
GLOWER
THIS GUY ALONE IS SCARY...
AND THIS ONE'S JUST CAMU'S UNDERLING!
YAY, A NEW MEMBER!
A SLAVE!

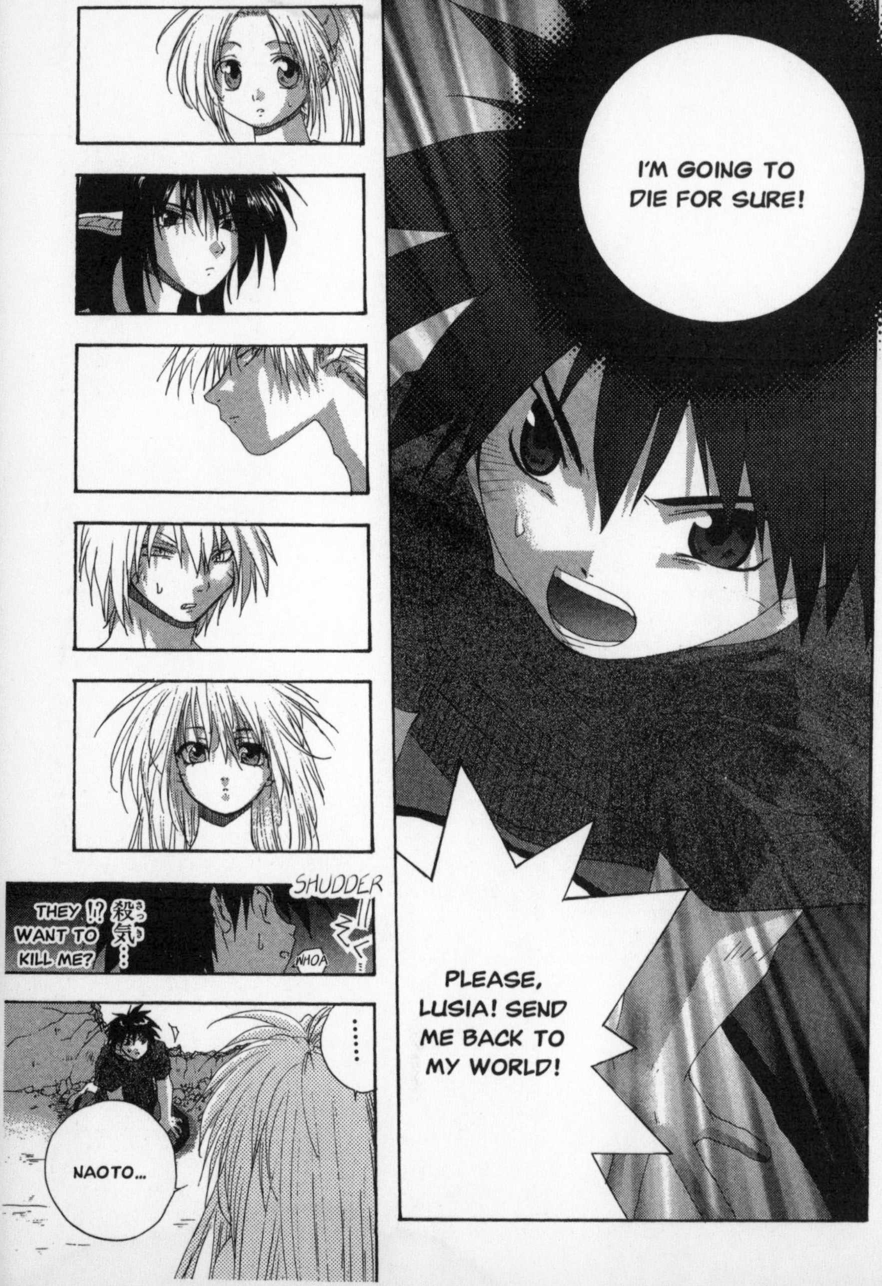
I'M GOING TO DIE FOR SURE!
PLEASE, LUSIA! SEND ME BACK TO MY WORLD!
SHUDDER
WHOA
殺気…
!?
THEY WANT TO KILL ME?
……
NAOTO...

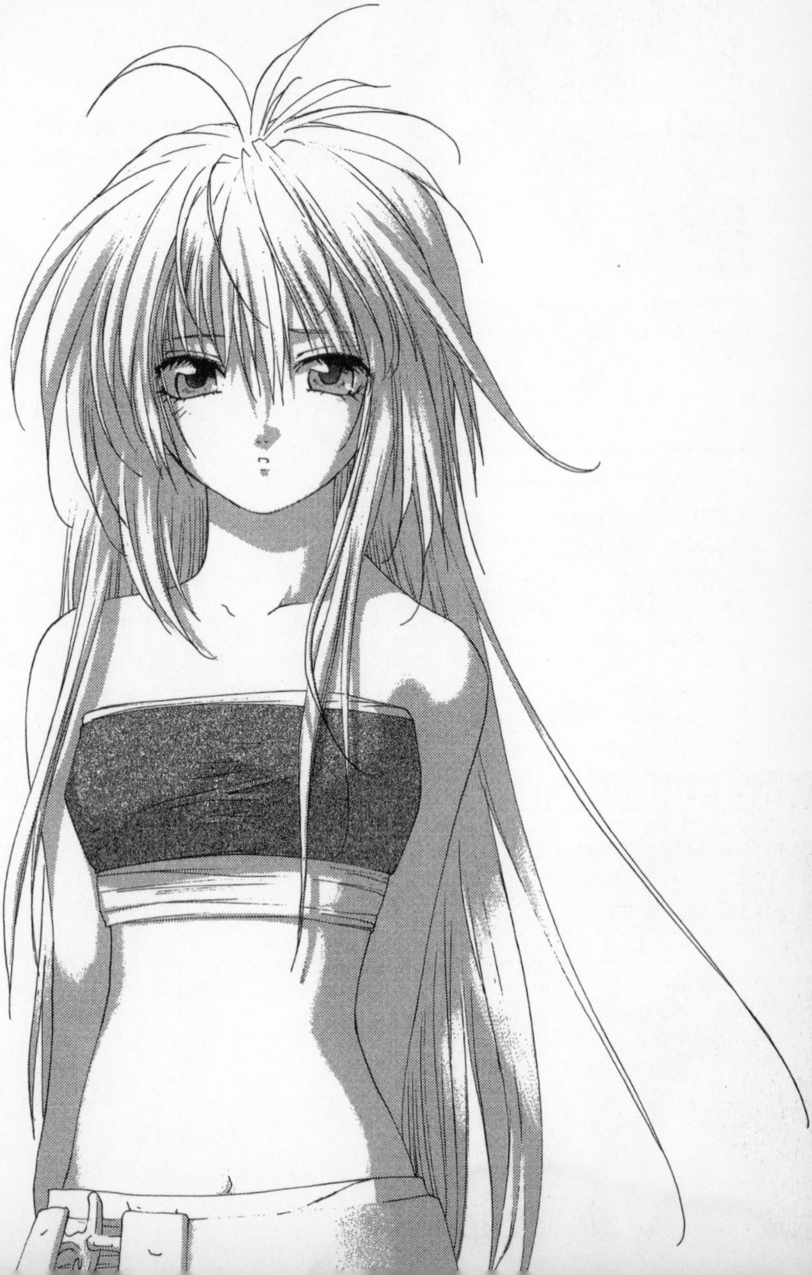

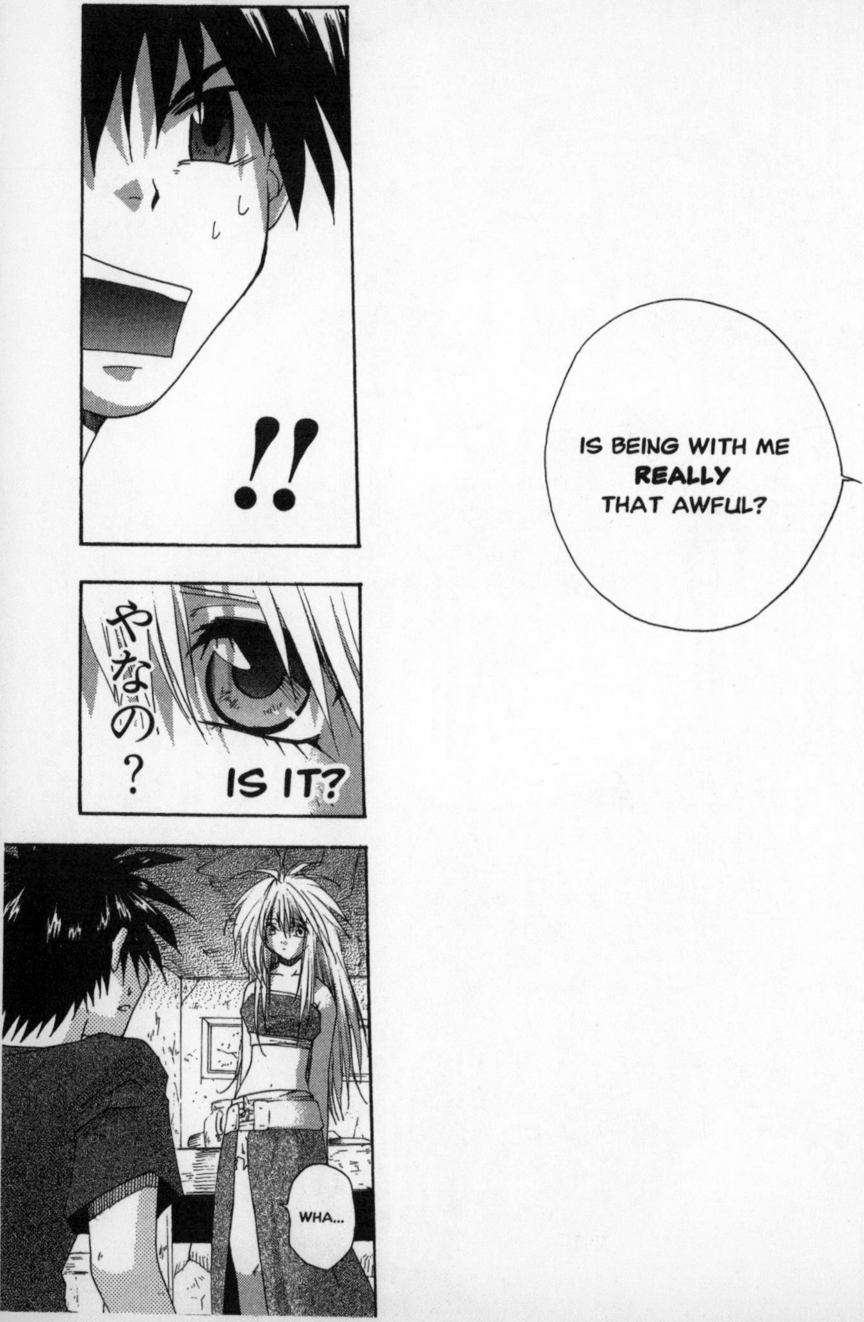
IS BEING WITH ME **REALLY** THAT AWFUL?
!!
やなの？
IS IT?
WHA...

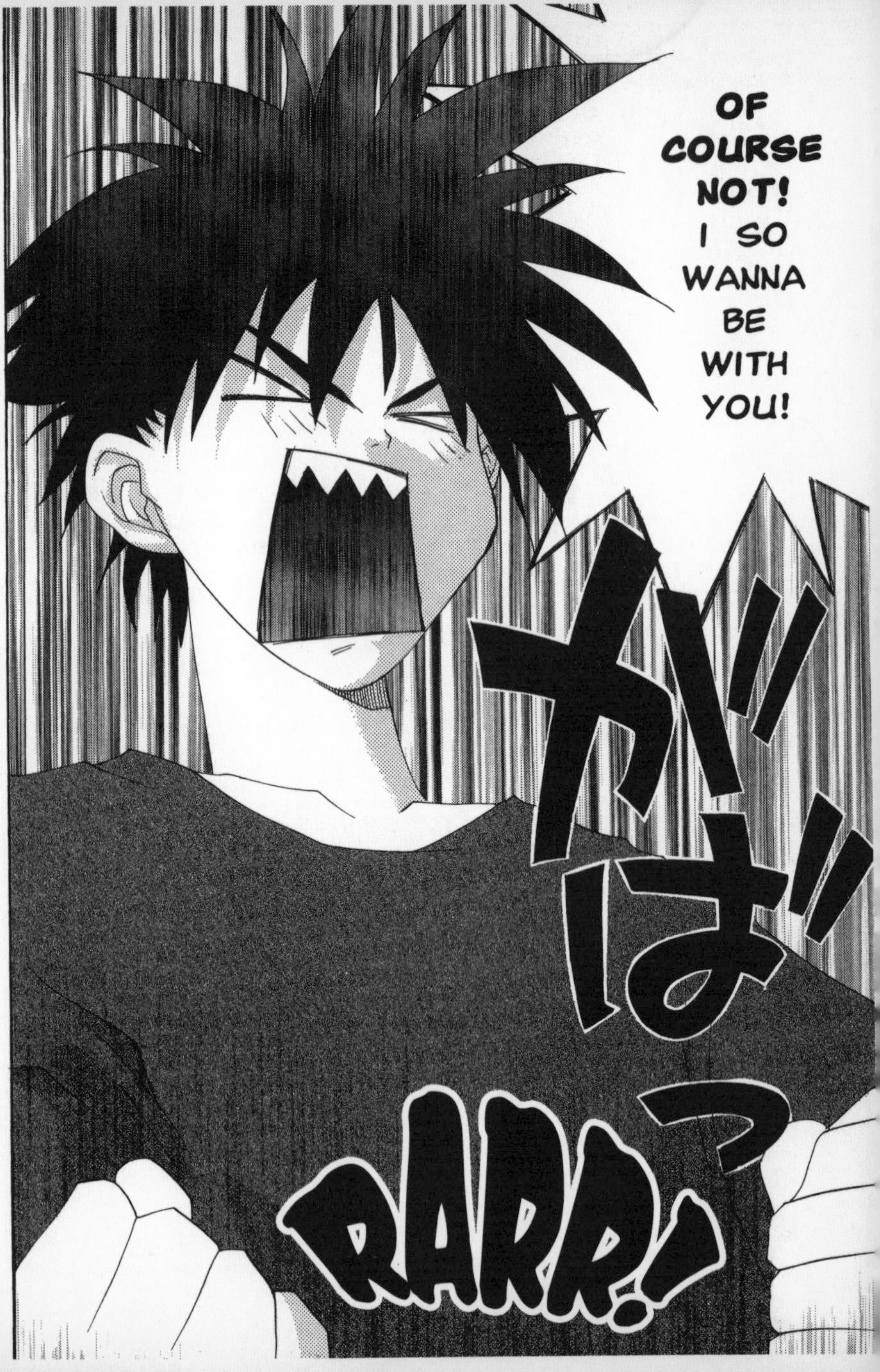
OF COURSE NOT! I SO WANNA BE WITH YOU!
がばっ
RARR!

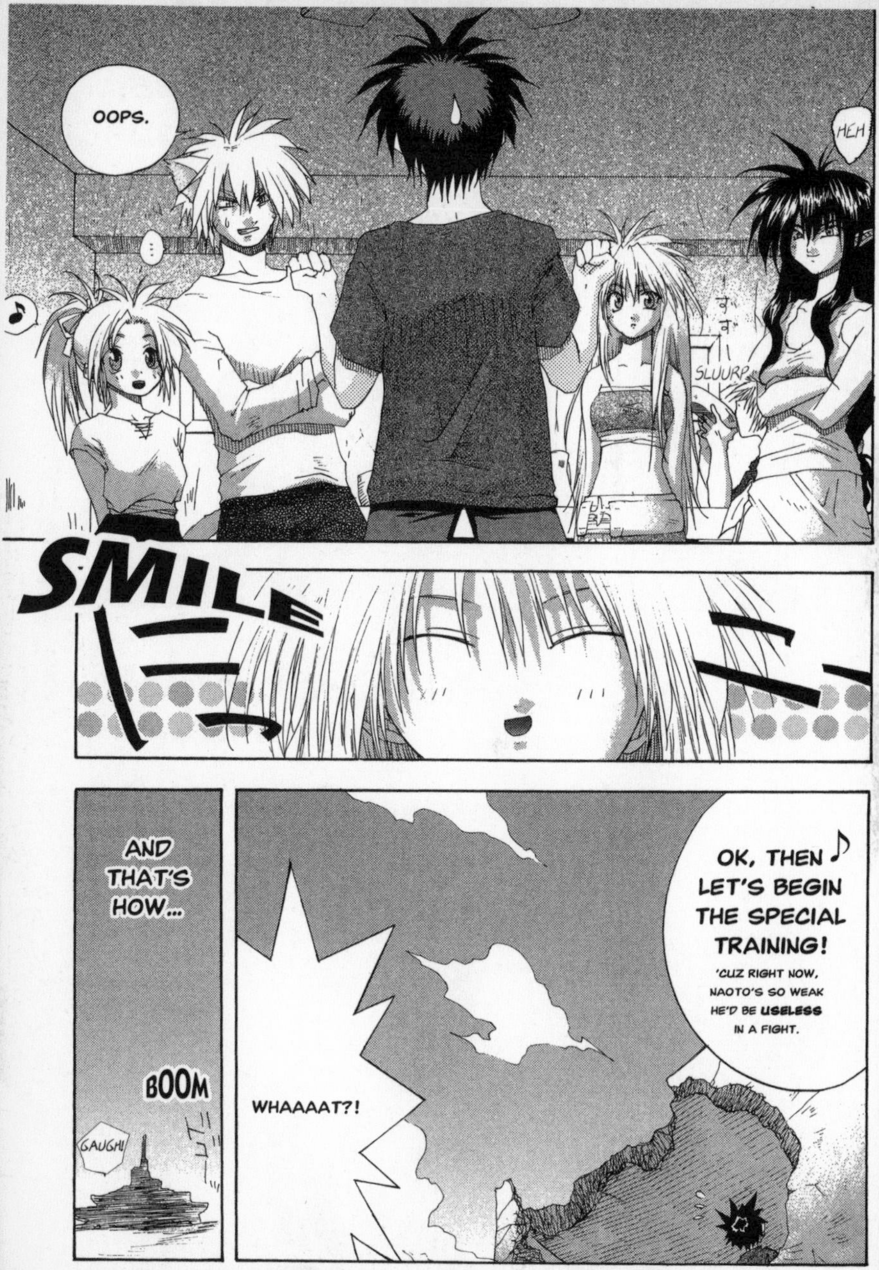
HEH
SLUURP
OOPS.
...
♪
SMILE
OK, THEN ♪ LET'S BEGIN THE SPECIAL TRAINING!
'CUZ RIGHT NOW, NAOTO'S SO WEAK HE'D BE USELESS IN A FIGHT.
WHAAAAT?!
AND THAT'S HOW...
BOOM
GAUGH!

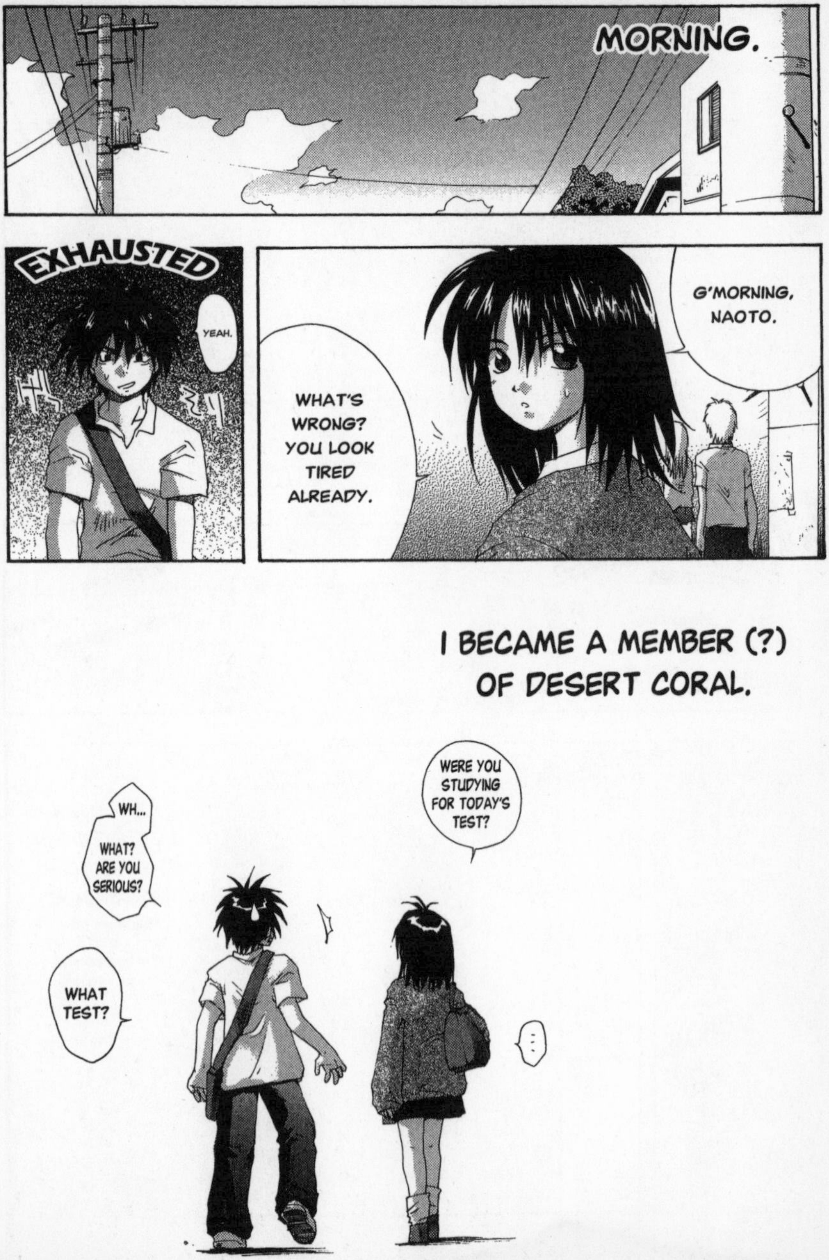
MORNING.
G'MORNING, NAOTO.
WHAT'S WRONG? YOU LOOK TIRED ALREADY.
EXHAUSTED
YEAH.
I BECAME A MEMBER (?) OF DESERT CORAL.
WERE YOU STUDYING FOR TODAY'S TEST?
WH...
WHAT? ARE YOU SERIOUS?
WHAT TEST?
...

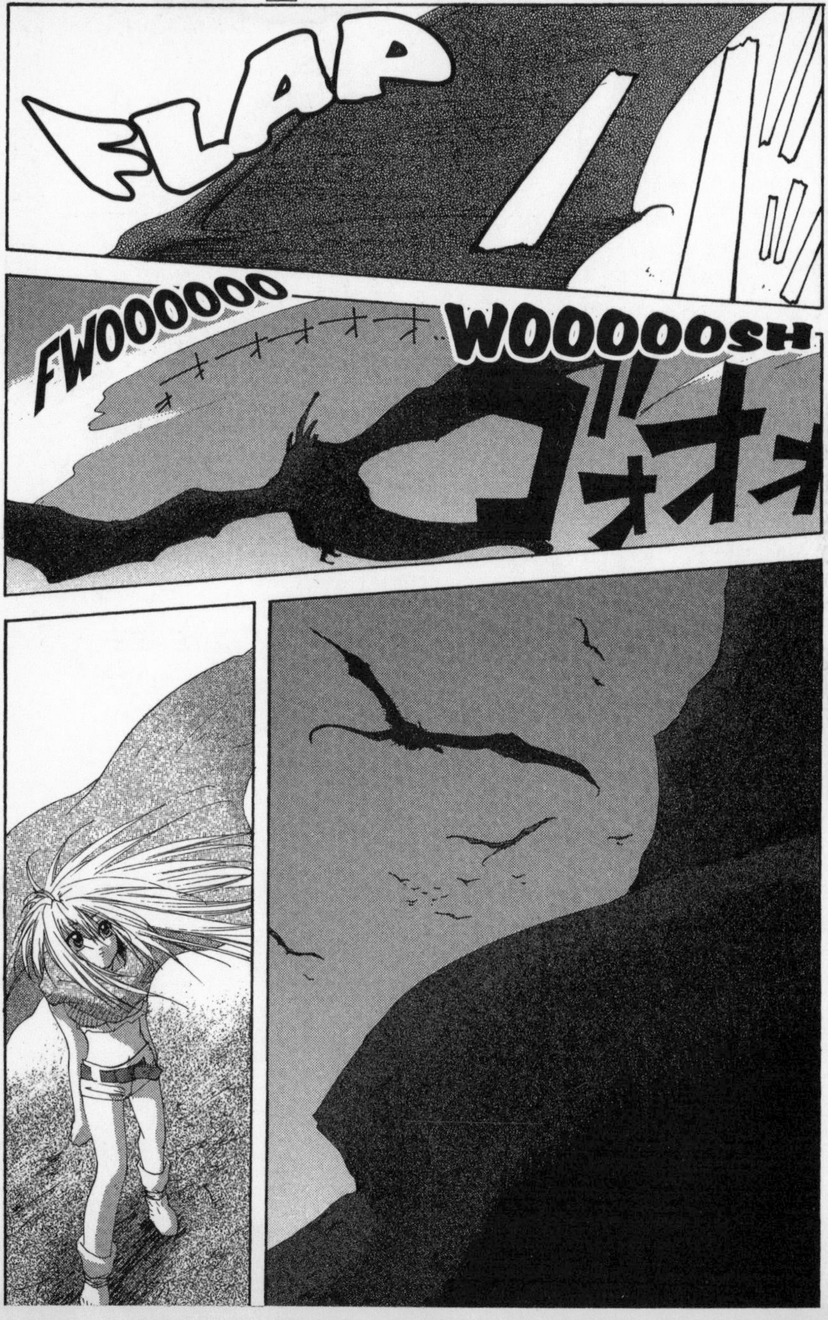
FLAP
FWOOOOOO
WOOOOOOSH

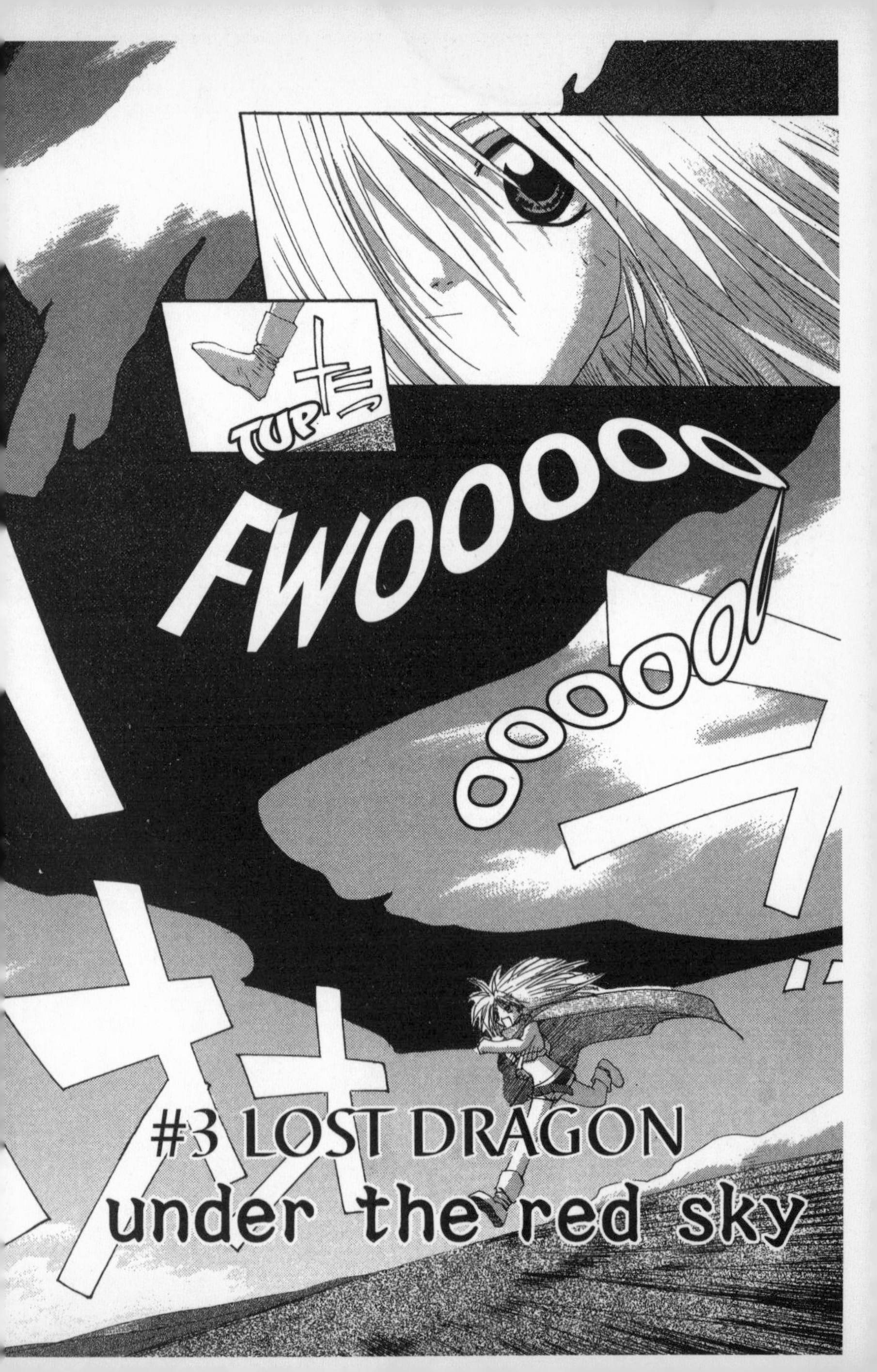
TUP
FWOOOOOOOOOOOO
#3 LOST DRAGON
under the red sky

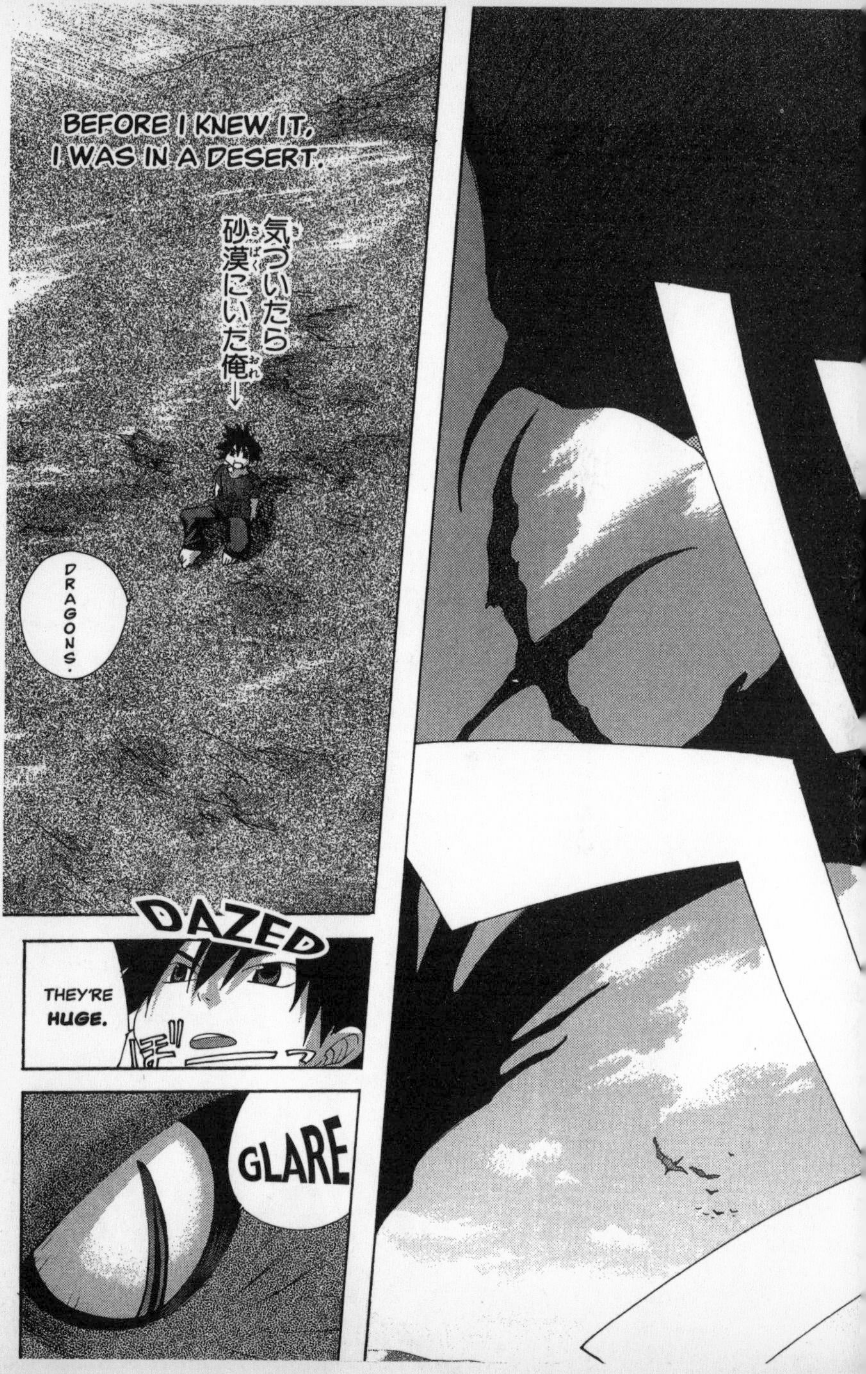
BEFORE I KNEW IT, I WAS IN A DESERT.
気づいたら砂漠にいた俺↓
DRAGONS.
DAZED
THEY'RE HUGE.
GLARE

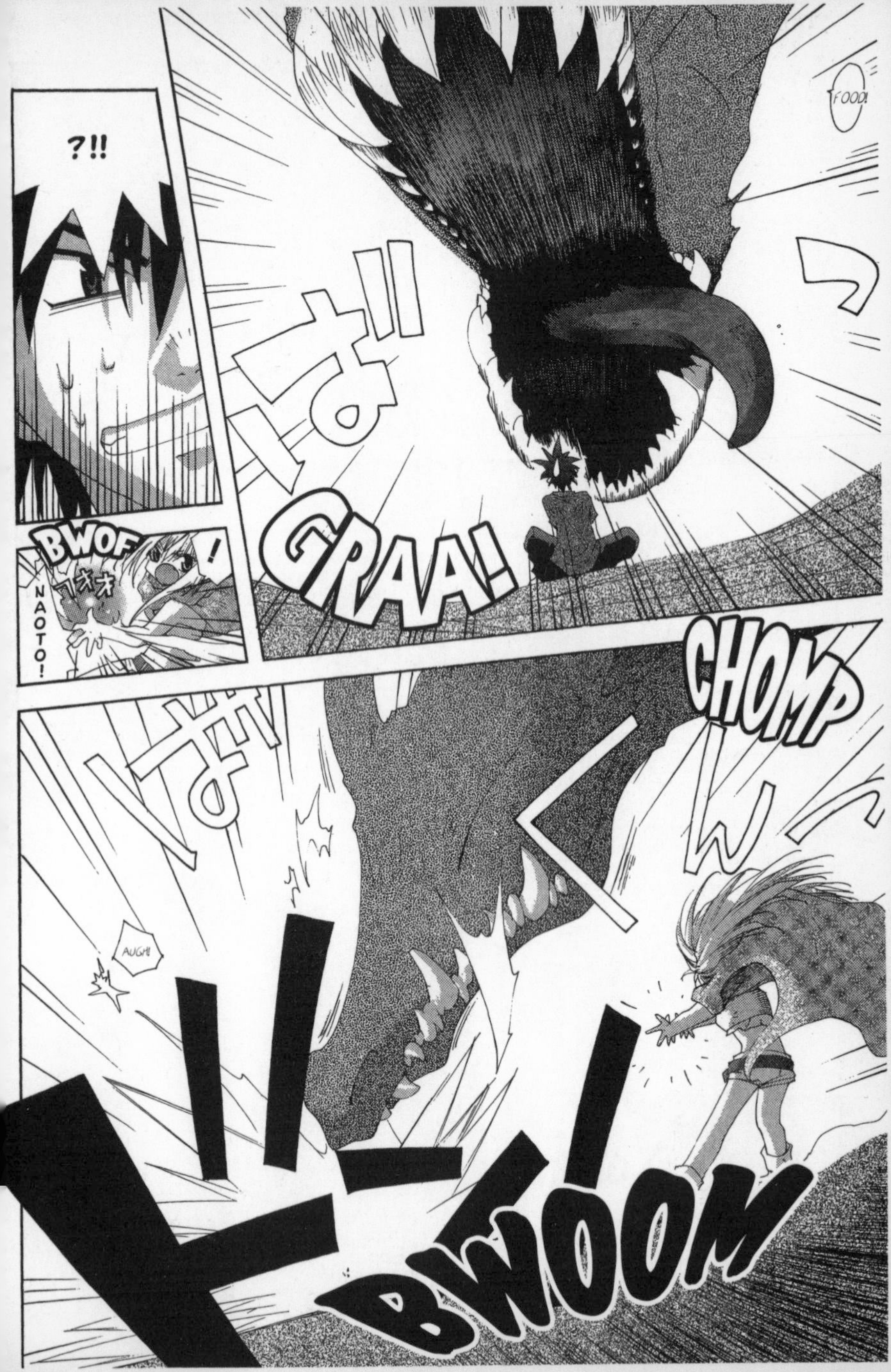
FOOD!
GRAA!
?!!
BWOF
!
NAOTO!
フォオ
CHOMP
AUGH!
BWOOM

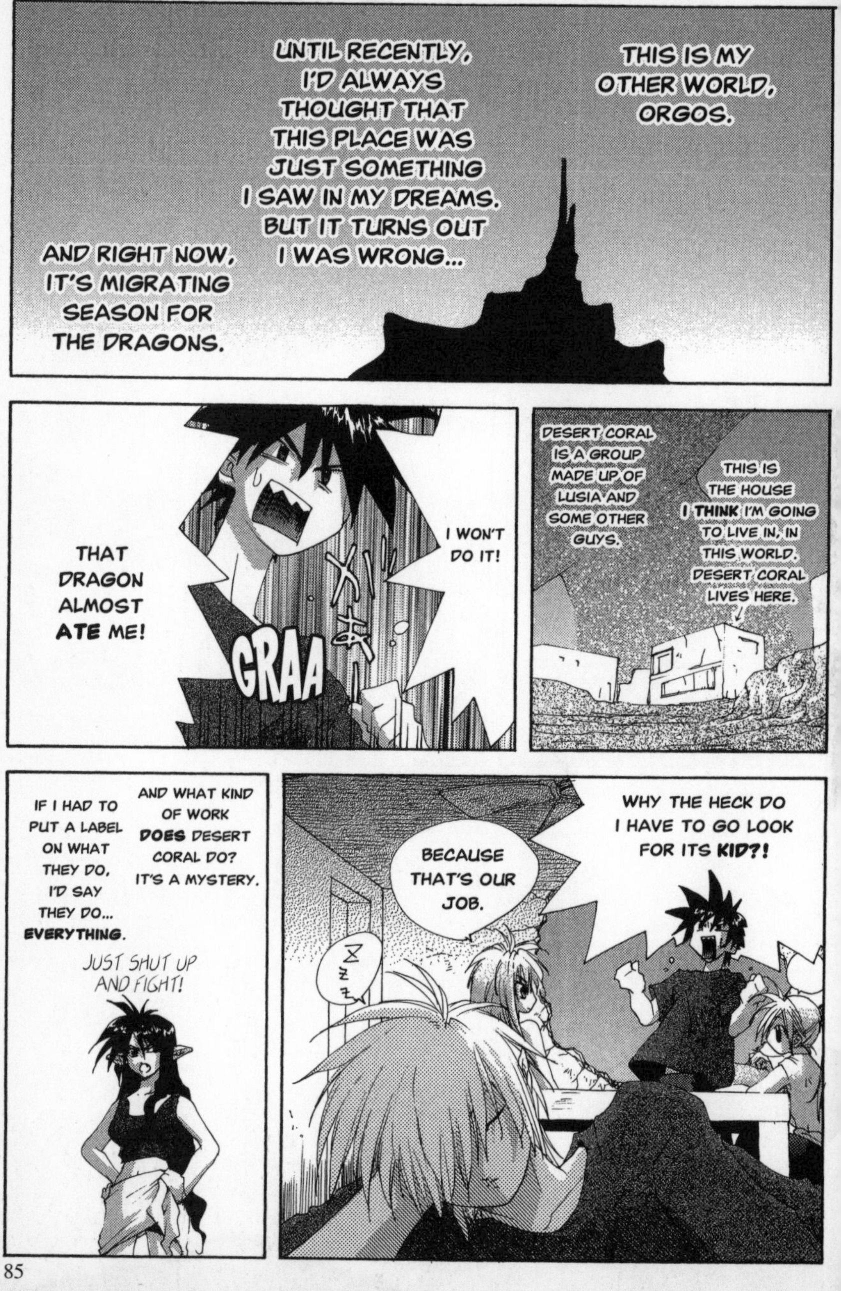
THIS IS MY OTHER WORLD, ORGOS.
UNTIL RECENTLY, I'D ALWAYS THOUGHT THAT THIS PLACE WAS JUST SOMETHING I SAW IN MY DREAMS. BUT IT TURNS OUT I WAS WRONG...
AND RIGHT NOW, IT'S MIGRATING SEASON FOR THE DRAGONS.
THIS IS THE HOUSE **I THINK** I'M GOING TO LIVE IN, IN THIS WORLD. DESERT CORAL LIVES HERE.
DESERT CORAL IS A GROUP MADE UP OF LUSIA AND SOME OTHER GUYS.
I WON'T DO IT!
GRAA
THAT DRAGON ALMOST **ATE** ME!
WHY THE HECK DO I HAVE TO GO LOOK FOR ITS **KID?!**
BECAUSE THAT'S OUR JOB.
AND WHAT KIND OF WORK **DOES** DESERT CORAL DO? IT'S A MYSTERY.
IF I HAD TO PUT A LABEL ON WHAT THEY DO, I'D SAY THEY DO... **EVERYTHING**.
JUST SHUT UP AND FIGHT!

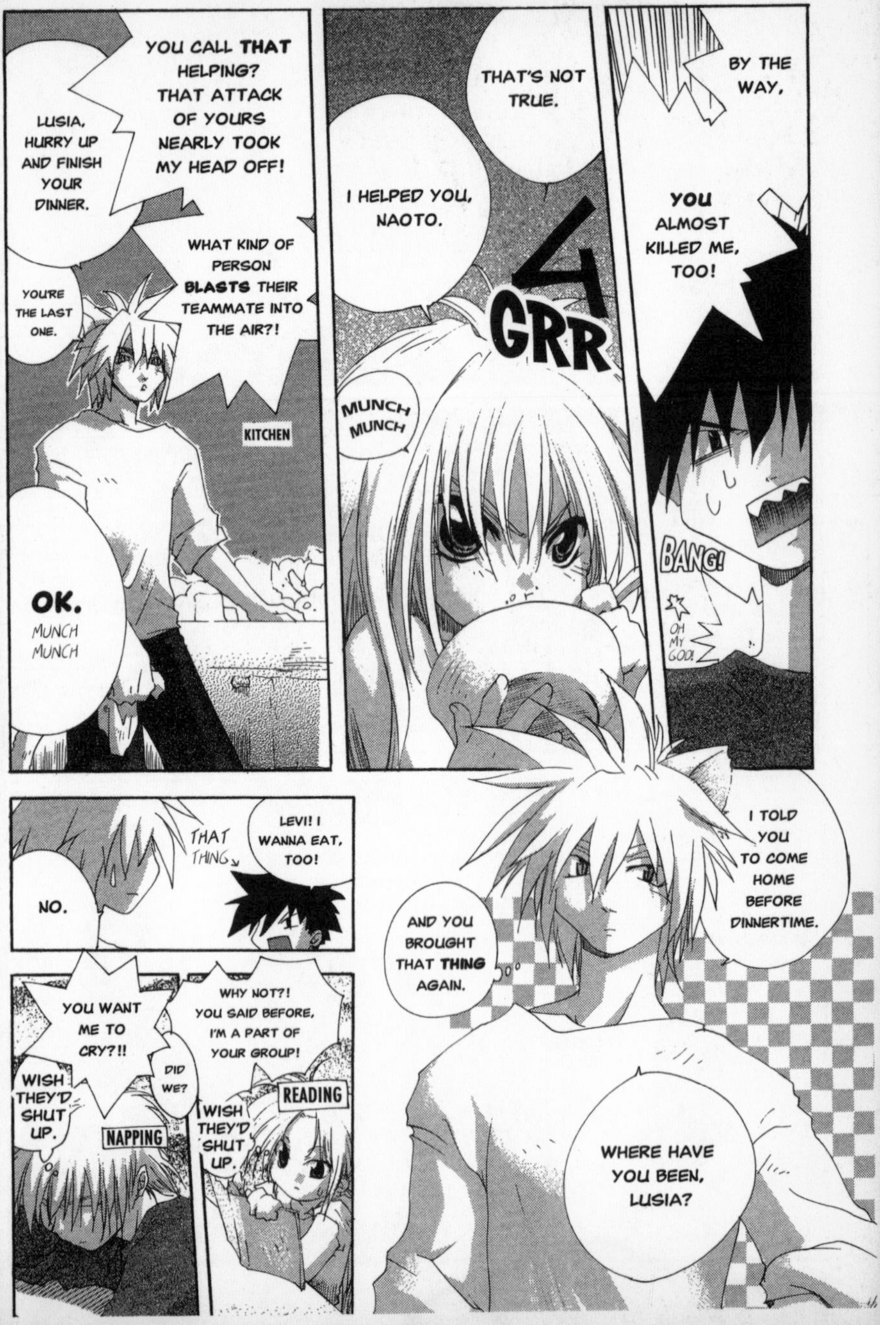
BY THE WAY,
YOU ALMOST KILLED ME, TOO!
BANG!
OH MY GOD!
THAT'S NOT TRUE.
I HELPED YOU, NAOTO.
GRR
MUNCH MUNCH
YOU CALL THAT HELPING? THAT ATTACK OF YOURS NEARLY TOOK MY HEAD OFF!
LUSIA, HURRY UP AND FINISH YOUR DINNER.
WHAT KIND OF PERSON BLASTS THEIR TEAMMATE INTO THE AIR?!
YOU'RE THE LAST ONE.
KITCHEN
OK.
MUNCH MUNCH
I TOLD YOU TO COME HOME BEFORE DINNERTIME.
AND YOU BROUGHT THAT THING AGAIN.
WHERE HAVE YOU BEEN, LUSIA?
LEVI! I WANNA EAT, TOO!
THAT THING
NO.
WHY NOT?! YOU SAID BEFORE, I'M A PART OF YOUR GROUP!
READING
DID WE?
WISH THEY'D SHUT UP.
YOU WANT ME TO CRY?!!
WISH THEY'D SHUT UP.
NAPPING

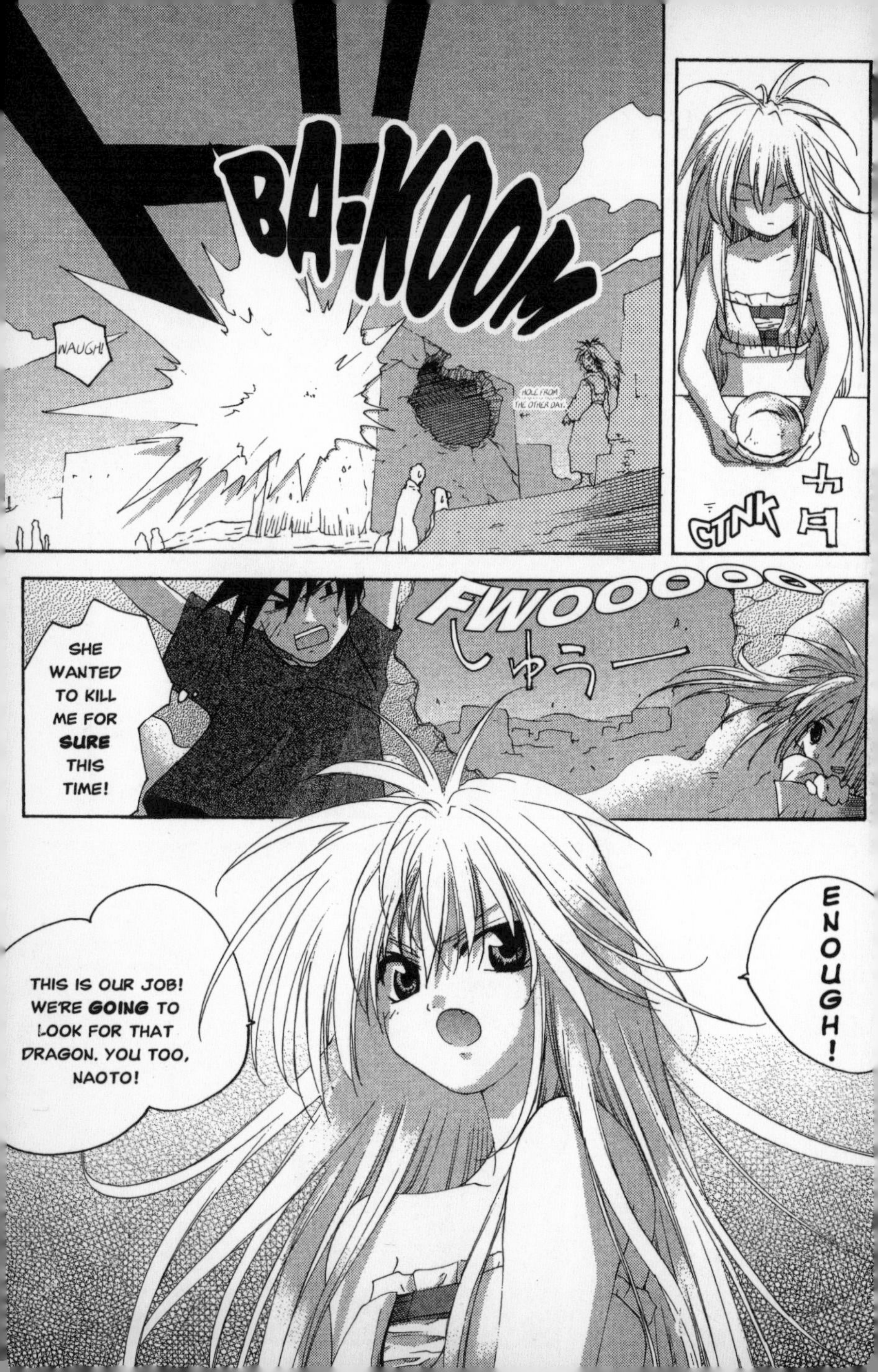
CTNK
BA-KOOM
WAUGH!
HOLE FROM THE OTHER DAY.
FWOOOOO
しゅうー
SHE WANTED TO KILL ME FOR **SURE** THIS TIME!
ENOUGH!
THIS IS OUR JOB! WE'RE **GOING** TO LOOK FOR THAT DRAGON. YOU TOO, NAOTO!

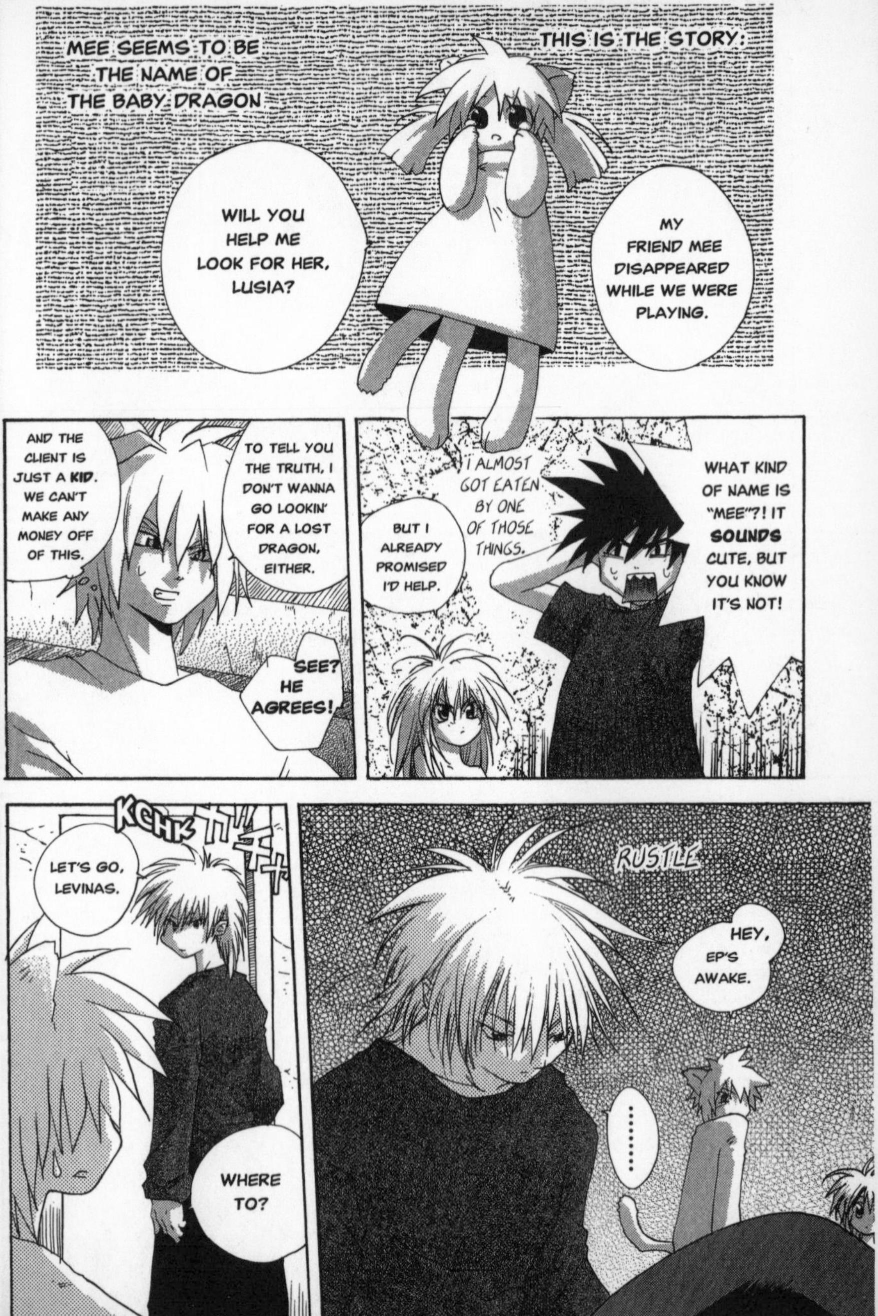
THIS IS THE STORY:
MY FRIEND MEE DISAPPEARED WHILE WE WERE PLAYING.
WILL YOU HELP ME LOOK FOR HER, LUSIA?
MEE SEEMS TO BE THE NAME OF THE BABY DRAGON
WHAT KIND OF NAME IS "MEE"?! IT SOUNDS CUTE, BUT YOU KNOW IT'S NOT!
I ALMOST GOT EATEN BY ONE OF THOSE THINGS.
BUT I ALREADY PROMISED I'D HELP.
TO TELL YOU THE TRUTH, I DON'T WANNA GO LOOKIN' FOR A LOST DRAGON, EITHER.
AND THE CLIENT IS JUST A KID. WE CAN'T MAKE ANY MONEY OFF OF THIS.
SEE? HE AGREES!
RUSTLE
HEY, EP'S AWAKE.
....
KCHK
LET'S GO, LEVINAS.
WHERE TO?

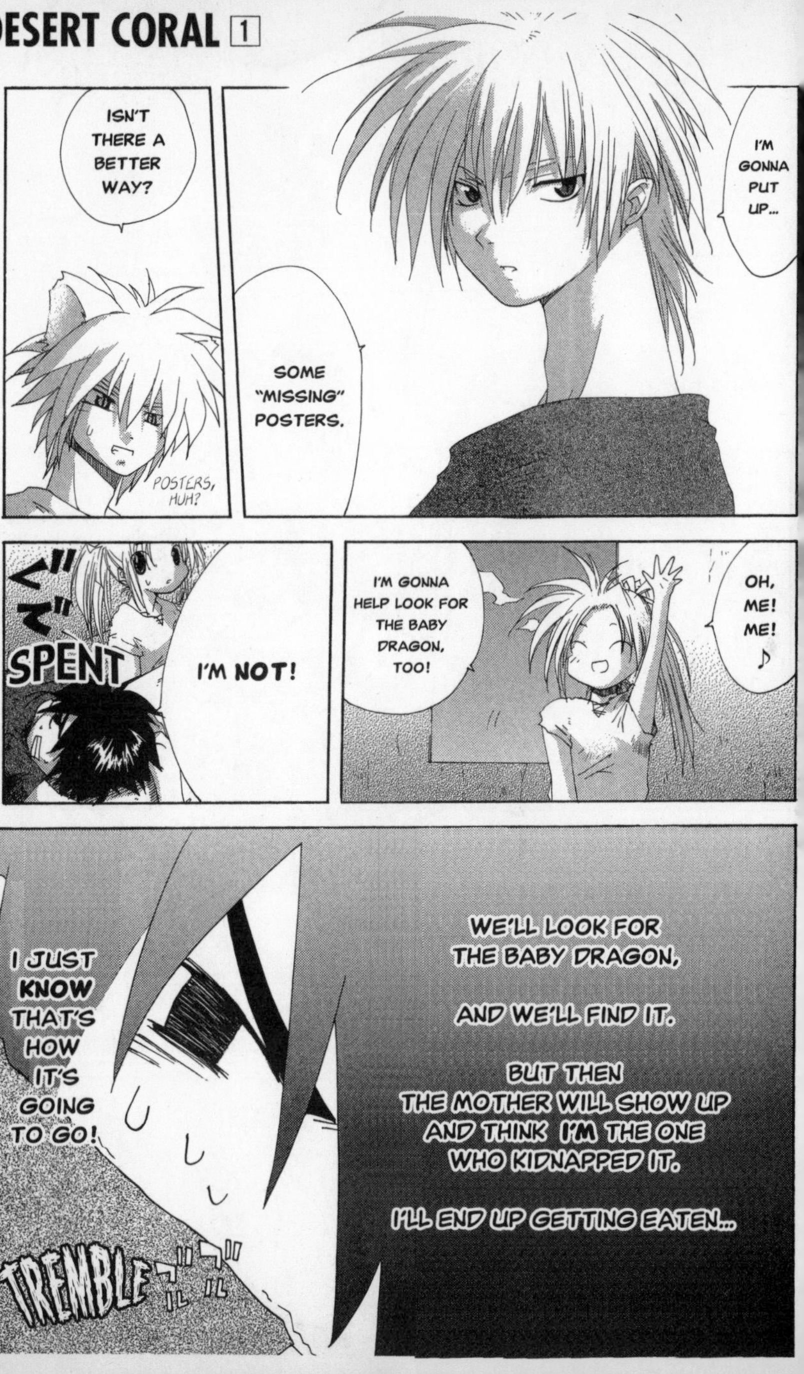
I'M GONNA PUT UP...
SOME "MISSING" POSTERS.
ISN'T THERE A BETTER WAY?
POSTERS, HUH?
OH, ME! ME! ♪
I'M GONNA HELP LOOK FOR THE BABY DRAGON, TOO!
I'M **NOT**!
SPENT
WE'LL LOOK FOR THE BABY DRAGON,
AND WE'LL FIND IT.
BUT THEN THE MOTHER WILL SHOW UP AND THINK **I'M** THE ONE WHO KIDNAPPED IT.
I'LL END UP GETTING EATEN...
I JUST **KNOW** THAT'S HOW IT'S GOING TO GO!
TREMBLE

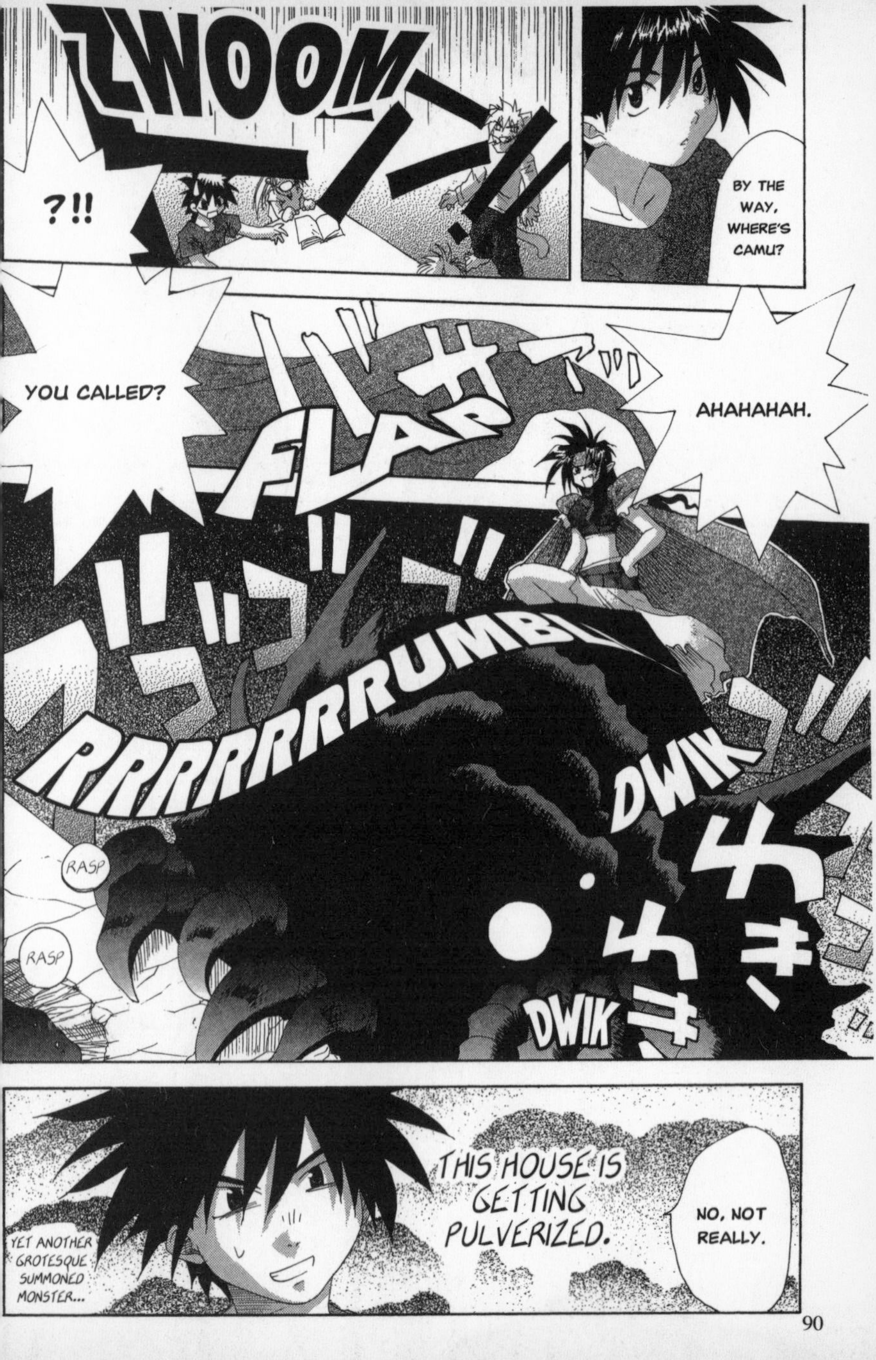
BY THE WAY, WHERE'S CAMU?
ZWOOM
?!!
AHAHAHAH.
YOU CALLED?
FLAP
RRRRRRRUMBL
DWIK
DWIK
RASP
RASP
NO, NOT REALLY.
THIS HOUSE IS GETTING PULVERIZED.
YET ANOTHER GROTESQUE SUMMONED MONSTER...

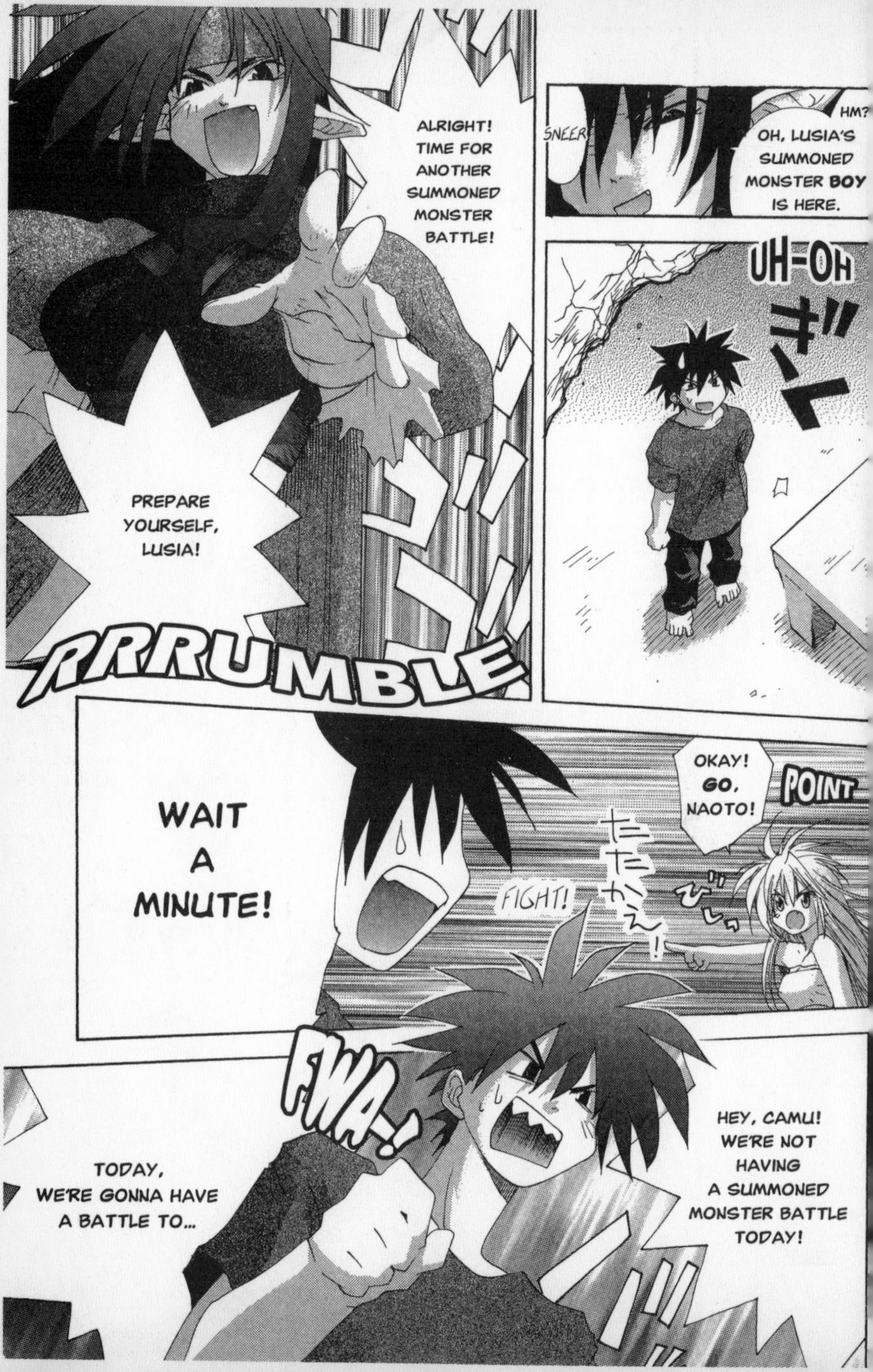
SNEER
HM? OH, LUSIA'S SUMMONED MONSTER **BOY** IS HERE.
UH-OH
ギン
ALRIGHT! TIME FOR ANOTHER SUMMONED MONSTER BATTLE!
PREPARE YOURSELF, LUSIA!
RRRUMBLE
OKAY! **GO,** NAOTO!
POINT
たたかえ！
FIGHT!
WAIT A MINUTE!
HEY, CAMU! WE'RE NOT HAVING A SUMMONED MONSTER BATTLE TODAY!
FWA-!
TODAY, WE'RE GONNA HAVE A BATTLE TO...

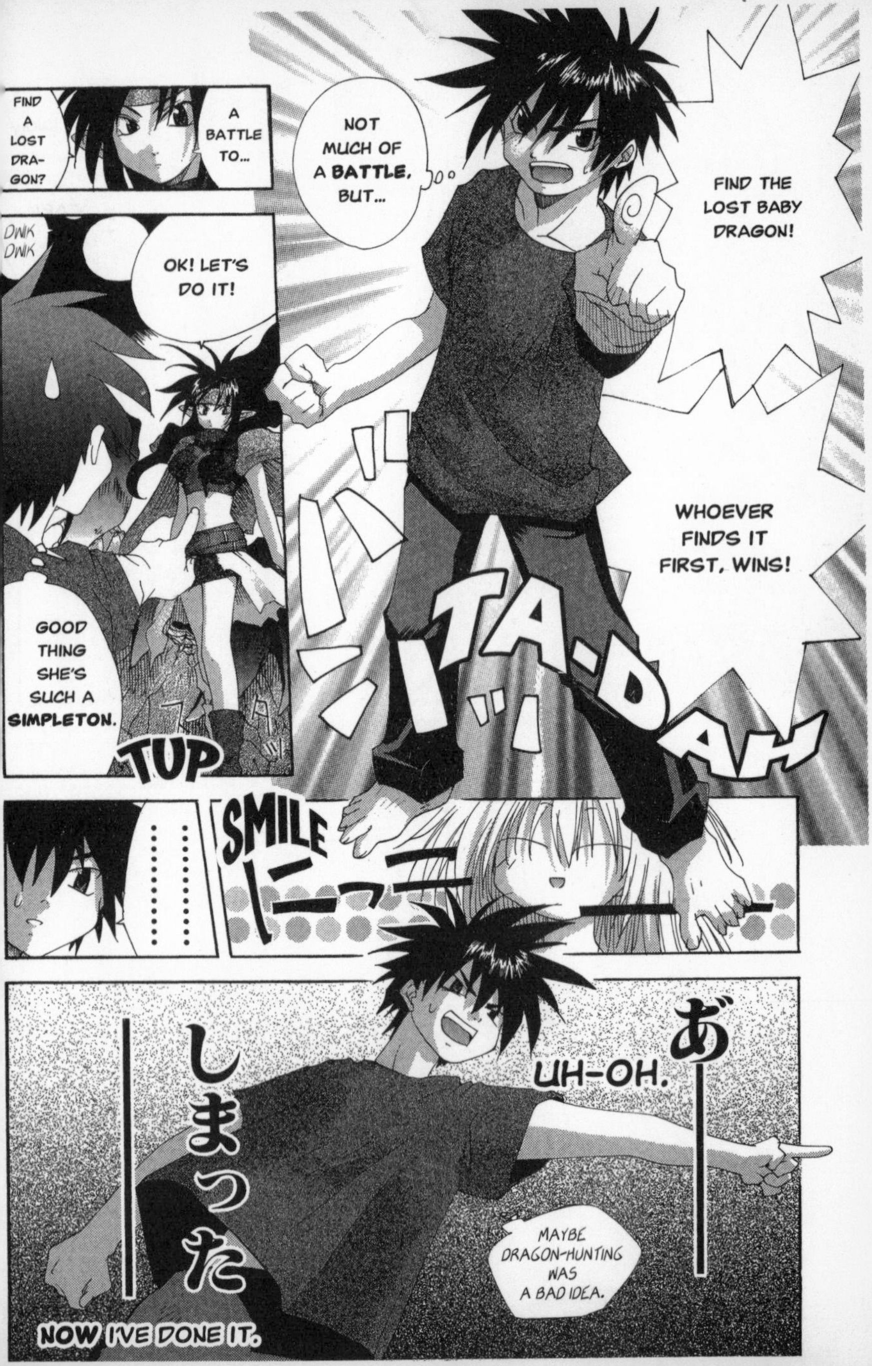
FIND THE LOST BABY DRAGON!
NOT MUCH OF A BATTLE, BUT...
WHOEVER FINDS IT FIRST, WINS!
TA-DAH
A BATTLE TO...
FIND A LOST DRAGON?
DWIK DWIK
OK! LET'S DO IT!
GOOD THING SHE'S SUCH A SIMPLETON.
TUP
SMILE
......
あー
UH-OH.
MAYBE DRAGON-HUNTING WAS A BAD IDEA.
しまった
NOW I'VE DONE IT.

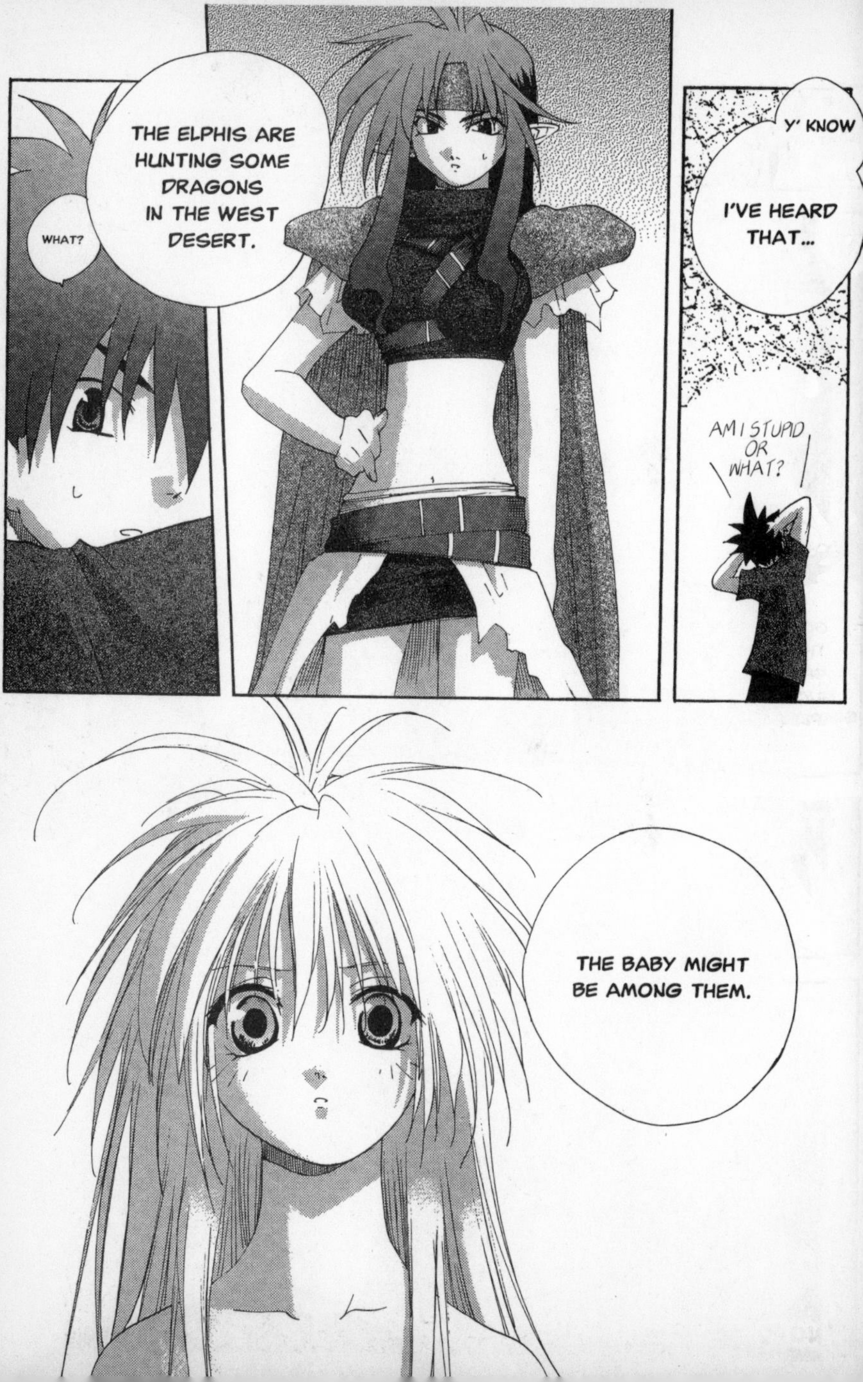
Y' KNOW
I'VE HEARD THAT...
AM I STUPID OR WHAT?
THE ELPHIS ARE HUNTING SOME DRAGONS IN THE WEST DESERT.
WHAT?
THE BABY MIGHT BE AMONG THEM.

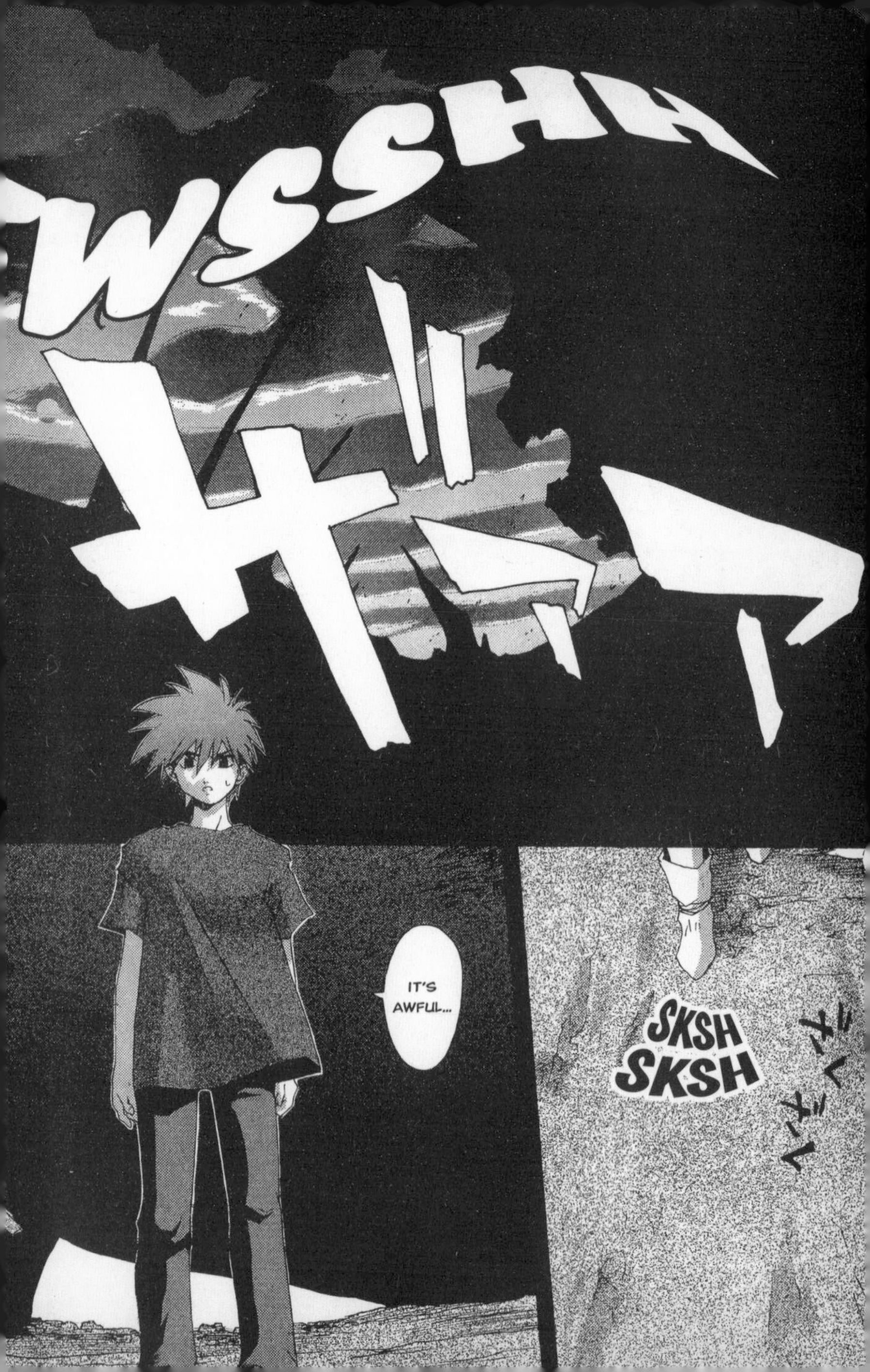
WSSHH
SKSH SKSH
IT'S AWFUL...

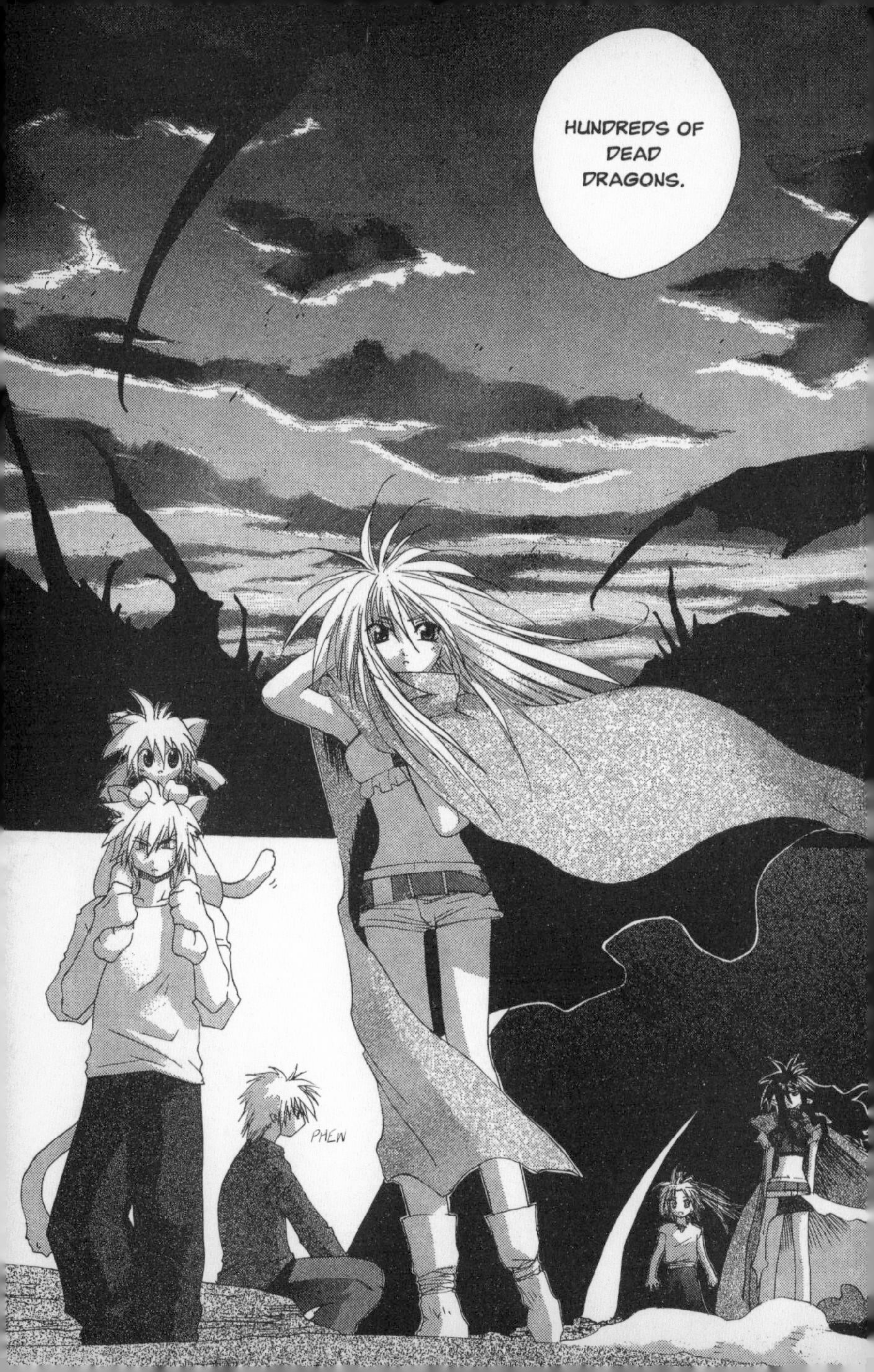
HUNDREDS OF DEAD DRAGONS.
PHEW

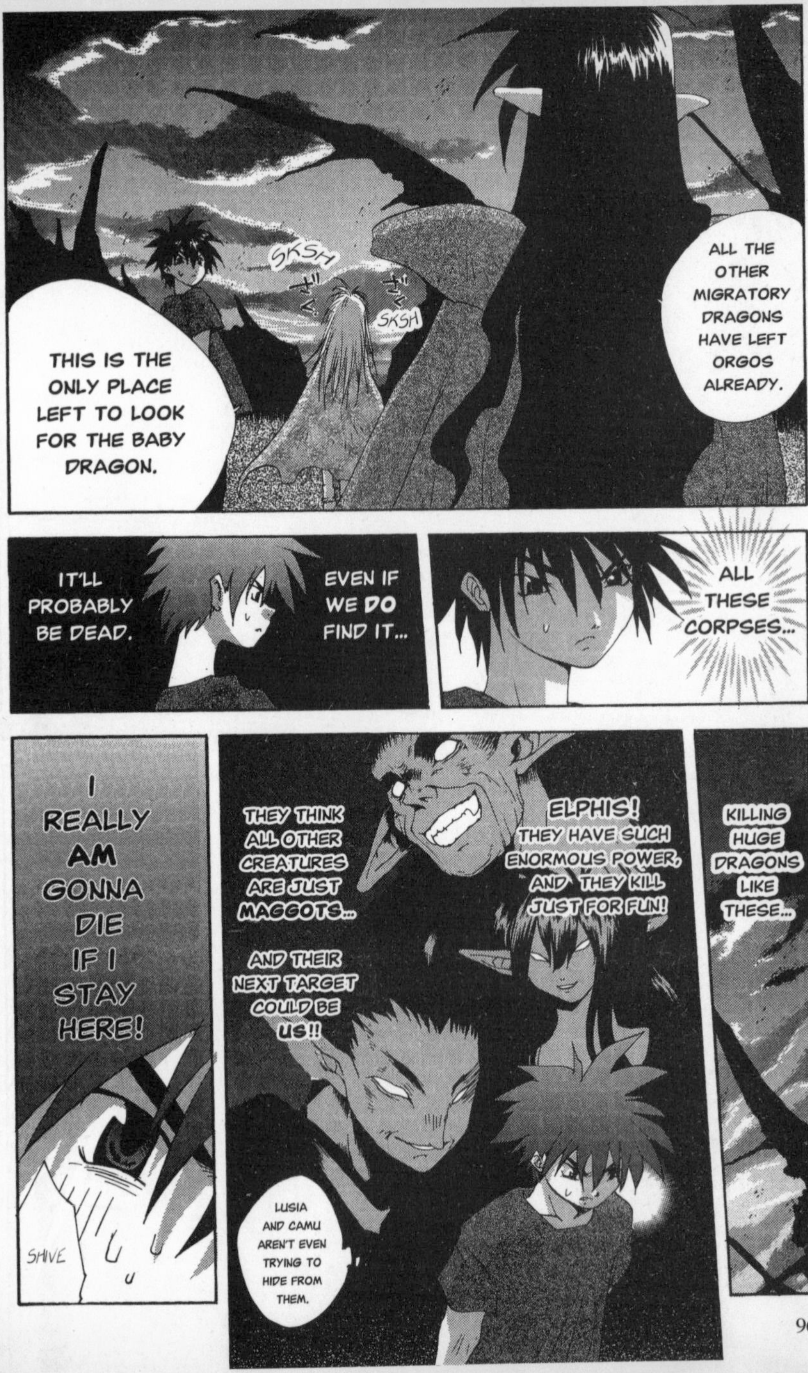

ALL THE OTHER MIGRATORY DRAGONS HAVE LEFT ORGOS ALREADY.
SKSH
SKSH
THIS IS THE ONLY PLACE LEFT TO LOOK FOR THE BABY DRAGON.
ALL THESE CORPSES...
EVEN IF WE DO FIND IT...
IT'LL PROBABLY BE DEAD.
KILLING HUGE DRAGONS LIKE THESE...
ELPHIS! THEY HAVE SUCH ENORMOUS POWER, AND THEY KILL JUST FOR FUN!
THEY THINK ALL OTHER CREATURES ARE JUST MAGGOTS...
AND THEIR NEXT TARGET COULD BE US!!
LUSIA AND CAMU AREN'T EVEN TRYING TO HIDE FROM THEM.
I REALLY AM GONNA DIE IF I STAY HERE!
SHIVE

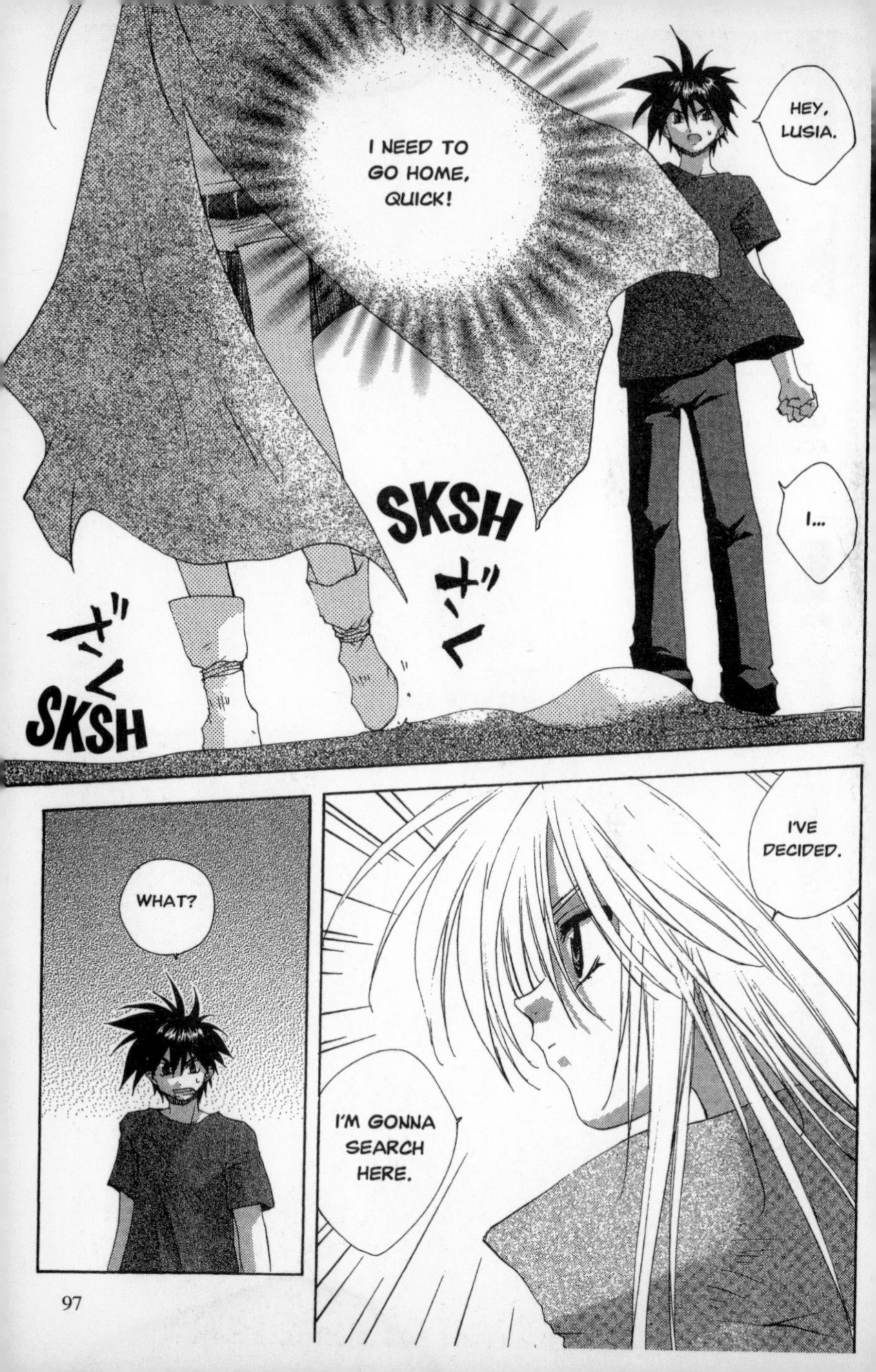
HEY, LUSIA.
I NEED TO GO HOME, QUICK!
I...
SKSH
ザッ
ザッ
SKSH
I'VE DECIDED.
I'M GONNA SEARCH HERE.
WHAT?

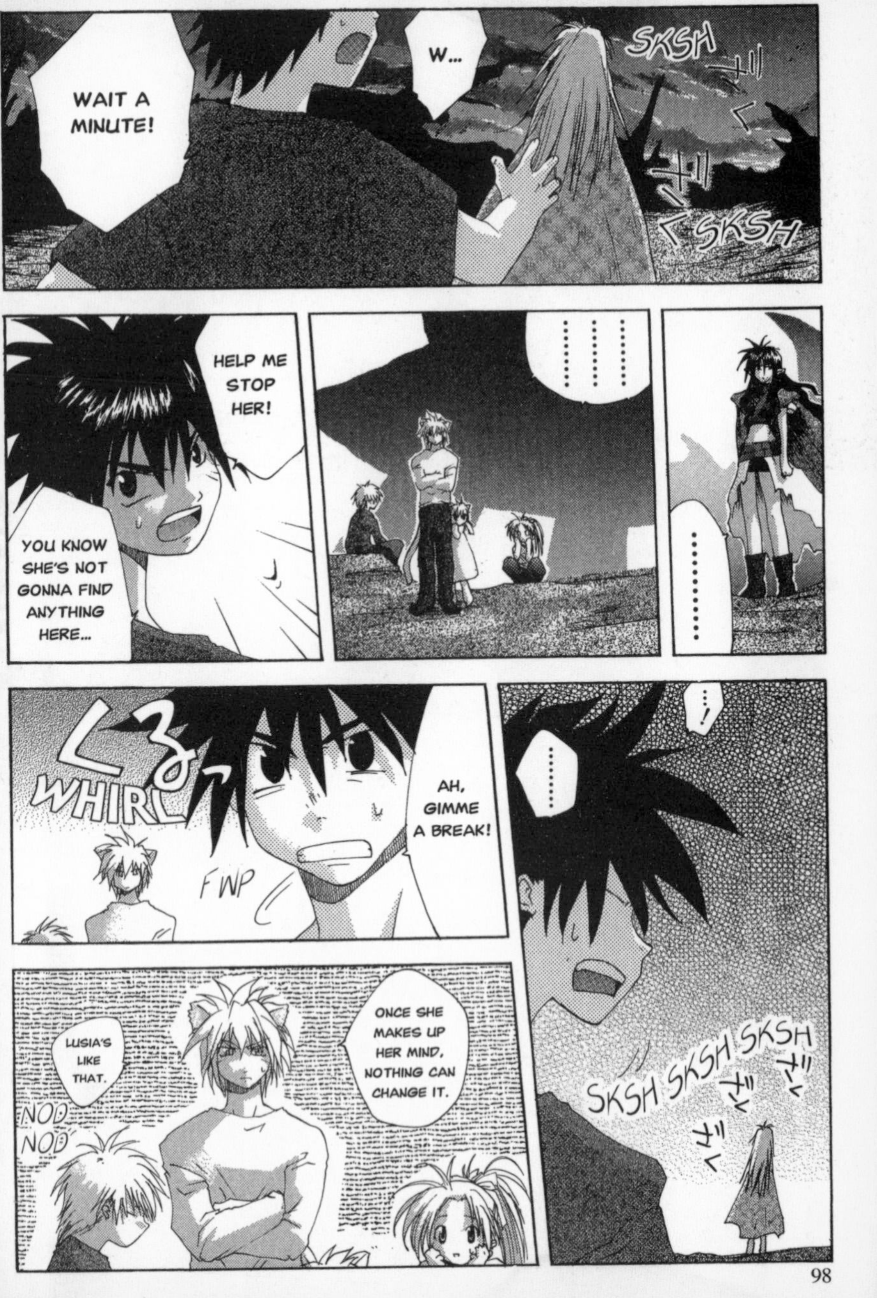
SKSH
W...
WAIT A MINUTE!
SKSH
......
......
HELP ME STOP HER!
YOU KNOW SHE'S NOT GONNA FIND ANYTHING HERE...
...!
......
SKSH SKSH SKSH
AH, GIMME A BREAK!
WHIRL
FWP
ONCE SHE MAKES UP HER MIND, NOTHING CAN CHANGE IT.
LUSIA'S LIKE THAT.
NOD NOD

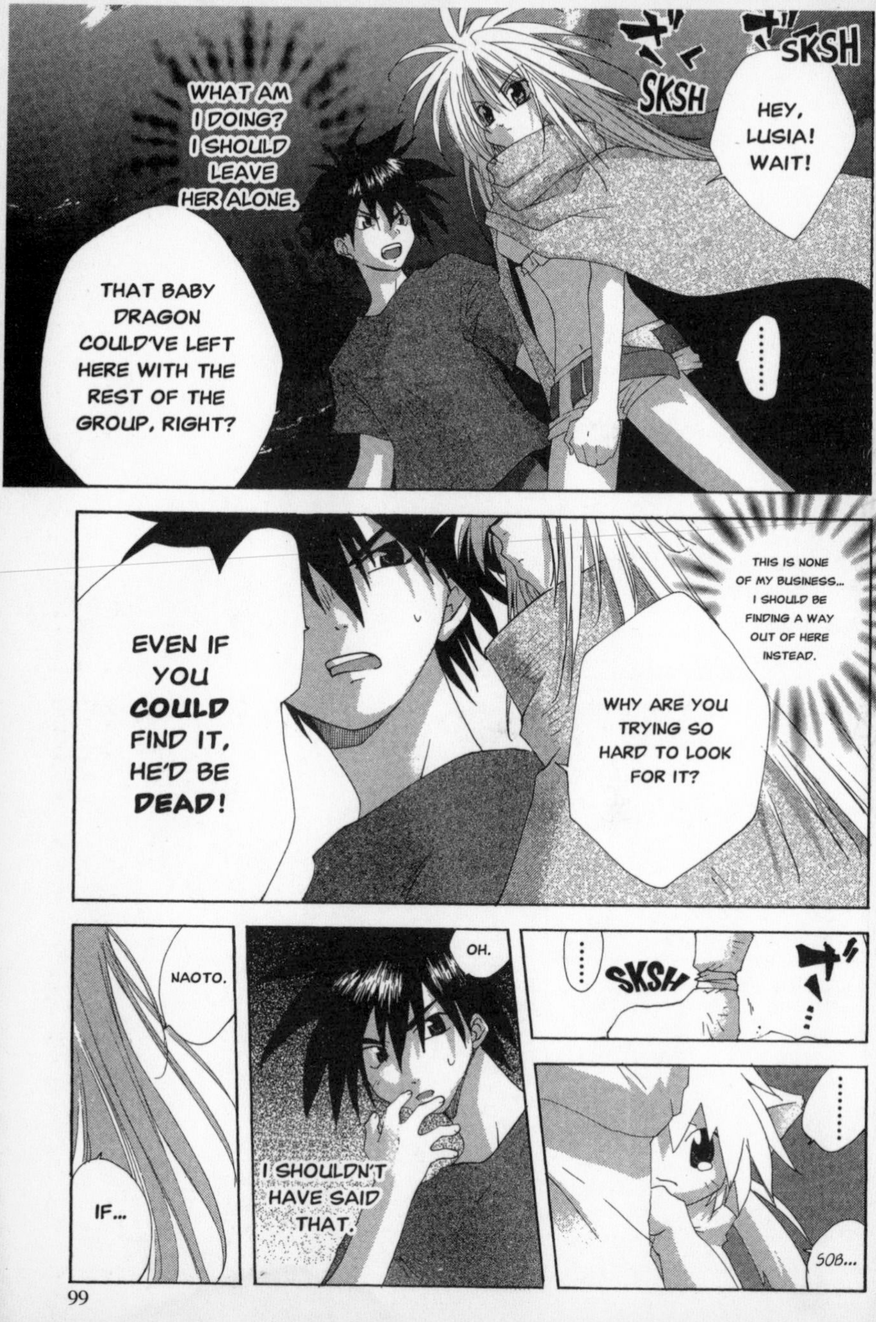
SKSH
HEY, LUSIA! WAIT!
SKSH
WHAT AM I DOING? I SHOULD LEAVE HER ALONE.
......
THAT BABY DRAGON COULD'VE LEFT HERE WITH THE REST OF THE GROUP, RIGHT?
THIS IS NONE OF MY BUSINESS... I SHOULD BE FINDING A WAY OUT OF HERE INSTEAD.
WHY ARE YOU TRYING SO HARD TO LOOK FOR IT?
EVEN IF YOU **COULD** FIND IT, HE'D BE **DEAD**!
......
SKSH
......
SOB...
OH.
I SHOULDN'T HAVE SAID THAT.
NAOTO.
IF...

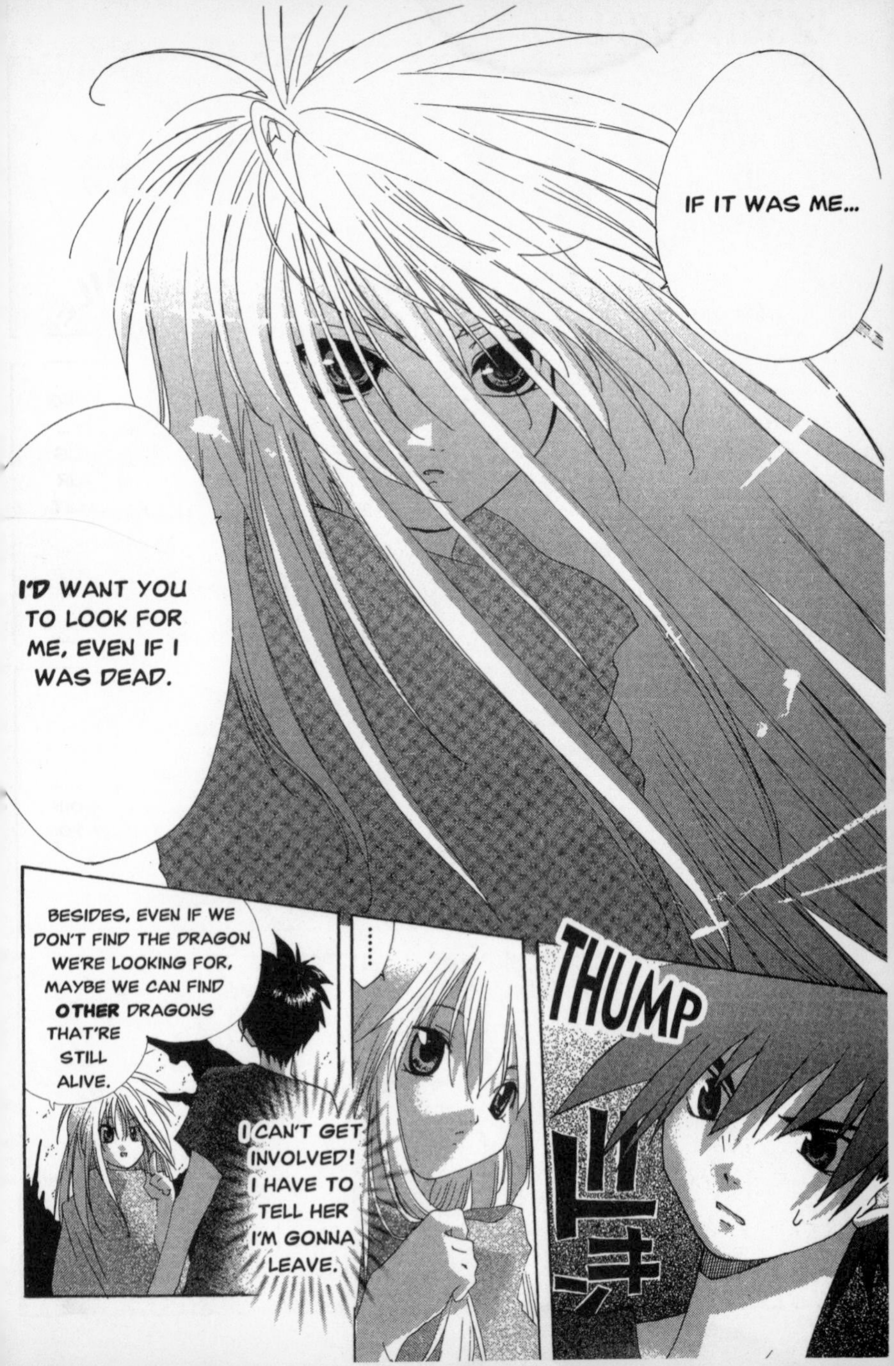
IF IT WAS ME...
I'D WANT YOU TO LOOK FOR ME, EVEN IF I WAS DEAD.
THUMP
......
I CAN'T GET INVOLVED! I HAVE TO TELL HER I'M GONNA LEAVE.
BESIDES, EVEN IF WE DON'T FIND THE DRAGON WE'RE LOOKING FOR, MAYBE WE CAN FIND OTHER DRAGONS THAT'RE STILL ALIVE.

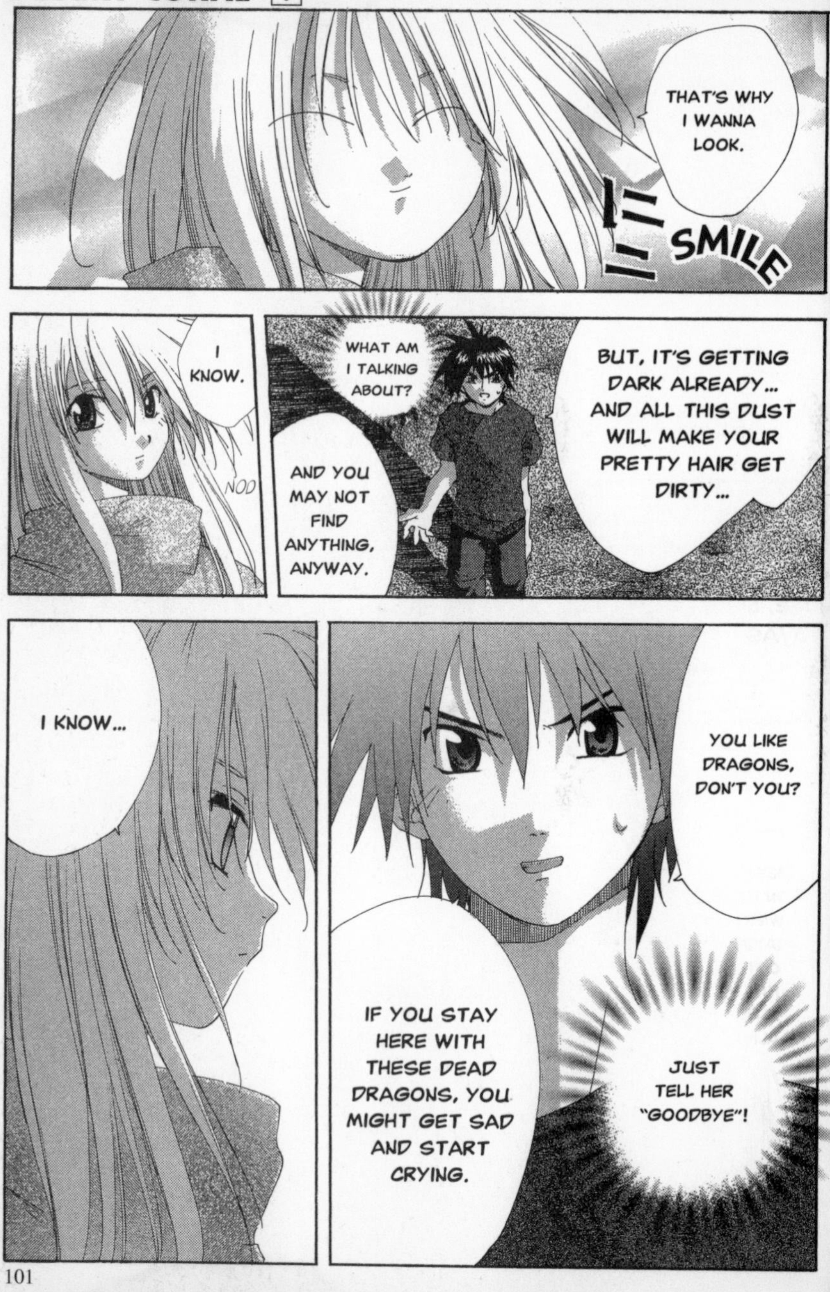
THAT'S WHY I WANNA LOOK.
SMILE
BUT, IT'S GETTING DARK ALREADY... AND ALL THIS DUST WILL MAKE YOUR PRETTY HAIR GET DIRTY...
WHAT AM I TALKING ABOUT?
AND YOU MAY NOT FIND ANYTHING, ANYWAY.
I KNOW.
NOD
YOU LIKE DRAGONS, DON'T YOU?
JUST TELL HER "GOODBYE"!
IF YOU STAY HERE WITH THESE DEAD DRAGONS, YOU MIGHT GET SAD AND START CRYING.
I KNOW...

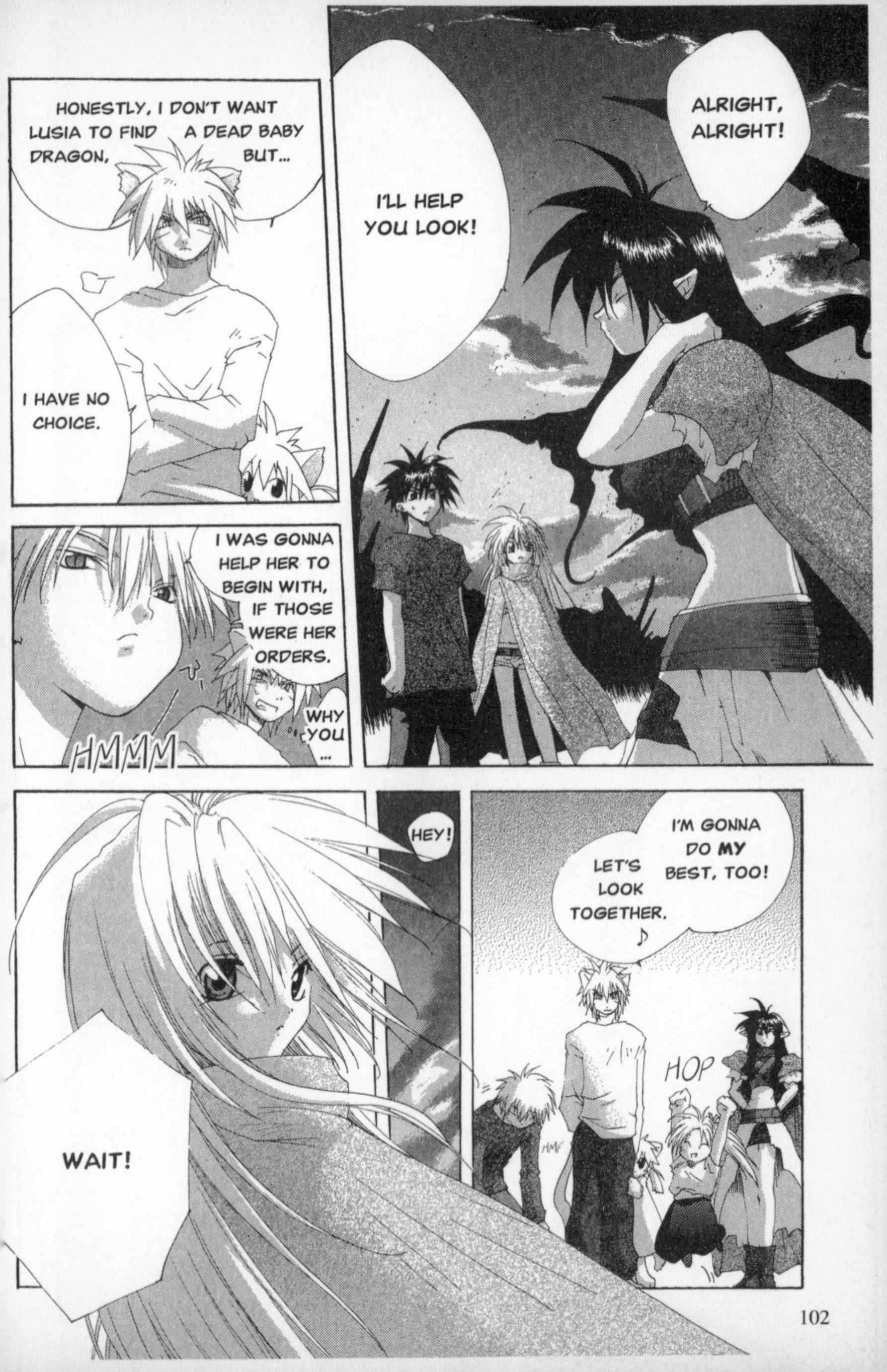

ALRIGHT, ALRIGHT!
I'LL HELP YOU LOOK!
HONESTLY, I DON'T WANT LUSIA TO FIND A DEAD BABY DRAGON, BUT...
I HAVE NO CHOICE.
I WAS GONNA HELP HER TO BEGIN WITH, IF THOSE WERE HER ORDERS.
WHY YOU ...
HMMM
I'M GONNA DO MY BEST, TOO!
LET'S LOOK TOGETHER. ♪
HOP
HEY!
WAIT!

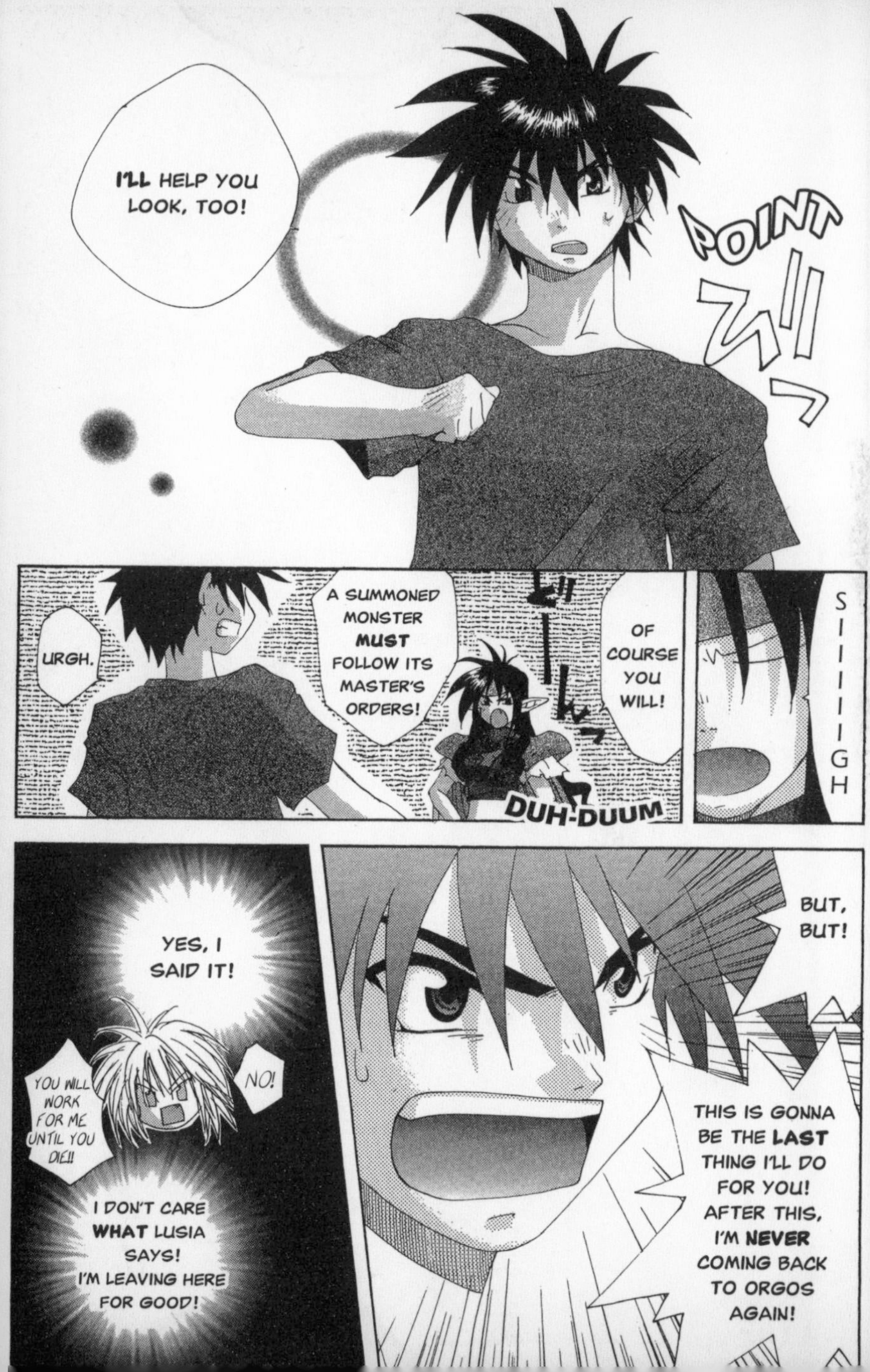
I'LL HELP YOU LOOK, TOO!
POINT
SIIIIIGH
OF COURSE YOU WILL!
A SUMMONED MONSTER MUST FOLLOW ITS MASTER'S ORDERS!
DUH-DUUM
URGH.
BUT, BUT!
THIS IS GONNA BE THE LAST THING I'LL DO FOR YOU! AFTER THIS, I'M NEVER COMING BACK TO ORGOS AGAIN!
YES, I SAID IT!
NO!
YOU WILL WORK FOR ME UNTIL YOU DIE!!
I DON'T CARE WHAT LUSIA SAYS! I'M LEAVING HERE FOR GOOD!

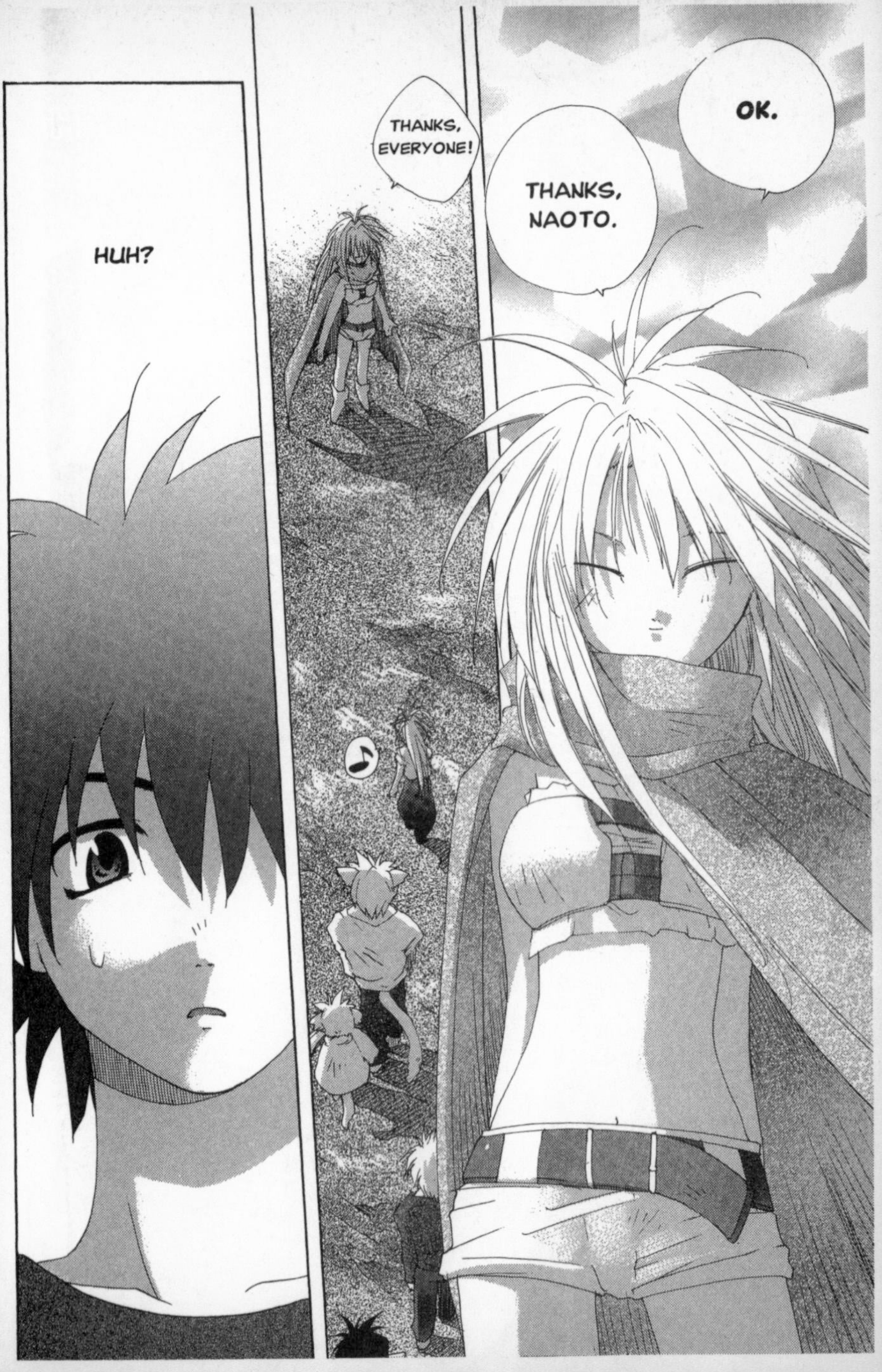
OK.
THANKS, NAOTO.
THANKS, EVERYONE!
♪
HUH?

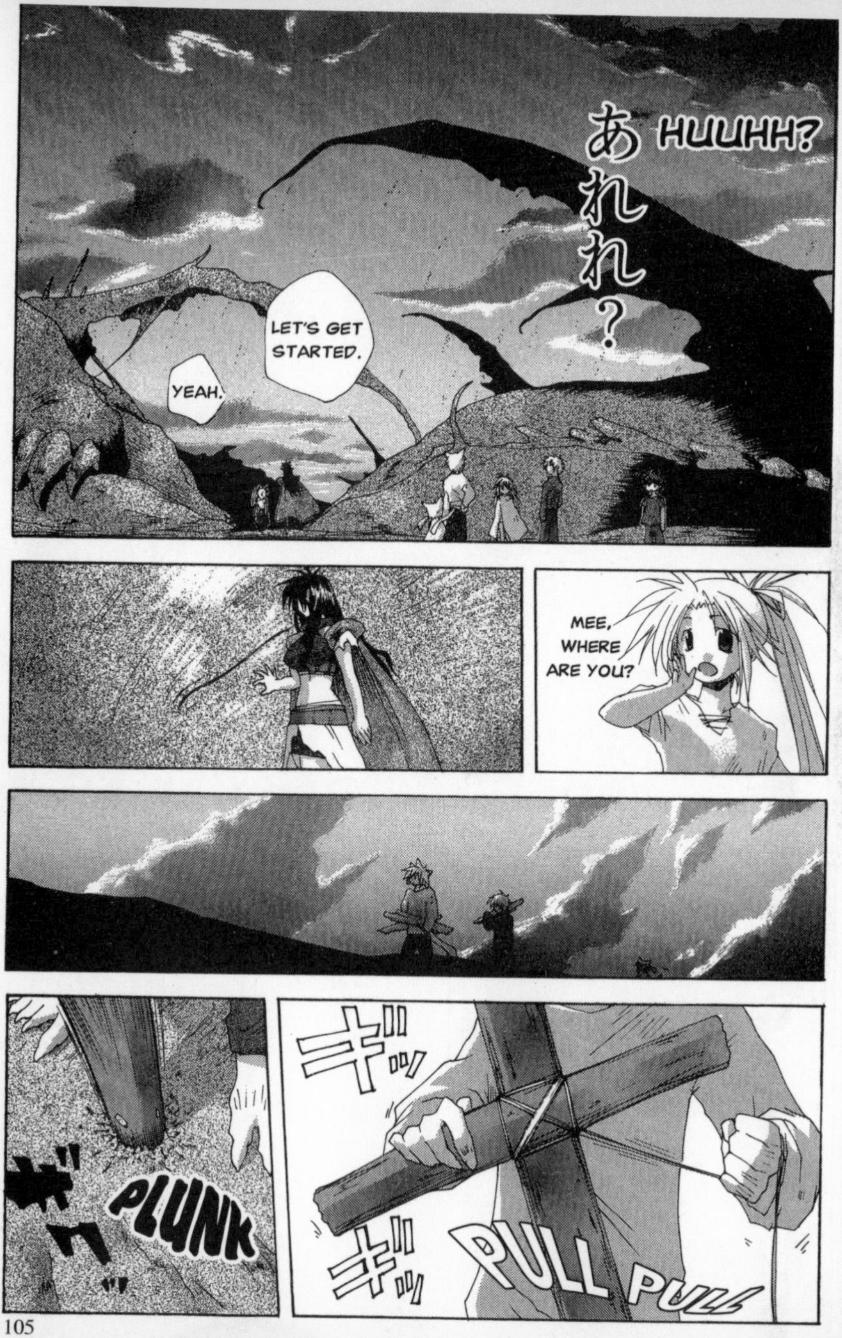
あれれ？
HUUHH?
LET'S GET STARTED.
YEAH.
MEE, WHERE ARE YOU?
ギッ
ギッ
PULL PULL
ギッ
PLUNK

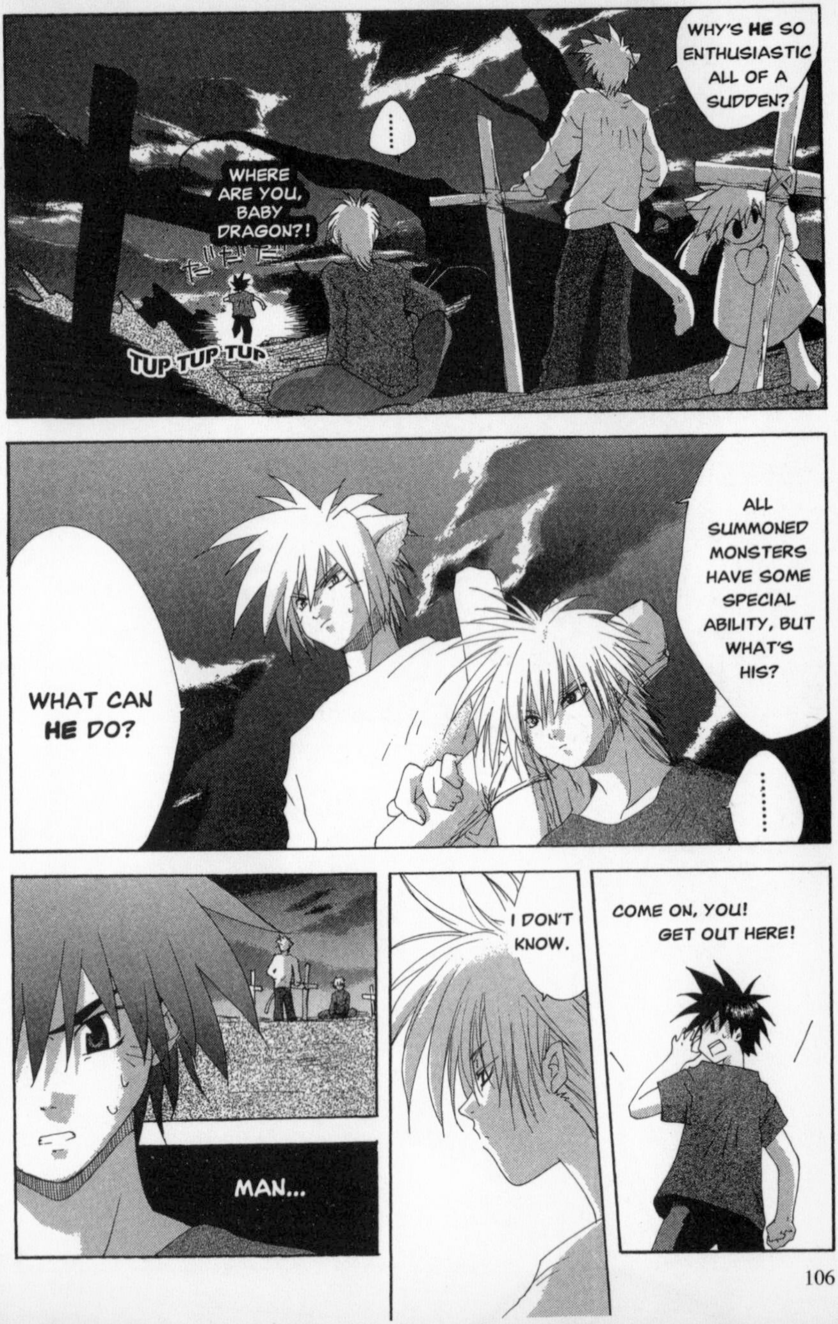
WHY'S HE SO ENTHUSIASTIC ALL OF A SUDDEN?
......
WHERE ARE YOU, BABY DRAGON?!
TUP TUP TUP
ALL SUMMONED MONSTERS HAVE SOME SPECIAL ABILITY, BUT WHAT'S HIS?
....
WHAT CAN HE DO?
COME ON, YOU! GET OUT HERE!
I DON'T KNOW.
MAN...

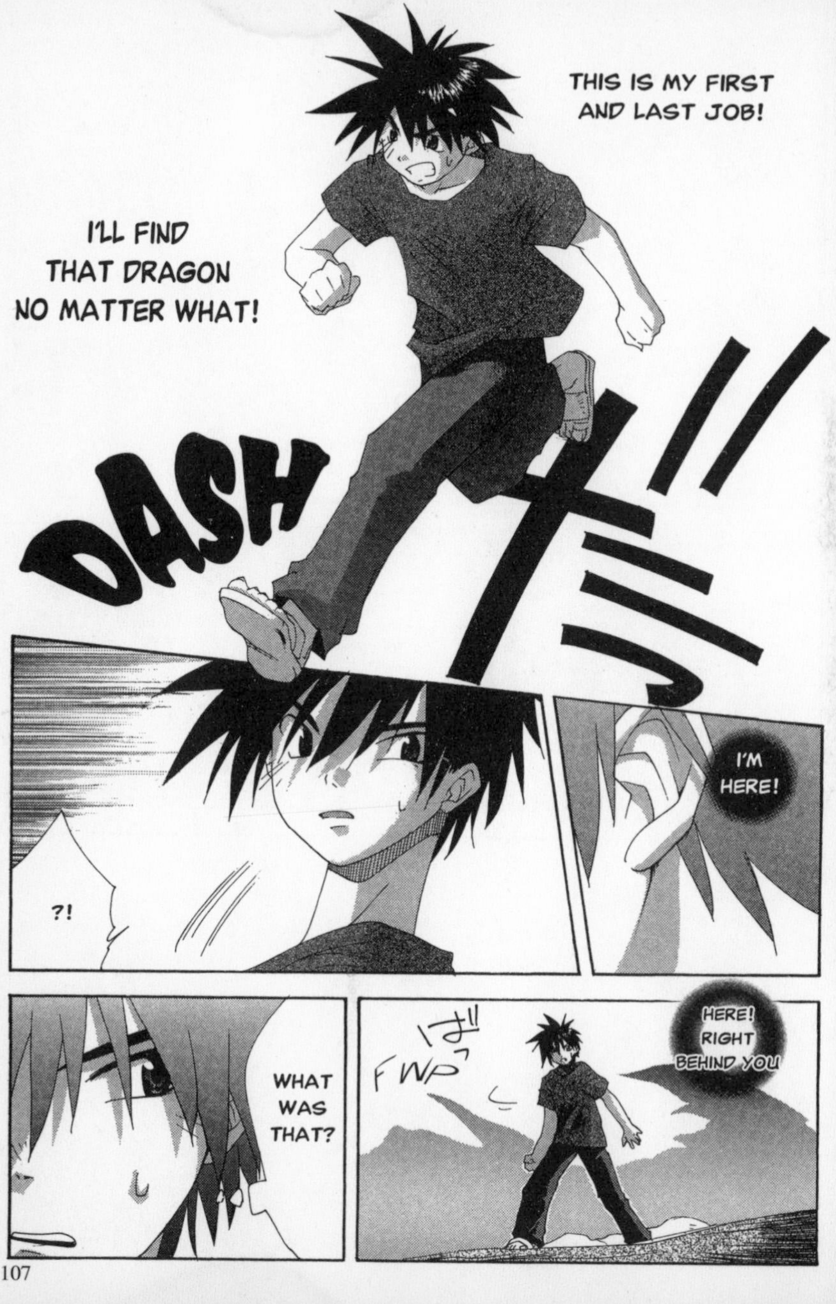
THIS IS MY FIRST AND LAST JOB!
I'LL FIND THAT DRAGON NO MATTER WHAT!
ダッ
DASH
I'M HERE!
?!
ばっ
FWP
HERE! RIGHT BEHIND YOU
WHAT WAS THAT?

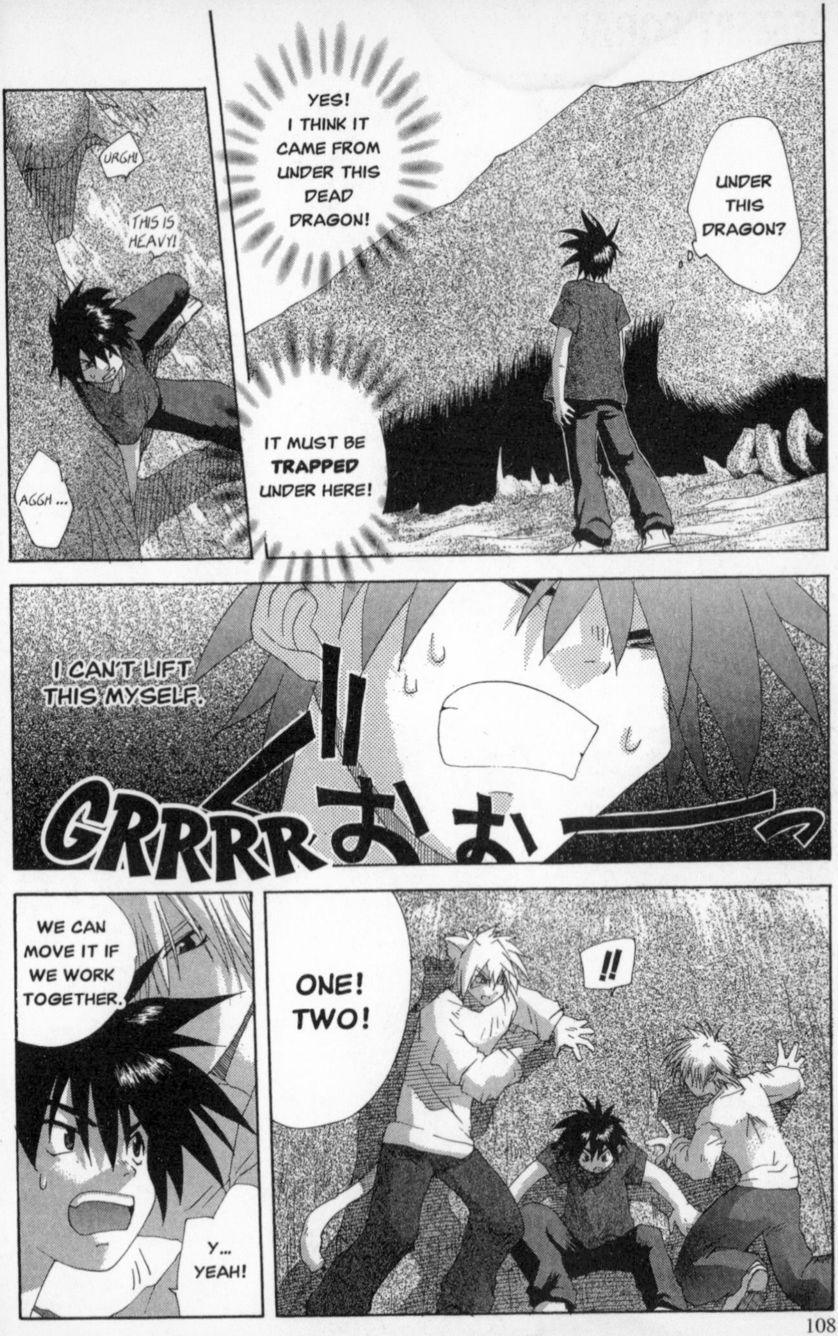
UNDER THIS DRAGON?
YES! I THINK IT CAME FROM UNDER THIS DEAD DRAGON!
IT MUST BE **TRAPPED** UNDER HERE!
URGH!
THIS IS HEAVY!
AGGH ...
I CAN'T LIFT THIS MYSELF.
GRRRRおおーーっ
!!
ONE! TWO!
WE CAN MOVE IT IF WE WORK TOGETHER.
Y... YEAH!

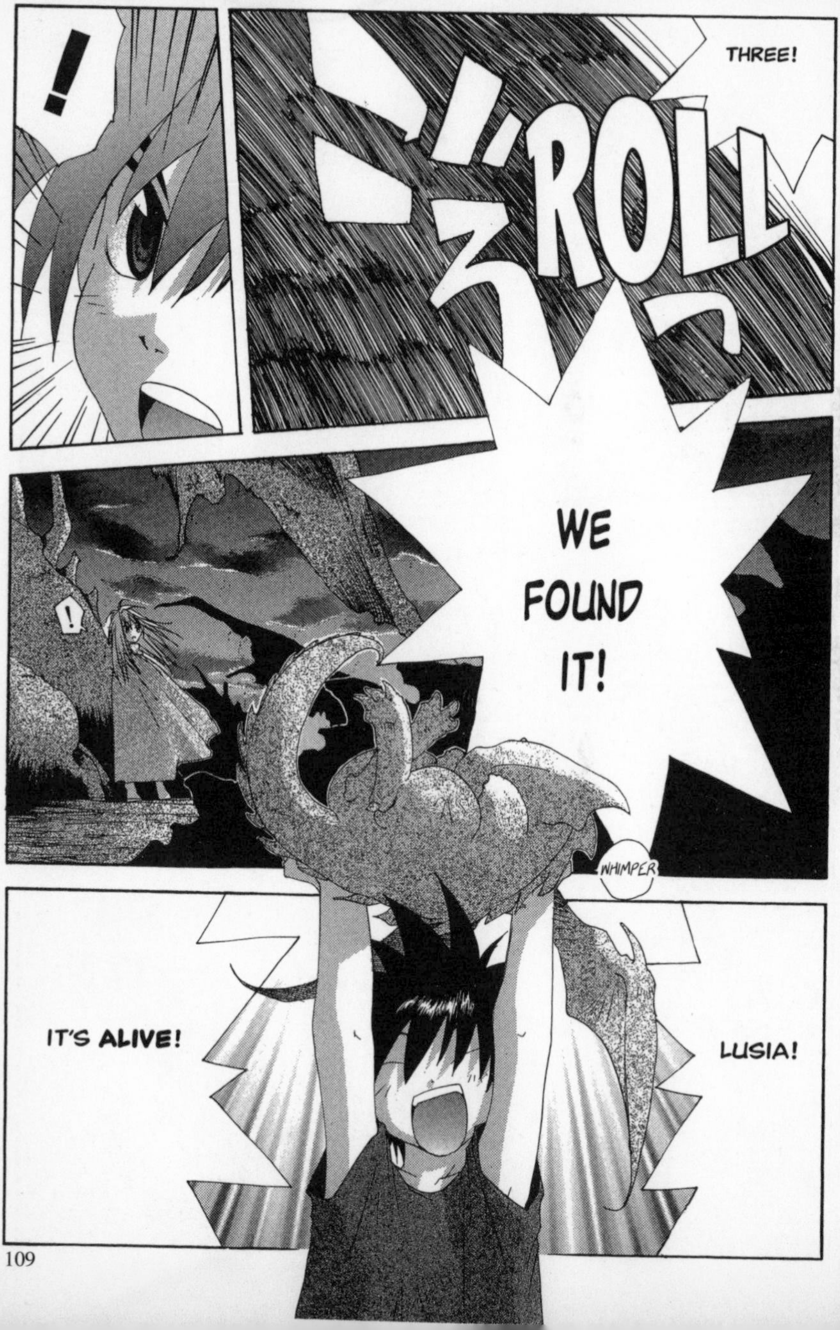
THREE!
ROLL
!
WE FOUND IT!
!
WHIMPER
LUSIA!
IT'S ALIVE!

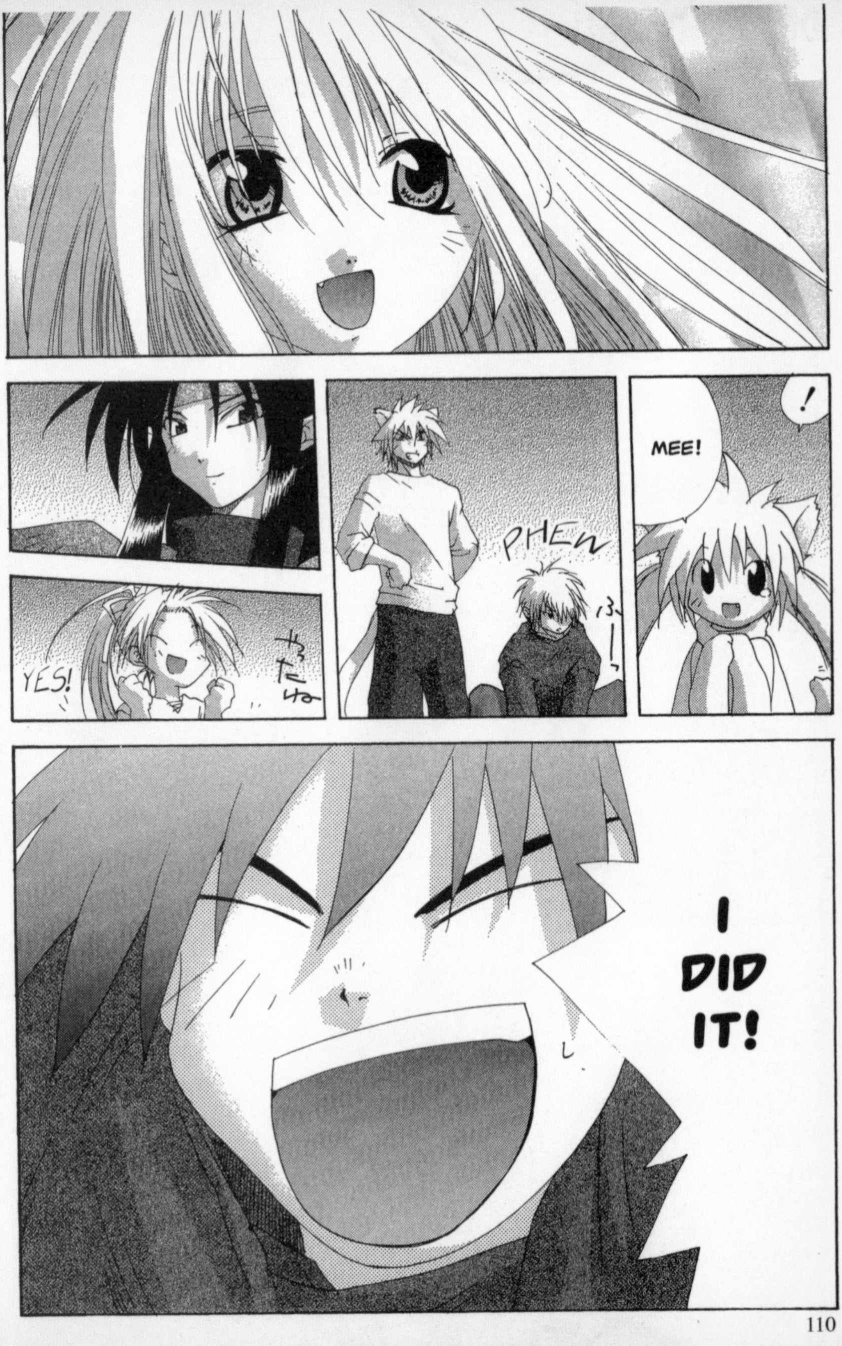
!
MEE!
PHEW
ふーっ
YES!
やったね
I DID IT!

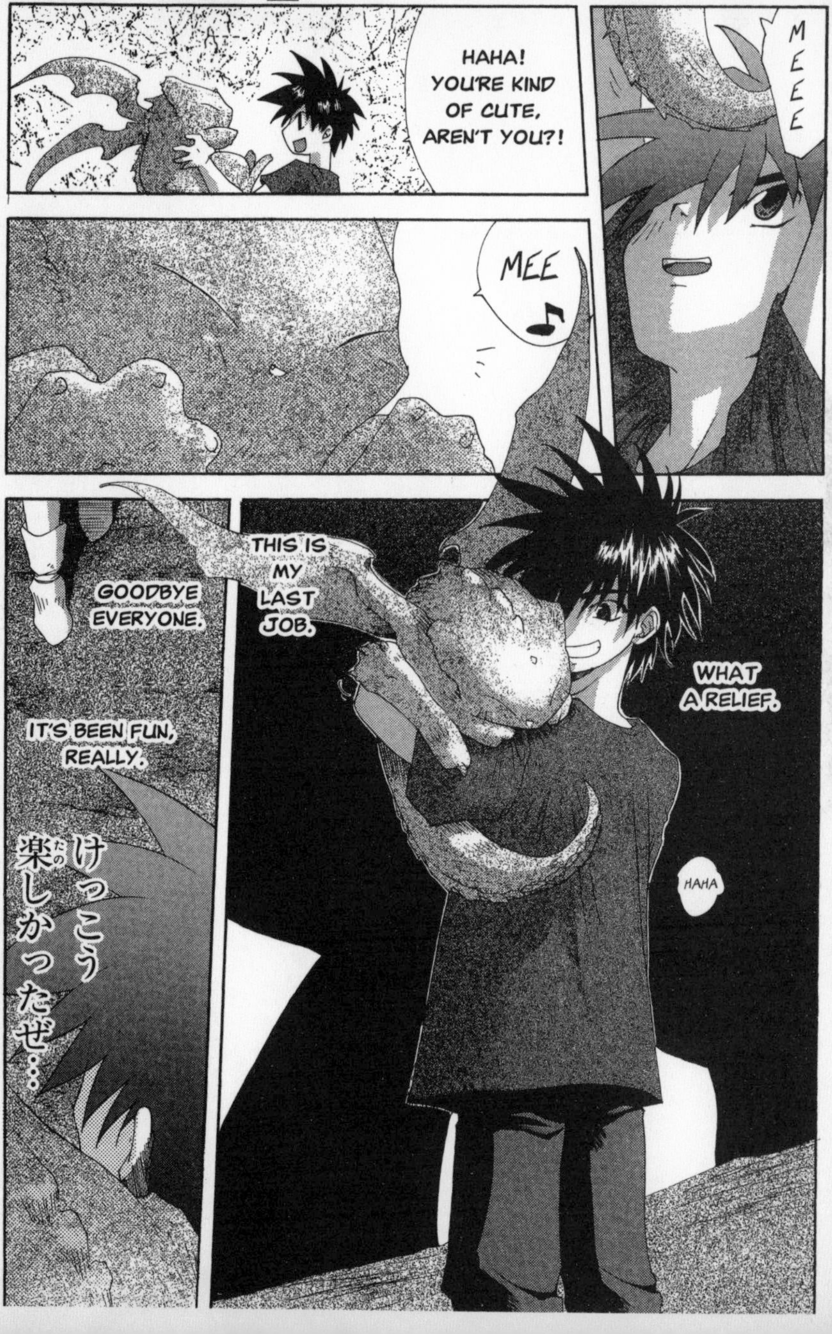
MEEE
HAHA! YOU'RE KIND OF CUTE, AREN'T YOU?!
MEE ♪
THIS IS MY LAST JOB.
WHAT A RELIEF.
HAHA
GOODBYE EVERYONE.
IT'S BEEN FUN, REALLY.
けっこう楽しかったぜ…

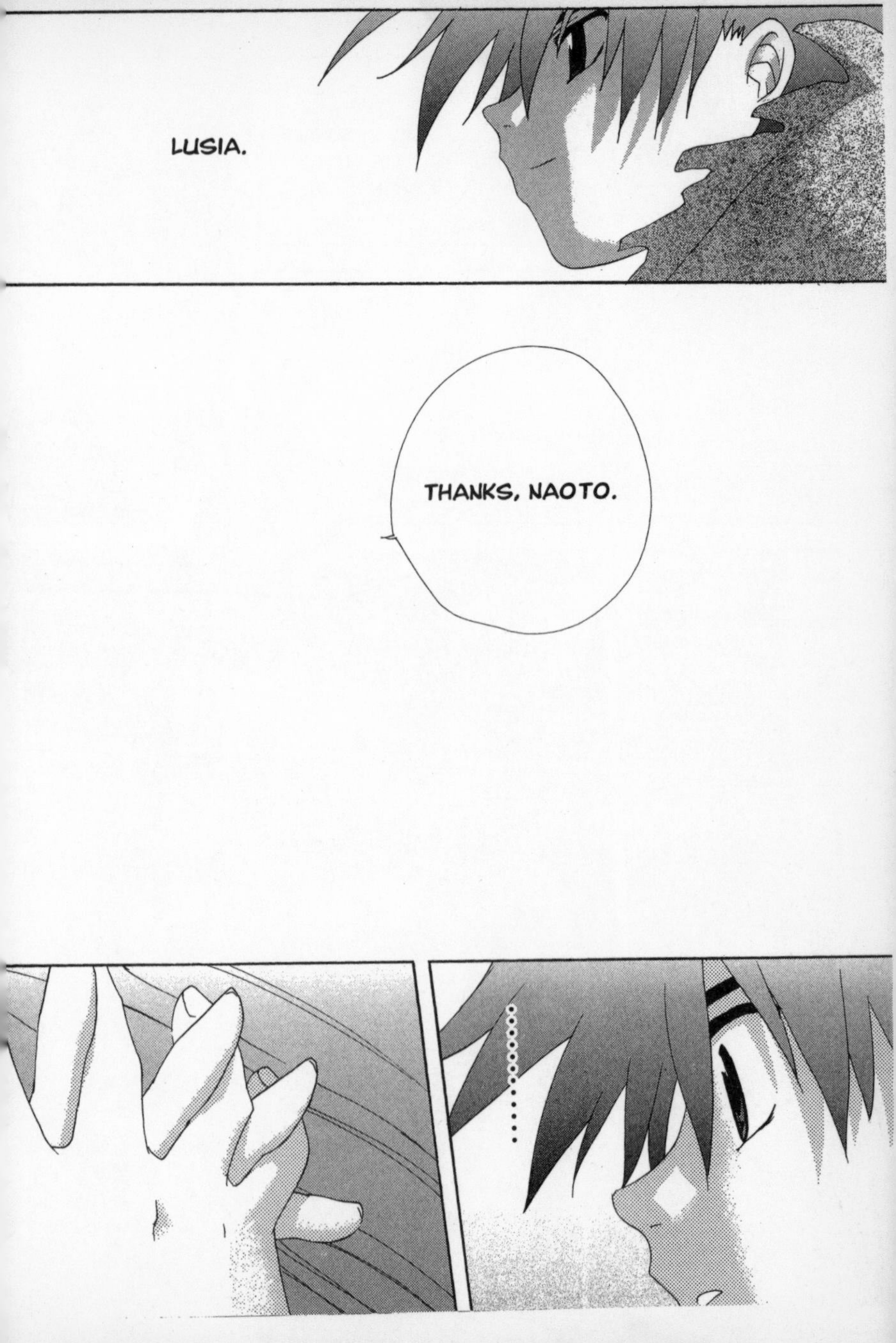
LUSIA.
THANKS, NAOTO.
......

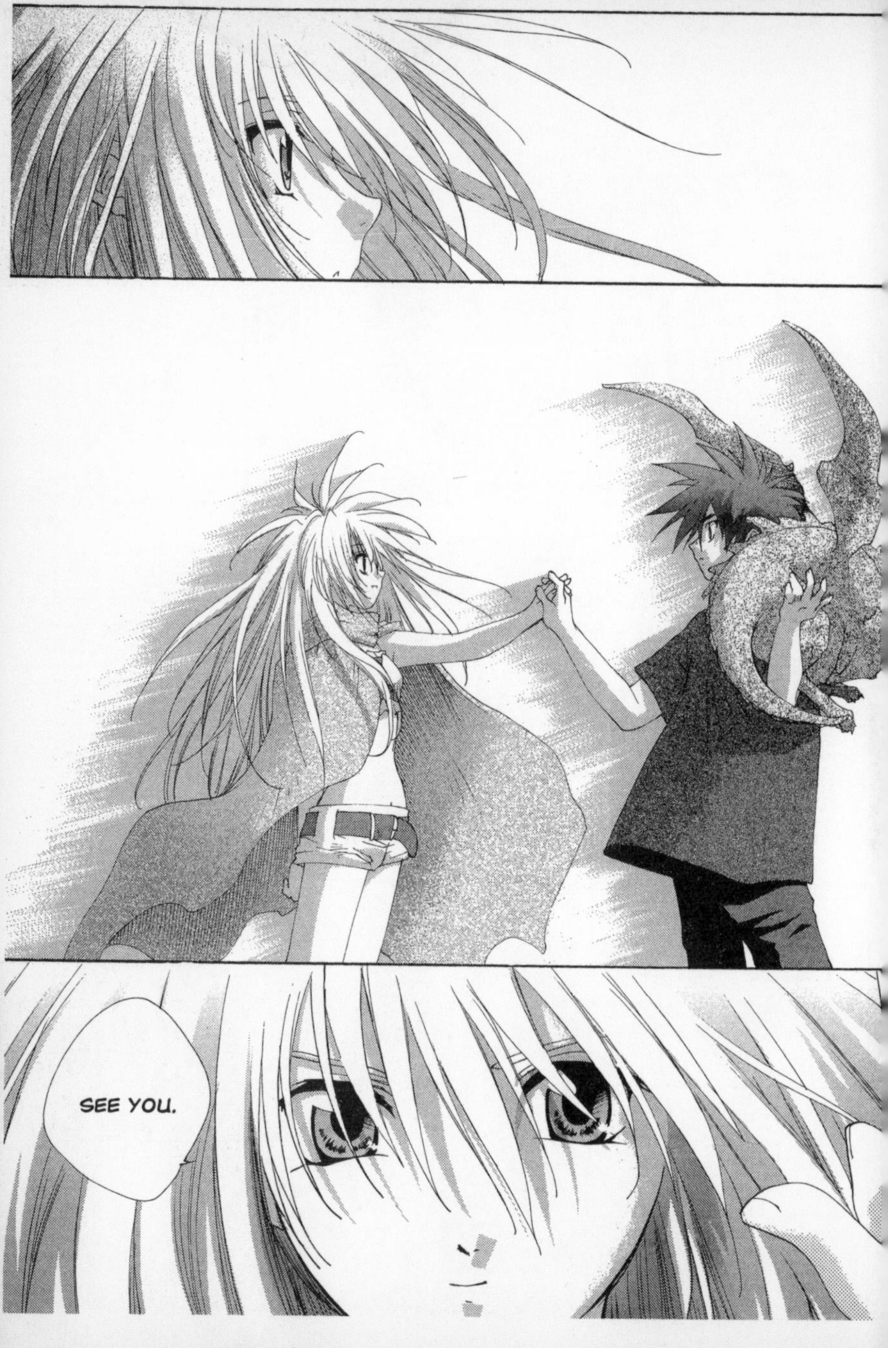
SEE YOU.

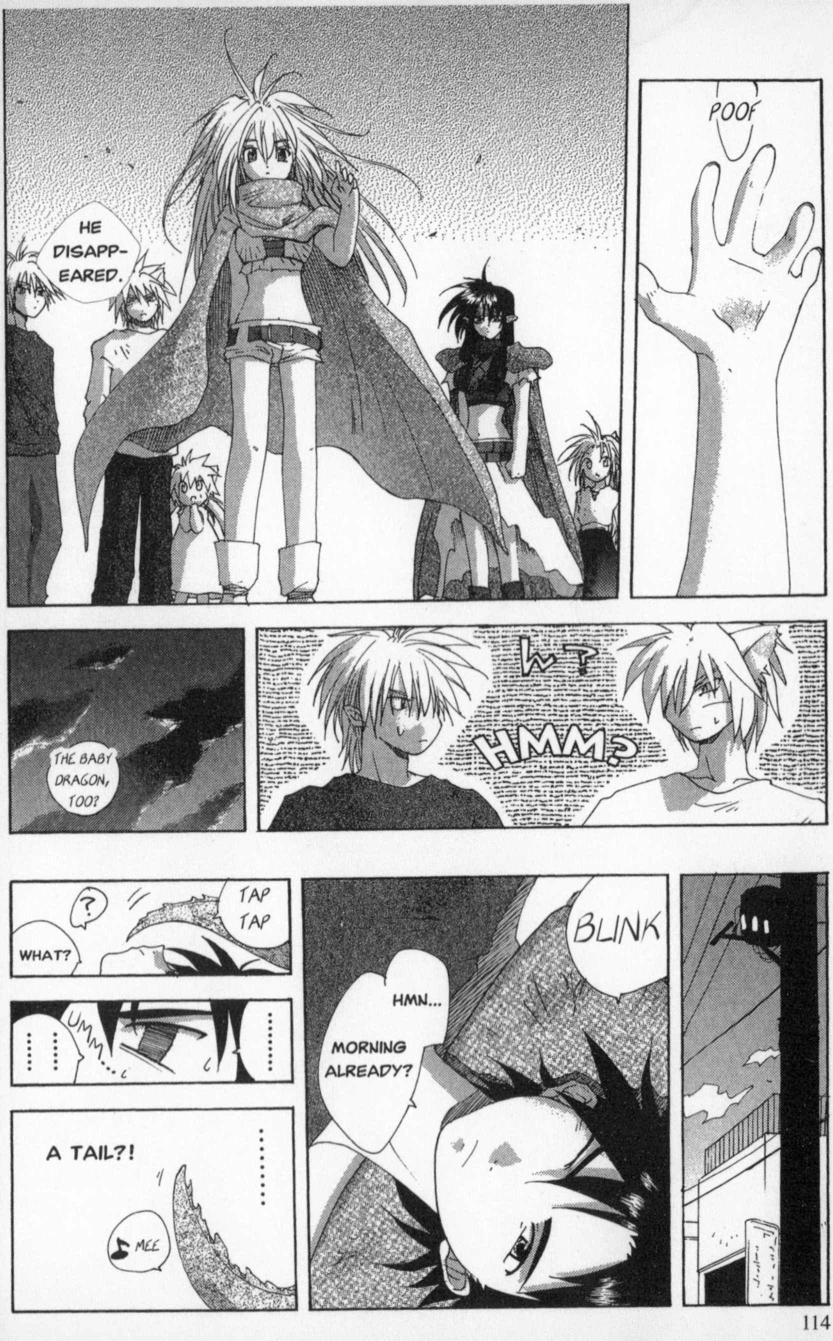

POOF
HE DISAPP-EARED.
ん?
HMM?
THE BABY DRAGON, TOO?
BLINK
HMN...
MORNING ALREADY?
TAP TAP
?
WHAT?
......
UMM...
......
......
A TAIL?!
MEE

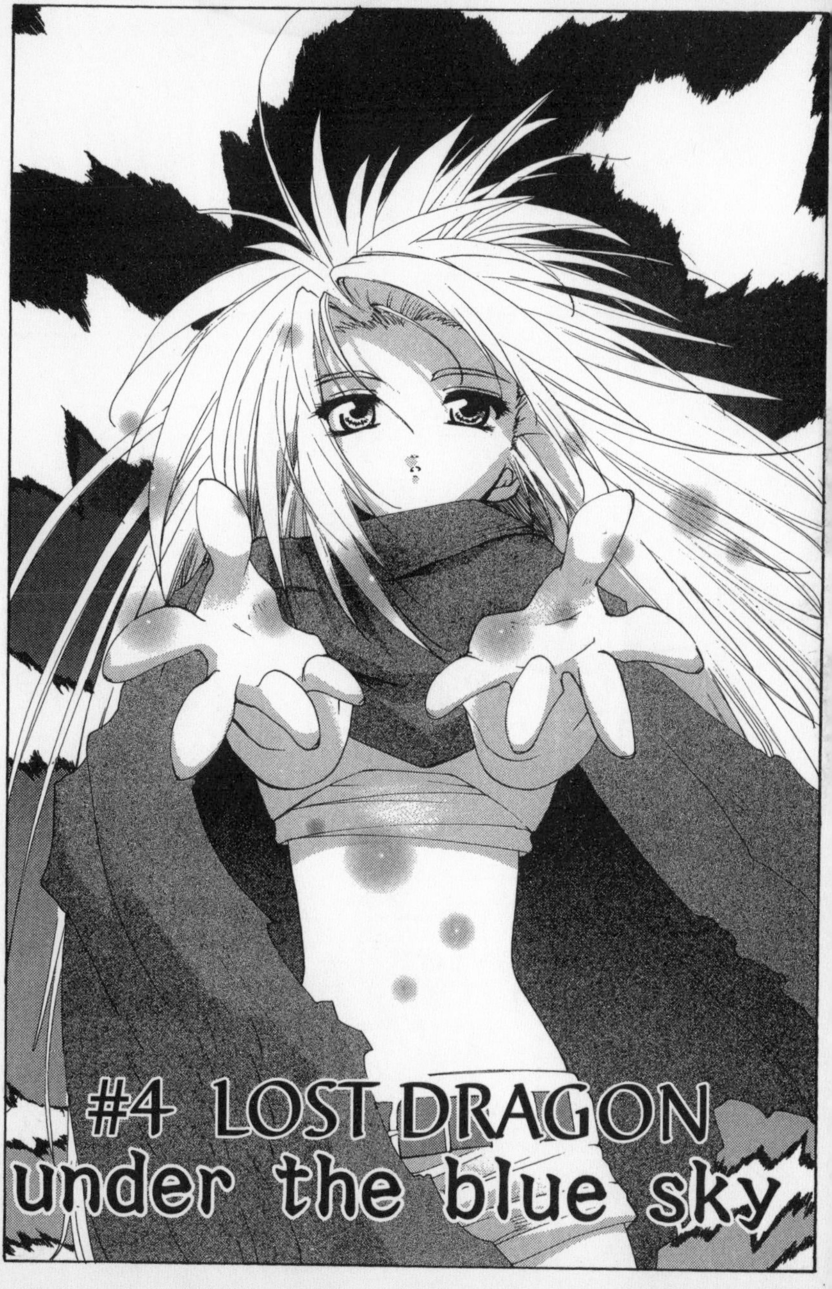
#4 LOST DRAGON
under the blue sky

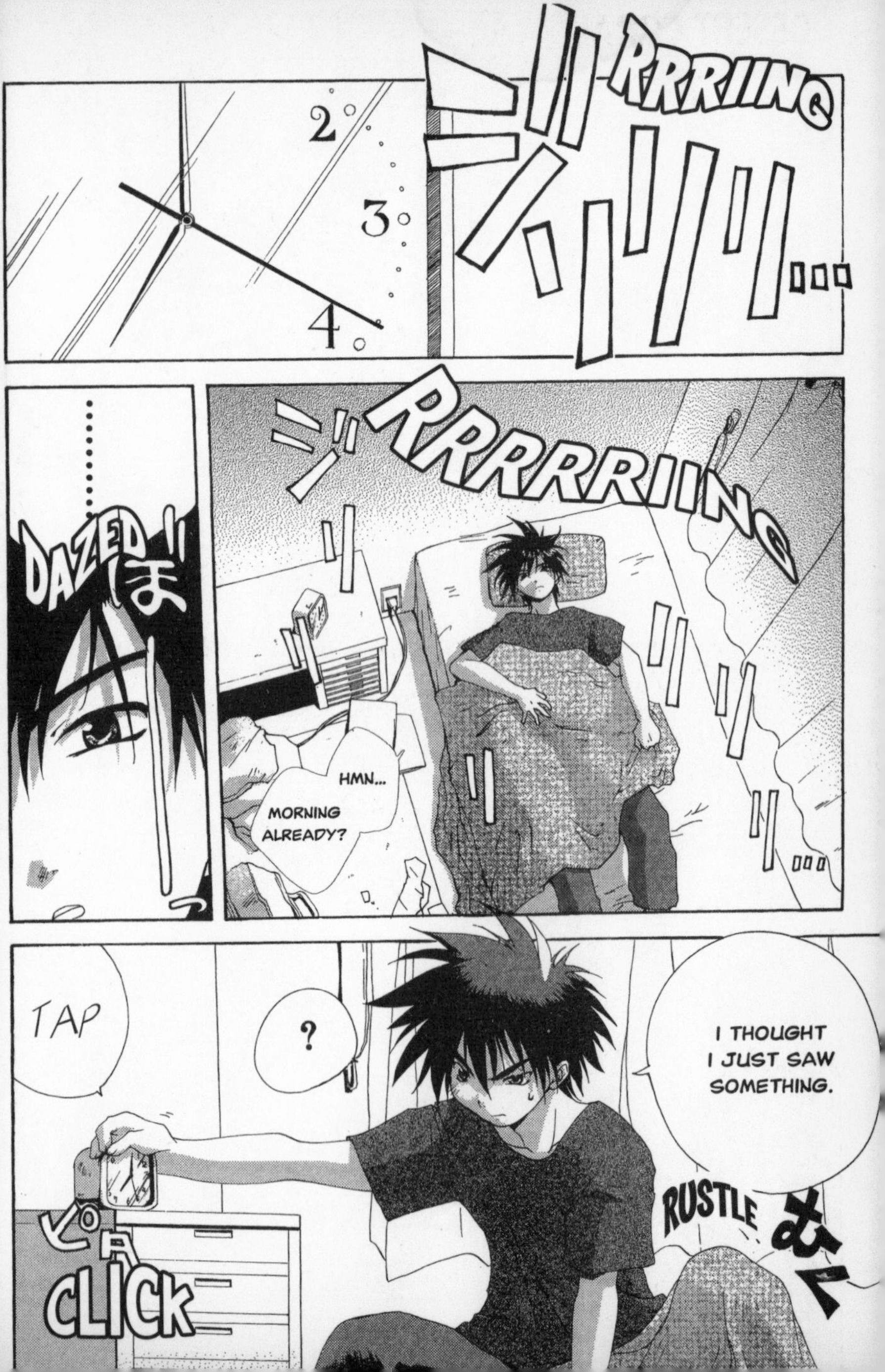
RRRIING
2
3
4
RRRRRRIING
HMN...
MORNING ALREADY?
DAZED
I THOUGHT I JUST SAW SOMETHING.
?
TAP
RUSTLE
CLICK

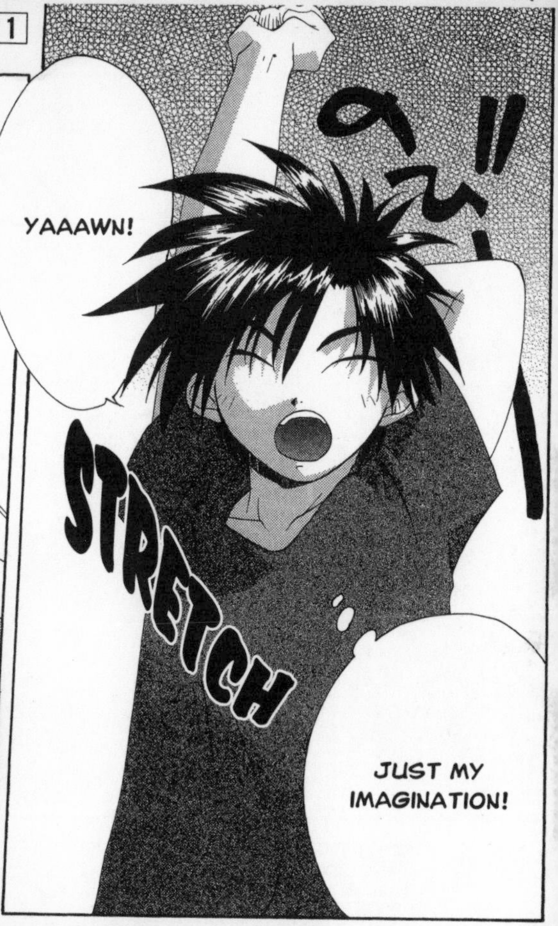
YAAAWN!
のびー!!
STRETCH
JUST MY IMAGINATION!

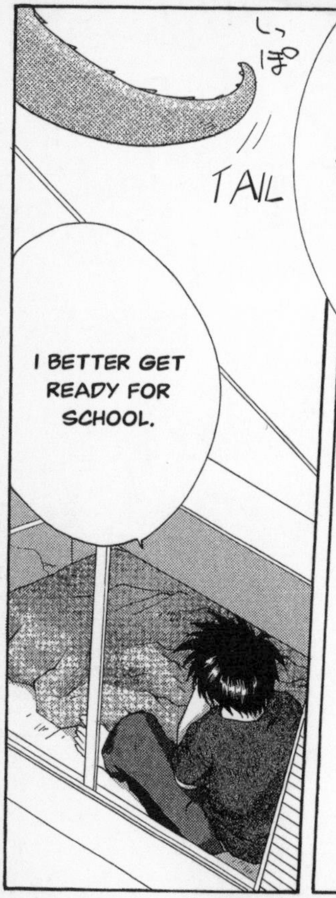
しっぽ
TAIL
I BETTER GET READY FOR SCHOOL.

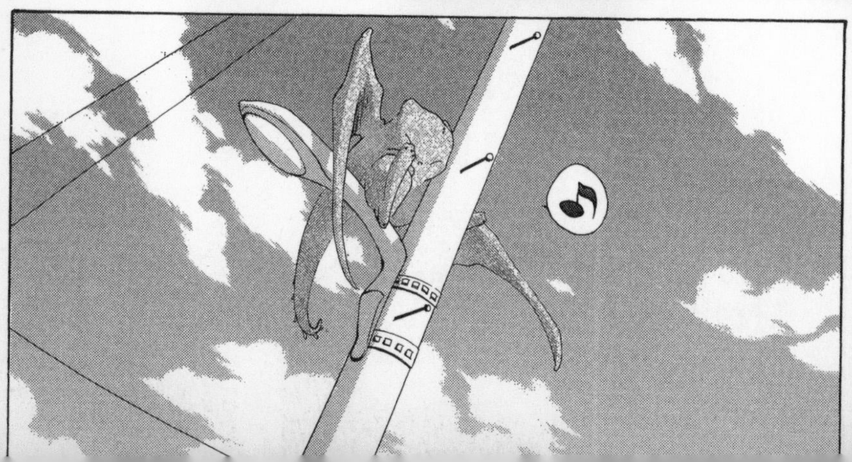

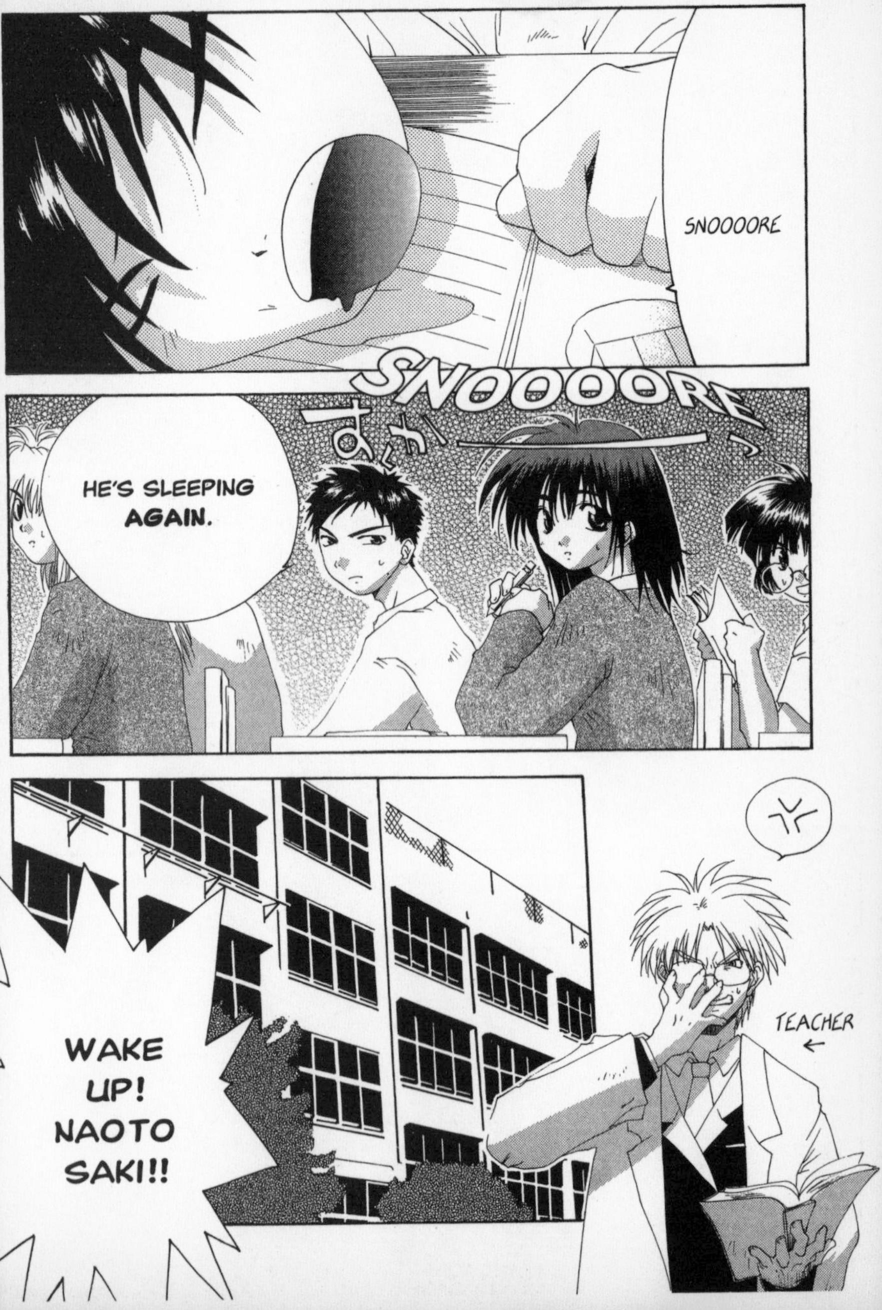
SNOOOORE
SNOOOORE
HE'S SLEEPING AGAIN.
TEACHER ←
WAKE UP! NAOTO SAKI!!

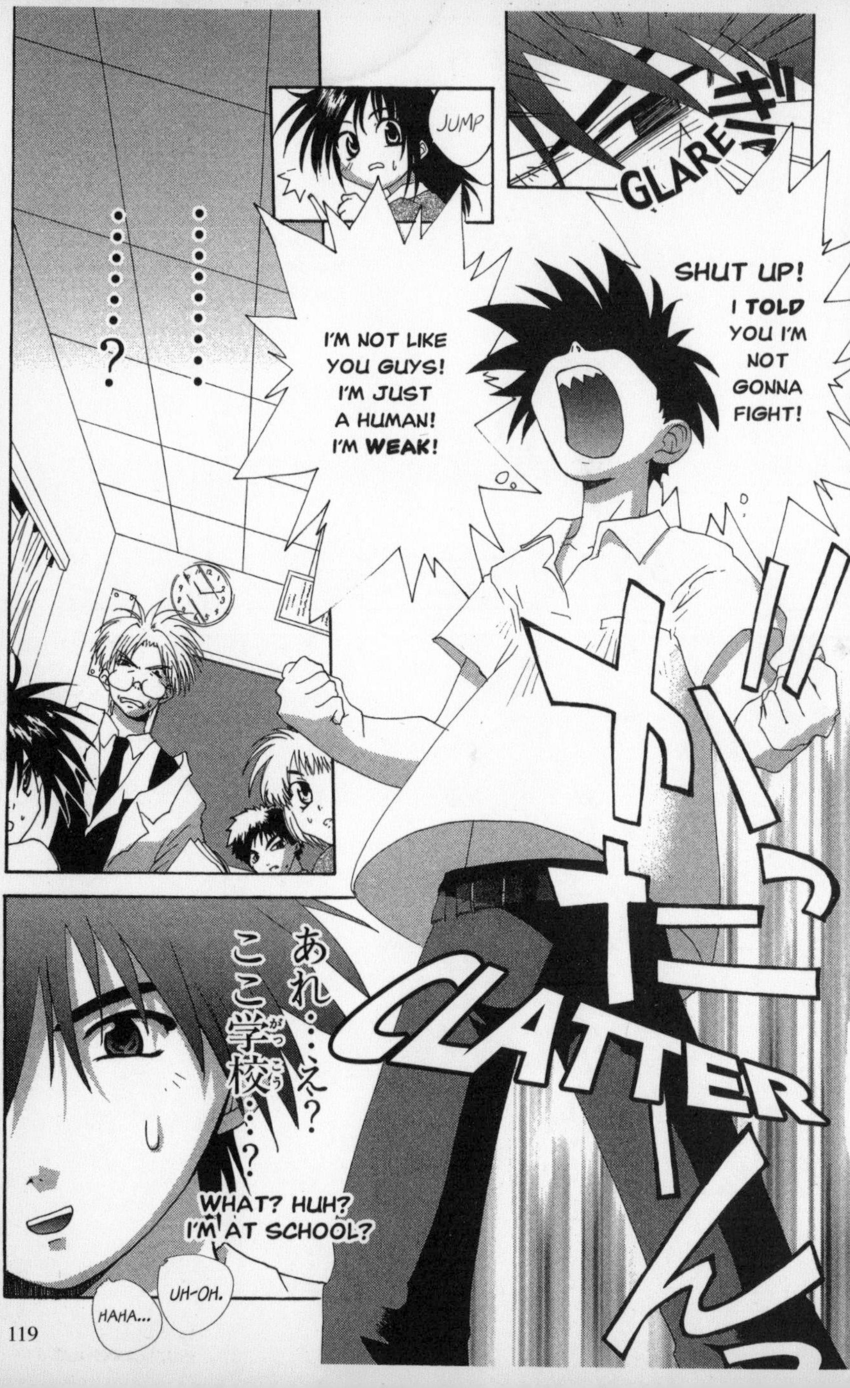
GLARE
JUMP
SHUT UP! I TOLD YOU I'M NOT GONNA FIGHT!
I'M NOT LIKE YOU GUYS! I'M JUST A HUMAN! I'M WEAK!
……?
………
CLATTER
あれ……え？
ここ学校……？
WHAT? HUH? I'M AT SCHOOL?
UH-OH.
HAHA...

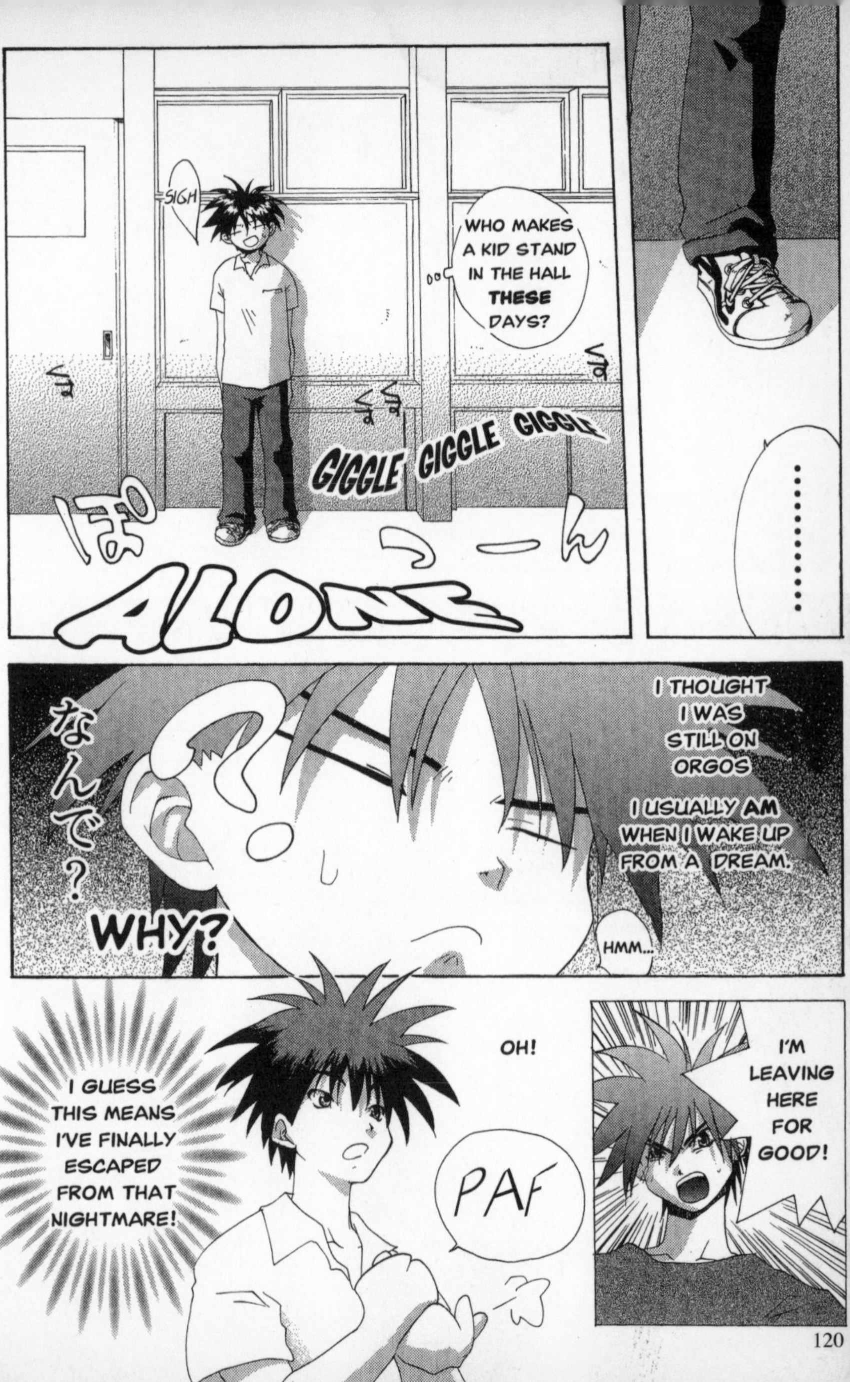
......
WHO MAKES A KID STAND IN THE HALL **THESE** DAYS?
SIGH
くす くす くす くす
GIGGLE GIGGLE GIGGLE
ぽつーん
ALONE
I THOUGHT I WAS STILL ON ORGOS
I USUALLY AM WHEN I WAKE UP FROM A DREAM.
HMM...
なんで？
WHY?
I'M LEAVING HERE FOR GOOD!
OH!
PAF
I GUESS THIS MEANS I'VE FINALLY ESCAPED FROM THAT NIGHTMARE!

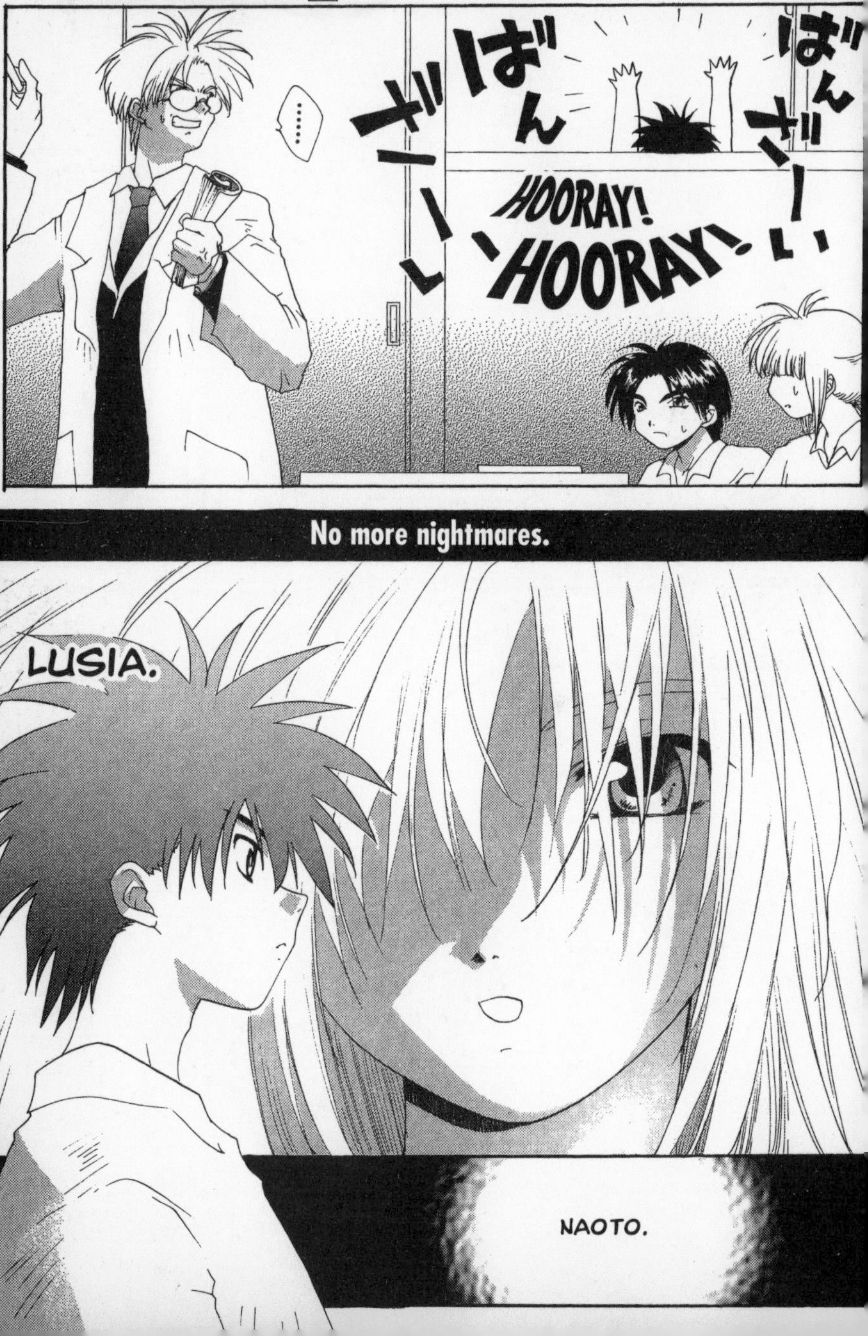
ばんざーい
HOORAY! HOORAY!
ばんざーい
……
No more nightmares.
LUSIA.
NAOTO.

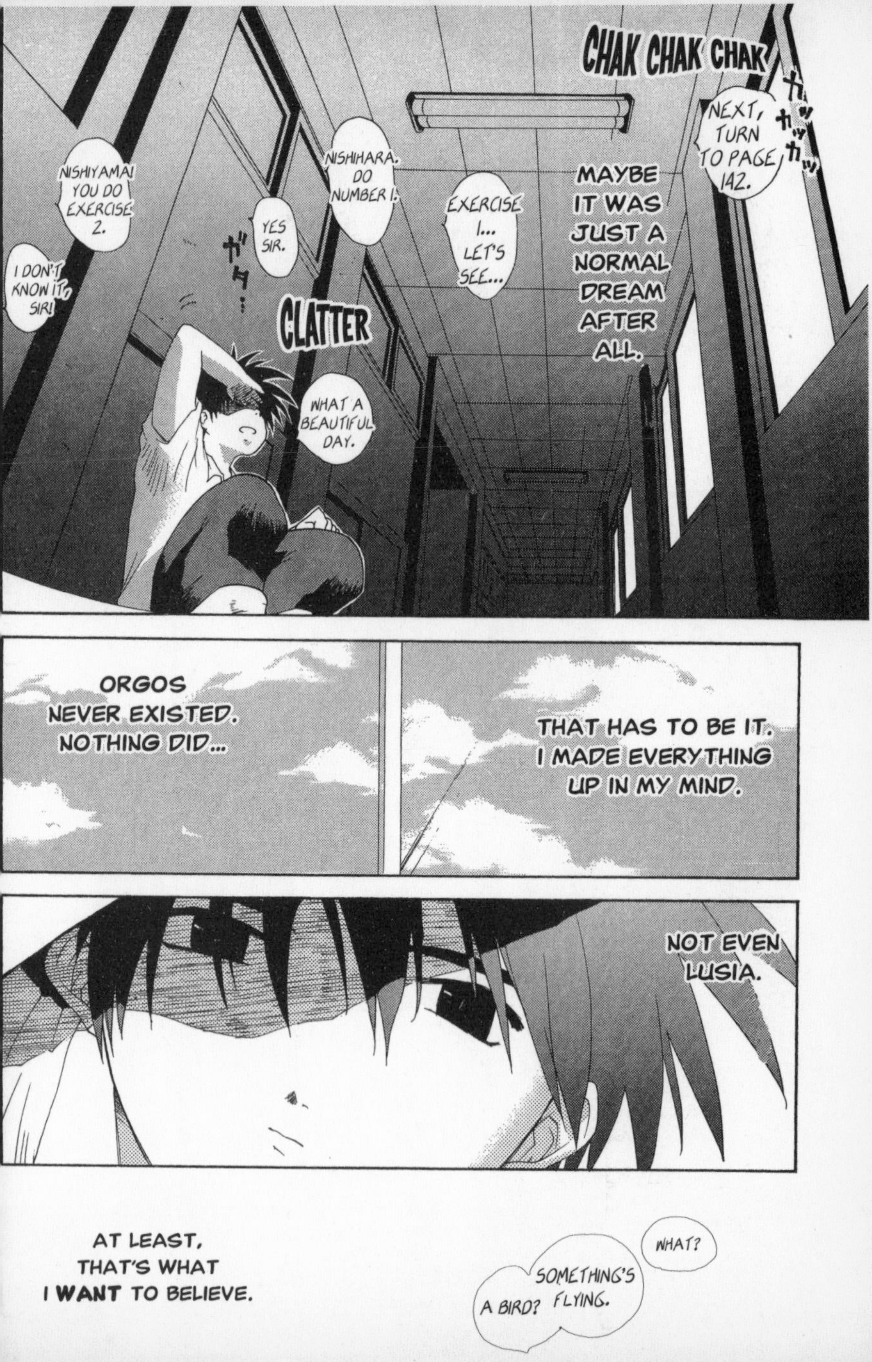
CHAK CHAK CHAK
カッ カッ カッ
NEXT, TURN TO PAGE 142.
MAYBE IT WAS JUST A NORMAL DREAM AFTER ALL.
EXERCISE 1... LET'S SEE...
NISHIHARA. DO NUMBER 1.
YES SIR.
ガタ
CLATTER
NISHIYAMA! YOU DO EXERCISE 2.
I DON'T KNOW IT, SIR!
WHAT A BEAUTIFUL DAY.
THAT HAS TO BE IT. I MADE EVERYTHING UP IN MY MIND.
ORGOS NEVER EXISTED. NOTHING DID...
NOT EVEN LUSIA.
WHAT?
SOMETHING'S FLYING.
A BIRD?
AT LEAST, THAT'S WHAT I **WANT** TO BELIEVE.

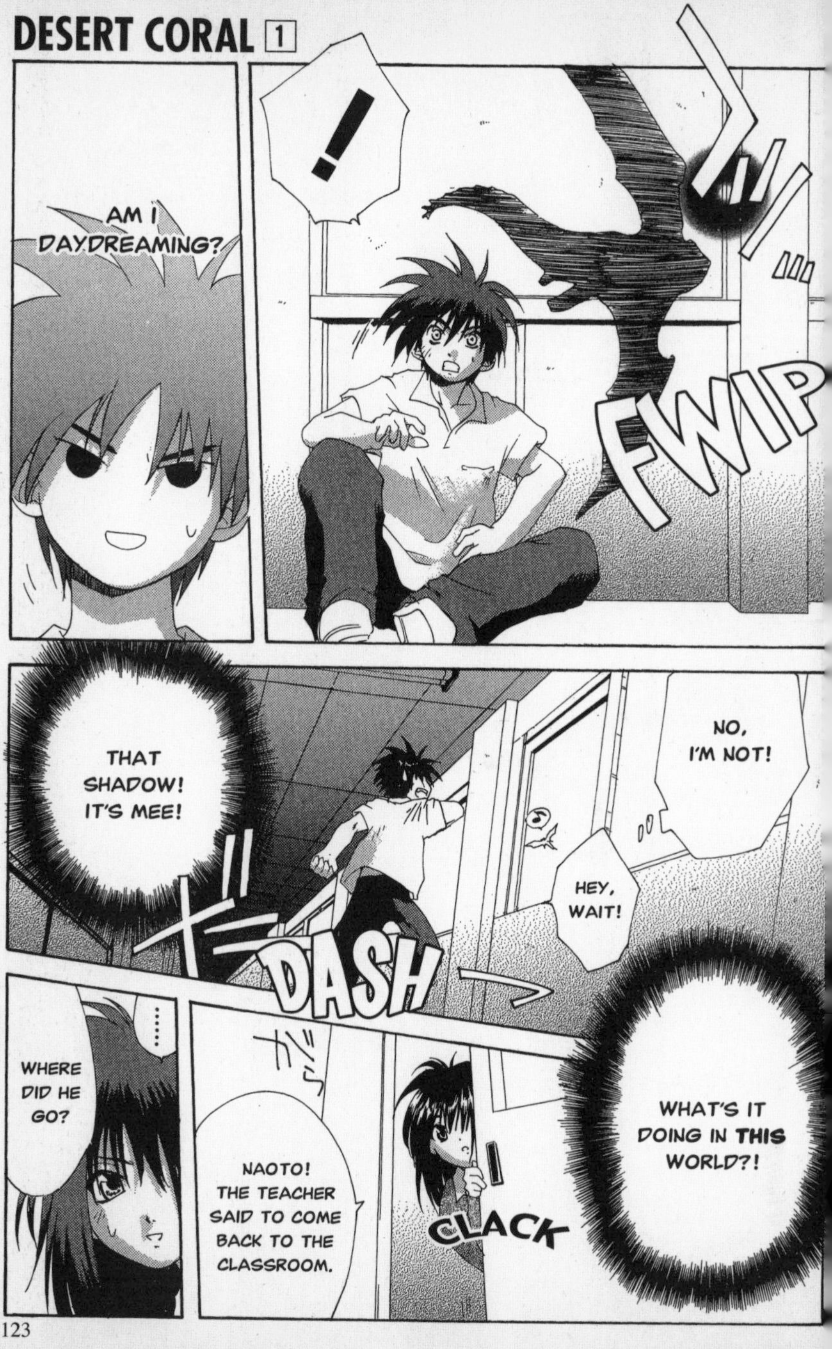
!
FWIP
AM I DAYDREAMING?
NO, I'M NOT!
HEY, WAIT!
DASH
THAT SHADOW! IT'S MEE!
WHAT'S IT DOING IN THIS WORLD?!
CLACK
NAOTO! THE TEACHER SAID TO COME BACK TO THE CLASSROOM.
......
WHERE DID HE GO?

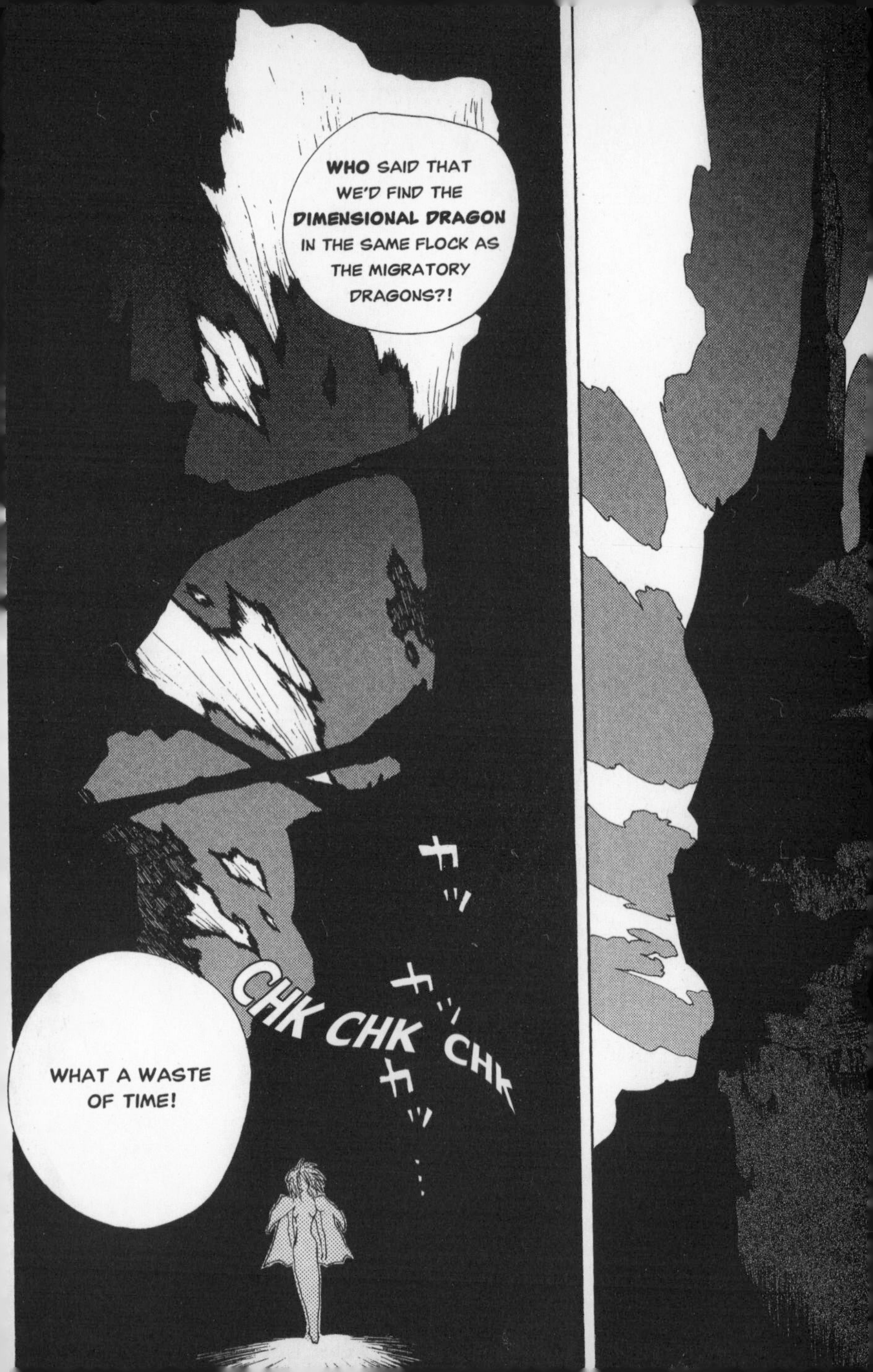
WHO SAID THAT WE'D FIND THE DIMENSIONAL DRAGON IN THE SAME FLOCK AS THE MIGRATORY DRAGONS?!
CHK CHK CHK
WHAT A WASTE OF TIME!

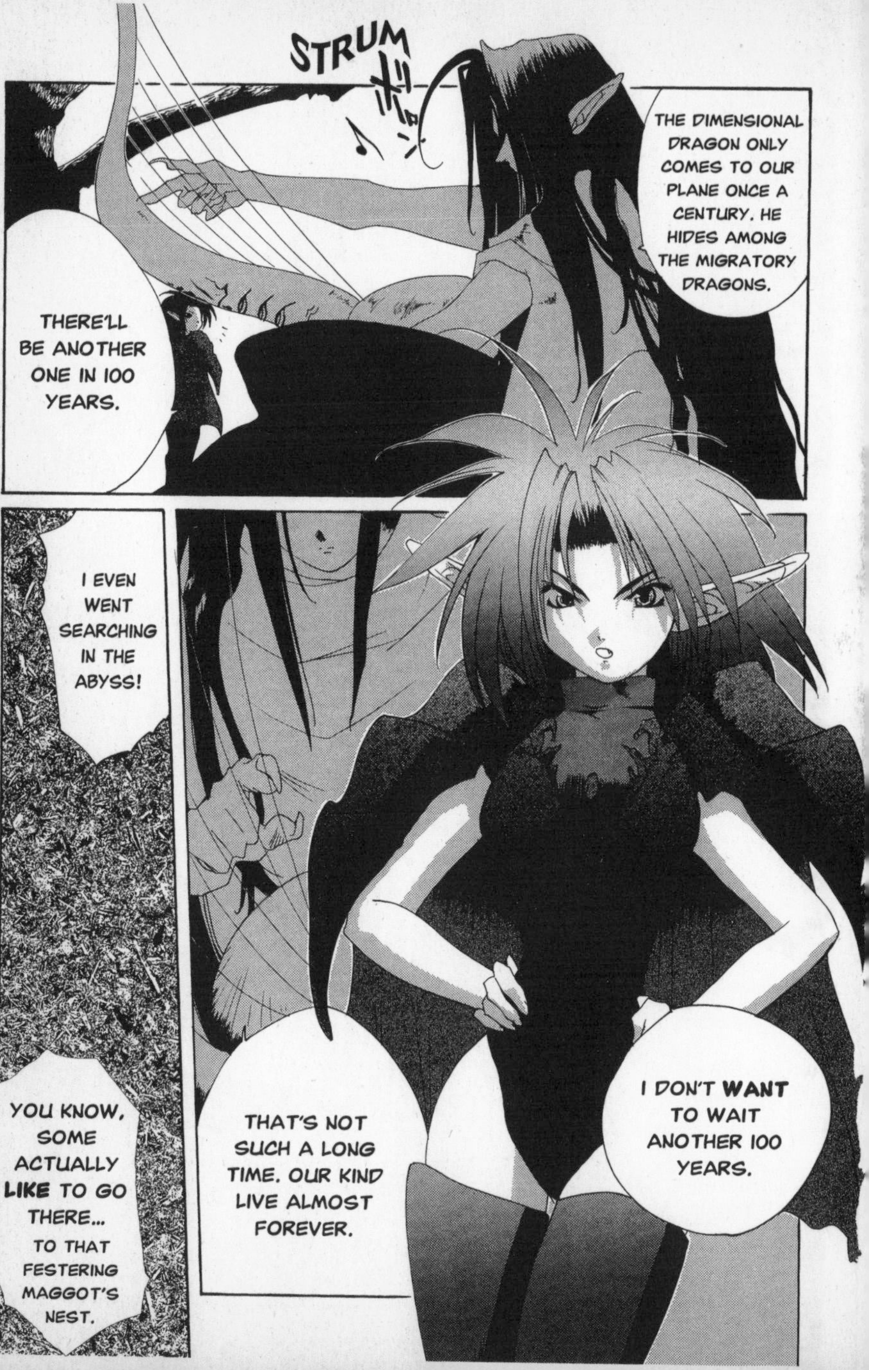
STRUM
THE DIMENSIONAL DRAGON ONLY COMES TO OUR PLANE ONCE A CENTURY. HE HIDES AMONG THE MIGRATORY DRAGONS.
THERE'LL BE ANOTHER ONE IN 100 YEARS.
I DON'T **WANT** TO WAIT ANOTHER 100 YEARS.
THAT'S NOT SUCH A LONG TIME. OUR KIND LIVE ALMOST FOREVER.
I EVEN WENT SEARCHING IN THE ABYSS!
YOU KNOW, SOME ACTUALLY **LIKE** TO GO THERE... TO THAT FESTERING MAGGOT'S NEST.

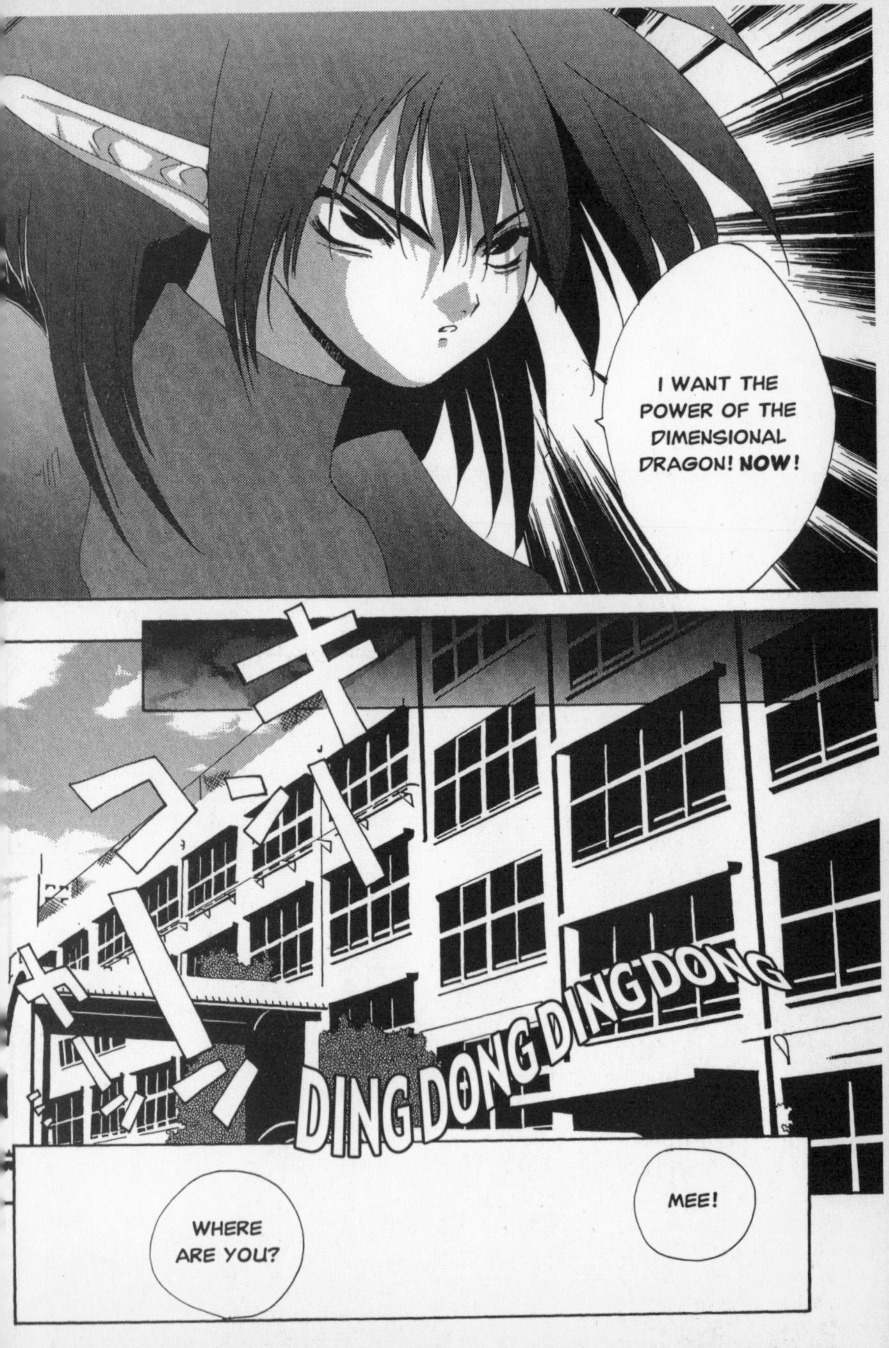
I WANT THE POWER OF THE DIMENSIONAL DRAGON! **NOW**!
DING DONG DING DONG
MEE!
WHERE ARE YOU?

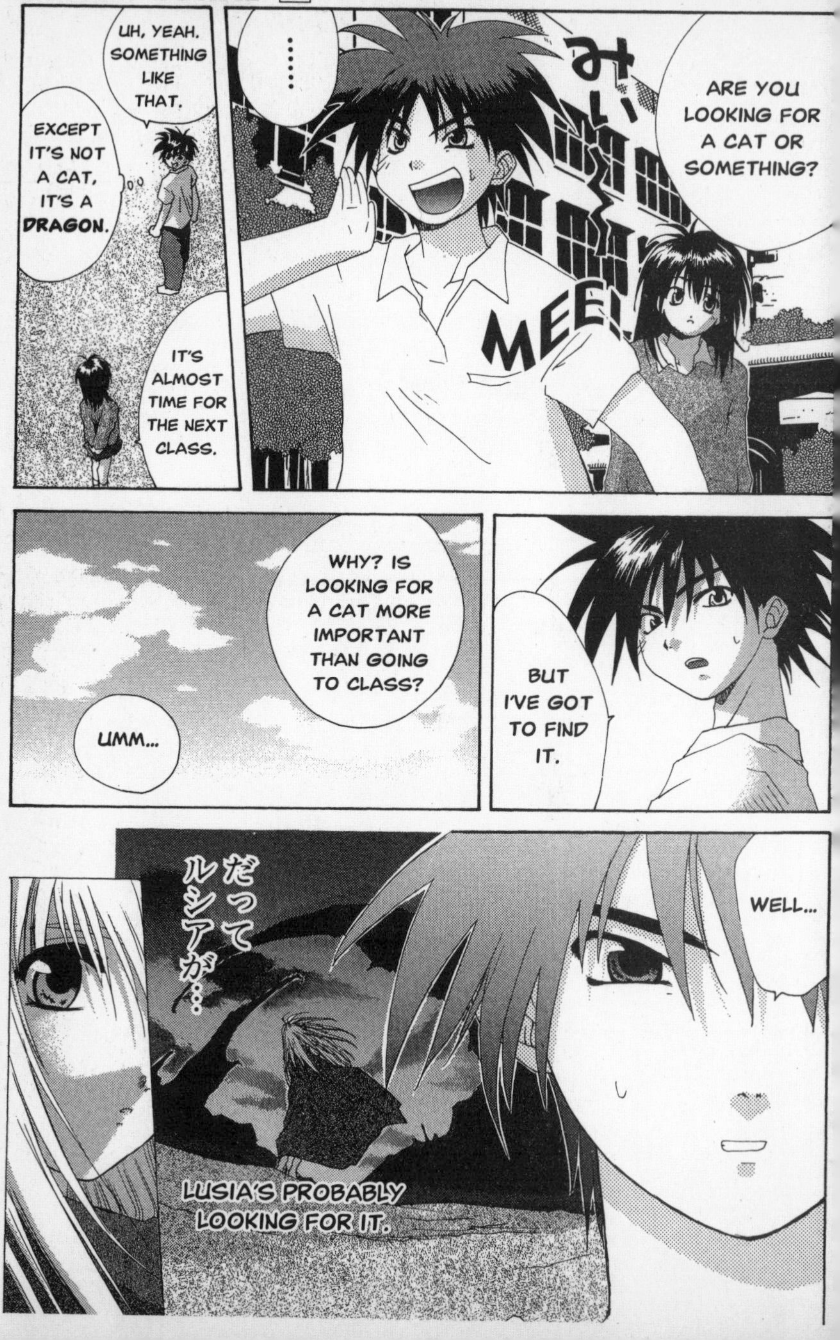
ARE YOU LOOKING FOR A CAT OR SOMETHING?
みぃ
MEE!
......
UH, YEAH. SOMETHING LIKE THAT.
EXCEPT IT'S NOT A CAT, IT'S A **DRAGON**.
IT'S ALMOST TIME FOR THE NEXT CLASS.
BUT I'VE GOT TO FIND IT.
WHY? IS LOOKING FOR A CAT MORE IMPORTANT THAN GOING TO CLASS?
UMM...
WELL...
だってルシアが…
LUSIA'S PROBABLY LOOKING FOR IT.

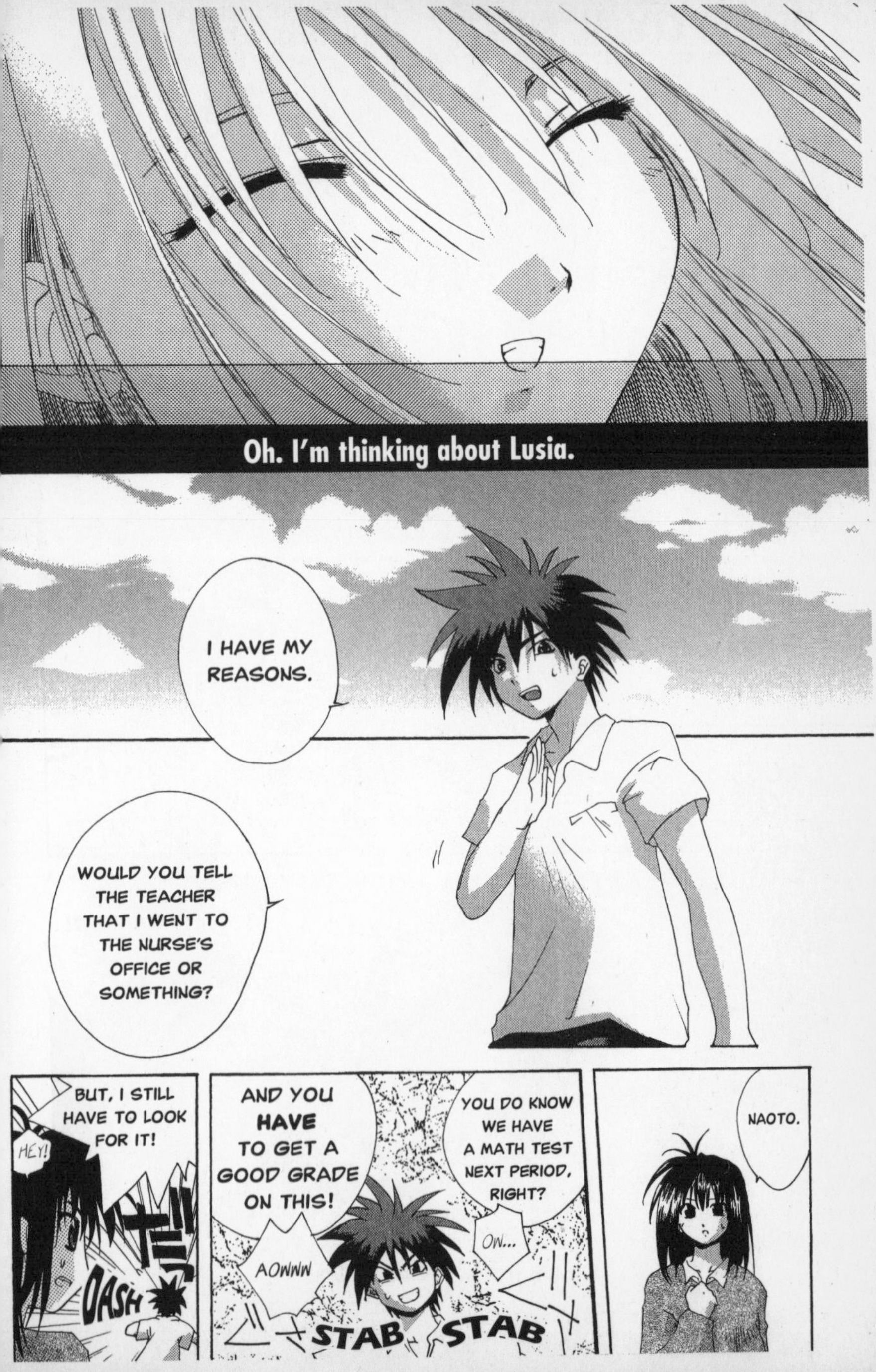
Oh. I'm thinking about Lusia.
I HAVE MY REASONS.
WOULD YOU TELL THE TEACHER THAT I WENT TO THE NURSE'S OFFICE OR SOMETHING?
NAOTO.
YOU DO KNOW WE HAVE A MATH TEST NEXT PERIOD, RIGHT?
AND YOU HAVE TO GET A GOOD GRADE ON THIS!
OW...
AOWWW
STAB STAB
BUT, I STILL HAVE TO LOOK FOR IT!
HEY!
DASH

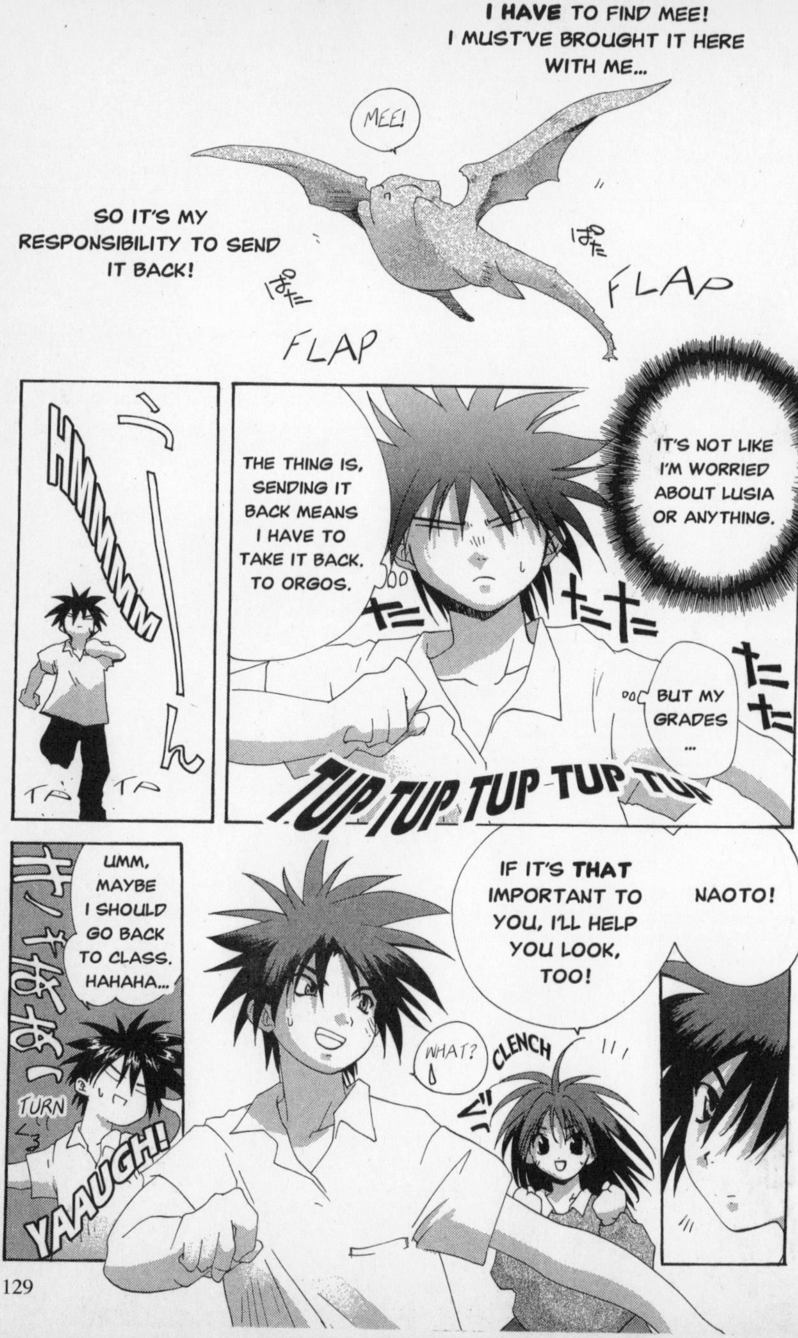
I HAVE TO FIND MEE! I MUST'VE BROUGHT IT HERE WITH ME...
MEE!
SO IT'S MY RESPONSIBILITY TO SEND IT BACK!
FLAP
FLAP
IT'S NOT LIKE I'M WORRIED ABOUT LUSIA OR ANYTHING.
THE THING IS, SENDING IT BACK MEANS I HAVE TO TAKE IT BACK. TO ORGOS.
BUT MY GRADES ...
TUP TUP TUP TUP TUP
HMMMMMM
NAOTO!
IF IT'S THAT IMPORTANT TO YOU, I'LL HELP YOU LOOK, TOO!
WHAT?
CLENCH
UMM, MAYBE I SHOULD GO BACK TO CLASS. HAHAHA...
TURN
YAAAUGH!

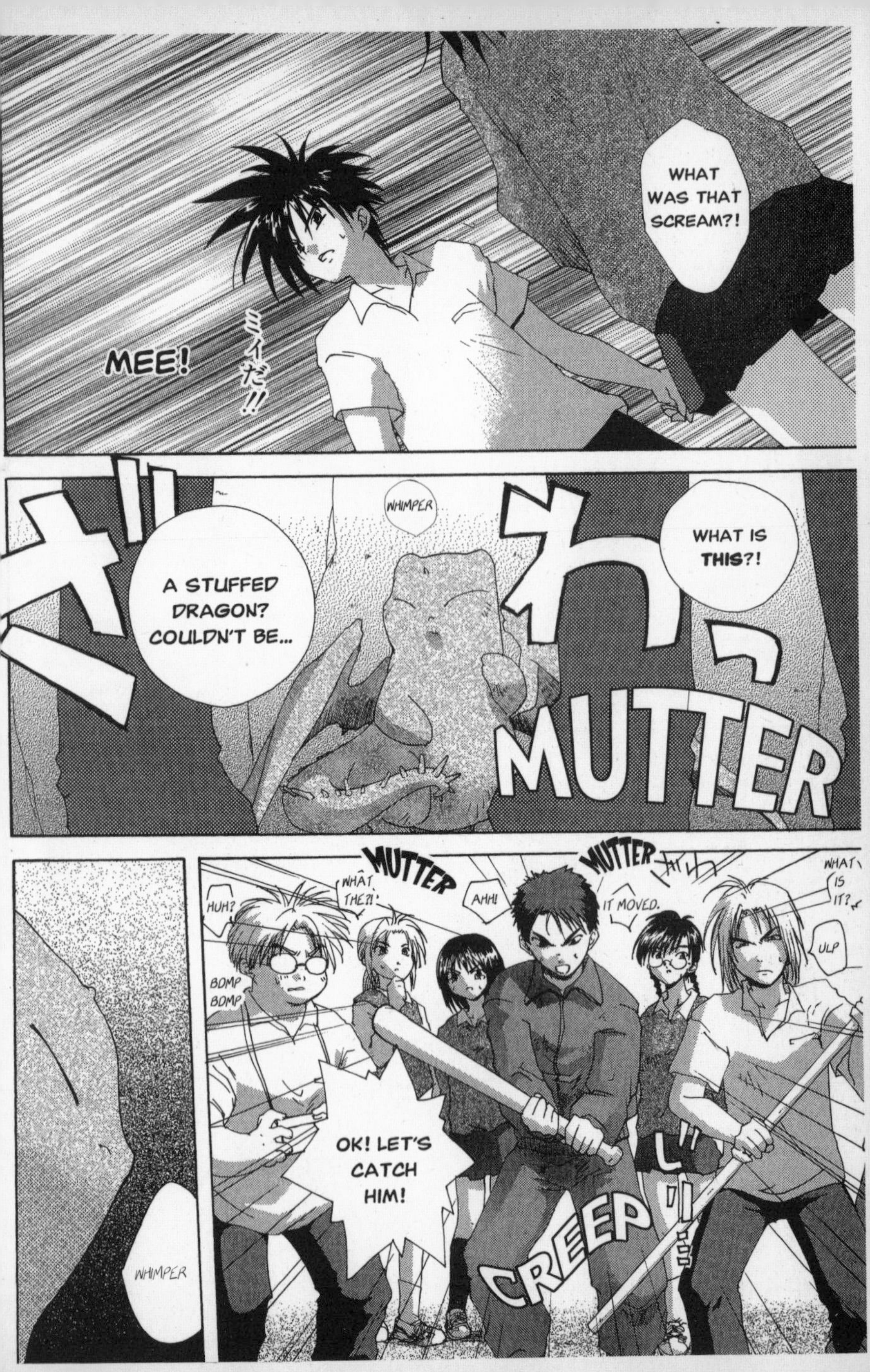
WHAT WAS THAT SCREAM?!
ミィだ!!
MEE!
WHAT IS THIS?!
MUTTER
WHIMPER
A STUFFED DRAGON? COULDN'T BE...
WHAT IS IT?!
ULP
MUTTER
IT MOVED.
AHH!
MUTTER
WHAT THE?!
HUH?
BOMP BOMP
OK! LET'S CATCH HIM!
CREEP
WHIMPER

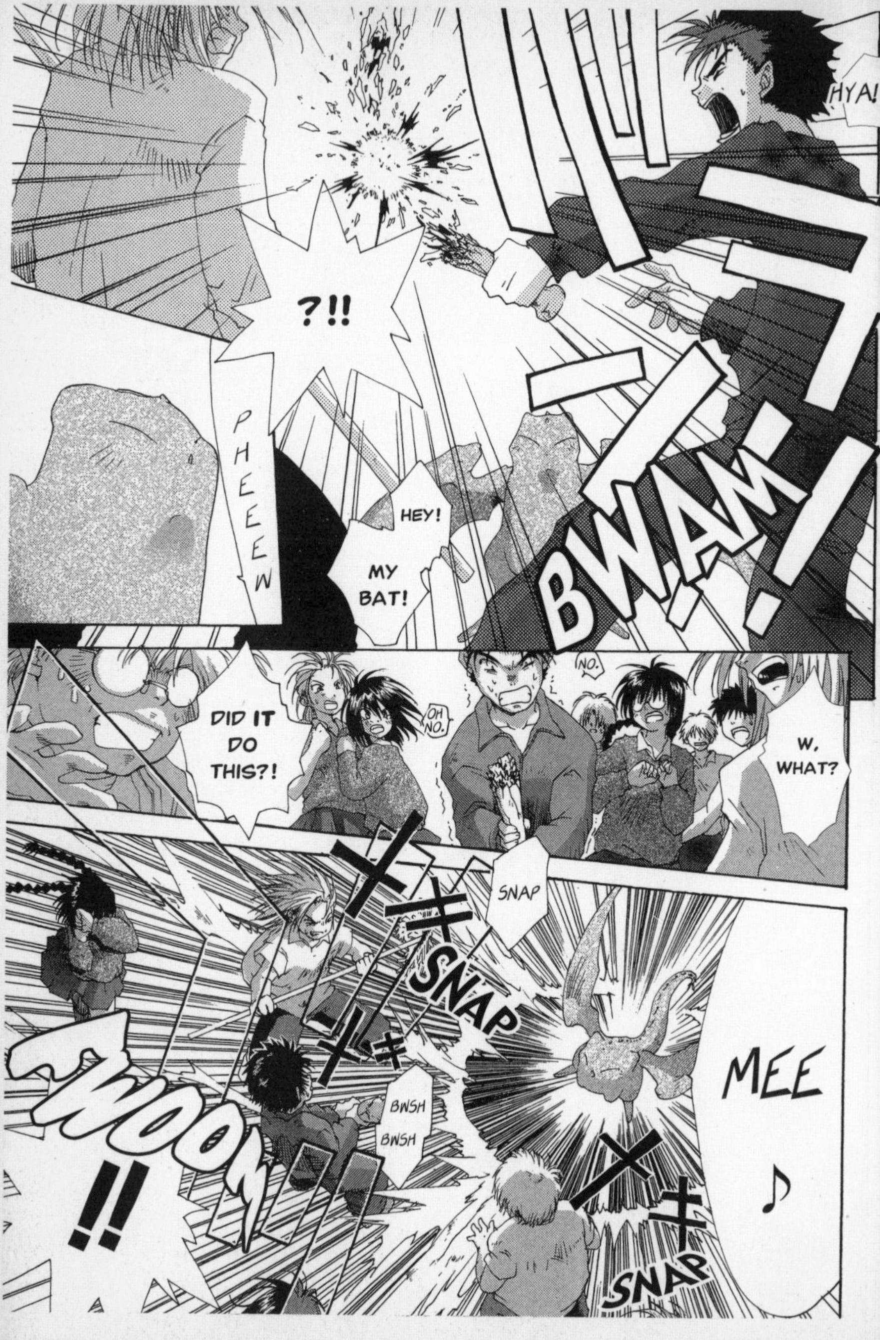
HYA!
BWAM!
?!!
HEY!
MY BAT!
PHEEEW
W. WHAT?
NO.
OH NO.
DID IT DO THIS?!
SNAP
SNAP
MEE ♪
SNAP
BWSH BWSH
FWOOM!!

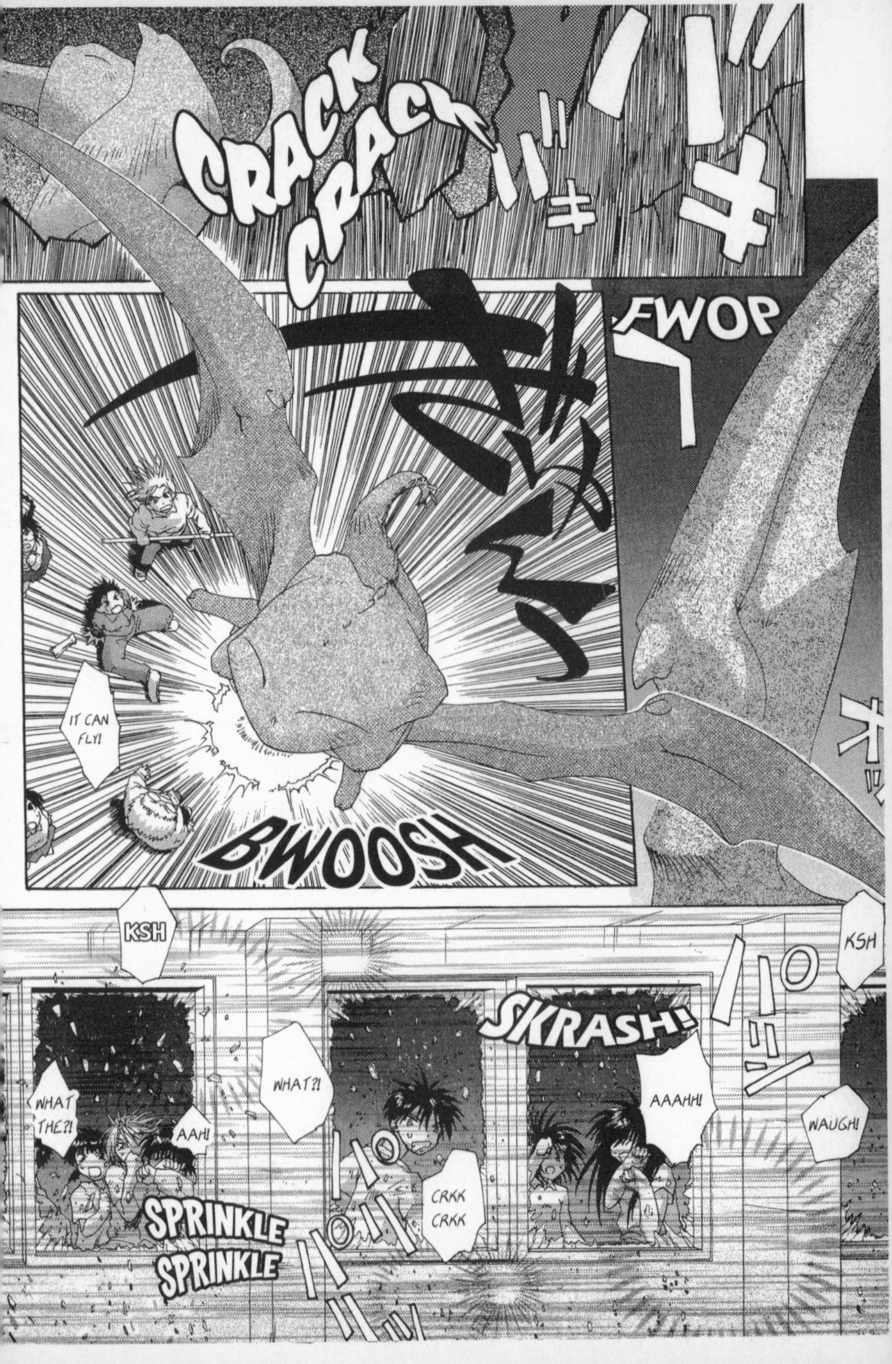
CRACK
CRACK
FWOP
IT CAN FLY!
BWOOSH
KSH
SKRASH!
WAUGH!
AAAHH!
CRKK CRKK
WHAT?!
KSH
AAH!
WHAT THE?!
SPRINKLE SPRINKLE

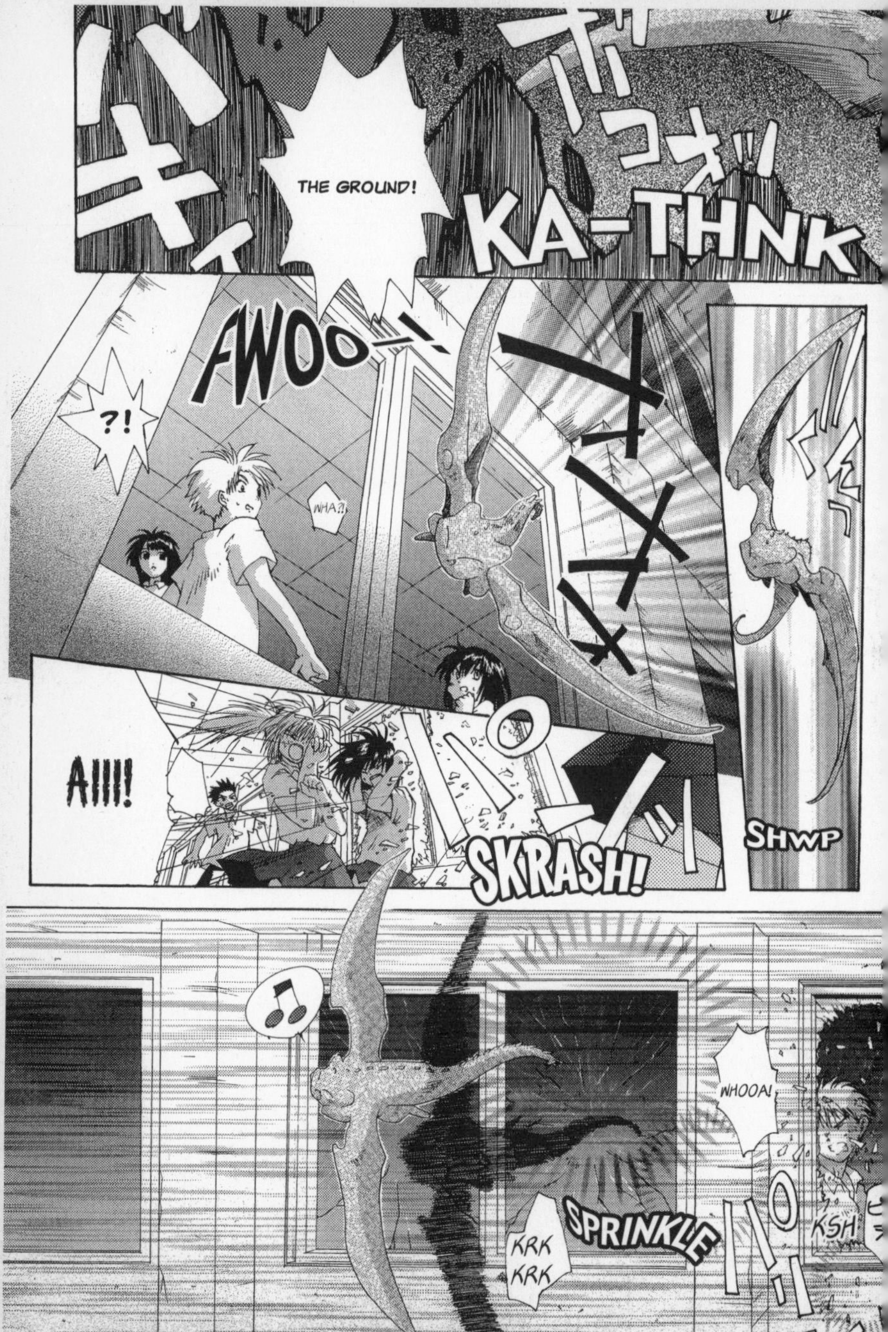
KA-THNK
THE GROUND!
SHWP
FWOO—!!
?!
WHA?!
SKRASH!
AIIII!
WHOOA!
KSH
SPRINKLE
KRK
KRK

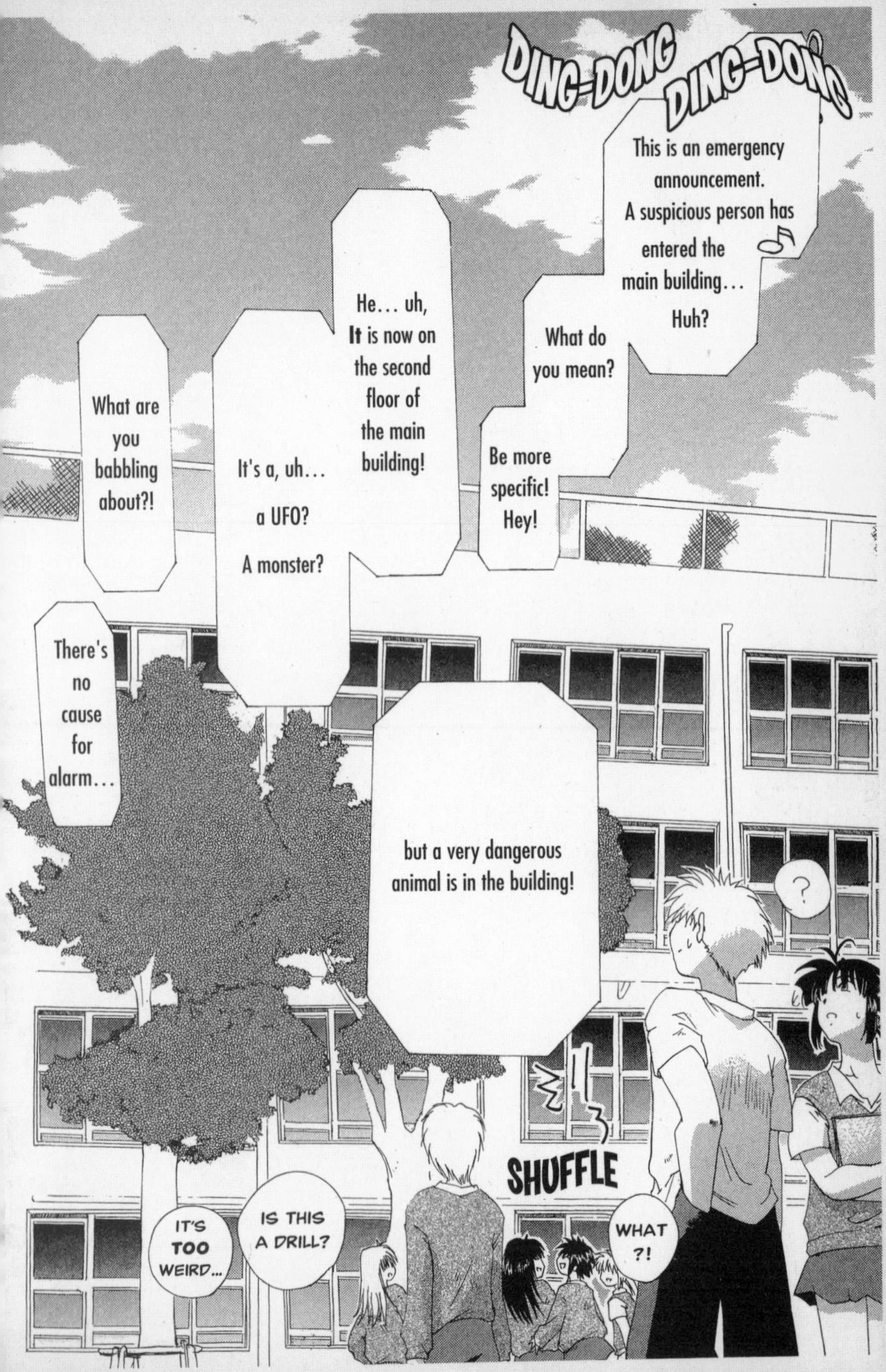
DING-DONG DING-DONG
This is an emergency announcement. A suspicious person has entered the main building... Huh?
What do you mean?
Be more specific! Hey!
He... uh, It is now on the second floor of the main building!
It's a, uh... a UFO? A monster?
What are you babbling about?!
There's no cause for alarm...
but a very dangerous animal is in the building!
?
WHAT?!
SHUFFLE
IS THIS A DRILL?
IT'S TOO WEIRD...

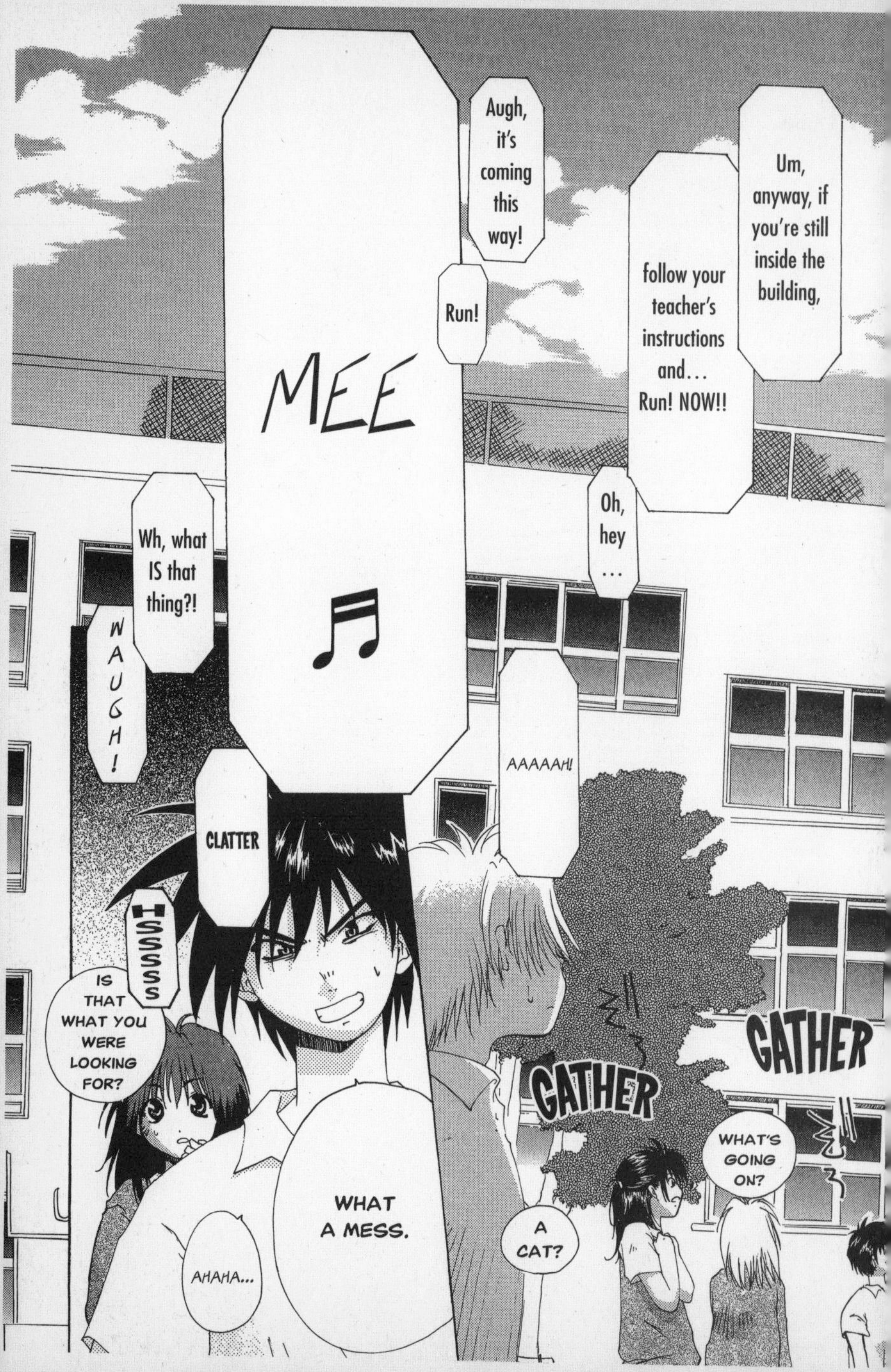
Um, anyway, if you're still inside the building,
follow your teacher's instructions and… Run! NOW!!
Augh, it's coming this way!
Run!
MEE ♫
Oh, hey…
Wh, what IS that thing?!
WAUGH!
AAAAAH!
CLATTER
HSSSSS
GATHER
GATHER
WHAT'S GOING ON?
A CAT?
WHAT A MESS.
IS THAT WHAT YOU WERE LOOKING FOR?
AHAHA...

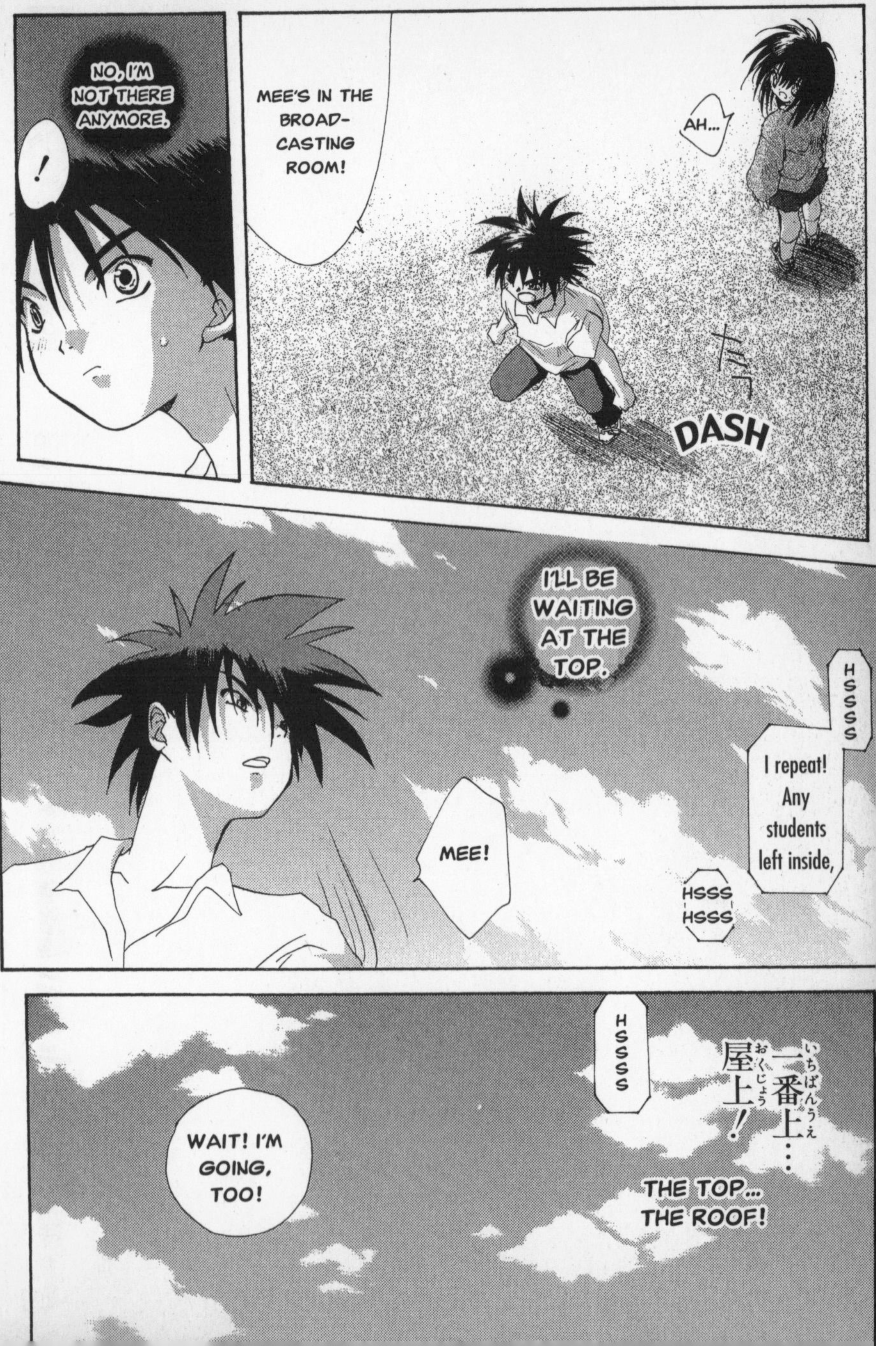
AH...
MEE'S IN THE BROAD-CASTING ROOM!
DASH
NO, I'M NOT THERE ANYMORE.
!
HSSSS
I repeat! Any students left inside,
HSSS HSSS
I'LL BE WAITING AT THE TOP.
MEE!
HSSSS
一番上（いちばんうえ）…屋上（おくじょう）！
THE TOP... THE ROOF!
WAIT! I'M GOING, TOO!

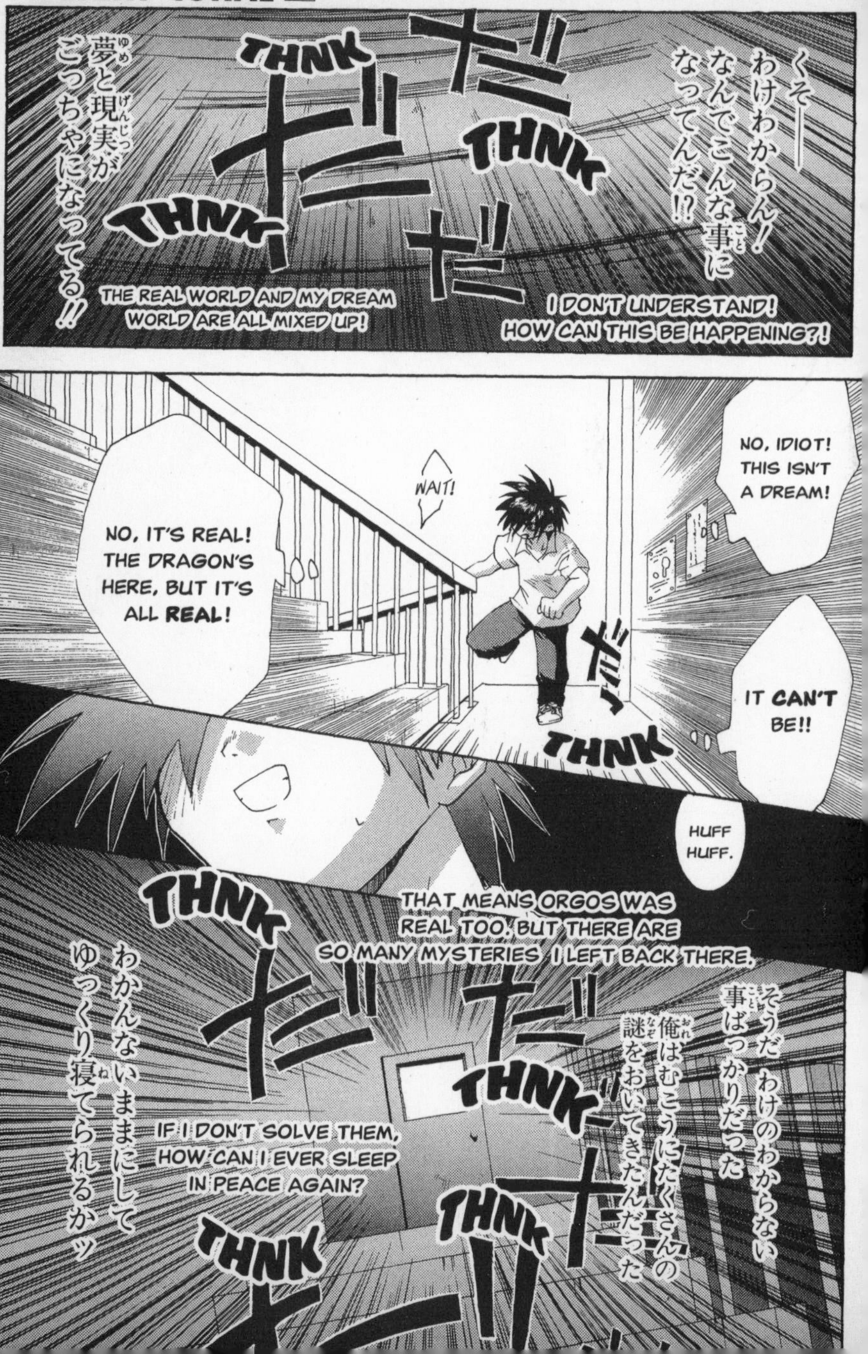
くそーわけわからん！なんでこんな事になってんだ!?
I DON'T UNDERSTAND! HOW CAN THIS BE HAPPENING?!
THNK
THNK
THNK
夢と現実がごっちゃになってる!!
THE REAL WORLD AND MY DREAM WORLD ARE ALL MIXED UP!
NO, IDIOT! THIS ISN'T A DREAM!
IT CAN'T BE!!
WAIT!
THNK
NO, IT'S REAL! THE DRAGON'S HERE, BUT IT'S ALL REAL!
HUFF HUFF.
そうだ わけのわからない事ばっかりだった 俺はむこうにたくさんの謎をおいてきたんだった
THAT MEANS ORGOS WAS REAL TOO. BUT THERE ARE SO MANY MYSTERIES I LEFT BACK THERE.
THNK
THNK
THNK
THNK
わかんないままにしてゆっくり寝てられるかッ
IF I DON'T SOLVE THEM, HOW CAN I EVER SLEEP IN PEACE AGAIN?

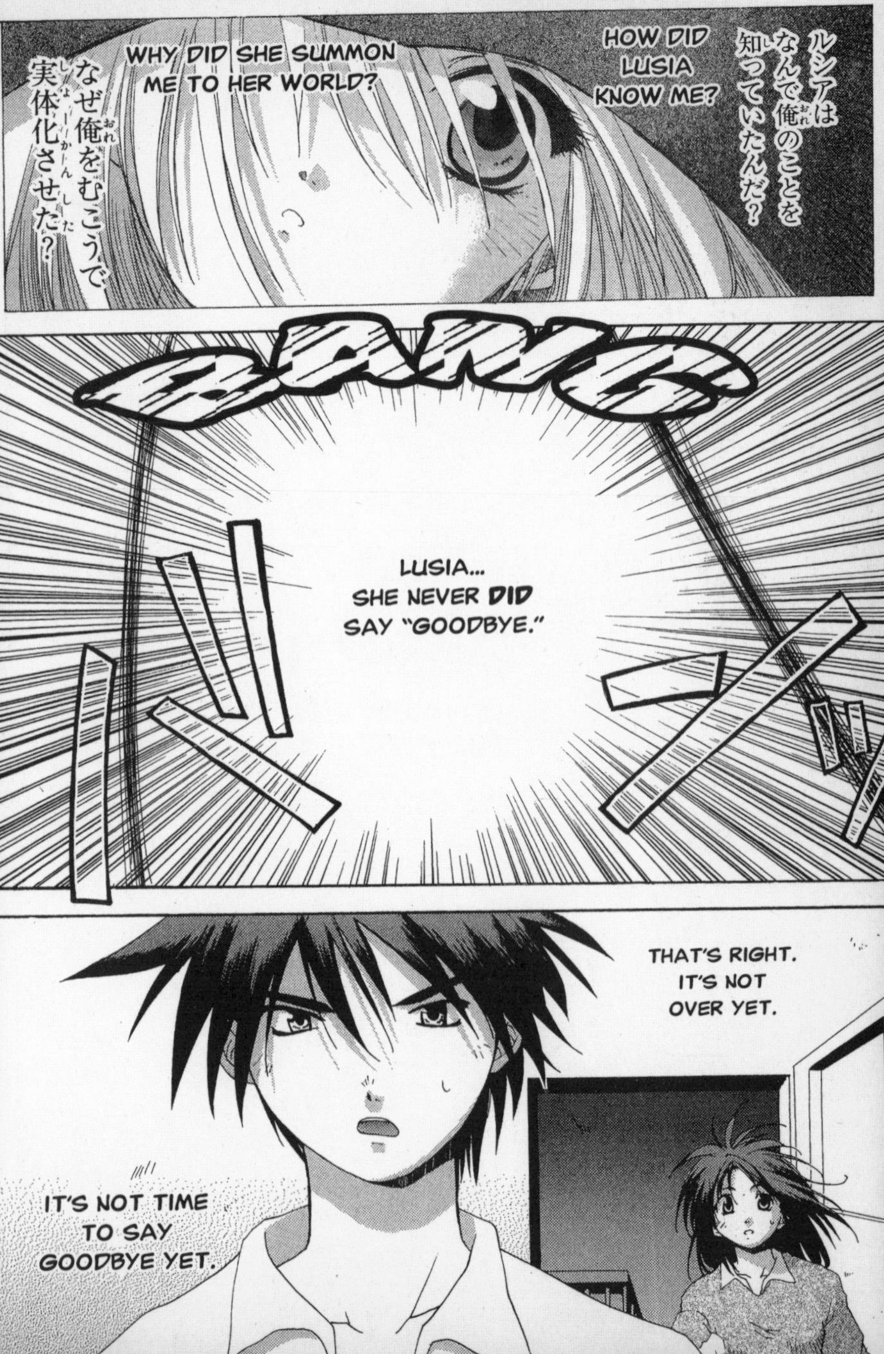
ルシアはなんで俺のことを知っていたんだ?
HOW DID LUSIA KNOW ME?
WHY DID SHE SUMMON ME TO HER WORLD?
なぜ俺をむこうで実体化させた?
BANG
LUSIA... SHE NEVER DID SAY "GOODBYE."
THAT'S RIGHT. IT'S NOT OVER YET.
IT'S NOT TIME TO SAY GOODBYE YET.

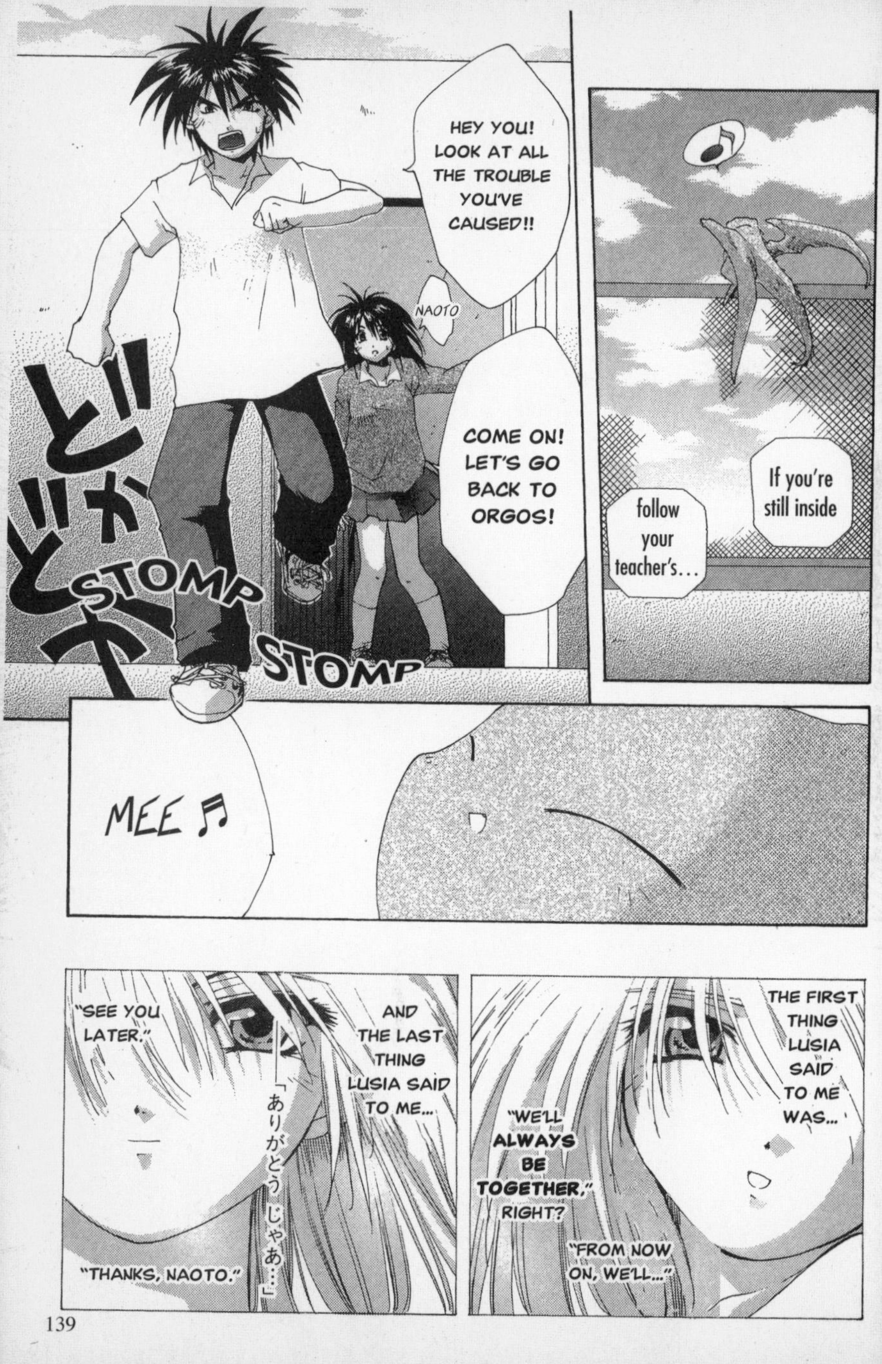
If you're still inside
follow your teacher's…
HEY YOU! LOOK AT ALL THE TROUBLE YOU'VE CAUSED!!
NAOTO
COME ON! LET'S GO BACK TO ORGOS!
STOMP
STOMP
MEE ♬
THE FIRST THING LUSIA SAID TO ME WAS…
"WE'LL ALWAYS BE TOGETHER," RIGHT?
"FROM NOW ON, WE'LL…"
AND THE LAST THING LUSIA SAID TO ME…
"SEE YOU LATER."
「ありがとう じゃあ…」
"THANKS, NAOTO."

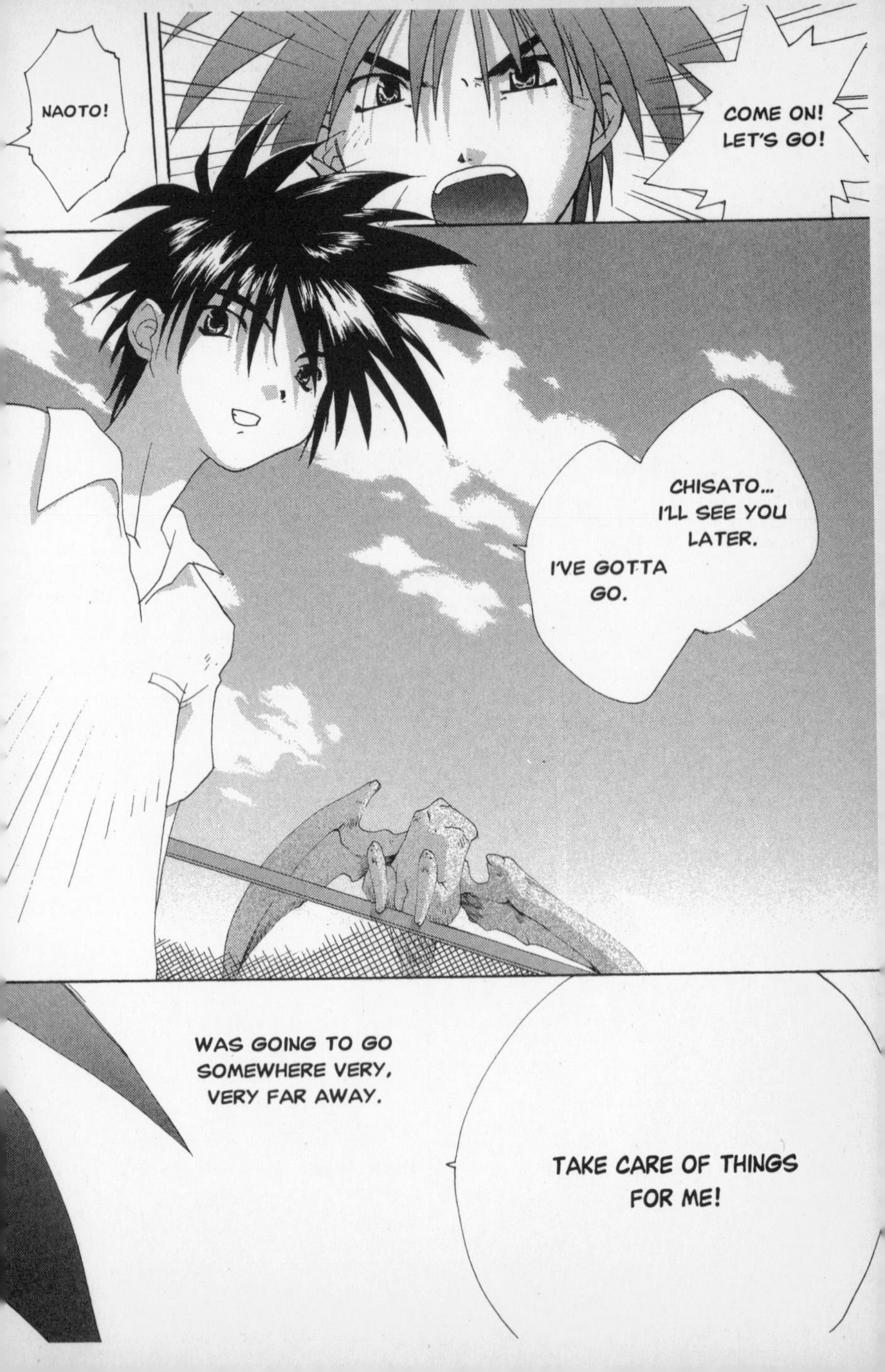
COME ON! LET'S GO!
NAOTO!
CHISATO... I'LL SEE YOU LATER.
I'VE GOTTA GO.
TAKE CARE OF THINGS FOR ME!
WAS GOING TO GO SOMEWHERE VERY, VERY FAR AWAY.

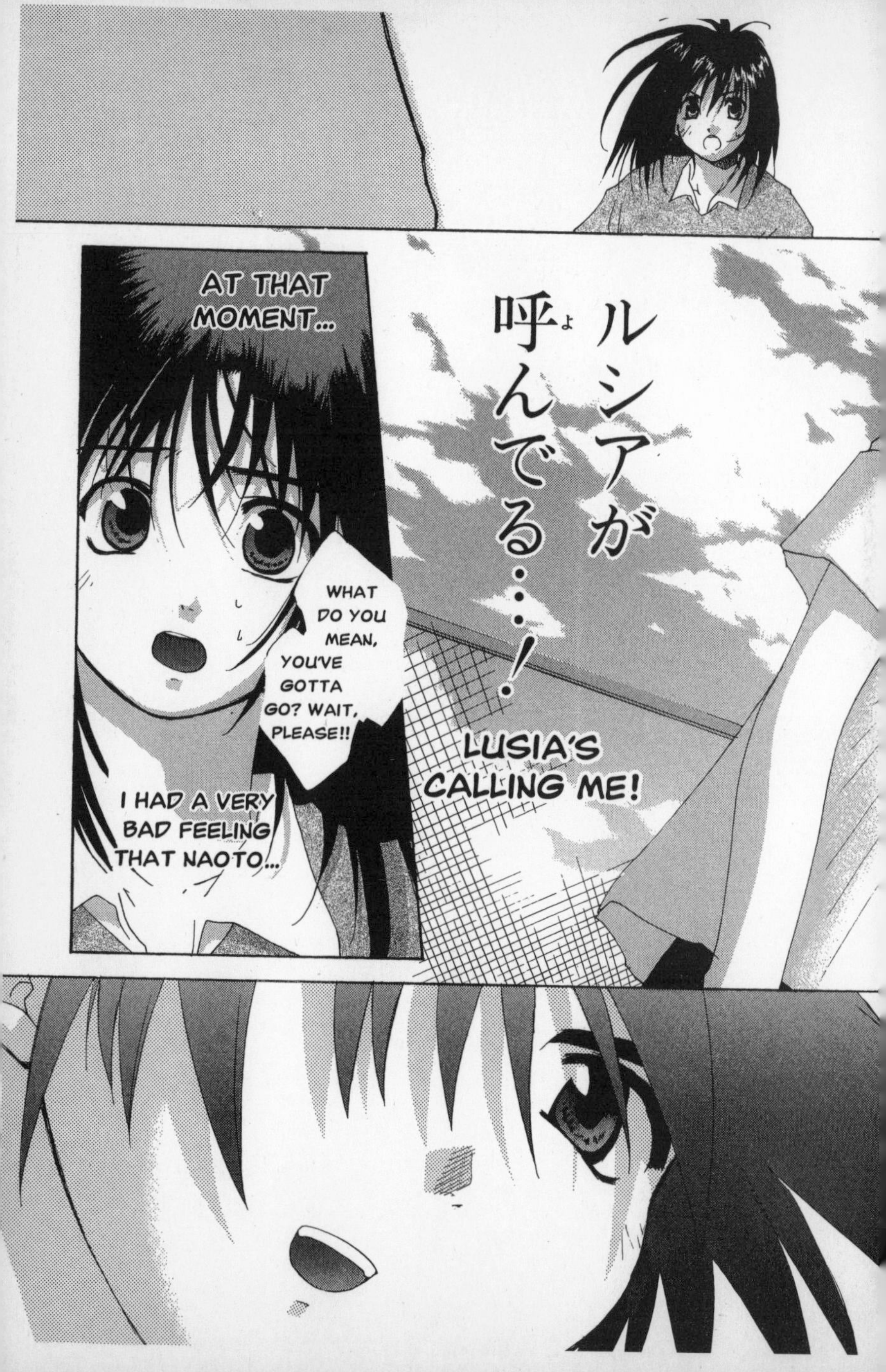
ルシアが呼んでる…！
LUSIA'S CALLING ME!
AT THAT MOMENT...
WHAT DO YOU MEAN, YOU'VE GOTTA GO? WAIT, PLEASE!!
I HAD A VERY BAD FEELING THAT NAOTO...

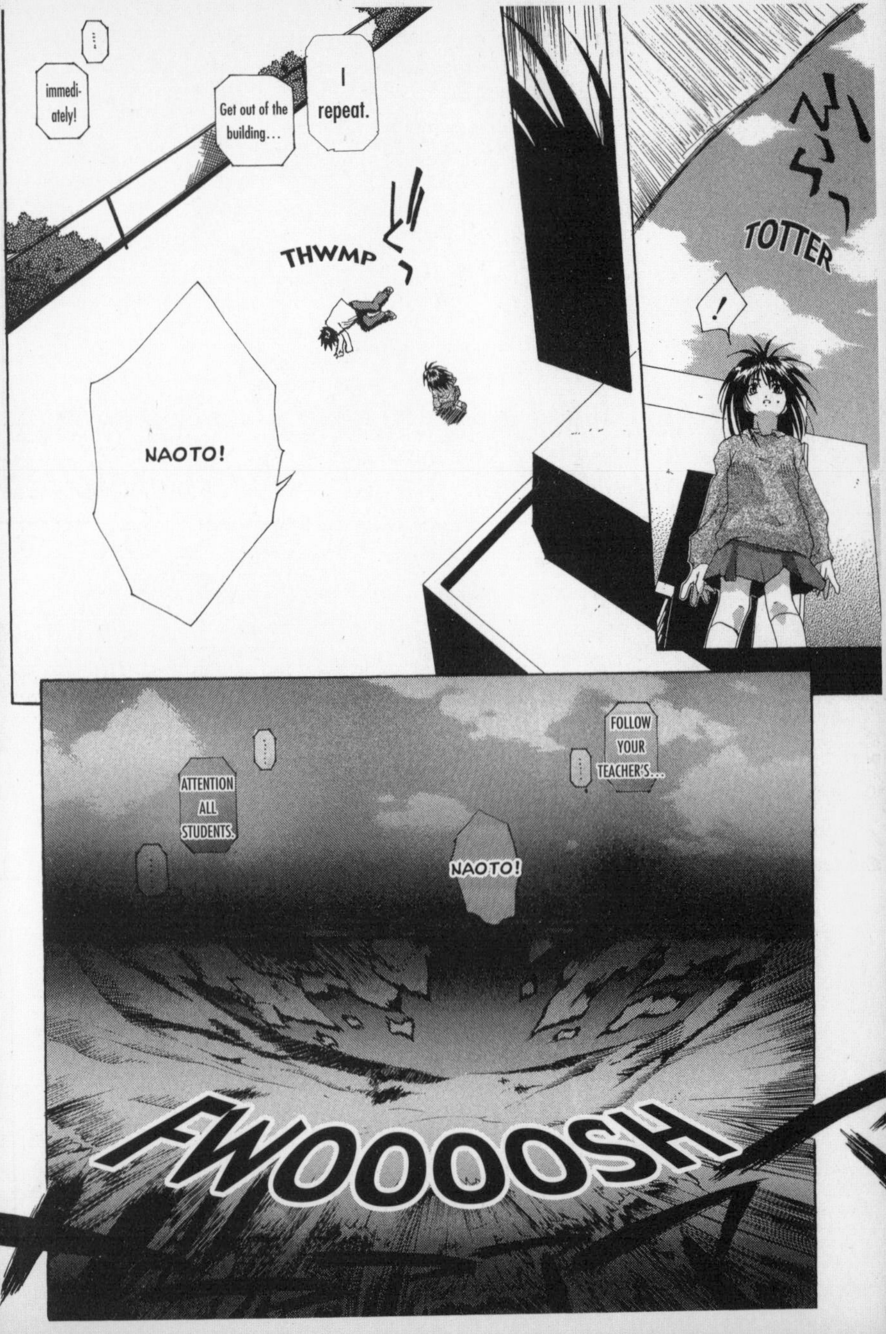

TOTTER
!
I repeat.
Get out of the building…
…
immedi-ately!
THWMP
NAOTO!
FOLLOW YOUR TEACHER'S…
…
…
ATTENTION ALL STUDENTS.
NAOTO!
…
FWOOOOSH

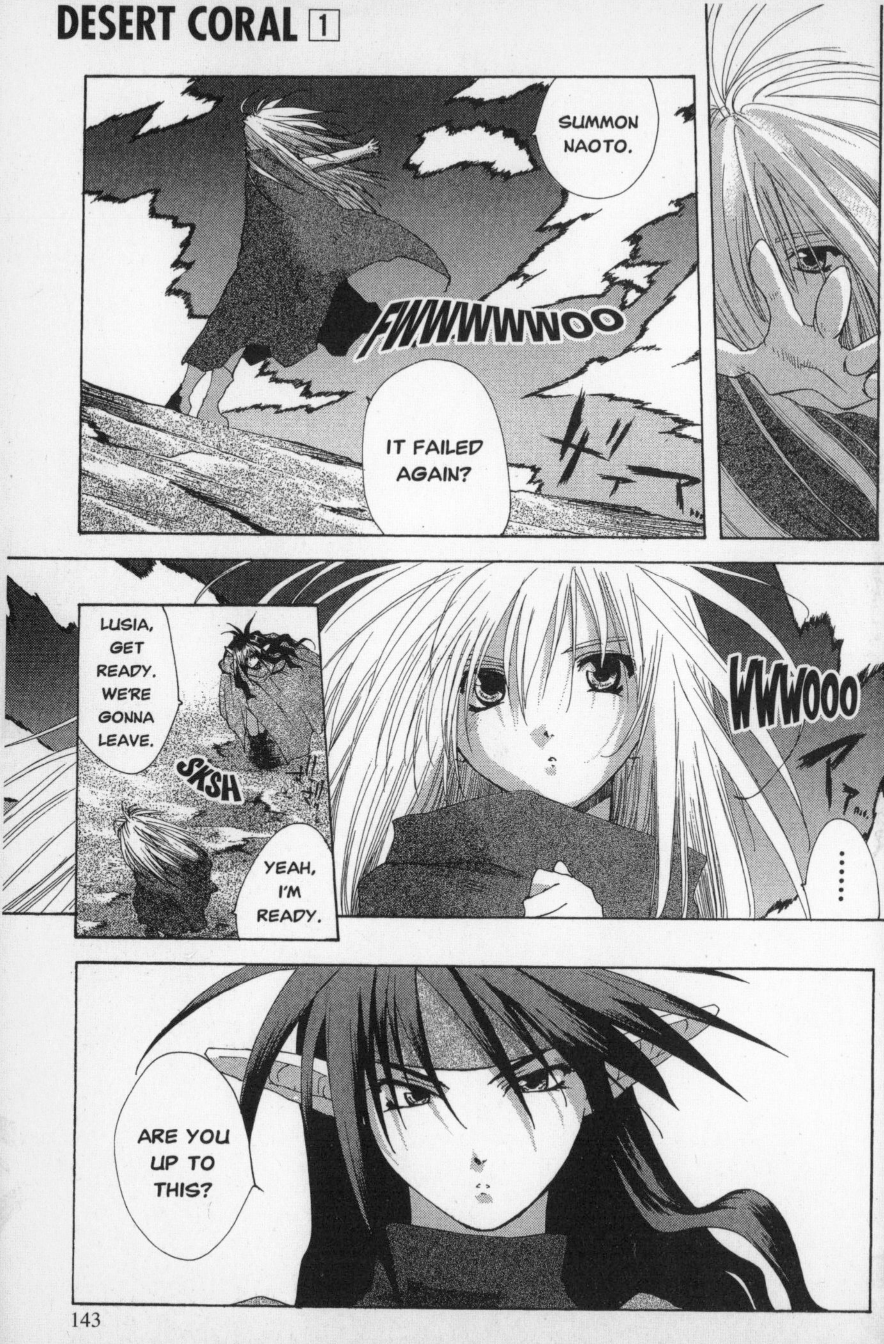
SUMMON NAOTO.
FWWWWWOO
IT FAILED AGAIN?
WWWOOO
......
LUSIA, GET READY. WE'RE GONNA LEAVE.
SKSH
YEAH, I'M READY.
ARE YOU UP TO THIS?

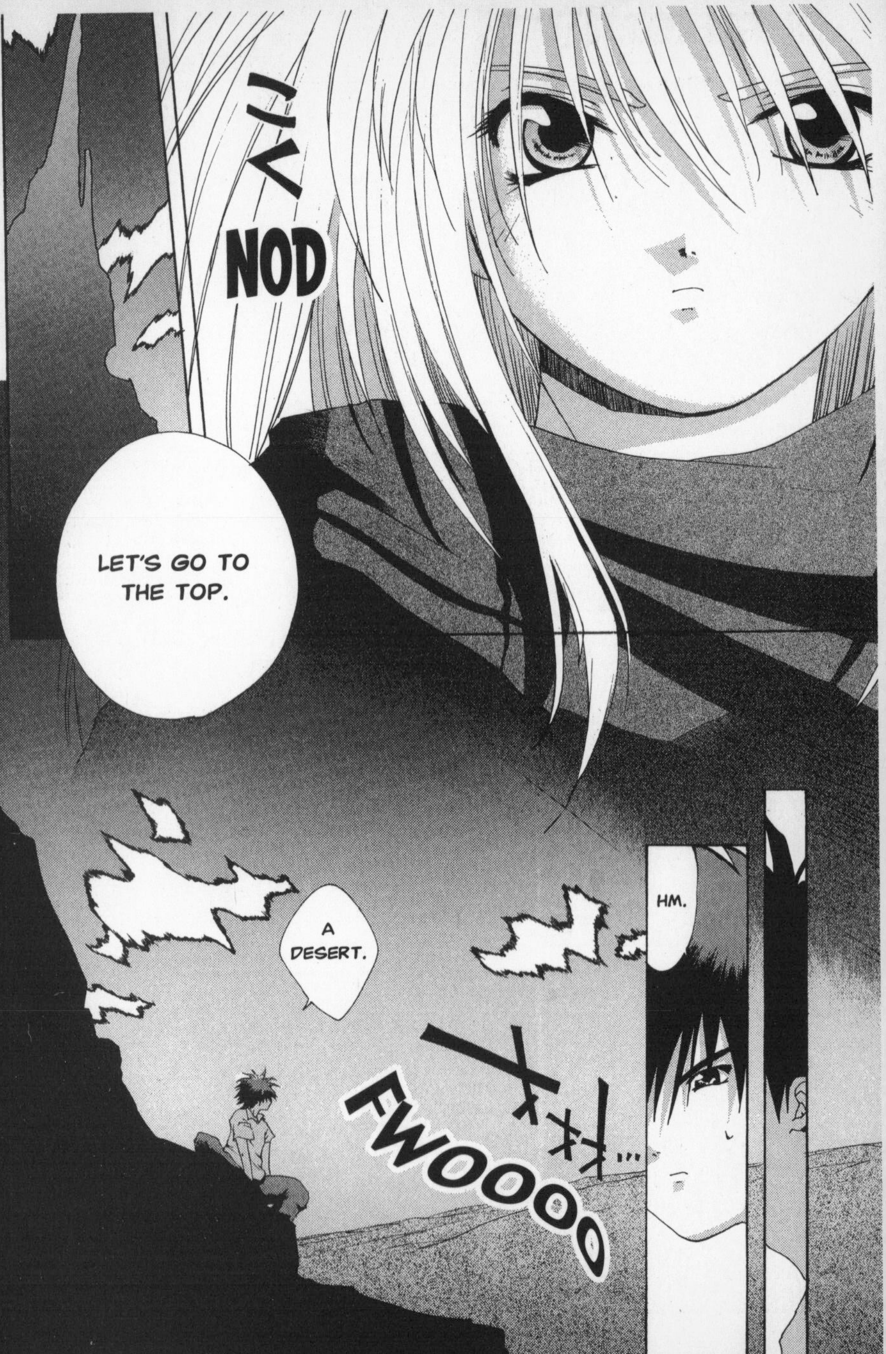
NOD
LET'S GO TO THE TOP.
A DESERT.
HM.
FWOOOO

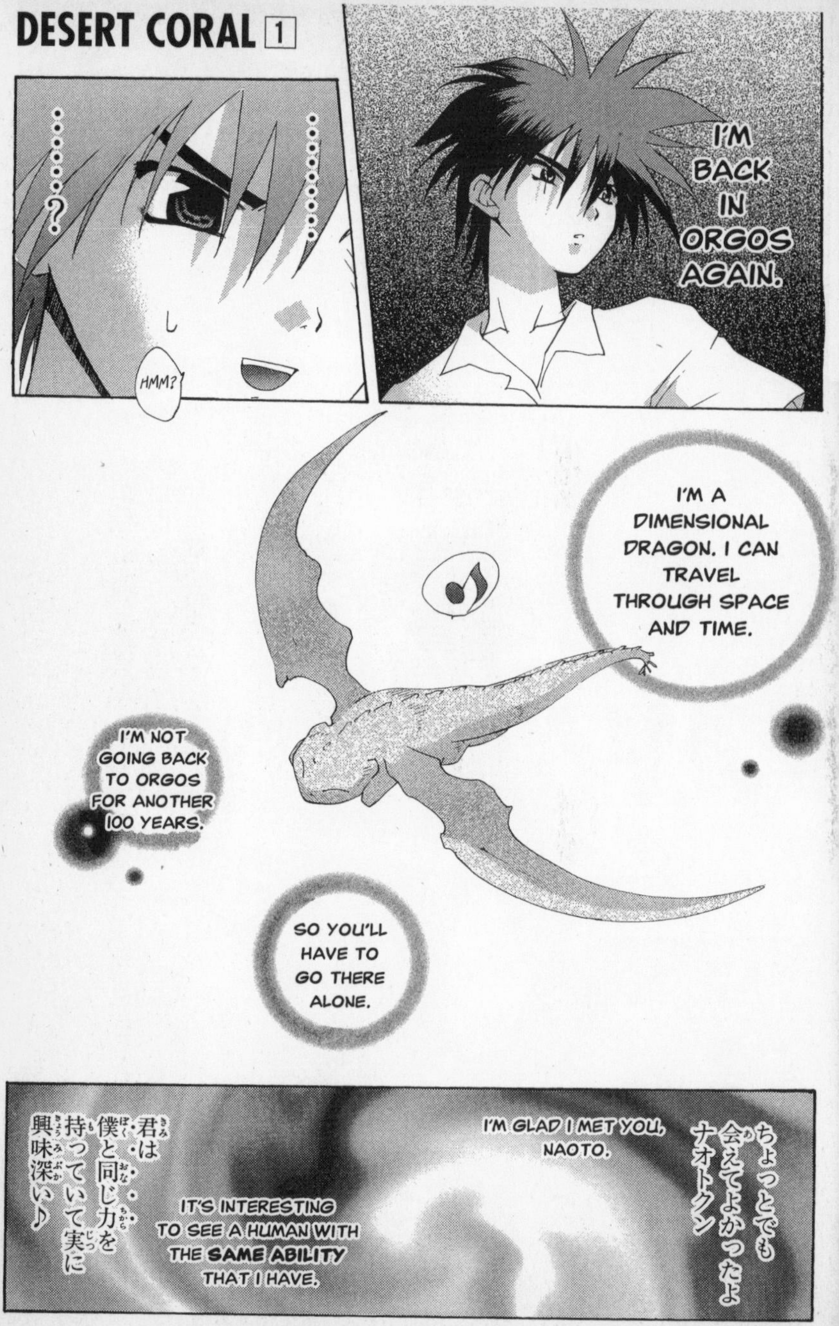
I'M BACK IN ORGOS AGAIN.
....
......?
HMM?
I'M A DIMENSIONAL DRAGON. I CAN TRAVEL THROUGH SPACE AND TIME.
♪
I'M NOT GOING BACK TO ORGOS FOR ANOTHER 100 YEARS.
SO YOU'LL HAVE TO GO THERE ALONE.
ちょっとでも会えてよかったよナオトクン
I'M GLAD I MET YOU, NAOTO.
君は・・僕と同じ力を持っていて実に興味深い♪
IT'S INTERESTING TO SEE A HUMAN WITH THE SAME ABILITY THAT I HAVE.

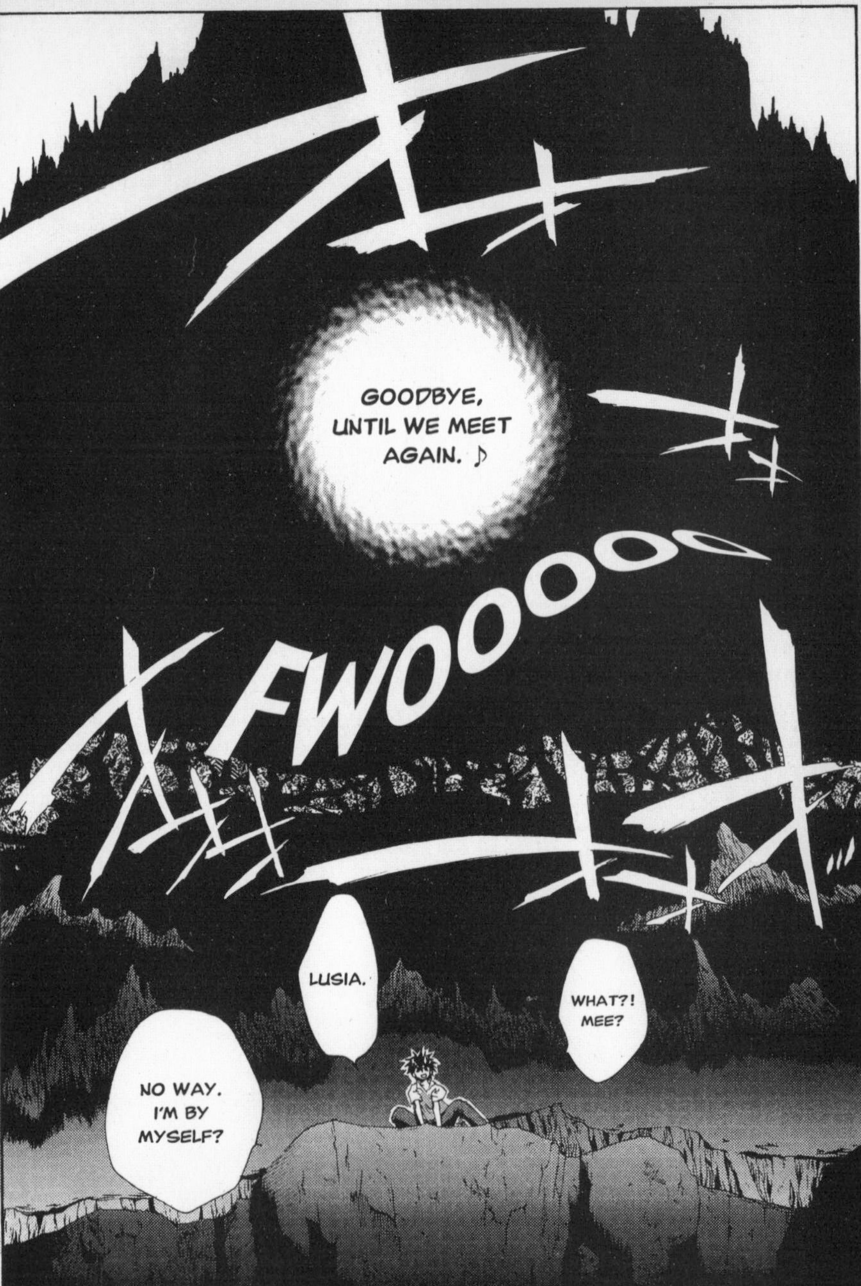
GOODBYE, UNTIL WE MEET AGAIN. ♪
FWOOOOOO
LUSIA.
WHAT?! MEE?
NO WAY. I'M BY MYSELF?

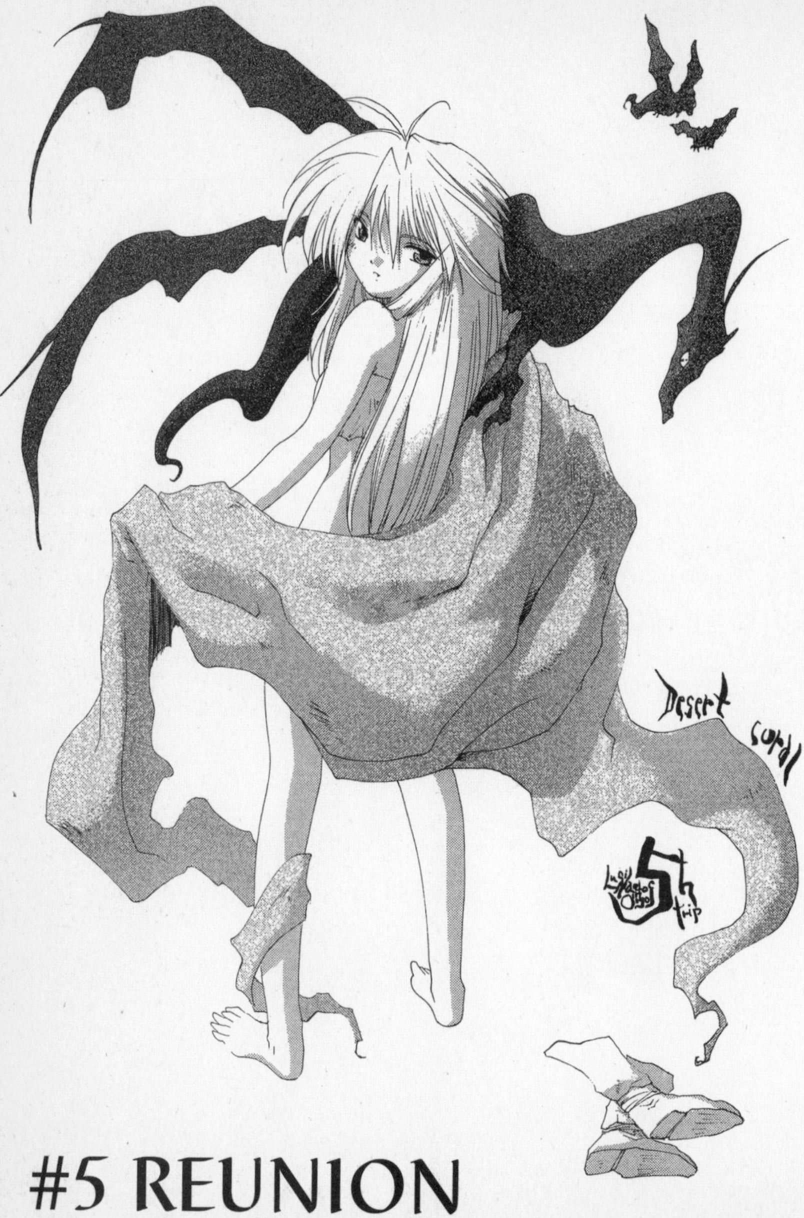
Desert coral
5th trip

#5 REUNION

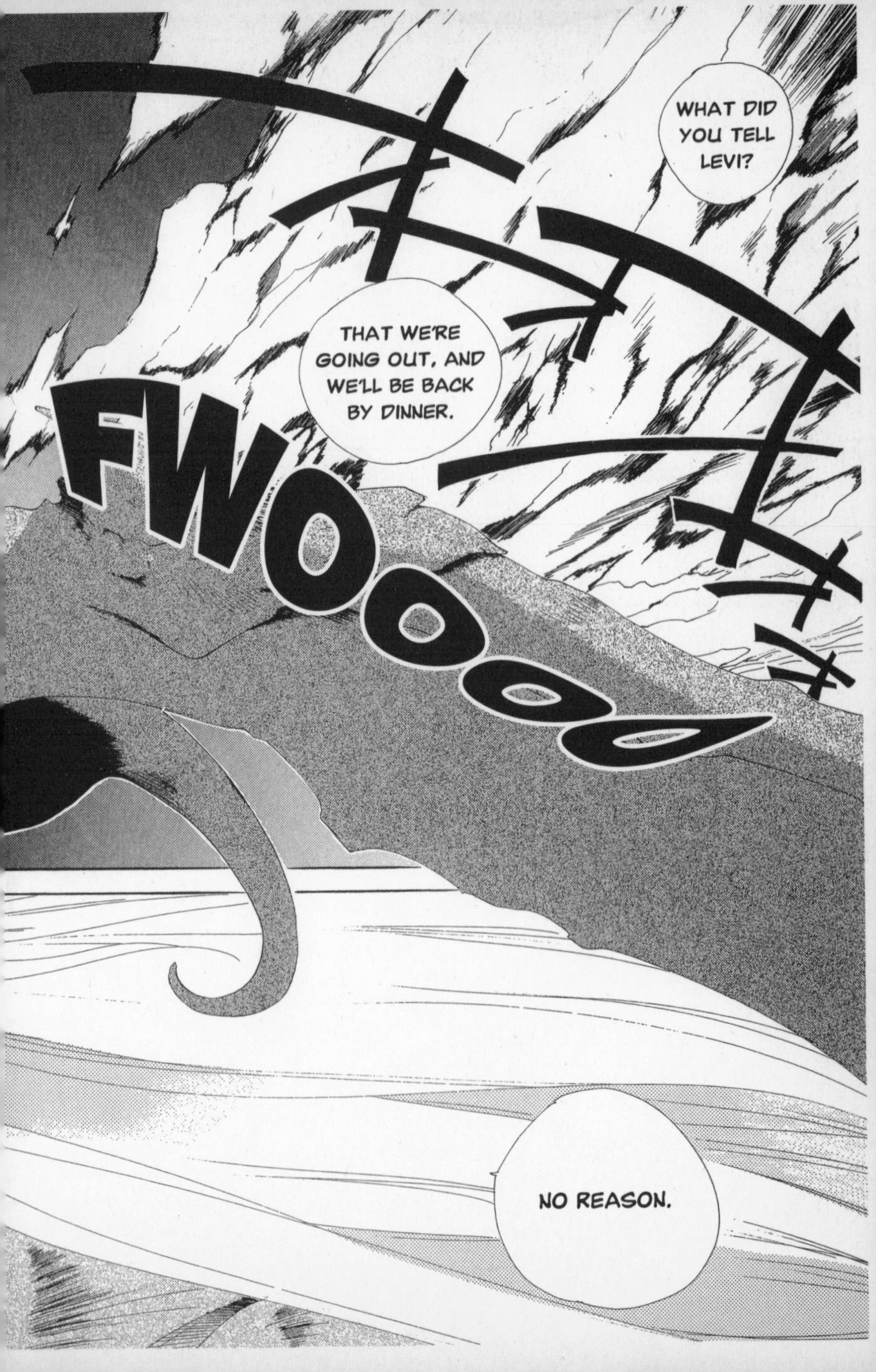
WHAT DID YOU TELL LEVI?
THAT WE'RE GOING OUT, AND WE'LL BE BACK BY DINNER.
FWOOOOO
NO REASON.

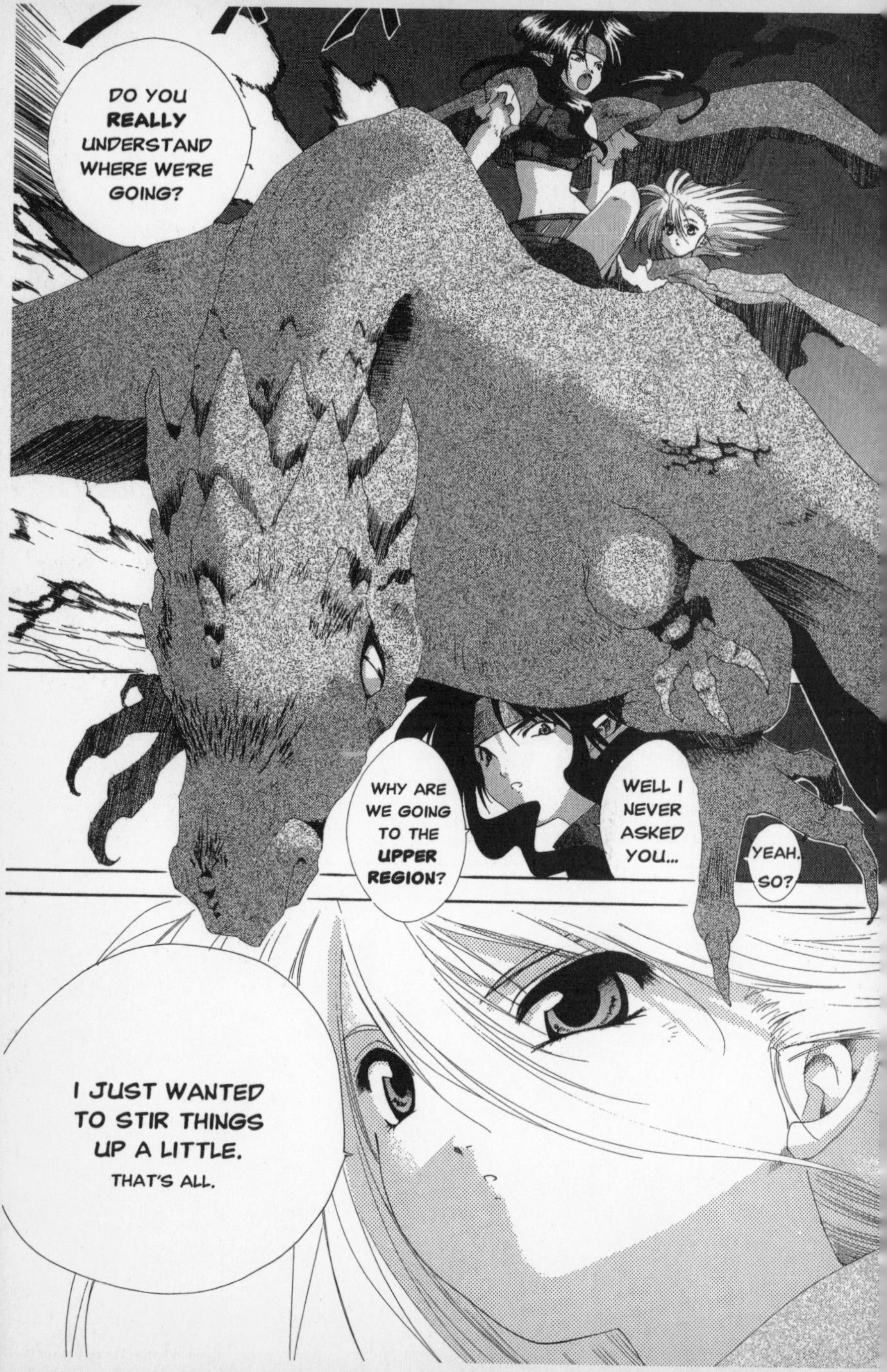
DO YOU **REALLY** UNDERSTAND WHERE WE'RE GOING?
YEAH. SO?
WELL I NEVER ASKED YOU...
WHY ARE WE GOING TO THE **UPPER REGION**?
I JUST WANTED TO STIR THINGS UP A LITTLE. THAT'S ALL.

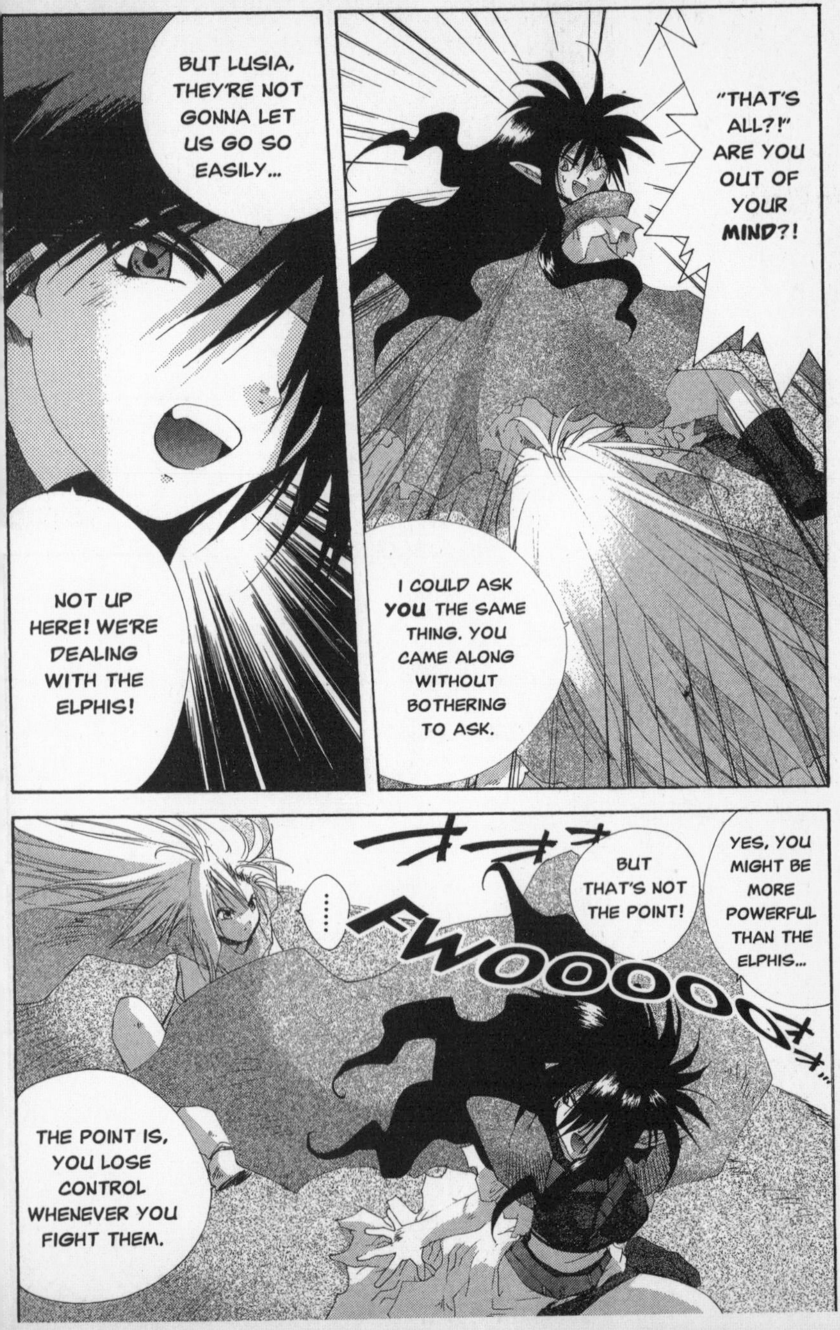
"THAT'S ALL?!" ARE YOU OUT OF YOUR MIND?!
I COULD ASK YOU THE SAME THING. YOU CAME ALONG WITHOUT BOTHERING TO ASK.
BUT LUSIA, THEY'RE NOT GONNA LET US GO SO EASILY...
NOT UP HERE! WE'RE DEALING WITH THE ELPHIS!
YES, YOU MIGHT BE MORE POWERFUL THAN THE ELPHIS...
BUT THAT'S NOT THE POINT!
......
FWOOOOOO
THE POINT IS, YOU LOSE CONTROL WHENEVER YOU FIGHT THEM.

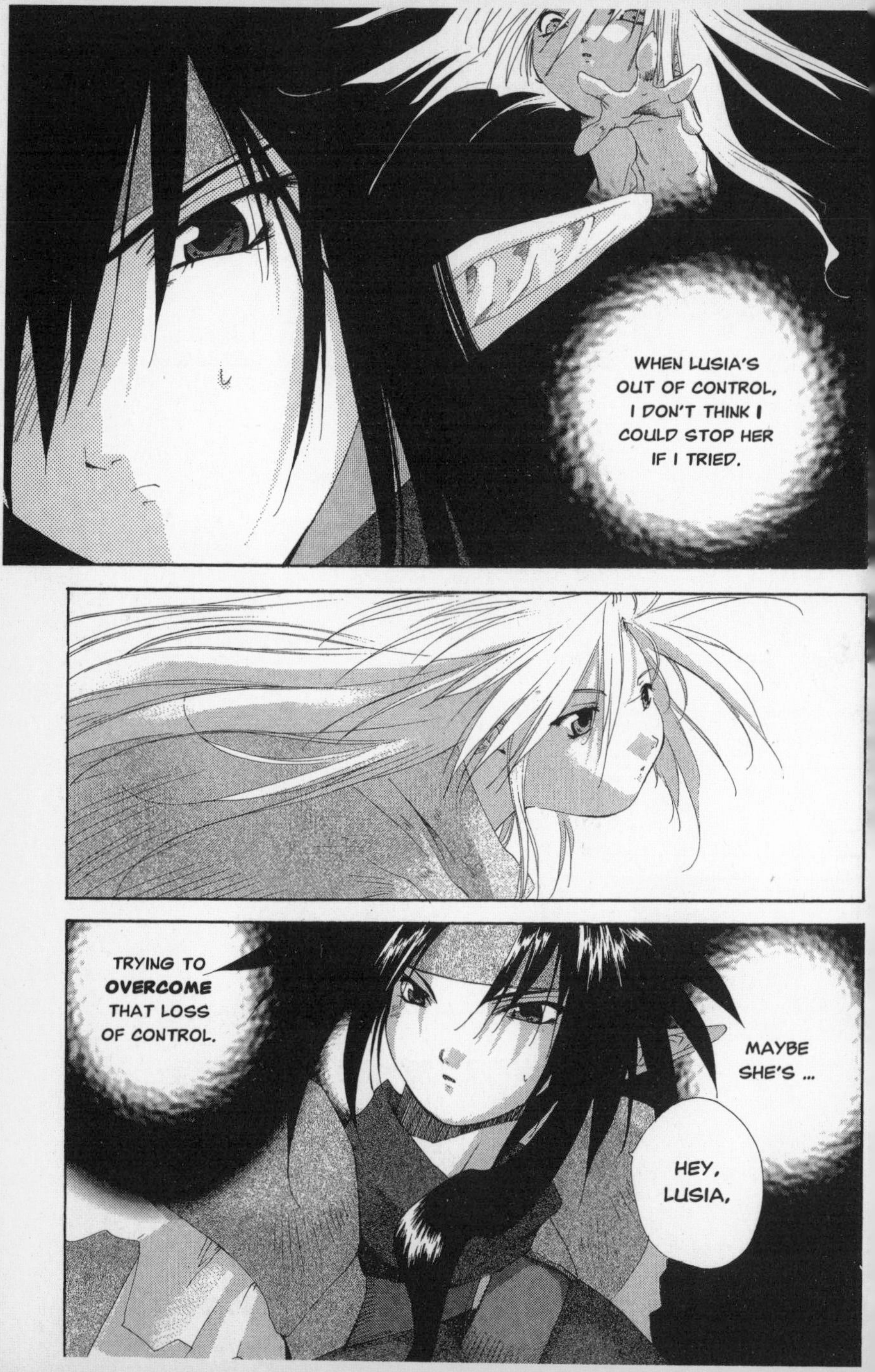
WHEN LUSIA'S OUT OF CONTROL, I DON'T THINK I COULD STOP HER IF I TRIED.
MAYBE SHE'S ...
TRYING TO **OVERCOME** THAT LOSS OF CONTROL.
HEY, LUSIA,

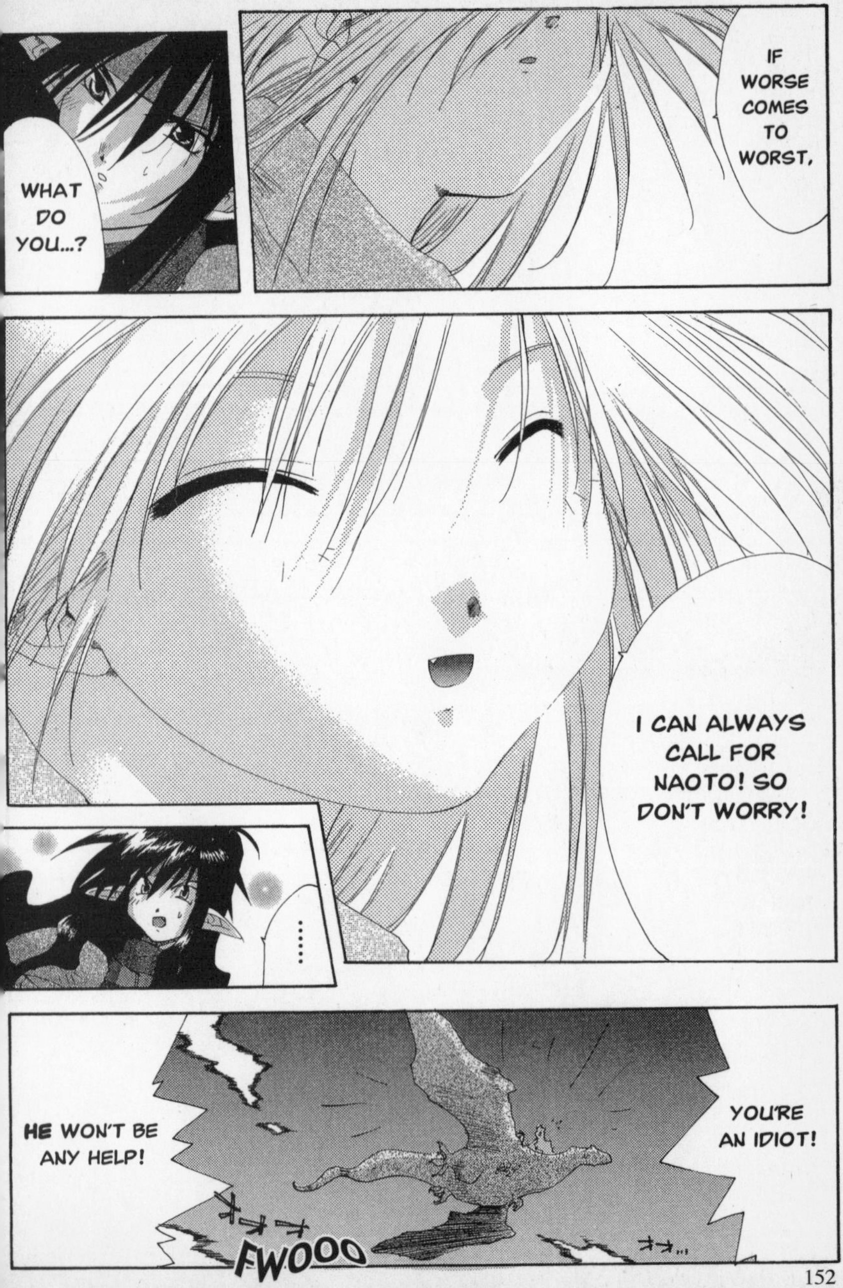
IF WORSE COMES TO WORST,
WHAT DO YOU...?
I CAN ALWAYS CALL FOR NAOTO! SO DON'T WORRY!
......
YOU'RE AN IDIOT!
HE WON'T BE ANY HELP!
FWOOO

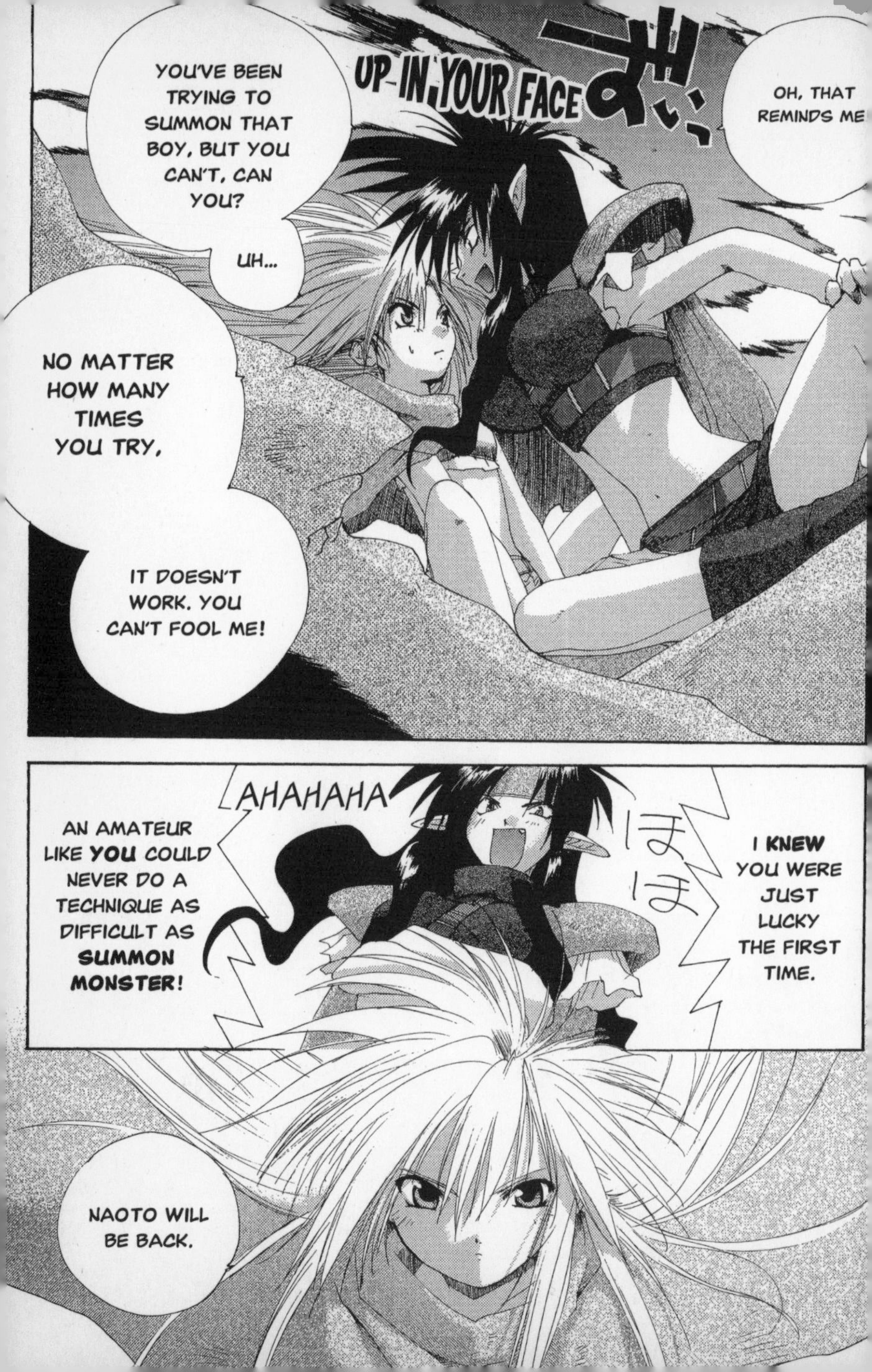
OH, THAT REMINDS ME
UP-IN-YOUR FACE
YOU'VE BEEN TRYING TO SUMMON THAT BOY, BUT YOU CAN'T, CAN YOU?
UH...
NO MATTER HOW MANY TIMES YOU TRY,
IT DOESN'T WORK. YOU CAN'T FOOL ME!
AHAHAHA
ほほ
I **KNEW** YOU WERE JUST LUCKY THE FIRST TIME.
AN AMATEUR LIKE **YOU** COULD NEVER DO A TECHNIQUE AS DIFFICULT AS **SUMMON MONSTER**!
NAOTO WILL BE BACK.

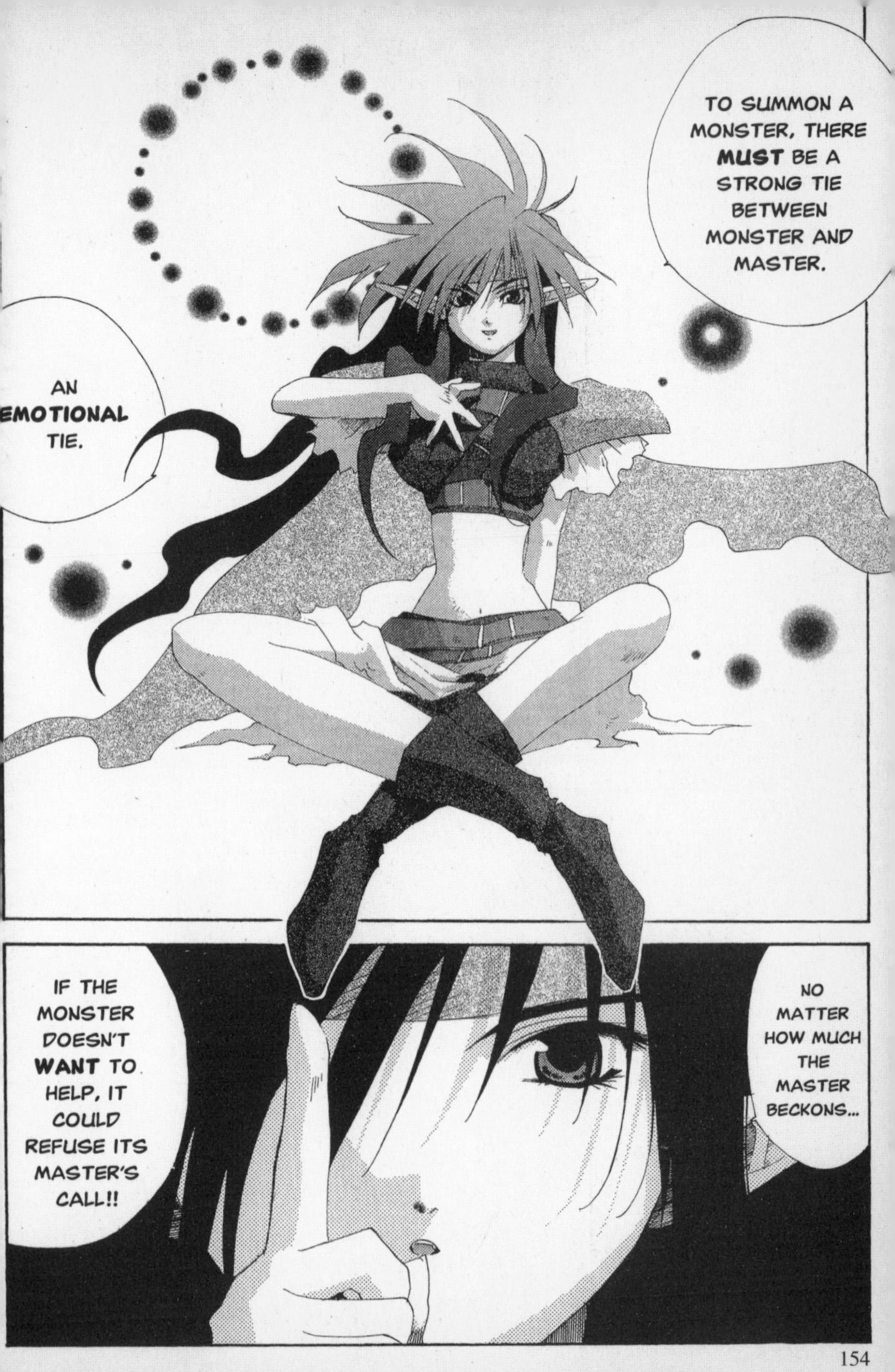
TO SUMMON A MONSTER, THERE **MUST** BE A STRONG TIE BETWEEN MONSTER AND MASTER.
AN **EMOTIONAL** TIE.
NO MATTER HOW MUCH THE MASTER BECKONS...
IF THE MONSTER DOESN'T **WANT** TO HELP, IT COULD REFUSE ITS MASTER'S CALL!!

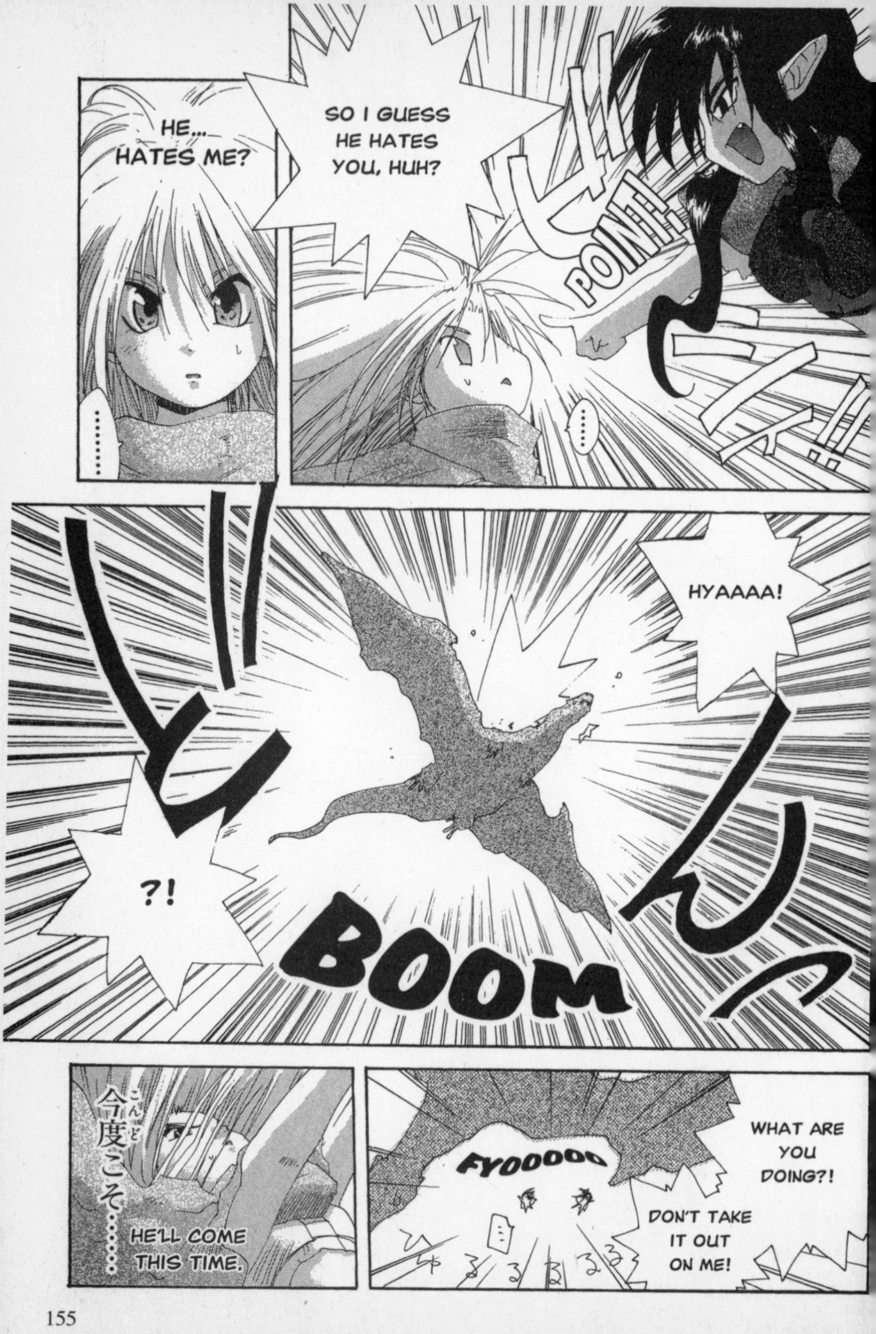
SO I GUESS HE HATES YOU, HUH?
POINT!!
...
HE... HATES ME?
......
HYAAAA!
?!
BOOM
WHAT ARE YOU DOING?!
FYOOOOO
DON'T TAKE IT OUT ON ME!
今度こそ……
HE'LL COME THIS TIME.

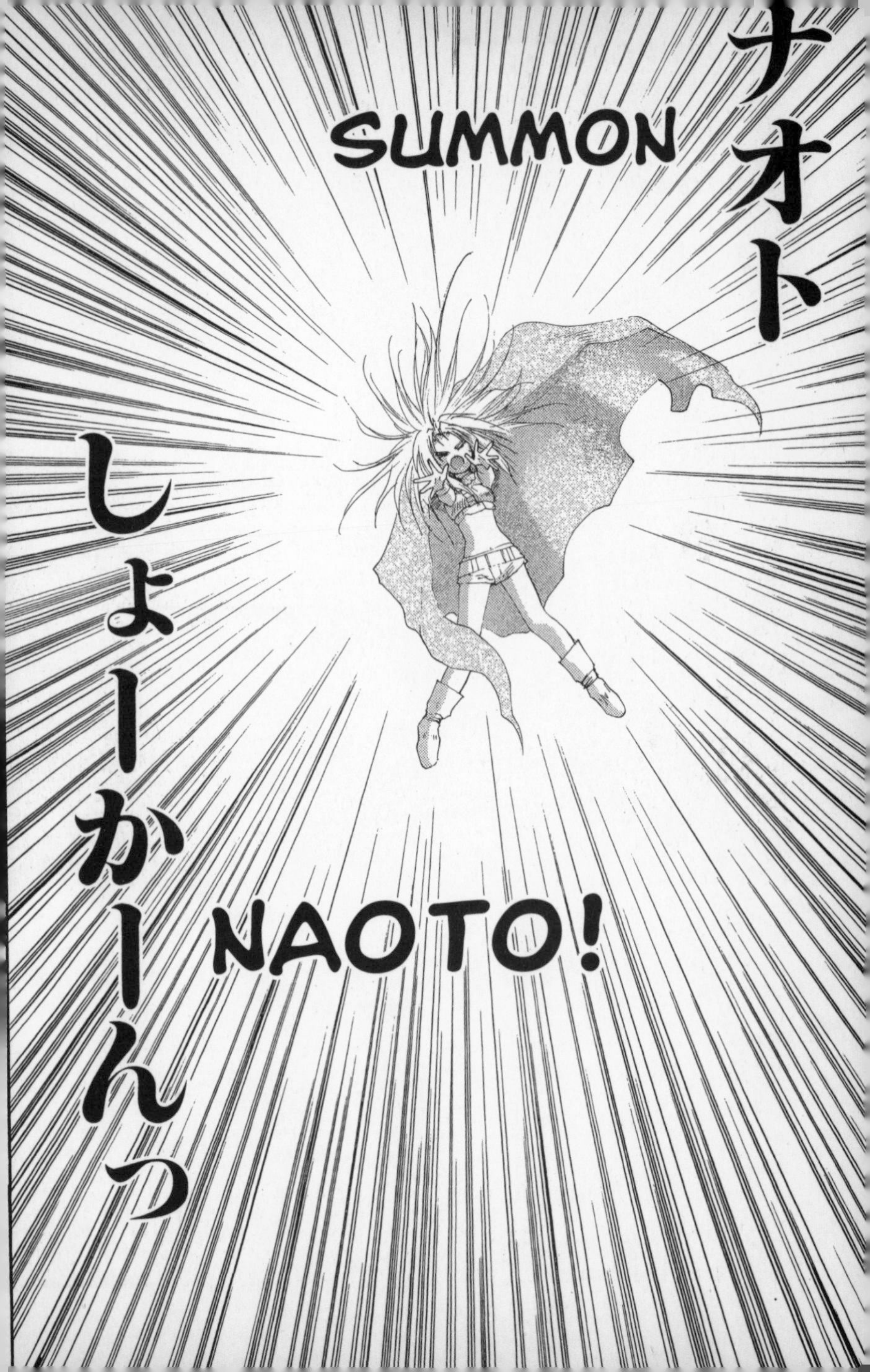
ナオト
SUMMON
しょーかーんっ
NAOTO!

WOOOO
FWWOOOO
WHERE IN THE HECK...
とぼとぼ
TRUDGE TRUDGE
はー
SIGH
AM I?

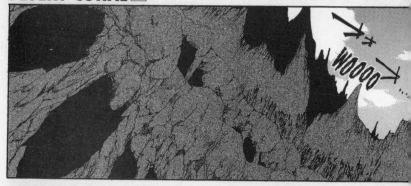

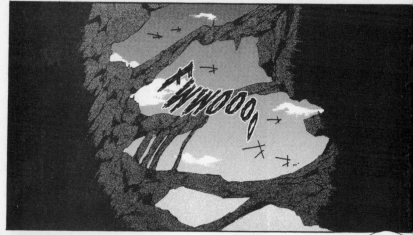

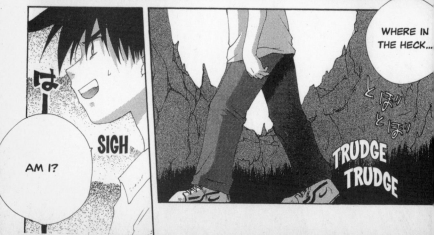

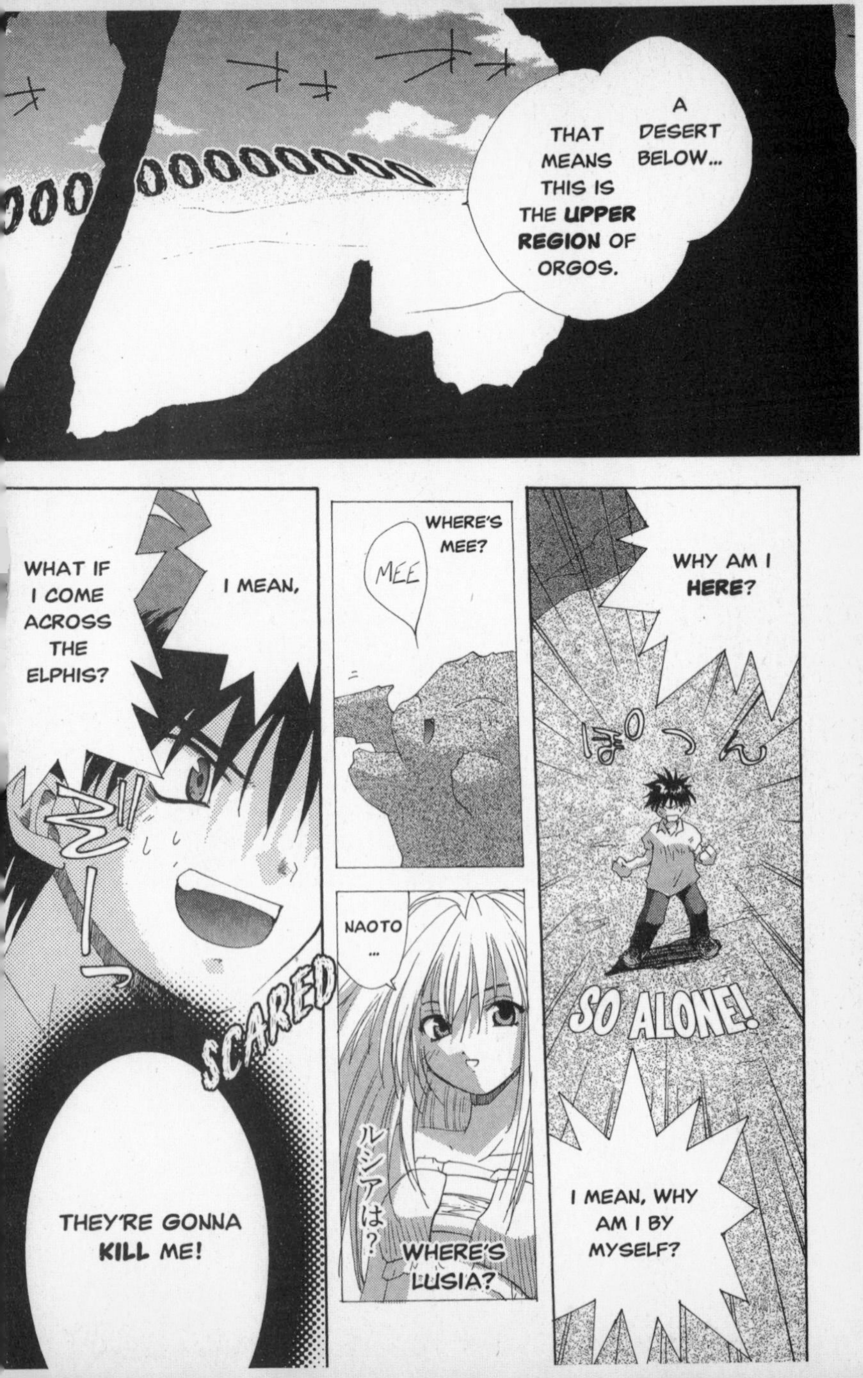

オオオオ
OOOOOOOOOOOOO
A DESERT BELOW...
THAT MEANS THIS IS THE **UPPER REGION** OF ORGOS.
WHY AM I **HERE**?
ぽつん
SO ALONE!
I MEAN, WHY AM I BY MYSELF?
WHERE'S MEE?
MEE
NAOTO ...
ルシアは？
WHERE'S LUSIA?
I MEAN,
WHAT IF I COME ACROSS THE ELPHIS?
SCARED
THEY'RE GONNA **KILL** ME!

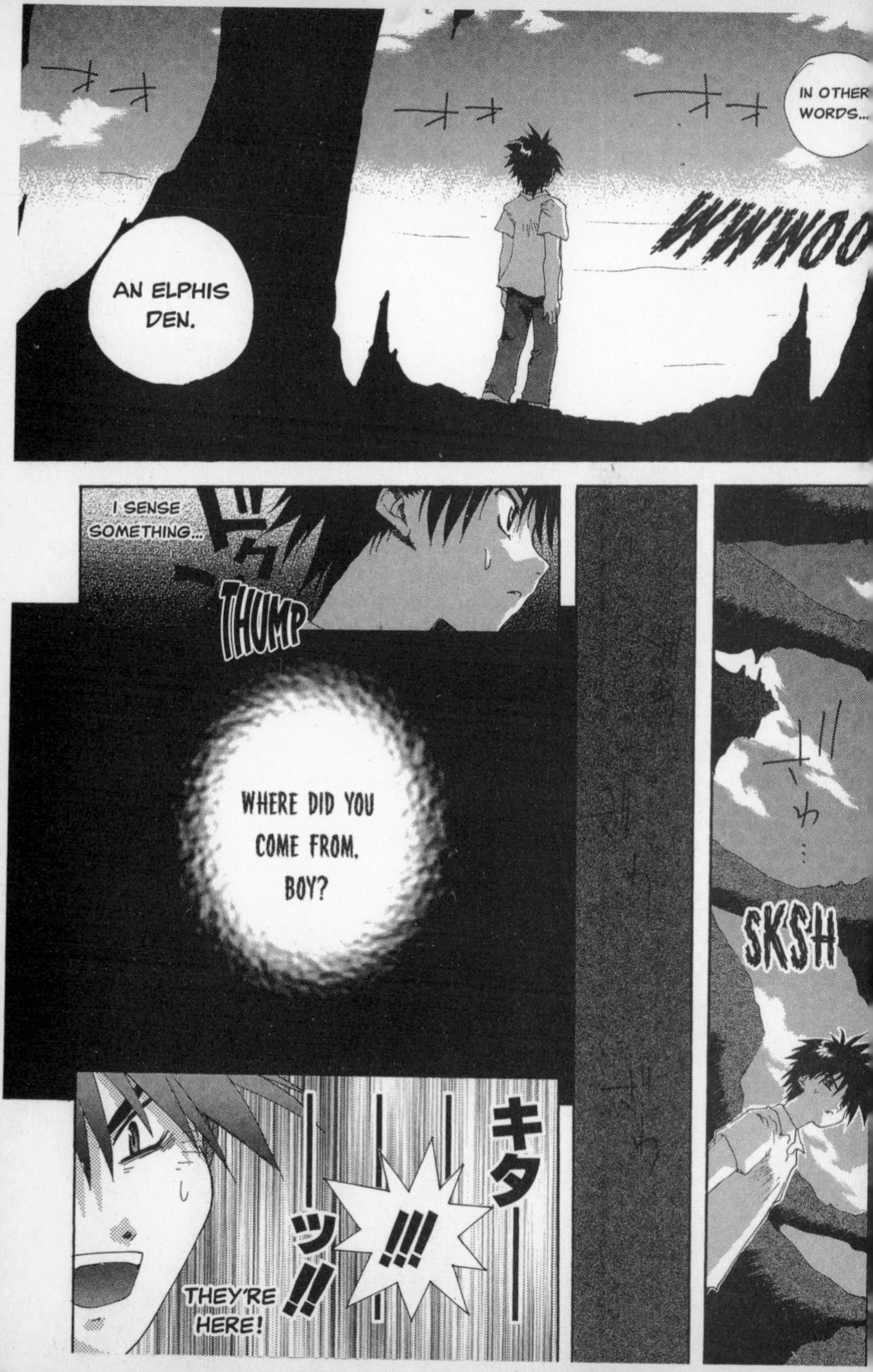
IN OTHER WORDS...
AN ELPHIS DEN.
SKSH
I SENSE SOMETHING...
THUMP
WHERE DID YOU COME FROM, BOY?
キターッ!!
!!!
THEY'RE HERE!

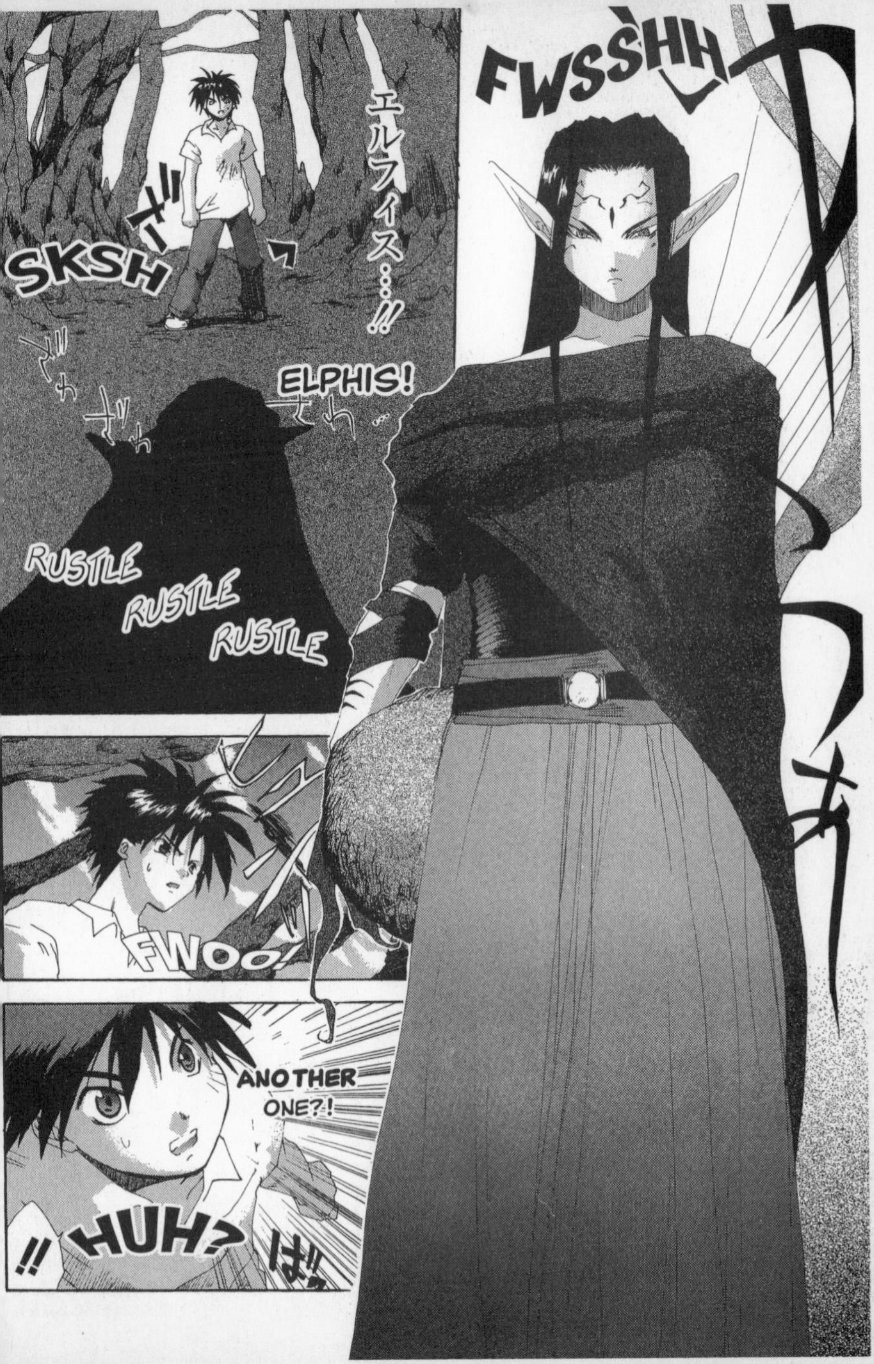
FWSSHH
エルフィス…!!
ELPHIS!
SKSH
RUSTLE
RUSTLE
RUSTLE
FWOO!
ANOTHER ONE?!
HUH?
!!
は!!

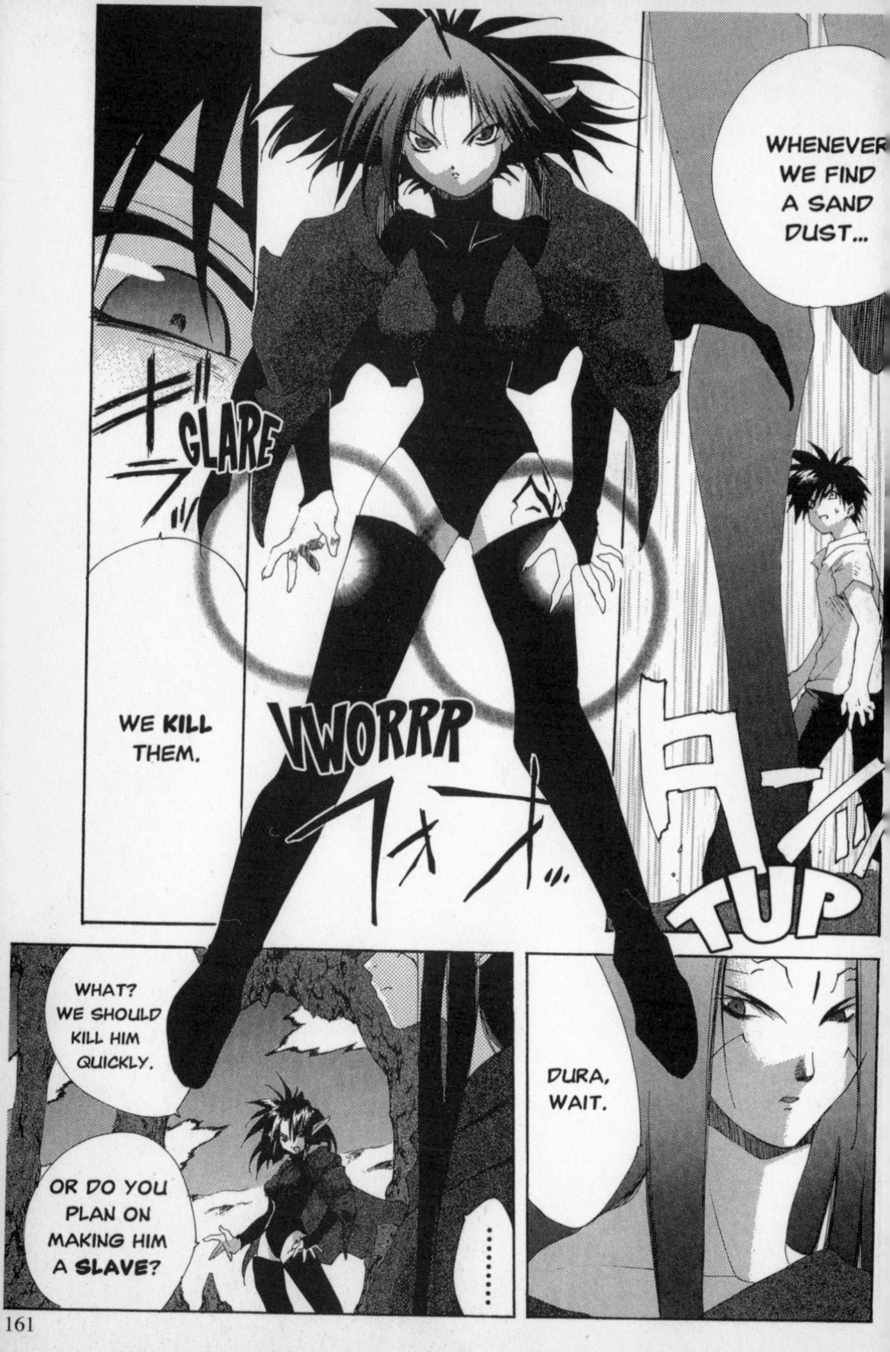

WHENEVER WE FIND A SAND DUST...
TUP
VWORRR
GLARE
WE KILL THEM.
DURA, WAIT.
WHAT? WE SHOULD KILL HIM QUICKLY.
OR DO YOU PLAN ON MAKING HIM A SLAVE?
......

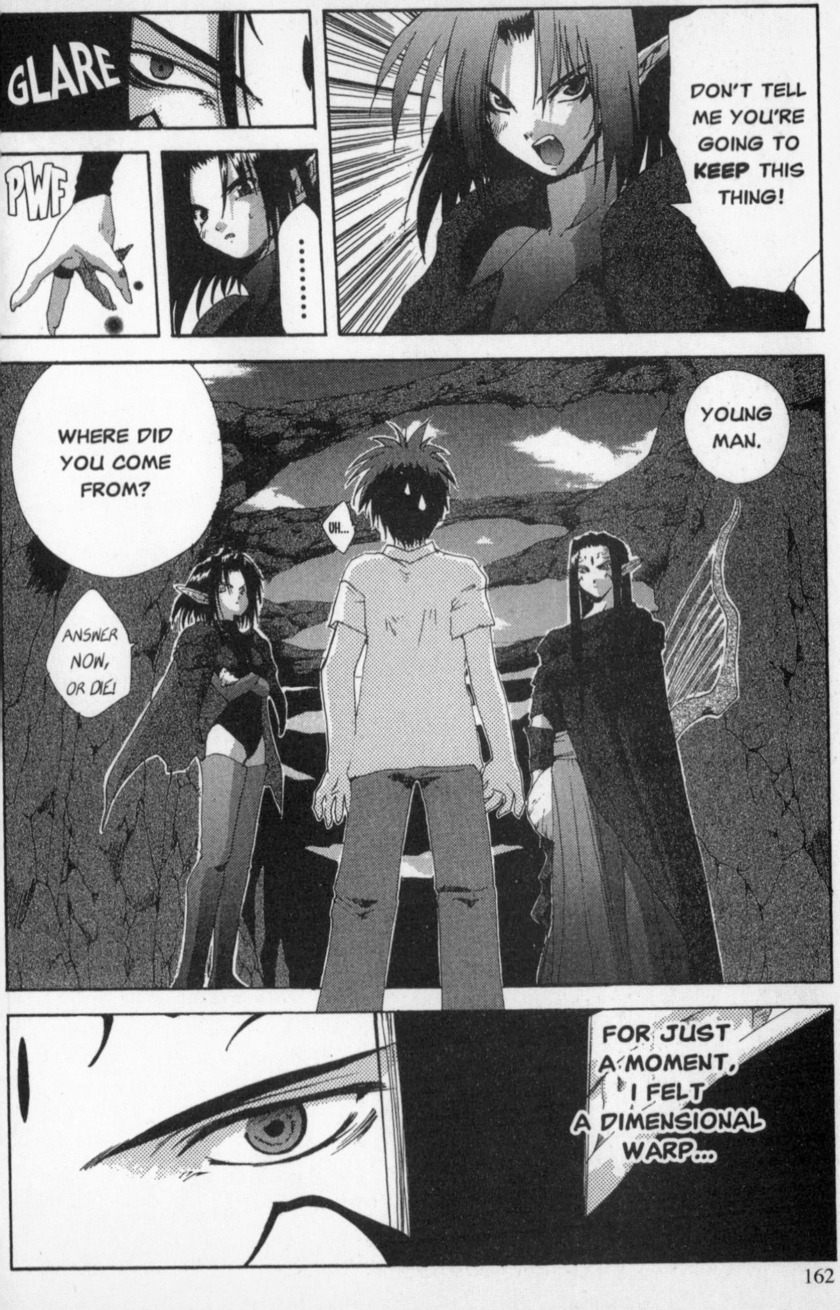
DON'T TELL ME YOU'RE GOING TO KEEP THIS THING!
GLARE
....
PWF
YOUNG MAN.
WHERE DID YOU COME FROM?
UH...
ANSWER NOW, OR DIE!
FOR JUST A MOMENT, I FELT A DIMENSIONAL WARP...

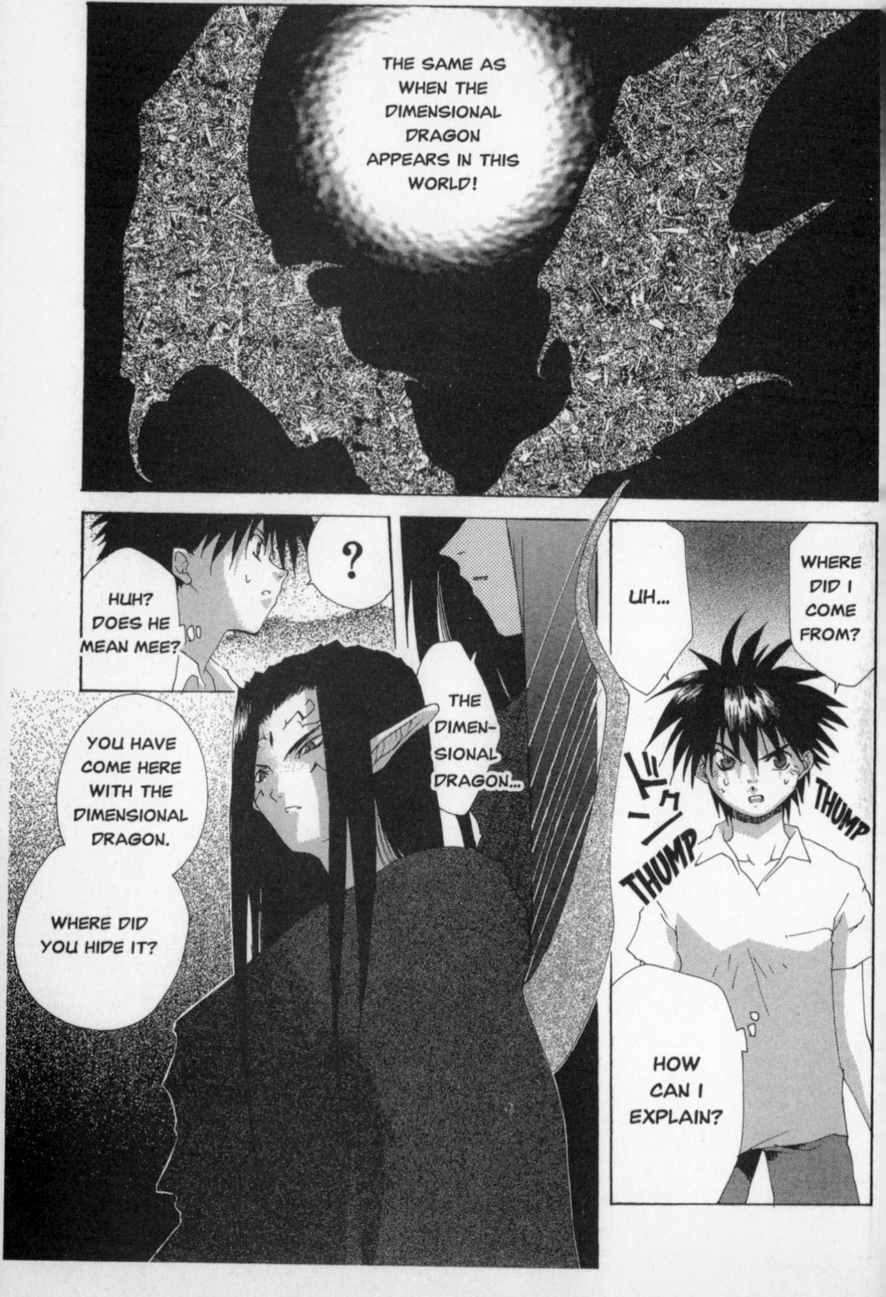
THE SAME AS WHEN THE DIMENSIONAL DRAGON APPEARS IN THIS WORLD!
WHERE DID I COME FROM?
UH...
THUMP
THUMP
HOW CAN I EXPLAIN?
?
HUH? DOES HE MEAN MEE?
THE DIMEN-SIONAL DRAGON...
YOU HAVE COME HERE WITH THE DIMENSIONAL DRAGON.
WHERE DID YOU HIDE IT?

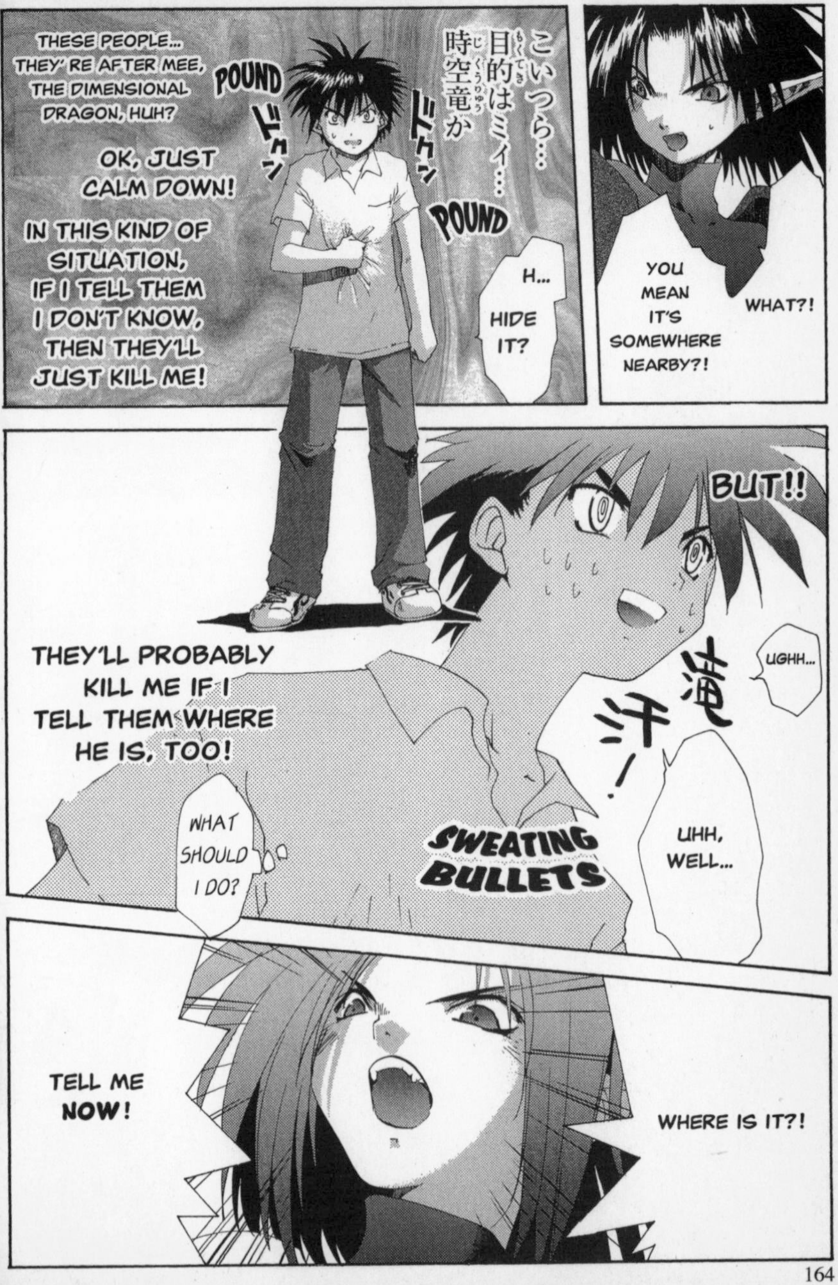
WHAT?!
YOU MEAN IT'S SOMEWHERE NEARBY?!
こいつら…目的はミィ…時空竜か
ドクン
POUND
ドクン
POUND
H... HIDE IT?
THESE PEOPLE... THEY' RE AFTER MEE, THE DIMENSIONAL DRAGON, HUH?
OK, JUST CALM DOWN!
IN THIS KIND OF SITUATION, IF I TELL THEM I DON'T KNOW, THEN THEY'LL JUST KILL ME!
BUT!!
UGHH...
滝汗!
UHH, WELL...
SWEATING BULLETS
THEY'LL PROBABLY KILL ME IF I TELL THEM WHERE HE IS, TOO!
WHAT SHOULD I DO?
WHERE IS IT?!
TELL ME NOW!

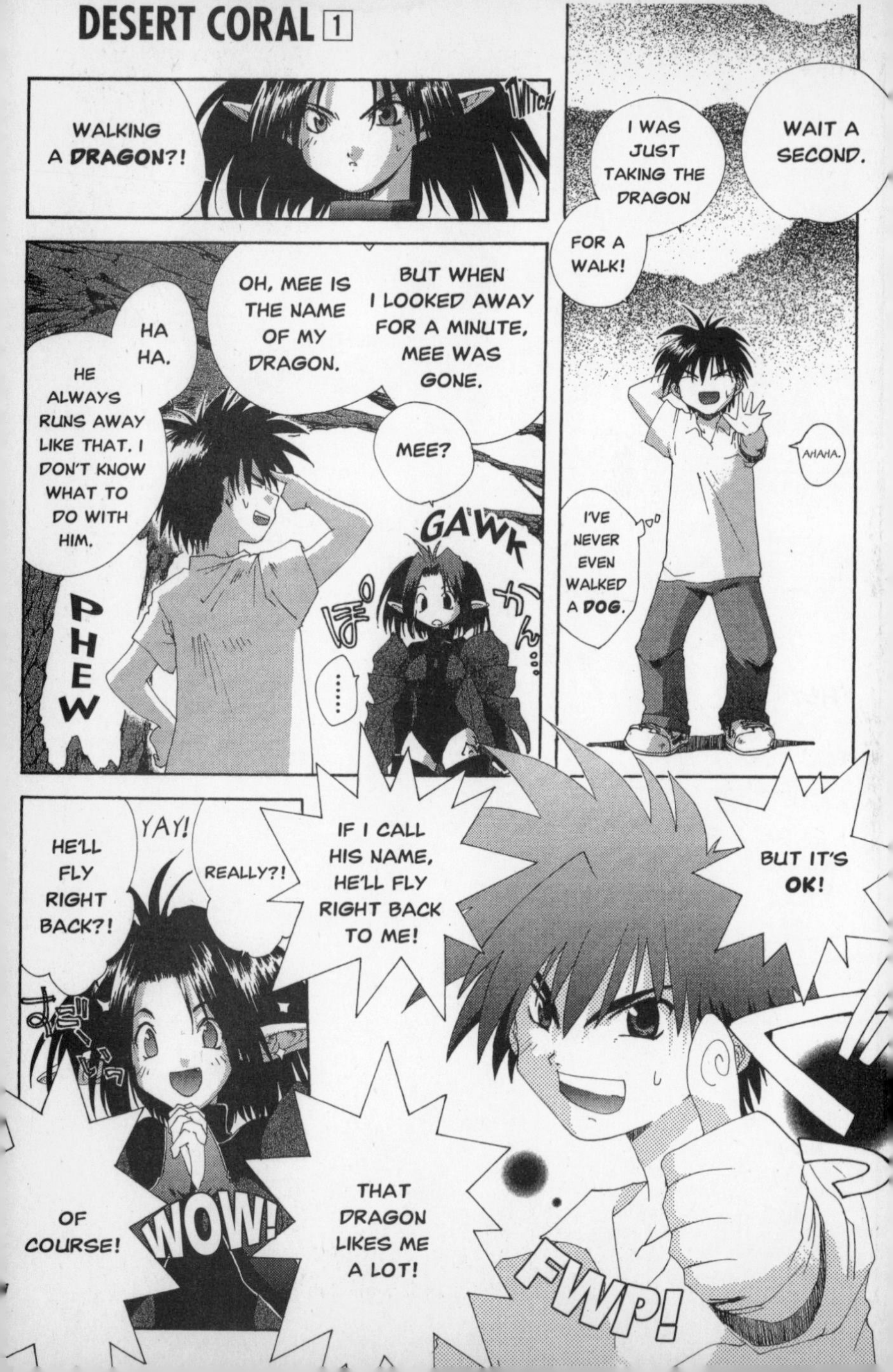
WAIT A SECOND.
I WAS JUST TAKING THE DRAGON
FOR A WALK!
AHAHA.
I'VE NEVER EVEN WALKED A DOG.
TWITCH
WALKING A **DRAGON**?!
BUT WHEN I LOOKED AWAY FOR A MINUTE, MEE WAS GONE.
OH, MEE IS THE NAME OF MY DRAGON.
HA HA.
HE ALWAYS RUNS AWAY LIKE THAT. I DON'T KNOW WHAT TO DO WITH HIM.
MEE?
GAWK
ぽかん…
......
PHEW
BUT IT'S **OK**!
IF I CALL HIS NAME, HE'LL FLY RIGHT BACK TO ME!
THAT DRAGON LIKES ME A LOT!
FWP!
YAY!
REALLY?!
HE'LL FLY RIGHT BACK?!
OF COURSE!
WOW!

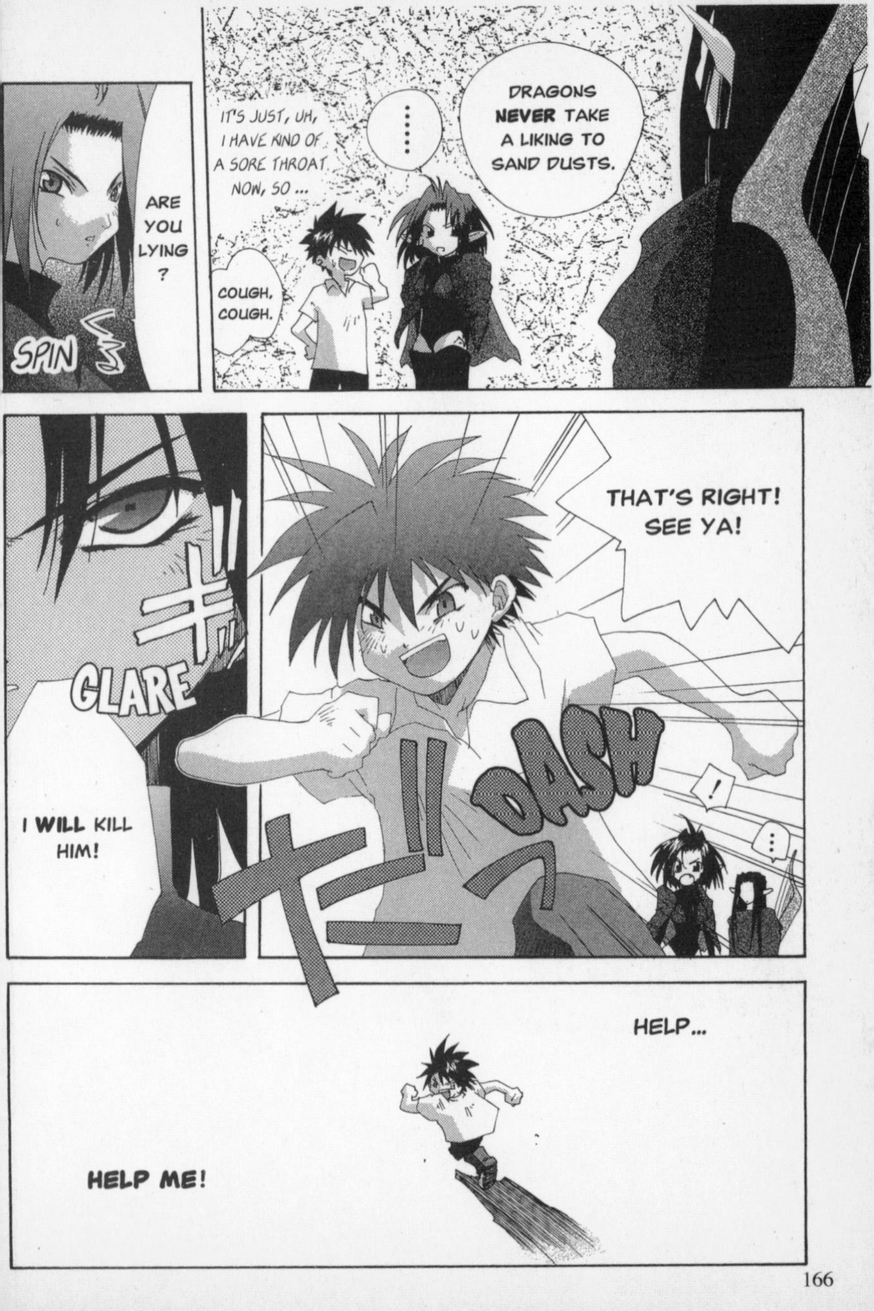
DRAGONS NEVER TAKE A LIKING TO SAND DUSTS.
......
IT'S JUST, UH, I HAVE KIND OF A SORE THROAT NOW, SO ...
COUGH, COUGH.
ARE YOU LYING?
SPIN
THAT'S RIGHT! SEE YA!
DASH
!
...
GLARE
I WILL KILL HIM!
HELP...
HELP ME!

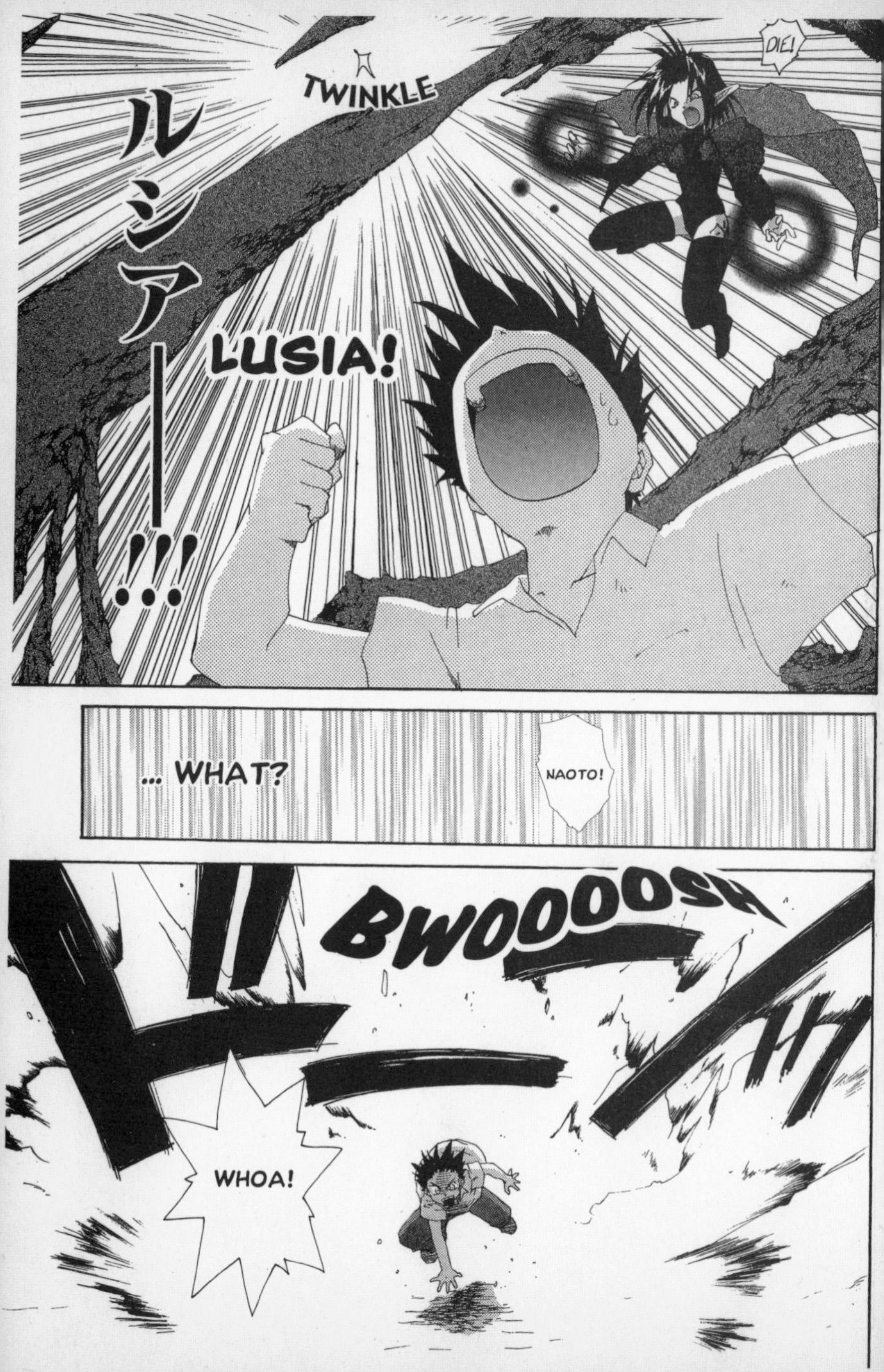
DIE!
TWINKLE
ルシアー!!!
LUSIA!
NAOTO!
... WHAT?
BWOOOOOSH
WHOA!

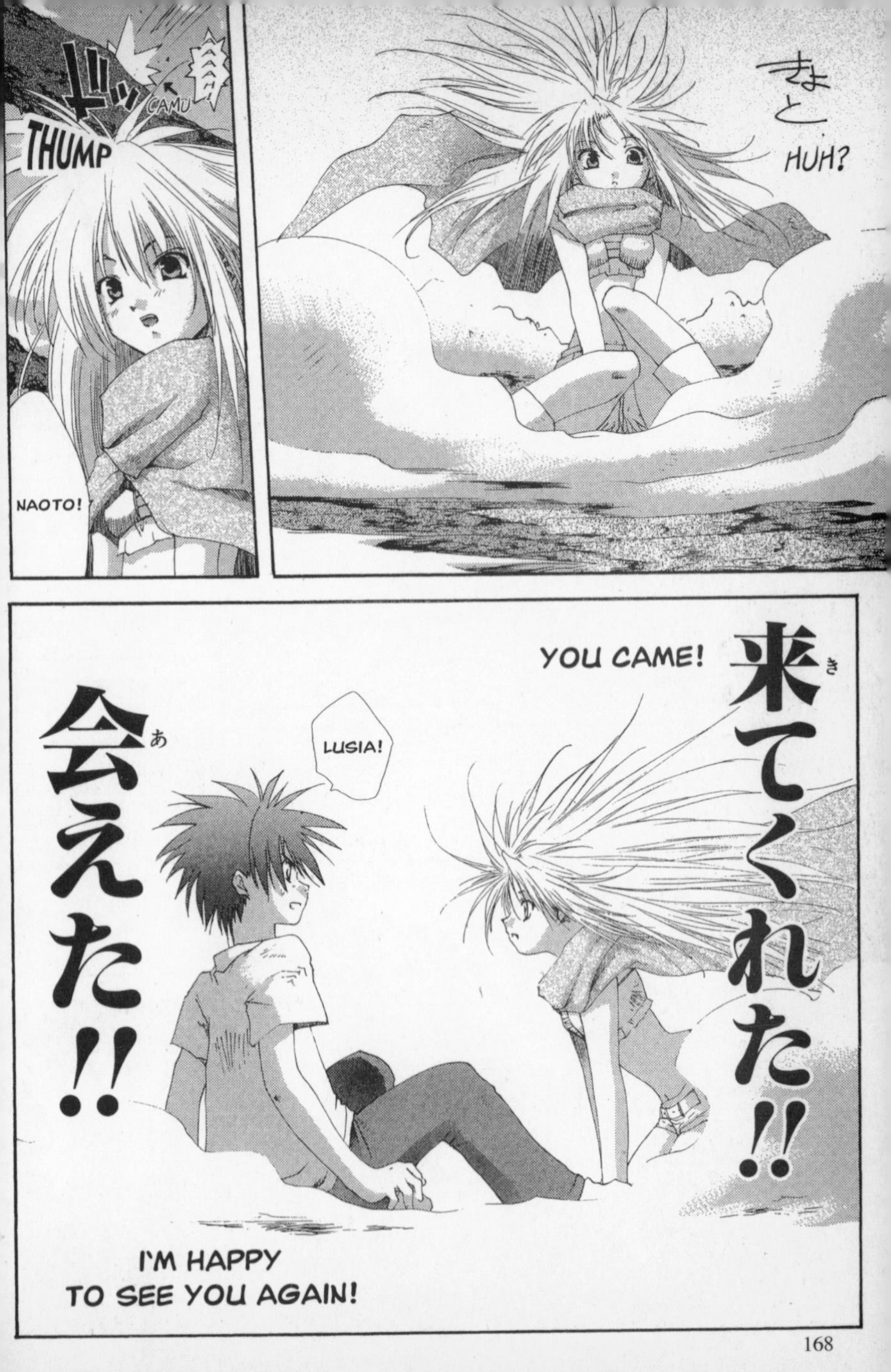
きょと
HUH?
ドッ
THUMP
CAMU
NAOTO!
YOU CAME!
来てくれた!!
LUSIA!
会えた!!
I'M HAPPY TO SEE YOU AGAIN!

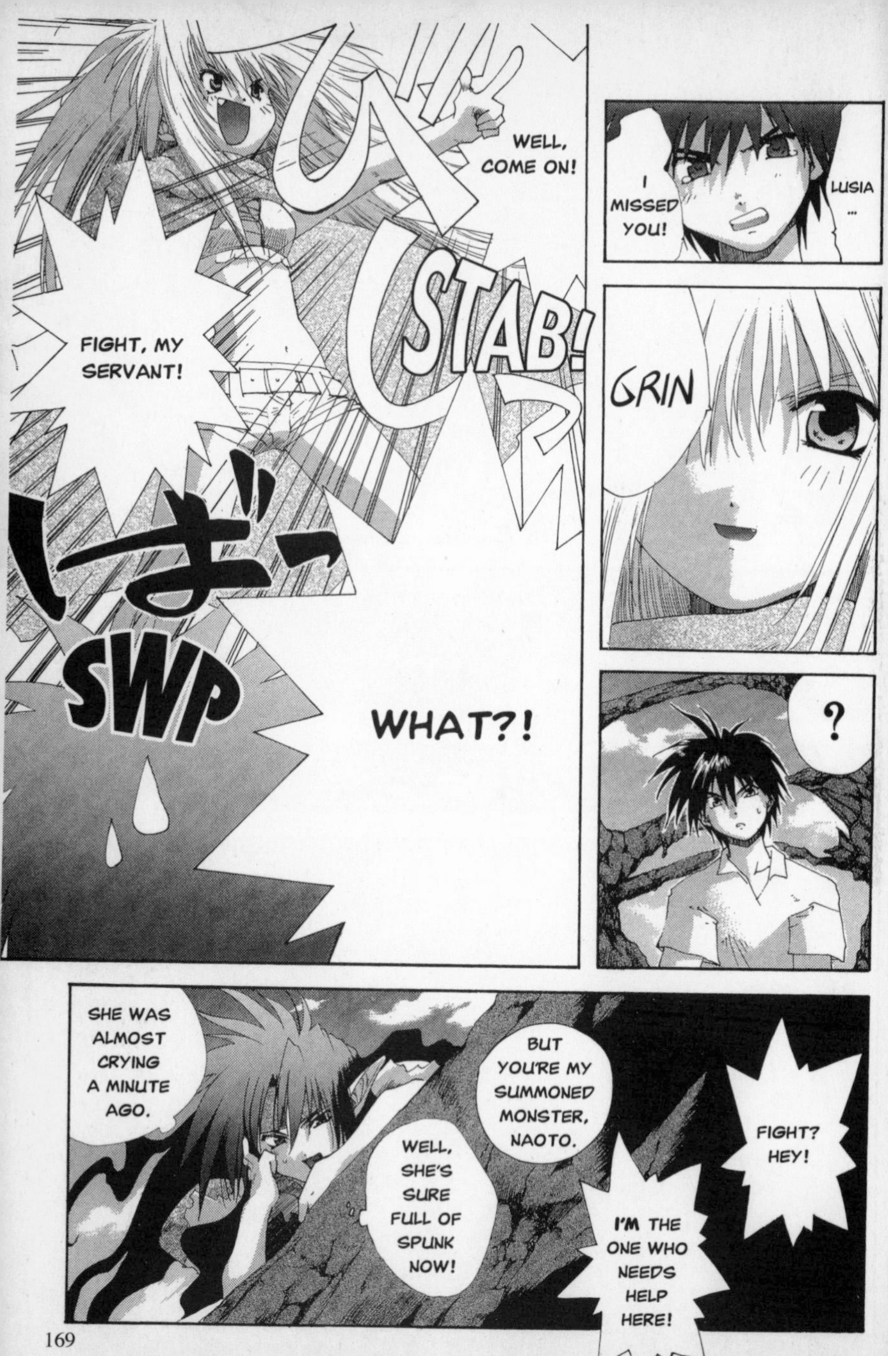
LUSIA ...
I MISSED YOU!
GRIN
?
WELL, COME ON!
STAB!
FIGHT, MY SERVANT!
SWP
WHAT?!
FIGHT? HEY!
I'M THE ONE WHO NEEDS HELP HERE!
BUT YOU'RE MY SUMMONED MONSTER, NAOTO.
WELL, SHE'S SURE FULL OF SPUNK NOW!
SHE WAS ALMOST CRYING A MINUTE AGO.

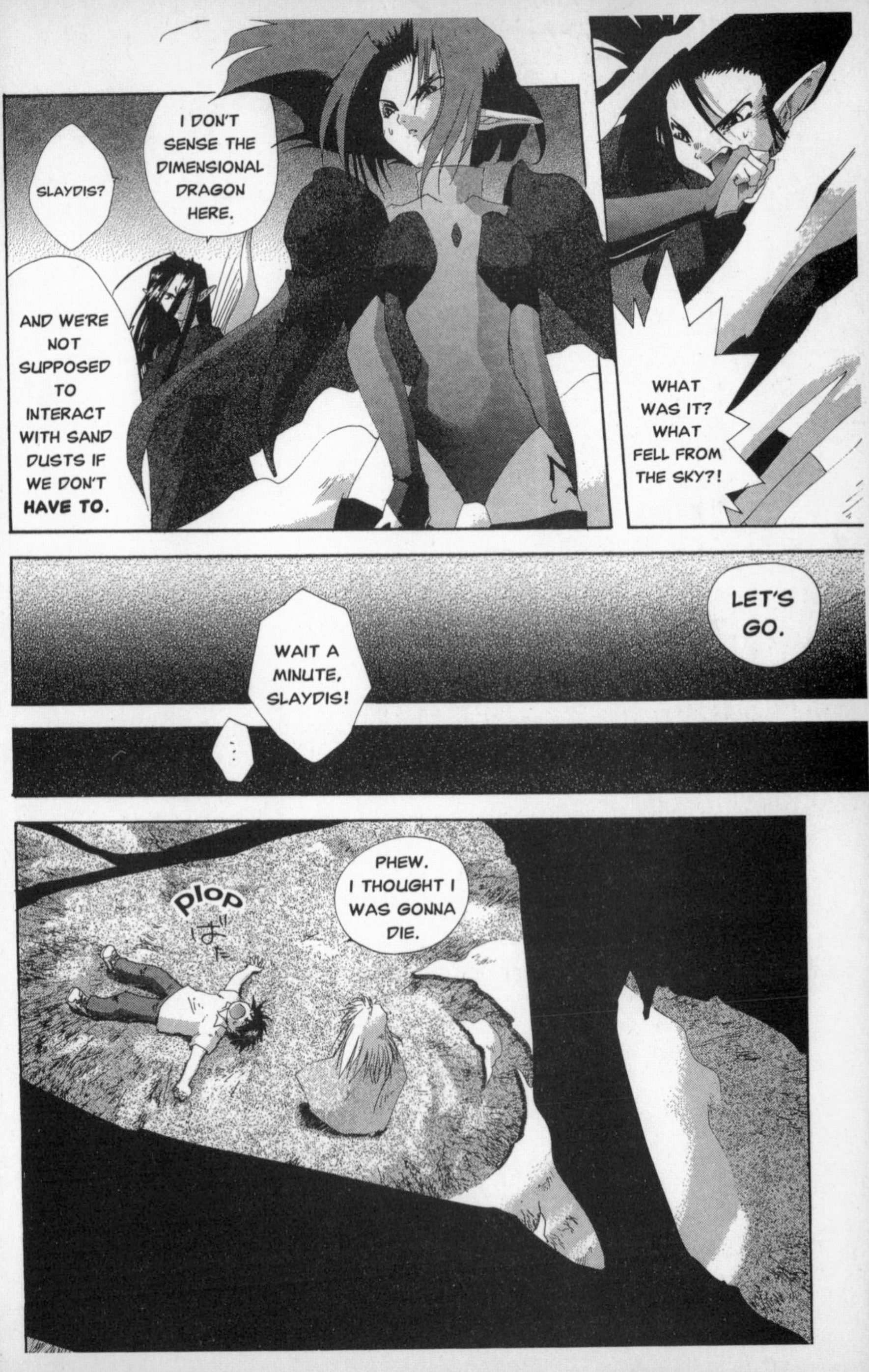
WHAT WAS IT? WHAT FELL FROM THE SKY?!
I DON'T SENSE THE DIMENSIONAL DRAGON HERE.
SLAYDIS?
AND WE'RE NOT SUPPOSED TO INTERACT WITH SAND DUSTS IF WE DON'T **HAVE TO**.
LET'S GO.
WAIT A MINUTE, SLAYDIS!
...
PHEW. I THOUGHT I WAS GONNA DIE.
plop
ばた

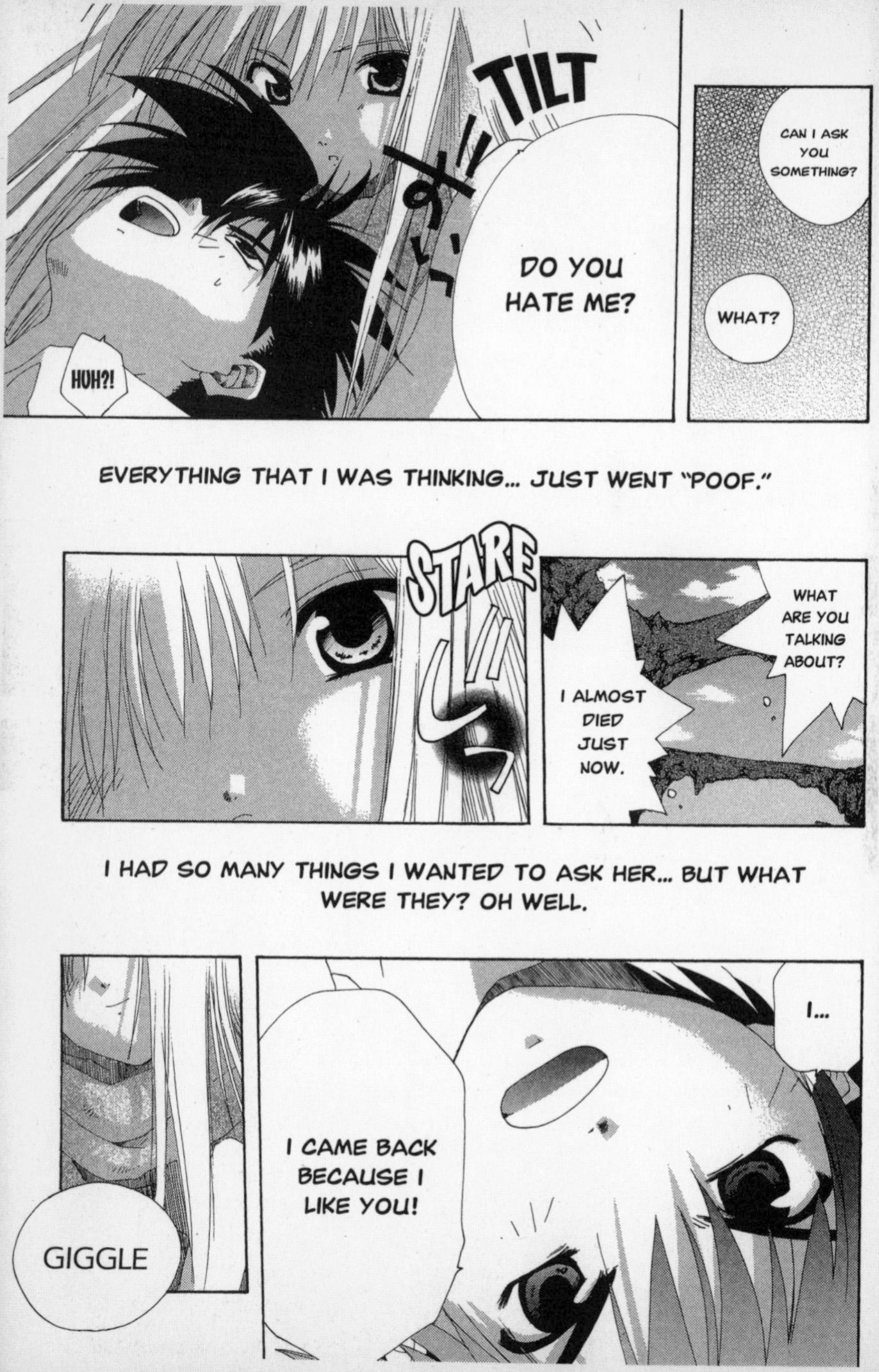
CAN I ASK YOU SOMETHING?
WHAT?
TILT
DO YOU HATE ME?
HUH?!
EVERYTHING THAT I WAS THINKING... JUST WENT "POOF."
WHAT ARE YOU TALKING ABOUT?
I ALMOST DIED JUST NOW.
STARE
I HAD SO MANY THINGS I WANTED TO ASK HER... BUT WHAT WERE THEY? OH WELL.
I...
I CAME BACK BECAUSE I LIKE YOU!
GIGGLE

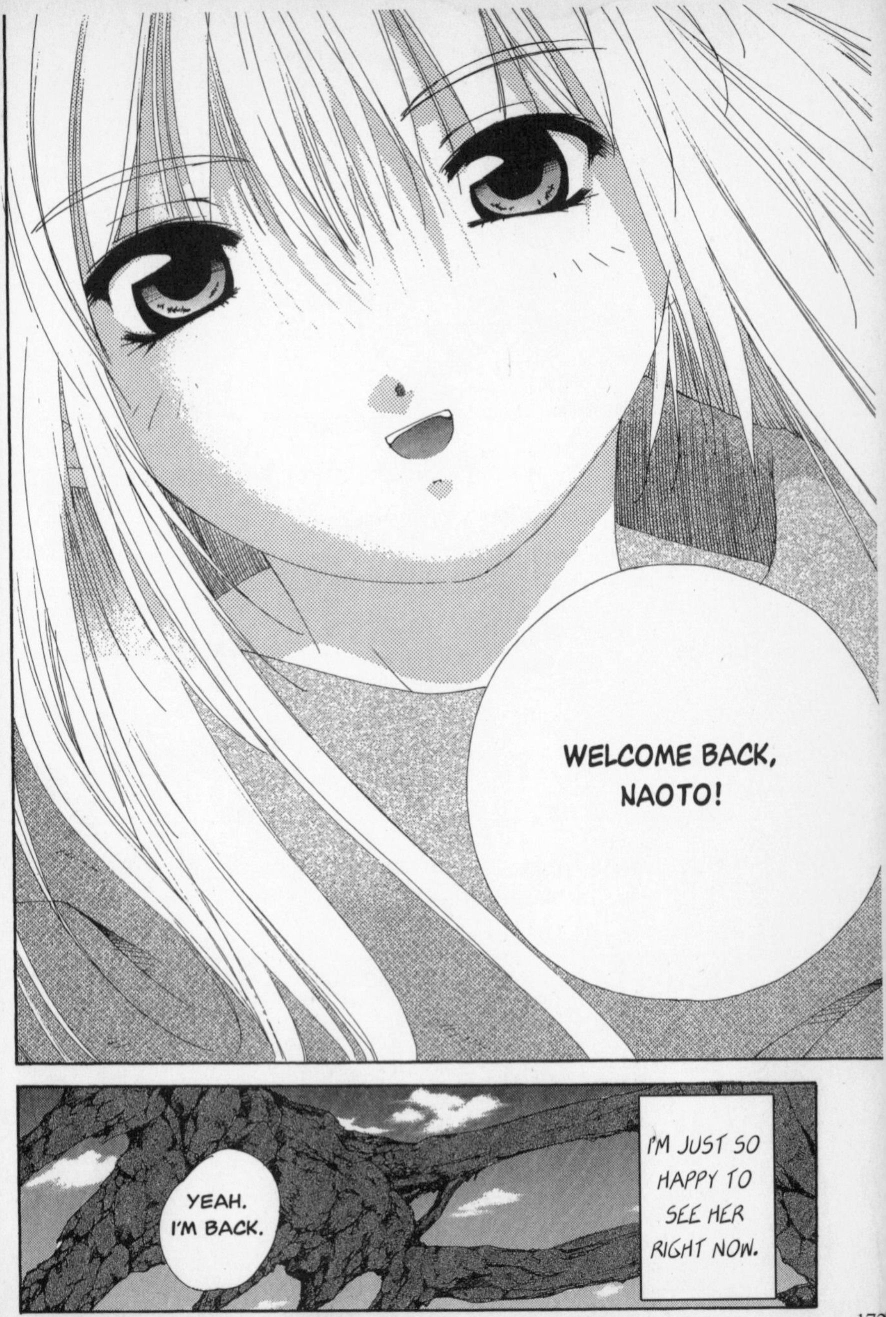
WELCOME BACK, NAOTO!
I'M JUST SO HAPPY TO SEE HER RIGHT NOW.
YEAH. I'M BACK.

DESERT CORAL 1 END

"ANYTHING GOES" CHARACTER DESIGN
CAST OF CHARACTERS (THE REAL WORLD)

NAOTO SAKI

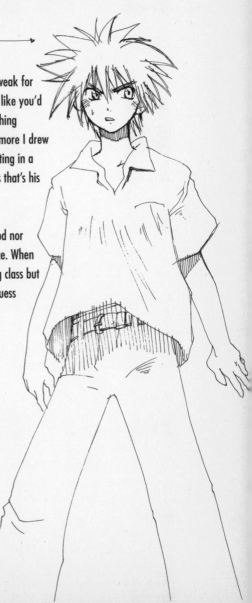

The main character of this manga
(well, he's supposed to be). He's pretty weak for
a protagonist. Naoto's just a regular kid like you'd
find anywhere, so I didn't give him anything
distinctive as far as looks... Except the more I drew
him, I realized that I was sometimes putting in a
furrow between his eyebrows. So I guess that's his
distinctive characteristic!

Naoto's grades at school are neither good nor
bad, just average. He's not bad at science. When
you consider he's always sleeping during class but
still manages to get average grades, I guess
he's actually rather smart.
He's pretty athletic, too—he runs fast
(and often).

He only has a couple of friends, and he
borrows notes from them for class. He
doesn't have as many friends as
it might seem.

Chisato is his childhood friend.

His hobby is sleeping.

CHISATO SHINO

Wow! Her last name is finally revealed! I hadn't even decided her first name until after a few installments.

As far as her appearance goes, I don't have many ideas. The only thing is that she's wearing long sleeves all the time for some reason.

Chisato is Naoto's childhood friend, but not his girlfriend. They went to the same elementary and junior high school together. She's a lot smarter than Naoto, but she went to the same high school so she could be with him.

Chisato is in the art, literature and drama clubs. She's an outstanding student who's good at both athletics and academics (unlike Naoto she has multiple talents). On top of that, she likes taking care of people. She has the potential to be popular, but since she's quiet she doesn't stand out very much in the classroom.

She has a strong sense of justice, and she's mature.

Ah, now **this** one is more like a main character...

DESERT CORAL VOLUME ONE

© WATARU MURAYAMA 2002
All rights reserved.
First published in 2002 by Mag Garden Co., Ltd., Tokyo, Japan.
English translation rights arranged with Mag Garden Co., Ltd.

Translator	**TOMOE SPENCER**
Lead Translator/Translation Supervisor	**JAVIER LOPEZ**
ADV Manga Translation Staff	**KAY BERTRAND, AMY FORSYTH, BRENDAN FRAYNE, EIKO McGREGOR**
Print Production/ Art Studio Manager	**LISA PUCKETT**
Pre-press Manager	**ERNIE ZUNIGA**
Art Production Manager	**RYAN MASON**
Sr. Designer/Creative Manager	**JORGE ALVARADO**
Graphic Designer/Group Leader	**SHANNON RASBERRY**
Graphic Designer	**NANAKO TSUKIHASHI**
Graphic Artists	**CHRIS LAPP, KRISTINA MILESKI, NATALIA MORALES, LANCE SWARTOUT**
Graphic Intern	**MARK MEZA**
International Coordinator	**TORU IWAKAMI**
International Coordinator	**ATSUSHI KANBAYASHI**
Publishing Editor	**SUSAN ITIN**
Assistant Editor	**MARGARET SCHAROLD**
Editorial Assistant	**VARSHA BHUCHAR**
Proofreader	**SHERIDAN JACOBS**
Research/ Traffic Coordinator	**MARSHA ARNOLD**
Excecutive, V.P., C.F.O, C.O.O	**KEVIN CORCORAN**
President, C.E.O & Publisher	**JOHN LEDFORD**

Email: editor@adv-manga.com
www.adv-manga.com
www.advfilms.com

For sales and distribution inquiries please call 1.800.282.7202

ADV MANGA™ is a division of A.D. Vision, Inc.
10114 W. Sam Houston Parkway, Suite 200, Houston, Texas 77099
English text © 2004 published by A.D. Vision, Inc. under exclusive license.
ADV MANGA is a trademark of A.D. Vision, Inc.

ISBN: 1-4139-0050-X
First printing, May 2004
10 9 8 7 6 5 4 3 2
Printed in Canada

THE ADVENTURE CONTINUES IN
DESERT CORAL
VOL.02

Naoto's fantastical dreamland has turned into an obsession. Once again, he returns to the magical and threatening world of Orgos, only to face the challenges of a place disturbed by violent unrest. Naoto, Lusia and the others continue to battle the evil Elphis, but Naoto's new friends have also become a source of problems. Camu spends most of her time with a bottle of booze and Lusia is on the verge of a meltdown, due to the constant pressures of her inner voice, Lucavifate, to kill the Elphis. Fantasy and reality intertwine as Naoto continues to struggle with his magical training, but he may risk more than he originally thought, especially if he projects his powers in the wrong direction— like, at himself!

COMING AUGUST 2004 FROM ADV MANGA

www.adv-manga.com

LETTER FROM THE ADV MANGA TRANSLATION STAFF

Dear Reader,

On behalf of the ADV Manga translation team, thank you for purchasing an ADV book. We are enthusiastic and committed to our work, and strive to carry our enthusiasm over into the book you hold in your hands.

Our goal is to retain the true spirit of the original Japanese book. While great care has been taken to render a true and accurate translation, some cultural or readability issues may require a line to be adapted for greater accessibility to our readers. At times, manga titles that include culturally-specific concepts will feature a "Translator's Notes" section, which explains noteworthy references to the original text.

We hope our commitment to a faithful translation is evident in every ADV book you purchase.

Sincerely,

Javier Lopez
Lead Translator

Eiko McGregor

Kay Bertrand

Brendan Frayne

Amy Forsyth

ADV Manga™
www.adv-manga.com

LETTTER FROM THE EDITOR

Dear Reader,

Thank you for purchasing an ADV Manga book. We hope you enjoyed the journey into Naoto's magical world in this thrilling tale, *Desert Coral*.

It is our sincere commitment in reproducing Asian comics and graphic novels to retain as much of the character of the original book as possible. From the right-to-left format of the Japanese books to the meaning of the story in the original language, the ADV Manga team is working hard to publish a quality book for our fans and readers. Write to us with your questions or comments, and tell us how you liked this and other ADV books. Be sure to visit our website at www.adv-manga.com and view the list of upcoming titles, sign up for special announcements, and fill out our survey.

The ADV Manga team of translators, designers, graphic artists, production managers, traffic managers, and editors hope you will buy more ADV books–there's a lot more in store from ADV Manga!

ADV MANGA™
www.adv-manga.com

Publishing Editor	Assistant Editor	Editorial Assistant
Susan B. Itin	Margaret Scharold	Varsha Bhuchar
Susan Itin	Margaret Scharold	VaBhu

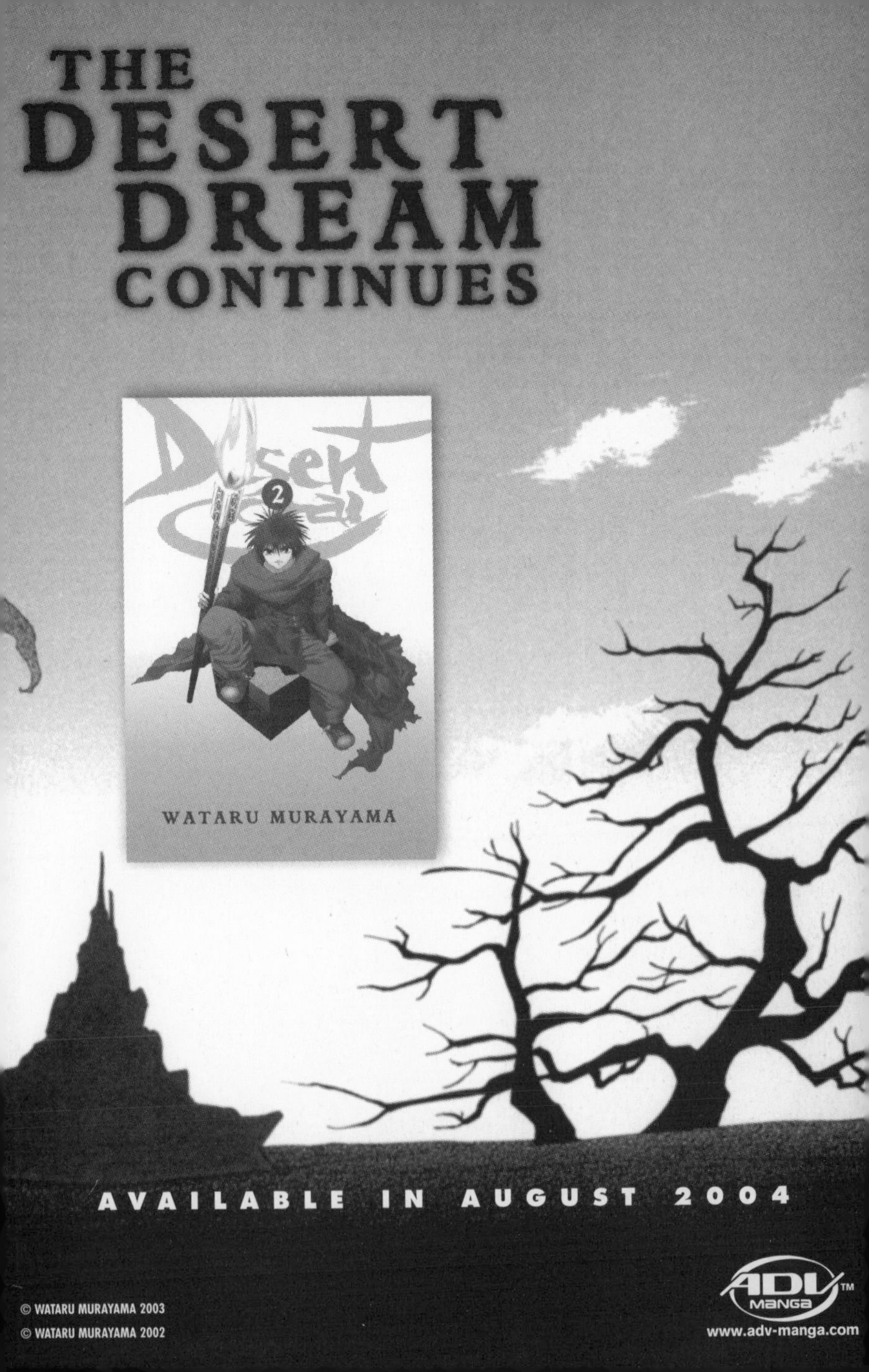
THE DESERT DREAM CONTINUES
2
WATARU MURAYAMA
AVAILABLE IN AUGUST 2004
© WATARU MURAYAMA 2003
© WATARU MURAYAMA 2002
ADV Manga™
www.adv-manga.com

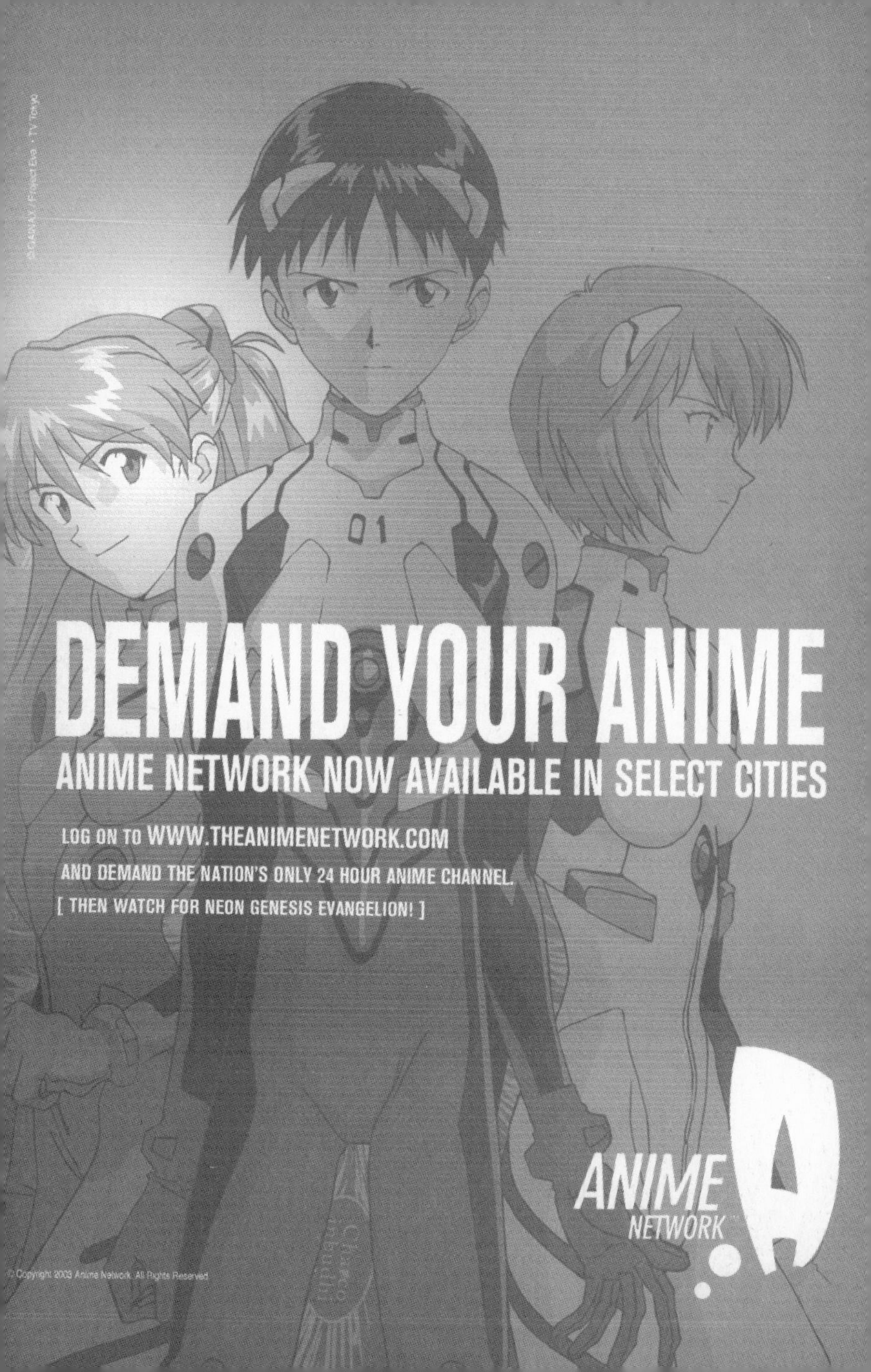
DEMAND YOUR ANIME
ANIME NETWORK NOW AVAILABLE IN SELECT CITIES
LOG ON TO WWW.THEANIMENETWORK.COM
AND DEMAND THE NATION'S ONLY 24 HOUR ANIME CHANNEL.
[THEN WATCH FOR NEON GENESIS EVANGELION!]
ANIME NETWORK
© Copyright 2003 Anime Network. All Rights Reserved

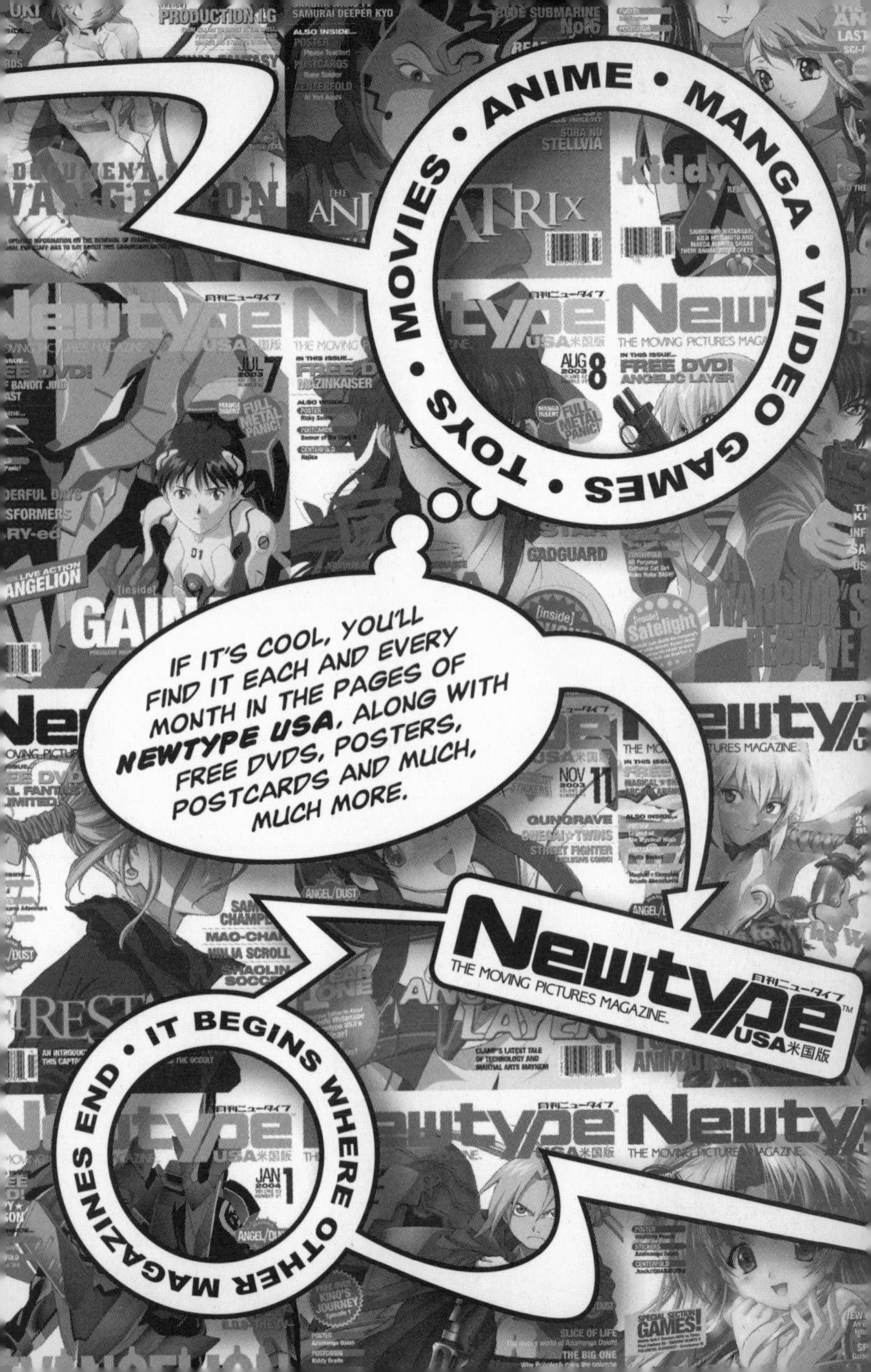

MOVIES • ANIME • MANGA • VIDEO GAMES • TOYS •
IF IT'S COOL, YOU'LL FIND IT EACH AND EVERY MONTH IN THE PAGES OF NEWTYPE USA, ALONG WITH FREE DVDS, POSTERS, POSTCARDS AND MUCH, MUCH MORE.
Newtype™ THE MOVING PICTURES MAGAZINE. 月刊ニュータイプ USA 米国版
IT BEGINS WHERE OTHER MAGAZINES END •

ADV MANGA

ADV Manga™ MANGA SURVEY

PLEASE MAIL THE COMPLETED FORM TO: EDITOR – ADV MANGA
c/o A.D. Vision, Inc. 10114 W. Sam Houston Pkwy., Suite 200 Houston, TX 77099

Name: ______________________________
Address: ______________________________
City, State, Zip: ______________________________
____
E-Mail: ______________________________
Male ☐ Female ☐ Age: ______________

☐ ***CHECK HERE IF YOU WOULD LIKE TO RECEIVE OTHER INFORMATION OR FUTURE OFFERS FROM ADV.***

All information provided will be used for internal purposes only. We promise not to sell or otherwise divulge your information.

1. Annual Household Income (*Check only one*)
- ☐ Under $25,000
- ☐ $25,000 to $50,000
- ☐ $50,000 to $75,000
- ☐ Over $75,000

2. How do you hear about new Manga releases? (*Check all that apply*)
- ☐ Browsing in Store
- ☐ Internet Reviews
- ☐ Anime News Websites
- ☐ Direct Email Campaigns
- ☐ Online forums (message boards and chat rooms)
- ☐ Carrier pigeon
- ☐ Other: ______________________
- ☐ Magazine Ad
- ☐ Online Advertising
- ☐ Conventions
- ☐ TV Advertising

3. Which magazines do you read? (*Check all that apply*)
- ☐ Wizard
- ☐ SPIN
- ☐ Animerica
- ☐ Rolling Stone
- ☐ Maxim
- ☐ DC Comics
- ☐ URB
- ☐ Polygon
- ☐ Original Play Station Magazine
- ☐ Entertainment Weekly
- ☐ YRB
- ☐ EGM
- ☐ Newtype USA
- ☐ SciFi
- ☐ Starlog
- ☐ Wired
- ☐ Vice
- ☐ BPM
- ☐ I hate reading
- ☐ Other: ______________

4. Have you visited the ADV Manga website?
- ☐ Yes
- ☐ No

5. Have you made any manga purchases online from the ADV website?
- ☐ Yes
- ☐ No

6. If you have visited the ADV Manga website, how would you rate your online experience?
- ☐ Excellent
- ☐ Good
- ☐ Average
- ☐ Poor

7. What genre of manga do you prefer?
(Check all that apply)
- ☐ adventure
- ☐ romance
- ☐ detective
- ☐ action
- ☐ horror
- ☐ sci-fi/fantasy
- ☐ sports
- ☐ comedy

8. How many manga titles have you purchased in the last 6 months?
- ☐ none
- ☐ 1-4
- ☐ 5-10
- ☐ 11+

9. Where do you make your manga purchases? *(Check all that apply)*
- ☐ comic store
- ☐ bookstore
- ☐ newsstand
- ☐ online
- ☐ other:_____
- ☐ department store
- ☐ grocery store
- ☐ video store
- ☐ video game store

10. Which bookstores do you usually make your manga purchases at?
(Check all that apply)
- ☐ Barnes & Noble
- ☐ Walden Books
- ☐ Suncoast
- ☐ Best Buy
- ☐ Amazon.com
- ☐ Borders
- ☐ Books-A-Million
- ☐ Toys "Я" Us
- ☐ Other bookstore:
_____

11. What's your favorite anime/manga website? *(Check all that apply)*
- ☐ adv-manga.com
- ☐ advfilms.com
- ☐ rightstuf.com
- ☐ animenewsservice.com
- ☐ animenewsnetwork.com
- ☐ Other:_____
- ☐ animeondvd.com
- ☐ anipike.com
- ☐ animeonline.net
- ☐ planetanime.com
- ☐ animenation.com